Seconds City

The Smart Shopper's Guide to Almost 1,000 Chicagoland Outlet Stores

Includes Illinois, Indiana, and Wisconsin

Susan Wolfson

CONTEMPORARY
BOOKS, INC.
CHICAGO ■ NEW YORK

Library of Congress Cataloging-in-Publication Data

Wolfson, Susan.
    Seconds city.

    Includes index.
    1. Outlet stores—Illinois—Chicago Region—
Directories.   2. Outlet stores—Wisconsin—Directories.
3. Outlet stores—Indiana—Directories.   I. Title.
TX335.W618   1986   380.1'45'000977311   86-2583
ISBN 0-8092-5179-5 (pbk.)

Published by Contemporary Books, Inc.
180 North Michigan Avenue, Chicago, Illinois 60601
Manufactured in the United States of America
Library of Congress Catalog Card Number: 86-2583
International Standard Book Number: 0-8092-5179-5

Published simultaneously in Canada by Beaverbooks, Ltd.
195 Allstate Parkway, Valleywood Business Park
Markham, Ontario L3R 4T8 Canada

This book is dedicated
In loving memory
To
A man of
Unconditional love
Unconditional trust
My sometime employer
My sometime coauthor
My inspiration
And advisor
And mentor
And friend
My stepfather
Ira J. Bach

CONTENTS

FOREWORD

After finding more than 3,000 nineteenth-century structures in the six-county metropolitan Chicago area, I spent much of the unpleasantly hot summer of 1980 in a car without air-conditioning, driving in circles throughout the suburbs, locating and evaluating the buildings for what was to become *A Guide to Chicago's Historic Suburbs On Wheels and On Foot* (Swallow/Ohio University Press, 1981). Driving in circles (six or seven days a week, ten to fourteen hours a day), I created a variety of things to amuse myself. I collected clean public washrooms; I collected wonderful bakeries; I collected interesting museums and friendly docents; I collected friendly reference librarians. I found (seasonally) warm/cool places to have a (seasonally) hot/cold drink. And I began to find scores of places in which to spend money.

Since my college days, when I somehow managed to survive on a mere $225 each month, I had kept a small number of outlet stores in mind and had prided myself on my "finds" of deli and bakery outlets. As I traveled through the suburbs, I found more and more places where I could buy goods at 20%, or 50%, or sometimes 90% less than their retail prices. I began to keep a file of these outlets.

My family and friends know of my "finds." As they located new outlets, they always took the time to let me know too. My list grew, and by 1983, when I was driving from Wisconsin to Indiana researching *A Guide to Chicago's Train Stations: Present and Past* (Swallow/Ohio University Press, 1986), I realized that these "finds" should be shared with a wider group.

Seconds City is a collection of nearly a thousand outlet stores in Illinois, Indiana, and Wisconsin, within driving distance of Chicago. Even at today's high gasoline prices, a well-planned shopping trip should save you more than the cost of this book the first time you use it.

"Cheap" need not necessarily mean "of lesser quality." I have tried to differentiate between "first quality" and other types of goods found in these outlet stores (see the *Glossary* for a list of terms). There will be times when $1.99/lb. corned beef will taste terrific, no matter how irregular the slices—and other times when you'll pay $3.99/lb. to have it look pretty—still a lot better than paying $5.98/lb. at your local deli counter. Only you can decide whether you would rather pay $79.95 to have the stripes at the seams match perfectly, or whether the wool sweater will keep you equally warm at $24.99.

I did not include "discount" or "off price" stores in this book. At the point at which my files reached nearly 2,000 listings, I decided to include only outlets. I'm sure most people know and recognize these stores, and, although prices at many of them are comparable to those at outlets, I know that with a quick look through the yellow pages you can locate most of them.

In these days of inflation and high prices, with careful shopping you, too, can learn to s-t-r-e-t-c-h your consumer dollars.

ACKNOWLEDGMENTS

I would like to thank a very special staff, whose dedication to this project and enthusiastic hard work made this book possible: Mark Soleau, Guy McKinney, Peter Nolan, Suzanne Chevrier, Wally Stearns, Bonnie deNoyelles, Erik Gregersen, Ingrid Gregersen, Maggie Gautier, and Lynn Kanter. Also Muriel Bach, Bob Beals, Flora Brown, John Carey, Rachel Chakrin, Dave Davis, Catherine Delaney, Sally Feldberg, Fred Hill, Stan Herzman, Vicki Hoffstedder, Mike James, Karen Kanter, Don Kelly, Howard Kilroy, Amy Klechner, Toni LaMorte, Mary Madison, Matthew Nolan, Mary O'Connor, Tom Robertson, Linda Ruiz, Virginia Shaw, Dave Tucker, Joseph Wolfson, and David Young.

I would also like to offer very special thanks to a very special person, Morton Weisman, for his encouragement, support, advice, and friendship.

WHAT IS AN OUTLET?

There are eight types of outlet stores listed in this book:

1. The **factory outlet store** is frequently at or next to the factory. It is owned by the factory and usually sells merchandise only from that factory (although some do sell related products made by another manufacturer, sometimes at little or no savings). The factory sends seconds, irregular or imperfect items, surplus, overruns, overstocks, end-of-season merchandise, customer returns (or anything left over in manufacturing, like fabric remnants) not sold through normal retail channels to the outlet, usually at savings that *begin* between 25% and 50% off normal retail prices.

2. The **manufacturer's outlet store** is usually owned by the manufacturer, but at a location away from the factory. It is often more similar in appearance to a retail store, but in most other respects it is like a factory outlet.

3. A **mill outlet** sells merchandise from a mill, like fabric, knit goods, carpets, etc. In most other ways, it is like a factory outlet.

4. **Sample shops** sell (usually one-of-a-kind) clothes that were made as samples for the manufacturer's salespeople to show to merchants who buy their lines. Sizes and colors are usually very limited.

5. **Outlets for chains of stores** sell merchandise left over from the retail stores, sometimes floor samples, end-of-season, damaged, or closeout items.

6. **Outlets for department stores** sell floor samples, damaged merchandise, end-of-season, discontinued lines, surplus, etc., that had sold at retail prices in their retail stores.

7. **Outlets for catalog merchandise** sell customer returns, last year's lines, end-of-season, discontinued, and other merchandise that will not be in the new catalog.

8. Outlet stores not listed above fall into two categories:

    Outlets that sell several manufacturers' goods with a common theme (such as crafts, linens, sportswear, or toys). They buy seconds, irregulars, surplus, overruns, overstocks, discontinued, and other merchandise from manufacturers, wholesalers, jobbers, etc.

    Outlets that buy odd lots, damaged shipments, salvage, or other merchandise at greatly reduced prices from jobbers or any source they find.

The line between outlets in these last two types, and "discount" or "off price" stores is very thin. In researching this book, we tried to eliminate discount and off price stores from our inventory. We always asked if the store was an outlet; if the manager or clerk said yes, I included it in the book.

Outlets come and go. Nearly a hundred that we researched less than a year ago were gone by the time we did a final check just before this book went to the publisher. New ones sprout just as quickly. There are probably a few (on the second floor, or off a back alley, of an obscure street, or in a remote town)—somewhere—that we missed.

Some of the "outlets" listed here may have "passed" our questions and visits. Some may have said they were outlets, when they were not, or some may offer little savings. If you know of an outlet that I missed, or feel a listing should be removed from this book, please write to me care of the publisher.

HOW TO USE THIS BOOK

To begin:

1. Look in the *Table of Contents* for the merchandise category you want. (If an outlet fits more than one, it's listed in the category covering the majority of its merchandise with only the outlet name and a reference to the main listing in the others.)

2. Turn to that chapter. Outlets in Chicago are listed first. The rest are listed alphabetically by state then by city or town.

3. If you need outlets open on Sunday, see the *Appendix A: Outlets Open on Sunday* (pp. 290–293).

4. If you are looking for the greatest savings, see the *Appendix B: Outlets with Discounts over 70%* (pp. 294–296).

5. If you want only first quality merchandise, see the *Appendix C: Outlets with All First Quality Merchandise* (pp. 297–299).

6. If you are looking for the annual sales, see the *Appendix D: Annual Sales (By Month or Season)* (pp. 300–305).

7. If you want to be notified of an outlet's special sales, see the *Appendix E: Outlets with Mailing Lists* (pp. 306–308).

8. If you are a senior citizen, see the *Appendix F: Outlets with Senior Citizens' Discounts* (pp. 309–310).

9. If you are looking for a particular brand name or a particular outlet, see the *Index* (pp. 311–320).

Every chapter begins with an introduction. The introduction has an overview of the outlets and merchandise in the chapter, suggestions of other chapters which may have additional, related items, and an evaluation of expected savings.

SAMPLE LISTING:

A.B.C. Outlet Store, 1234 N. 5th Avenue, Chicago, IL 60633; (312) 123-4567
This outlet sells specific merchandise at savings that begin at 25% off retail price on first quality merchandise. Savings can go as high as 75% on seconds, discontinued, last year's lines, and closeout items.

SUN.	MON.	TUE.	WED.	THU.	FRI.	SAT.
closed*	9–6	9–6	9–6	9–9	9–6	9–5

SAVINGS: 30%–50% off   *Mailing List*   *All First Quality*
BRAND NAMES: Official Name, Good Name, Other Name
SALE DAYS: Tuesday
SPECIAL SALES: monthly
ANNUAL SALES: January, August
SPECIAL DISCOUNTS: senior citizens, 10% off Wednesday
PARKING: street, meters
PAYMENT: cash, checks (amount of purchase only, with proper I.D.), MasterCard, VISA
 ($10 minimum)

—————
*They are open Sunday 9–4 from Thanksgiving to Christmas.

How to Read the Listings:

1. The *NAME* of the outlet (sometimes followed by a second name or further description) is always on the first line.
2. The street *ADDRESS* (or name of the mall it's in), *CITY, STATE*, and *ZIP CODE*, along with the *AREA CODE* and *PHONE NUMBER* are also provided.
3. a. The main listing for a store gives information on:
    i. what they sell
    ii. how much you will save
    iii. suggested best buys
    iv. quality of merchandise
    v. locations of other stores in the chain
   b. Additional listings in the same chapter refer you to the city with the main listing. If the name is different, the referral is to the correct name and city.
   c. Additional listings in *another* chapter refer you to the chapter with the main listing.
4. The *HOURS* the outlet is open each day are given in an easy-to-read table.
5. The *SAVINGS* off retail prices you can expect to find at that outlet are given as percentages. Frequently the manager or clerk was reluctant to make a clear statement; occasionally it was difficult to compare prices (because retail prices were not listed, or quality was not comparable). In these cases, I estimated the percentages. Where a discrepancy exists between the savings reported in the descriptive paragraph and this listing, it may indicate variances between outlets within the chain, or differences in information from researchers or outlet managers.
6. If merchandise was *ALL FIRST QUALITY* (no seconds, irregulars, damaged, etc.), I said so.

7. If an outlet at which you plan to shop has a *MAILING LIST*, ask to have your name added so you will know of upcoming special sales and be able to take advantage of the extra savings.
8. *BRAND NAMES* found in each store are listed. If there are many brands sold, I listed only the major ones for which they said they were an outlet; otherwise, I omitted the category.
9. *SALE DAYS* are the days of the week on which (some or all) merchandise was discounted further (usually 10%–20% off already reduced prices). When the sale days varied, I said so and recommended you phone ahead to find out when to go to that outlet.
10. *SPECIAL SALES* fell somewhere between sale days and annual sales. If sales did not come with regularity, they are listed here.
11. *ANNUAL SALES* occur at the same time each year and I tried to list these as a month or season. However, many clerks did not know when an annual sale was scheduled, so a call ahead is suggested.
12. *SPECIAL DISCOUNTS* are usually listed according to:
    a. who gets it (most frequently senior citizens)
    b. how much (listed as a percent off the already reduced prices)
    c. when (assume all the time unless specified)
    d. restrictions (an I.D. card)
13. *PARKING* is listed as lot or street. If it is street, we asked if there were meters. In congested areas, we asked if it were difficult. In downtown Chicago, I suggest you inquire when you enter the lot to find out if the parking is free or reduced, and if you need to validate a ticket.
14. *PAYMENT* is listed in this order:
    a. cash
    b. checks (followed by any restrictions on the use of checks)
    c. credit cards (followed by any restrictions on the use of credit cards)
    d. other means of payment (food stamps, travelers checks)
15. If there is additional information about any of the above categories, there is an asterisk and the information appears at the end of the listing.

GLOSSARY

"as is"—Merchandise that is sold "as is" is frequently damaged, has been a floor sample, or has a flaw; it is not returnable

bolt ends—The remnant at the end of a bolt of fabric or carpeting; usually first quality

broken pieces—Normally associated with baked goods; usually greatly discounted

bruised—Usually a floor sample, sometimes damaged in shipping; usually furniture or appliances; usually cosmetic damage that does not affect the use of an item (see also "dents")

closeouts—Either merchandise no longer being made by the manufacturer or end-of-season merchandise in a store; usually first quality

customer returns—Merchandise previously sold, then returned; custom-made merchandise made to wrong specifications (color, size, etc.)

damaged—Usually damaged in shipping or while on display in the store (see also "as is")

day-old—Usually bakery goods that are brought to the outlet after one day on the route deliveryman's truck (see also "end of code")

dents—Usually first quality food in a dented can; also floor sample furniture or appliances (see also "bruised")

discontinued—A style, color, or design no longer being produced by the manufacturer; usually first quality (see also "closeouts")

end of code—Usually bakery or other food items with a "freshness code" date approaching after which the item may no longer be sold

end-of-season—Seasonal goods, usually clothes whose season has passed (swimming suits in September, snow gear in May)

ends and pieces—Chunks of food too small to go through the slicing machine (cheese, sausage, delicatessen products); fabric pieces too small for commercial use (see also "bolt ends," "mill ends," and "remnants")

first quality—Merchandise manufactured to specification (see also "perfect")

imperfect—An item with a flaw that may or may not affect its use (see also "seconds" and "irregulars")

irregulars—An item with a minor flaw (see also "imperfect" and "seconds")

jobber—A middleman between the manufacturer and the retailer

labels removed—Usually major designer's merchandise that may not be advertised as such; sometimes first quality; can be (and see also) "end-of-season," "samples," "closeouts," "overruns," and "surplus"

last year's line—Styles, colors, or designs that were part of the past season's goods of a manufacturer; usually first quality

mill ends—See "bolt ends"

odd lots—Merchandise in excess of a quantity ordered; the salvageable part of a damaged shipment

overruns—Merchandise in excess of orders placed to the manufacturers; usually first quality (see also "overstock")

overstock—Excess merchandise at the manufacturer or outlet store; usually first quality (see also "overruns")

perfect—Merchandise manufactured to specification (see also "first quality")

reconditioned—Used or defective merchandise that was returned (usually under warranty) and repaired

rust—First quality merchandise, in rusted cans

salvage—Merchandise damaged in shipment, in a fire, or an accident; merchandise from a shipment that is still usable after the insurance company has paid off on the rest of the lot

samples—Clothing (usually handmade, one-of-a-kind items in limited sizes and colors; frequently of better quality than the mass-produced merchandise that follows) used by the manufacturer's representative to sell the line to retailers; floor samples; items displayed at a retail store or outlet; an item made to see if it will sell; cookies on the counter (see also "test runs")

seconds—An item that does not meet the specifications to which it was manufactured; usually sold at a fraction of the usual retail price (see also "irregular" and "imperfect")

slightly damaged—Small cosmetic flaws; usually furniture or appliances, sometimes clothing

surplus—Merchandise in excess of the orders of a manufacturer; merchandise that has not sold after a specified time (see also "overruns" and "overstocks")

test runs—An item manufactured (frequently one-of-a-kind) to see if it will sell; the merchandise produced during a test of the production process

unlabeled—First quality merchandise (usually canned) without the label

unwrapped—Merchandise that is usually sold packaged, without the packaging; sometimes first quality, sometimes seconds

1
APPLIANCES

This chapter includes large and small kitchen appliances and most electronic audio and video components and systems. Other items are also grouped here because they are electric or mechanical. You may also want to look in Chapter 10, *Department Stores*, and Chapter 15, *Housewares*, for other outlets that sell appliances.

Appliances can be an excellent category in which to save. Discontinued and last year's line frequently mean only minor changes in appearance or in color. Seconds, floor models, samples, damaged, and "dents" usually mean there is a cosmetic flaw which will not affect the item's use. If you are going to place a refrigerator against a wall or cabinet, a dent or scratch on that side will not matter, and even a scratch on the front can be fixed (if you are a bit handy) with a paint touch-up kit for only a few dollars. Before you buy, I would suggest you narrow your choices to a brand or two and a few models and become acquainted with the retail prices. Decide if you have to have first quality, if cosmetic considerations are important to you, and which compromises you can make in order to save money. Then, when you go to the outlet, you will be able to make an informed choice, and get the greatest savings.

ILLINOIS

CHICAGO, IL

Chicago Speakerworks, 5700 N. Western Avenue, Chicago, IL 60659; (312) 769-5640
Some excellent buys on speakers and turntables are available at this outlet. Although there are very few seconds, they are the best buy at up to 70% off retail price.

SUN.	MON.	TUE.	WED.	THU.	FRI.	SAT.
closed	11–9	11–6	11–6	11–9	11–6	11–6

SAVINGS: 50%–70% off　　　　　　　　　　　　　　　*Mailing List*
ANNUAL SALES: Christmas
PARKING: lot
PAYMENT: cash, checks (amount of purchase only, with proper I.D.), MasterCard, VISA, American Express, Diners Club

American Family Scale
See listing under *Baby Accessories* in Chicago, Illinois.

Polk Brothers Outlet, 3500 W. Grand Avenue, Chicago, IL 60651; (312) 772-5800
This is the outlet for the Polk Brothers stores. They sell all kinds of brand name appliances and rugs. Most merchandise is surplus and overstock from their retail stores.

SUN.	MON.	TUE.	WED.	THU.	FRI.	SAT.
10-6	9-7	9-7	9-7	9-7	9-7	9-7

SAVINGS: 20%-70% off
PARKING: street
PAYMENT: cash, checks (amount of purchase only, with proper I.D.), MasterCard, VISA, American Express

ARLINGTON HEIGHTS, IL

The Treadle Machine
See listing under *Sewing Supplies and Equipment* in Arlington Heights, Illinois.

DOWNERS GROVE, IL

Sunbeam Appliance Service Company, 1644 W. Ogden Avenue, Downers Grove, IL 60515; (312) 852-1550
This is the outlet for Sunbeam and Oster appliances. Savings are greatest on factory seconds, samples, dented, discontinued, overstocks, and closeout merchandise. They also sell some "as is" and reconditioned small appliances. They have other stores in Niles and Evergreen Park, Illinois.

SUN.	MON.	TUE.	WED.	THU.	FRI.	SAT.
closed	8:30-5	8:30-5	8:30-5	8:30-5	8:30-5	9-noon

SAVINGS: 30%-60% off
BRAND NAMES: Sunbeam, Oster, Northern
PARKING: lot
PAYMENT: cash, checks, MasterCard, VISA

EVANSTON, IL

Andrews Company Sewing Machines, 1016 W. Davis Street, Evanston, IL 60201; (312) 866-9595
This is an outlet for Singer and Bernina Sewing Machines. Savings vary from 25%-40% off retail price, with greater saving on irregulars and discontinued models. They also sell notions, threads, and used sewing machines.

SUN.	MON.	TUE.	WED.	THU.	FRI.	SAT.
closed	9:30-5:30	9:30-5:30	9:30-5:30	9:30-9	9:30-5:30	9:30-5

SAVINGS: 25%-40% off
BRAND NAMES: Singer, White, Bernina, Viking
PARKING: street
PAYMENT: cash, checks (amount of purchase only, with proper I.D.), MasterCard, VISA

EVERGREEN PARK, IL

Sunbeam Appliance Service Company, 3523 W. 95th Street, Evergreen Park, IL 60642; (312) 425-7134
See listing in Downers Grove, Illinois.

SUN.	MON.	TUE.	WED.	THU.	FRI.	SAT.
closed	closed	8:30-5	8:30-5	8:30-5	8:30-5	9-5

SAVINGS: 20%-40% off   *Mailing List*
BRAND NAMES: Sunbeam, Oster
PARKING: lot
PAYMENT: cash, checks (amount of purchase only, with proper I.D.), MasterCard, VISA

Big "D" Closeouts, 1973 Bloomingdale Road, Glendale Heights, IL 60137; (312) 529-6243

Look through a large assortment of tools, radios, stereos, and more for savings from 35%–80% off retail price on closeout merchandise. They have an interesting pricing structure: most merchandise costs either $2.00, $5.00, or $10.00. They have other stores in Palatine and Schaumburg, Illinois.

SUN.	MON.	TUE.	WED.	THU.	FRI.	SAT.
10-5	10-6	10-9	10-9	10-5	10-9	10-6

SAVINGS: 35%–80% off
PARKING: lot
PAYMENT: cash, checks (amount of purchase only, with proper I.D.), MasterCard, VISA

Ace Washer and Dryer Company, 5614 W. Dempster Street, Morton Grove, IL 60053; (312) 966-4900

This is an outlet for Maytag. Savings average 20% off retail price on washers and dryers, as well as other major appliances. The greatest savings are on seconds, irregular, damaged, and used models.

SUN.	MON.	TUE.	WED.	THU.	FRI.	SAT.
closed	9-9	9-5	9-9	9-5	9-5	9-5

SAVINGS: 20%–25% off
PARKING: street
PAYMENT: cash, checks (with proper I.D.), MasterCard, VISA, American Express

Sunbeam Appliance Service Company, 7427 N. Harlem Avenue, Niles, IL 60648; (312) 647-8250

See listing in Downers Grove, Illinois.

SUN.	MON.	TUE.	WED.	THU.	FRI.	SAT.
closed	8:30-5	8:30-5	8:30-5	8:30-5	8:30-5	9-3

SAVINGS: 20%–40% off   *Mailing List*
BRAND NAMES: Sunbeam, Oster
PARKING: lot
PAYMENT: cash, checks (amount of purchase only, with proper I.D.), MasterCard, VISA

Big "D" Closeouts, 1631 N. Baldwin Road, Palatine, IL 60074; (312) 359-4488

See listing in Glendale Heights, Illinois.

SUN.	MON.	TUE.	WED.	THU.	FRI.	SAT.
10-5	10-6	10-9	10-9	10-9	10-9	10-6

SAVINGS: 35%–80% off
PARKING: lot
PAYMENT: cash, checks (amount of purchase only, with proper I.D.), MasterCard, VISA

Big "D" Closeouts, 634 S. Roselle Road, Schaumburg, IL 60193; (312) 980-0230

See listing in Glendale Heights, Illinois.

SUN.	MON.	TUE.	WED.	THU.	FRI.	SAT.
10-5	10-6	10-9	10-9	10-9	10-9	10-6

SAVINGS: 30%–80% off
PARKING: lot
PAYMENT: cash, checks (amount of purchase only, with proper I.D.), MasterCard, VISA

Big "D" Closeouts, 1710 W. Wise Road, Schaumburg, IL 60193; (312) 980-9764
See listing in Glendale Heights, Illinois.

SUN.	MON.	TUE.	WED.	THU.	FRI.	SAT.
10-5	10-6	10-9	10-9	10-9	10-9	10-5

SAVINGS: 30%–80% off
PARKING: lot
PAYMENT: cash, checks (amount of purchase only, with proper I.D.), MasterCard, VISA

Friedman's, 219 W. Golf Road, Schaumburg, IL 60195; (312) 882-2255
This store sells major brands of microwave ovens at savings of about 10% off retail price. Some items are seconds, dents, overruns, overstocks, and closeouts.

SUN.	MON.	TUE.	WED.	THU.	FRI.	SAT.
noon-5	10-9	10-9	10-9	10-9	10-9	10-6

SAVINGS: about 10% off
BRAND NAMES: Amana, Frigidaire, Tappan
PARKING: lot
PAYMENT: cash, checks (with proper I.D.), MasterCard, VISA, American Express

VILLA PARK, IL

Jim's Bargain Corner, 336 E. St. Charles Road, Villa Park, IL 60181; (312) 832-4456
This outlet sells several brands of regular and heavy duty tools, general merchandise, sanders, electric drills, and tape recorders at savings up to 60% off retail price.

SUN.	MON.	TUE.	WED.	THU.	FRI.	SAT.
11-5	10-8	10-8	10-8	10-8	10-8	10-6

SAVINGS: up to 60% off   *All First Quality*
PARKING: lot
PAYMENT: cash, checks (amount of purchase only, with proper I.D.)

WISCONSIN
HARTFORD, WI

Hartford Vacuum, 28 E. Jackson Street, Hartford, WI 53027; (414) 673-6420
The front of this store has vacuum cleaners at discount prices, but check the back room. They are an outlet for Regal Ware, Mirro, and Chef-Mate. There are lots of small appliances and cookware at savings that begin at 50% off retail price on first quality and go as high as 80% on some seconds, samples, discontinued, and closeout items.

SUN.	MON.	TUE.	WED.	THU.	FRI.	SAT.
closed	9-5	9-5	9-5	9-5	9-8	9-5

SAVINGS: 50%–80% off
BRAND NAMES: Regal Ware, Mirro, Chef-Mate
SPECIAL SALES: coupon specials, 10% discount card (ask)
SPECIAL DISCOUNTS: senior citizens, 10% off
PARKING: street
PAYMENT: cash, checks (amount of purchase only, with proper I.D.), MasterCard, VISA

KEWASKUM, WI

Regal Ware Outlet Store, 1308 Fond du Lac Avenue, Kewaskum, WI 53040; (414) 626-2121

This is the factory outlet for Regal Ware. They sell coffee makers, electric knives, microwave cookware, and pots and pans. Savings begin at 30% off retail price on first quality, and can go as high as 50% on some seconds, overruns, overstocks, closeouts, and "bruised" merchandise. They also have a store in West Bend, Wisconsin.

SUN.	MON.	TUE.	WED.	THU.	FRI.	SAT.
closed	9-5	9-5	9-5	9-5	9-5	9-2

SAVINGS: up to 50% off
BRAND NAMES: Regal Ware
SPECIAL SALES: weekly
PARKING: lot
PAYMENT: cash, checks (amount of purchase only, with proper I.D.)

REEDSBURG, WI

Hankscraft Outlet Store, 273 Main Street, Reedsburg, WI 53959; (414) 524-4347
This is the factory outlet for Hankscraft vaporizers and humidifiers. They also sell Gerber baby accessories. Savings average 33% off retail price on first quality merchandise, and higher on a few seconds, samples, test runs, last year's lines, discontinued, and closeout items.

SUN.	MON.	TUE.	WED.	THU.	FRI.	SAT.
closed	9-5:30	9-5:30	9-5:30	9-5:30	9-8	9-5

SAVINGS: 33%-50% off
BRAND NAMES: Hankscraft, Gerber
ANNUAL SALES: July
SPECIAL SALES: 20% off in the summer
PARKING: lot
PAYMENT: cash, checks (amount of purchase only, with proper I.D.)

WEST BEND, WI

E K Outlet
See listing under *Clothing—Accessories* in West Bend, Wisconsin.

Regal Ware Outlet Store, West Bend Outlet Mall, 180 Island Avenue, West Bend, WI 53095; (414) 334-9445
See listing in Kewaskum, Wisconsin.

SUN.	MON.	TUE.	WED.	THU.	FRI.	SAT.
noon-5	9:30-5	9:30-5	9:30-5	9:30-5	9:30-8	9:30-5

SAVINGS: 30%-50% off
BRAND NAMES: Regal Ware
PARKING: lot
PAYMENT: cash, checks

West Bend Company—Employees Cash Sales Store, 445 Western Avenue, West Bend, WI 53095; (414) 334-2311
This factory outlet store sells West Bend appliances, Thermo Serv plastic housewares, and Nappe-Babcock insulated and non-insulated bags. Savings are greatest on seconds, irregulars, test runs, discontinued, and closeout merchandise.

SUN.	MON.	TUE.	WED.	THU.	FRI.	SAT.
closed	9:30-5	9:30-5	9:30-5	9:30-5	9:30-6	9-1

SAVINGS: about 20% off
BRAND NAMES: West Bend, Thermo Serv, Nappe-Babcock
PARKING: lot
PAYMENT: cash, checks (amount of purchase only, with proper I.D.)

West Bend Vacuum Center, 220 S. Main Street, West Bend, WI 53095; (414)
334-7085
   The front of this store has vacuum cleaners at discount prices, but check the back
room. They are an outlet for Regal Ware, Mirro, and Chef-Mate. There are lots of small
appliances and cookware savings that begin at 50% off retail price on first quality and
go as high as 80% on some seconds, samples, discontinued, and closeout items.

SUN.	MON.	TUE.	WED.	THU.	FRI.	SAT.
closed	9-5	9-5	9-5	9-5	9-8	9-5

SAVINGS: 50%–80% off
BRAND NAMES: Regal Ware, Mirro, Chef-Mate
SPECIAL SALES: coupon specials, 10% discount card (ask)
SPECIAL DISCOUNTS: senior citizens, 10% off
PARKING: street
PAYMENT: cash, checks (amount of purchase only, with proper I.D.), MasterCard, VISA

2
AUTOMOTIVE

Most stores I found selling automotive supplies were retail or, if they did have savings, were discount stores rather than outlets. The best savings I could find were on car mats and custom-made vehicle seats.

Delfast Corporation Factory Outlet, 1528 W. Armitage Avenue, Chicago, IL 60622; (312) 486-0440 or 1 (800) 621-4616
    This factory outlet sells car mats. You pay retail price for a custom-made mat cut while you wait; ready-made merchandise savings average 10%; however, customer returns, closeouts, seconds, and overstocks can save you up to 50% off the retail price.

SUN.	MON.	TUE.	WED.	THU.	FRI.	SAT.
closed	8–4:30	8–4:30	8–4:30	8–4:30	8–4:30	closed

SAVINGS: 0%–50% off
BRAND NAMES: Fibremats, Sisalmats, Ultimats
PARKING: lot
PAYMENT: cash, checks, MasterCard, VISA, American Express, Diners Club

Factory Tire Outlet, 850 W. Washington Street, Chicago, IL 60607; (312) 666-6400
    This is one of several outlets for Michelin tires. Some also sell other brands at savings that average 20%–40% off retail price. They have other stores in Des Plaines, Downers Grove, Elmhurst, Mount Prospect, Mundelein, Oak Lawn, and Wooddale, Illinois.

SUN.	MON.	TUE.	WED.	THU.	FRI.	SAT.
closed	7–6	7–6	7–6	7–6	7–6	8–4

SAVINGS: 20%–40% off   *Mailing List*
BRAND NAMES: Michelin
SPECIAL SALES: vary
SPECIAL DISCOUNTS: senior citizens, 10% off
PARKING: lot
PAYMENT: cash, checks (amount of purchase only, with proper I.D.), MasterCard, VISA, American Express, Diners Club

Freedman Seating Company Factory Outlet, 4043 N. Ravenswood Avenue, Chicago, IL 60613; (312) 929-5666
    This is the factory outlet for Freedman Seating Company. They manufacture seats for RVs, vans, pickup trucks, and 4-wheel drive vehicles. They also sell sofa beds and dining and lounge furniture. Savings begin at 20% off retail price on first quality, and can go as high as 40% on some closeouts.

SUN.	MON.	TUE.	WED.	THU.	FRI.	SAT.
closed	9–5	9–5	9–5	9–5	9–5	9–5

SAVINGS: 20%–40% off
BRAND NAMES: Freedman Seats
ANNUAL SALES: seasonal
PARKING: street
PAYMENT: cash, checks (amount of purchase only, with proper I.D.), MasterCard, VISA

Merlin's Muffler Outlet, 3055 W. Devon Avenue, Chicago, IL 60659; (312) 338-0448
      This is the factory outlet for Merlin's Mufflers. Typical savings are 15% off prices at "discount" muffler shops, and as much as 50% off dealer-installed mufflers. They also do brakes and shocks for 15%–50% off dealer price.

SUN.	MON.	TUE.	WED.	THU.	FRI.	SAT.
closed	8–6	8–6	8–6	8–6	8–6	8–3

SAVINGS: 15%–50% off
PARKING: lot
PAYMENT: cash, checks, MasterCard, VISA, American Express

DES PLAINES, IL

Factory Tire Outlet, 1700 E. Oakton Street, Des Plaines, IL 60018; (312) 297-7690
      See listing in Chicago, Illinois.

SUN.	MON.	TUE.	WED.	THU.	FRI.	SAT.
closed	8–6	8–6	8–6	8–6	8–6	8–4

SAVINGS: 20%–40% off   *All First Quality*
BRAND NAMES: Michelin
SPECIAL SALES: ask
PARKING: lot
PAYMENT: cash, checks (amount of purchase only, with proper I.D.), MasterCard,
      VISA, American Express, Diners Club, Carte Blanche, B.F. Goodrich credit card

DOWNERS GROVE, IL

Factory Tire Outlet, 523 W. Ogden Avenue, Downers Grove, IL 60515; (312) 960-4510
      See listing in Chicago, Illinois.

SUN.	MON.	TUE.	WED.	THU.	FRI.	SAT.
closed	8–6	8–6	8–6	8–6	8–6	8–4

SAVINGS: 20%–40% off   *Mailing List*   *All First Quality*
BRAND NAMES: Michelin
SPECIAL SALES: vary
SPECIAL DISCOUNTS: senior citizens, 5%–10% off
PARKING: lot
PAYMENT: cash, checks (amount of purchase only, with proper I.D.), MasterCard,
      VISA, American Express, Diners Club

Factory Tire Outlet, 153 N. Addison Street, Elmhurst, IL 60126; (312) 833-0750
See listing in Chicago, Illinois.

SUN.	MON.	TUE.	WED.	THU.	FRI.	SAT.
closed	8-6	8-6	8-6	8-6	8-6	8-4

SAVINGS: 20%–40% off   *Mailing List*   *All First Quality*
BRAND NAMES: Michelin
SPECIAL SALES: vary
SPECIAL DISCOUNTS: senior citizens, 5%–10% off
PARKING: lot
PAYMENT: cash, checks (amount of purchase only, with proper I.D.), MasterCard,
  VISA, American Express, Diners Club

Factory Tire Outlet, 1881 W. Algonquin Road, Mount Prospect, IL 60056; (312)
439-9672
See listing in Chicago, Illinois.

SUN.	MON.	TUE.	WED.	THU.	FRI.	SAT.
closed	8-6	8-6	8-6	8-6	8-6	8-2

SAVINGS: 20%–40% off   *Mailing List*   *All First Quality*
BRAND NAMES: Michelin
SPECIAL SALES: most holidays
PARKING: lot
PAYMENT: cash, checks (amount of purchase only, with proper I.D.), MasterCard,
  VISA, American Express, Diners Club

Factory Tire Outlet, 309 N. Lake Street, Mundelein, IL 60060; (312) 949-6300
See listing in Chicago, Illinois.

SUN.	MON.	TUE.	WED.	THU.	FRI.	SAT.
closed	8-6	8-6	8-6	8-6	8-6	8-4

SAVINGS: 20%–40% off   *All First Quality*
BRAND NAMES: Michelin
SPECIAL SALES: vary
SPECIAL DISCOUNTS: senior citizens, 5% off
PARKING: lot
PAYMENT: cash, checks (amount of purchase only, with proper I.D.), MasterCard,
  VISA, American Express, Diners Club, Carte Blanche

Factory Tire Outlet, 6161 W. 95th Street, Oak Lawn, IL 60453; (312) 636-1281
See listing in Chicago, Illinois.

SUN.	MON.	TUE.	WED.	THU.	FRI.	SAT.
closed	8-7	8-7	8-7	8-7	8-7	8-4

SAVINGS: 20%–40% off   *All First Quality*
BRAND NAMES: Michelin
SPECIAL SALES: vary
SPECIAL DISCOUNTS: senior citizens, 10% off
PARKING: lot
PAYMENT: cash, checks (amount of purchase only, with proper I.D.), MasterCard,
  VISA, American Express, Diners Club

Factory Tire Outlet, 321 Georgetown Square Mall, Wooddale, IL 60191; (312) 595-0050
See listing in Chicago, Illinois.

SUN.	MON.	TUE.	WED.	THU.	FRI.	SAT.
closed	7:30–5:30	7:30–5:30	7:30–5:30	7:30–5:30	7:30–5:30	8–4

SAVINGS: 20%–40% off   *All First Quality*
BRAND NAMES: Michelin
SPECIAL SALES: vary
SPECIAL DISCOUNTS: senior citizens, 10% off
PARKING: lot
PAYMENT: cash, checks (amount of purchase only, with proper I.D.), MasterCard, VISA, American Express, Diners Club, B.F. Goodrich credit card

INDIANA

GARY, IN

Brady's This Is It—Factory Outlet Store—Home and Auto
See listings under *Ceramics* and *Plates, Glassware, and Tableware* in Gary, Indiana.

SHIPPSHEWANA, IN

Mastercraft
See listing under *Furniture* in Shippshewana, Indiana.

WISCONSIN

JANESVILLE, WI

Norwood Mills Outlet Store
See listing under *Fabrics* in Janesville, Wisconsin.

3
BABY ACCESSORIES

This chapter includes items for the baby, but not clothing (see Chapter 7, *Clothing—Babies'*) and toys (see Chapter 27, *Toys*). You will probably also want to look at Chapter 4, *Beds, Mattresses, and Box Springs*, for cribs. Most outlets that handle baby clothes carry baby accessories, and most of these outlets sell other merchandise as well.

ILLINOIS

CHICAGO, IL

American Family Scale, 3718 S. Ashland Avenue, Chicago, IL 60609; (312) 376-6811
This factory outlet sells kitchen scales, bathroom scales, and baby scales. They also sell microwave cookware, timers, baby booster seats, and baby feeding dishes. Everything in the store is 30% off retail price on first quality merchandise.

SUN.	MON.	TUE.	WED.	THU.	FRI.	SAT.
closed	8:30–4	8:30–4	8:30–4	8:30–4	8:30–4	closed

SAVINGS: 30% off   *All First Quality*
BRAND NAMES: American Family
PARKING: lot
PAYMENT: cash, checks (amount of purchase only, with proper I.D.), MasterCard, VISA

Rubens Baby Factory
See listing under *Clothing—Babies'* in Chicago, Illinois.

INDIANA

COLUMBUS, IN

Cosco Store, 2525 State Street, Columbus, IN 47201; (812) 372-0141
This outlet sells Cosco baby products: baby beds, cribs, rockers, cradles, as well as Cosco bar stools and bridge furniture. They also sell gas and electric weed trimmers and edgers. Savings are greatest on seconds, irregulars, imperfects, discontinued, and "as is" items.

SUN.	MON.	TUE.	WED.	THU.	FRI.	SAT.
closed	10–6	10–6	10–6	10–6	10–6	closed*

SAVINGS: 30%–50% off
BRAND NAMES: Cosco, Nockonwood, K & S Industrials
PARKING: lot
PAYMENT: cash, checks (amount of purchase only, with proper I.D.)

---

*They are open on Saturday, 10:00–2:00, from October through December only.

Kewaunee Equipment Company, 401 Park Street, Kewaunee, WI 54216; (414) 388-3232

This is the outlet for Kewaunee playpens, strollers, potty chairs, and booster chairs for children. Most merchandise is first quality, but best savings are on seconds and irregulars.

SUN.	MON.	TUE.	WED.	THU.	FRI.	SAT.
closed	8–3	8–3	8–3	8–3	8–3	8–3

SAVINGS: 40% off
BRAND NAMES: Kewaunee
ANNUAL SALES: twice a year
PARKING: lot
PAYMENT: cash, checks (amount of purchase only, with proper I.D)

REEDSBURG, WI

Hankscraft Outlet Store
See listing under *Appliances* in Reedsburg, Wisconsin.

4
BEDS, MATTRESSES, AND BOX SPRINGS

Savings on mattresses and box springs were among the best I found while researching this book. I found 50% off retail price a usual starting point. The major changes from year to year are in the pattern of the fabric covers; so, assuming you will use a mattress cover, a mismatched set shouldn't make much difference.

Before you buy, decide on the brand, firmness, and length of warranty you will want. Look for last year's lines, discontinued, and mismatched sets. Most retailers told me it was very important to match the mattress and box springs, but they were referring to the quality, not the cover pattern, and I haven't heard much on that subject from consumers.

Waterbeds and futons are also included in this chapter. You will probably also want to look in Chapter 13, *Furniture*, and Chapter 10, *Department Stores*, for other stores that sell beds. If you are looking for cribs or crib mattresses, also look in Chapter 3, *Baby Accessories*.

ILLINOIS

CHICAGO, IL

American Sleep—Waveland Mattress Company, 2850 W. Irving Park Road, Chicago, IL 60618; (312) 549-4733
This is the factory outlet for Waveland Mattress Company. Savings on their own brands of mattresses, box springs, and futons are approximately 75% off retail price for first quality. They also sell several brands of sofas and sofa beds. They carry Purified Down comforters and pillows. Savings begin at 37% off retail price on sofa beds, and go up to 60% off retail price on comforters and pillows, and up to 75% off on the mattresses.

SUN.	MON.	TUE.	WED.	THU.	FRI.	SAT.
closed	9-5	9-5	9-5	9-5	9-5	9-5

SAVINGS: 37%–75% off
BRAND NAMES: Schweiger, Carlton, Kroehler, Purified Down, Waveland
PARKING: street
PAYMENT: cash, checks (Telecheck), MasterCard, VISA

Bedding Specialists, 5115 N. Harlem Avenue, Chicago, IL 60656; (312) 774-7011
This is an outlet for Sealy mattresses. Savings run as high as 50% off retail price on some items. They also sell major brands of headboards and bed frames. They have other stores in Cicero, Lansing, and Oak Lawn, Illinois.

SUN.	MON.	TUE.	WED.	THU.	FRI.	SAT.
closed	10–7:30	10–6	10–6	10–7:30	10–6	10–4

SAVINGS: about 20% off   *All First Quality*
BRAND NAMES: Sealy, Soma, Basset
PARKING: street
PAYMENT: cash, checks (amount of purchase only, with proper I.D., no out-of-state
  checks), MasterCard, VISA

Factory Bedding, 4820 S. Ashland Avenue, Chicago, IL 60609; (312) 927-9796
  This store sells Sealy and Therapeutic mattresses and box springs. They also sell
frames and headboards.

SUN.	MON.	TUE.	WED.	THU.	FRI.	SAT.
closed	9–7	9–6	9–6	9–6	9–7	9–6

SAVINGS: up to 50% off   *All First Quality*
BRAND NAMES: Sealy, Therapeutic
SALE DAYS: vary
PARKING: street, meters
PAYMENT: cash, checks (amount of purchase only, with proper I.D., merchandise held
  until the check clears), MasterCard, VISA

Factory to You Sales—Made-Rite Bedding Company, 1517 W. Haddon Avenue,
  Chicago, IL 60622; (312) 276-6886
  This is the factory outlet for Made-Rite bedding. Savings on mattresses, box
springs, headboards, bed frames, folding beds, and bunk beds can go as high as 50%
off retail price on first quality merchandise.

SUN.	MON.	TUE.	WED.	THU.	FRI.	SAT.
closed	8–4:30	8–4:30	8–4:30	8–4:30	8–4:30	closed

SAVINGS: up to 50% off   *All First Quality*
BRAND NAMES: Made-Rite
PARKING: street, can be difficult
PAYMENT: cash, checks (amount of purchase only, with proper I.D.), MasterCard, VISA

Marjen of Chicago Discount Furniture and Bedding
  See listing under *Furniture* in Chicago, Illinois.

Mattress King, 1203 W. Belmont Avenue, Chicago, IL 60657; (312) 472-5120
  This store sells major brands of mattresses. They also sell roll-away beds,
waterbeds, baby cribs, and bed frames. They claim that their prices are the lowest in
the city.

SUN.	MON.	TUE.	WED.	THU.	FRI.	SAT.
11–4:30	11–8	11–6	11–6	11–8	11–6	closed

SAVINGS: at least 50%   *All First Quality*
BRAND NAMES: Sealy, Serta, Restonic, Therapeutic, King Koil, Mantua, Weshco
SPECIAL DISCOUNTS: senior citizens, 10% off
PARKING: lot
PAYMENT: cash, checks (amount of purchase only, with proper I.D., no out-of-state
  checks), MasterCard, VISA

National Bedding and Furniture Company, 3718 W. Fullerton Avenue, Chicago, IL
  60647; (312) 252-0678
  This store sells Berkshire brass beds, and Sealy and Therapeutic mattresses and
box springs. Savings can run up to 75% off retail price on overruns, discontinued, and
last year's line.

SUN.	MON.	TUE.	WED.	THU.	FRI.	SAT.
closed	10–8	10–5	closed	10–8	10–5	10–5

SAVINGS: up to 75% off   *Mailing List*
BRAND NAMES: Sealy, Therapeutic, Berkshire
SPECIAL SALES: seasonal sales
SPECIAL DISCOUNTS: police officers and fire fighters, 10% off
PARKING: lot
PAYMENT: cash, checks (with proper I.D.), MasterCard, VISA

Peppers Waterbeds—Warehouse Clearance Outlet, 4405 N. Clark Street,
   Chicago, IL 60640; (312) 275-0330
      This is an outlet for the Peppers retail stores. Savings on waterbeds and
headboards can run as high as 75% off retail price on discontinued items. They also
sell some imperfects. They have another store in Itasca, Illinois.

SUN.	MON.	TUE.	WED.	THU.	FRI.	SAT.
noon–5:30	11–8	11–8	11–8	11–8	11–8	11–5:30

SAVINGS: up to 75% off
BRAND NAMES: Burlington
SALE DAYS: periodic
PARKING: street, meters
PAYMENT: cash, checks (amount of purchase only, with proper I.D.), MasterCard, VISA

ADDISON, IL

Marjen Discount Furniture and Bedding Warehouse
   See listing under *Furniture* in Addison, Illinois.

BENSENVILLE, IL

Astro Bedding Corporation—The Mattress Factory, 107 O'Leary Drive,
   Bensenville, IL 60106; (312) 860-1445
      This is the outlet for Astro mattresses. They also sell Dresher, Brass Roots, and
Berkshire brass beds, brass headboards, and bed frames. Most merchandise is first
quality, but savings rise to 40% off retail on overruns and overstocks.

SUN.	MON.	TUE.	WED.	THU.	FRI.	SAT.
closed	10–9	10–6	10–6	10–9	10–6	10–5

SAVINGS: 10%–40% off   *All First Quality*
BRAND NAMES: Astro, Dresher, Brass Roots, Berkshire
SALE DAYS: specials once a week
PARKING: lot
PAYMENT: cash, checks (amount of purchase only, with proper I.D.), Mastercard, VISA

BLOOMINGTON, IL

Direct Factory Outlet
   See listing under *Furniture* in Bloomington, Illinois.

CICERO, IL

Bedding Specialists, 5222 W. 25th Street, Cicero, IL 60650; (312) 780-0155
   See listing in Chicago, Illinois.

SUN.	MON.	TUE.	WED.	THU.	FRI.	SAT.
closed	9:30–7:30	9:30–5	9:30–5	9:30–7:30	9:30–5	9–5

SAVINGS: up to 40% off
BRAND NAMES: Sealy
PARKING: street
PAYMENT: cash, checks (amount of purchase only, with proper I.D.), MasterCard, VISA

Bedding Specialists, 5434 W. 25th Street, Cicero, IL 60650; (312) 780-0157
   See listing in Chicago, Illinois.

SUN.	MON.	TUE.	WED.	THU.	FRI.	SAT.
closed	9:30–7:30	9:30–5:30	9:30–5:30	9:30–7:30	9:30–5:30	9–5

SAVINGS: about 20% off   *All First Quality*
BRAND NAMES: Sealy, Bedding Specialists
PARKING: street
PAYMENT: cash, checks (amount of purchase only, with proper I.D.), MasterCard, VISA

CRYSTAL LAKE, IL

Verlo Mattress Factory, 7107-A Pingree Road, Crystal Lake, IL 60014; (815) 455-2570
   This is the factory outlet for Verlo mattresses. Savings average 40%–60% off retail price on ten lines of first quality mattresses and box springs. They also sell bed frames. They have other stores in Naperville, and Wheeling, Illinois; and in Whitewater, Wisconsin.

SUN.	MON.	TUE.	WED.	THU.	FRI.	SAT.
11–4	9–5	9–5	9–5	9–8	9–8	9–5

SAVINGS: 40%–60% off   *All First Quality*
BRAND NAMES: Verlo
SPECIAL DISCOUNTS: senior citizens, 5% off
PARKING: lot
PAYMENT: cash, checks (amount of purchase only, with proper I.D.)

HEBRON, IL

Mattress Liquidations, 10002 Main Street, Hebron, IL 60034; (815) 648-4300
   This shop sells mattresses and box springs. Best buys are on seconds, irregulars, samples, test runs, surplus, overruns, last year's lines, discontinued, and "as is" merchandise. They sell the bedding in their store next door (see p. 233).

SUN.	MON.	TUE.	WED.	THU.	FRI.	SAT.
10–5	closed	closed	closed	10–5	10–5	10–5

SAVINGS: 30%–60% off   *Mailing List*
BRAND NAMES: King Koil, Sealy, Serta
ANNUAL SALES: December
PARKING: street
PAYMENT: cash, MasterCard, VISA, American Express

HIGHWOOD, IL

North Shore Bedding, 425 N. Sheridan Road, Highwood, IL 60040; (312) 433-6660
   This outlet sells Heller Brothers box springs, Sealy mattresses, Berkshire and Brass Roots headboards and footboards, and bedroom furniture accessories. Savings average 40%–60% off retail price.

SUN.	MON.	TUE.	WED.	THU.	FRI.	SAT.
11–5	10–8	10–8	10–8	10–8	10–8	10–6

SAVINGS: 40%–60% off   *All First Quality*
BRAND NAMES: Heller Brothers, Sealy, Berkshire, Brass Roots
PARKING: lot
PAYMENT: cash, checks (amount of purchase only, with proper I.D.)

ITASCA, IL

Peppers Waterbeds, 1151 Bryn Mawr, Itasca, IL 60143; (312) 773-6706
   See listing in Chicago, Illinois.

SUN.	MON.	TUE.	WED.	THU.	FRI.	SAT.
10–5	10–9	10–9	10–9	10–9	10–9	10–6

SAVINGS: 30%–50% off

SALE DAYS: vary
PARKING: lot
PAYMENT: cash, checks (amount of purchase only, with proper I.D., no out-of-state checks), MasterCard, VISA

LANSING, IL

Bedding Specialists, 17839 S. Torrence Avenue, Lansing, IL 60433; (312) 895-5020
See listing in Chicago, Illinois.

SUN.	MON.	TUE.	WED.	THU.	FRI.	SAT.
closed	10-8	10-5	10-5	10-8	10-8	10-4

SAVINGS: up to 50% off   *All First Quality*
BRAND NAMES: Sealy, Soma, Bassett
PARKING: lot
PAYMENT: cash, checks (amount of purchase only, with proper I.D.), MasterCard, VISA

MORTON GROVE, IL

Beds And Spreads, 6949 W. Dempster Street, Morton Grove, IL 60053; (312) 965-6710
This shop sells major brands of sheets, mattresses, and bedspreads at savings that average 20%–30% off retail prices.

SUN.	MON.	TUE.	WED.	THU.	FRI.	SAT.
noon-5	10-8:30	10-5:30	10-5:30	10-8:30	10-5:30	10-5:30

SAVINGS: 20%–30% off   *All First Quality*
PARKING: lot
PAYMENT: cash, checks (with proper I.D.), MasterCard, VISA

NAPERVILLE, IL

Verlo Mattress Factory, 422 W. 5th Avenue, Naperville, IL 60540; (312) 961-9191
See listing in Crystal Lake, Illinois.

SUN.	MON.	TUE.	WED.	THU.	FRI.	SAT.
11-4	9-8	9-5	9-5	9-8	9-8	9-5

SAVINGS: 50%–70% off   *All First Quality*
BRAND NAMES: Verlo
PARKING: lot
PAYMENT: cash, checks (amount of purchase only, with proper I.D.), MasterCard, VISA

NILES, IL

JJ's Bedding & Furniture Discount, Dempster Plaza Shopping Center, 8780 W. Dempster Street, Niles, IL 60648; (312) 297-3130
This is an outlet for Sealy mattresses and box springs. Savings range from 40%–60% off retail price. They also sell headboards and several brands of living room furniture at savings up to 80% off retail price on overstocks.

SUN.	MON.	TUE.	WED.	THU.	FRI.	SAT.
11-5	10-9	closed	closed	closed	10-9	10-5

SAVINGS: 40%–80% off
BRAND NAMES: Sealy
SALE DAYS: vary
PARKING: lot
PAYMENT: cash, checks (with proper I.D.), MasterCard, VISA

OAK LAWN, IL

Bedding Specialists, 5368 W. 95th Street, Oak Lawn, IL 60453; (312) 424-4499
See listing in Chicago, Illinois.

SUN.	MON.	TUE.	WED.	THU.	FRI.	SAT.
closed	10–7:30	10–5:30	10–5:30	10–7:30	10–5:30	10–4

SAVINGS: 40%–50% off   *All First Quality*
BRAND NAMES: Sealy, Bedding Specialists, Dresher, Berkshire, Brass Roots, Karel of
  Cumberland
PARKING: lot
PAYMENT: cash, checks (amount of purchase only, with proper I.D.), MasterCard, VISA

SCHAUMBURG, IL

Schaumburg Mattress Factory, 909 S. Roselle Road, Schaumburg, IL 60193; (312)
  529-0118
  This factory outlet sells its own brand of mattresses. Savings begin at 40% off
retail price on first quality and can go as high as 60% off on some seconds. They also
sell bed frames and headboards.

SUN.	MON.	TUE.	WED.	THU.	FRI.	SAT.
11–3	10–8:30	10–8:30	10–8:30	10–8:30	10–8:30	10–5

SAVINGS: 40%–60% off
PARKING: lot
PAYMENT: cash, checks (amount of purchase only, with proper I.D.), MasterCard, VISA

WHEELING, IL

Verlo Mattress Factory, 82 E. Dundee Road, Wheeling, IL 60090; (312) 541-1234
  See listing in Crystal Lake, Illinois.

SUN.	MON.	TUE.	WED.	THU.	FRI.	SAT.
noon–5	10–8	10–8	10–8	10–8	10–8	9–5

SAVINGS: 50%–60% off   *All First Quality*
BRAND NAMES: Verlo
PARKING: lot
PAYMENT: cash, checks (amount of purchase only, with proper I.D.), MasterCard,
  VISA, American Express

INDIANA
SHIPPSHEWANA, IN

Mastercraft
  See listing under *Furniture* in Shippshewana, Indiana.

WISCONSIN
WHITEWATER, WI

Verlo Mattress Factory, Route 4 and Highway 59, Box 298, Whitewater, WI 53190;
  (414) 473-4339
  See listing in Crystal Lake, Illinois.

SUN.	MON.	TUE.	WED.	THU.	FRI.	SAT.
closed	8–6	8–6	8–6	8–6	8–8	8–5

SAVINGS: 45%–50% off   *All First Quality*
BRAND NAMES: Verlo
ANNUAL SALES: twice a year
PARKING: lot
PAYMENT: cash, checks (amount of purchase only, with proper I.D.), MasterCard,
  VISA, American Express

5
CARPETING, RUGS, AND FLOOR COVERINGS

Carpeting is one of the most expensive categories in this book. It is also one of the best purchases on which to save. If you take the time to compare price and quality before you buy, you may well find the brand and color carpeting you prefer among the mill ends or remnants most discounted at the outlet. Seconds in carpeting may mean an irregularity in color or texture. If your room is smaller than the width of the piece of carpeting with the flaw, you may be able to trim away the problem area and get the equivalent of perfect carpets at seconds prices.

Measure carefully before you go shopping. Know how many yards you will need. Try to bring a sample of the paint, wallpaper, or fabric you want to match. Be sure to ask if delivery and/or padding and installation are included in the price; they may not be at these prices.

I found prices were best on merchandise that was in stock; however, many outlets were willing to special order at lesser savings. This, of course, lost one of the advantages to outlet shopping: that the carpeting doesn't take weeks or months to arrive.

ILLINOIS

CHICAGO, IL

Caravans Awry, 318 W. Grand Avenue, Chicago, IL 60610; (312) 644-5395
This shop sells a variety of oriental rugs at discounts up to 75% off retail price. Examples would be a 9 × 12 handmade Chinese rug (retail $5,000, here $2,160), a 9 × 12 handmade Pakistani room rug (retail $3,200, here $1,800).

SUN.	MON.	TUE.	WED.	THU.	FRI.	SAT.
noon–6	10–7	10–7	10–7	10–7	10–7	10–6

SAVINGS: 20%–75% off   *All First Quality*
BRAND NAMES: Eastern Accents
ANNUAL SALES: annual "over-the-hump" sale (call for information)
PARKING: lot
PAYMENT: cash, checks (amount of purchase only, with proper I.D.), MasterCard, VISA, American Express

Carpet Factory Outlet, 2100 S. Marshall Boulevard, Chicago, IL 60623; (312) 542-5800
This outlet sells major brands of carpet and vinyl floor covering at savings from 40%–75% off retail price. The best buys are on some seconds, imperfects, ends and pieces, discontinued, overruns, and closeout merchandise.

19

SUN.	MON.	TUE.	WED.	THU.	FRI.	SAT.
closed	9–4:30	9–4:30	9–4:30	9–4:30	9–4:30	9–4:30

SAVINGS: 40%–75% off
BRAND NAMES: Galaxy, Evans-Black, Armstrong, Congoleum, Ozite, World, Salem,
  Philadelphia, Masland
PARKING: lot
PAYMENT: cash, MasterCard, VISA

Carpet Wholesalers, 5022 N. Kedzie Avenue, Chicago, IL 60625; (312) 463-3336
   This is one of several outlets that sell most major brands of carpeting and vinyl
flooring. Best buys are on test runs, ends and pieces, overruns, overstocks, last year's
lines, discontinued patterns, and mill ends. They have other stores in Berwyn, Fox
River Grove, Lombard, Morton Grove, Oak Lawn, and Schaumburg, Illinois.

SUN.	MON.	TUE.	WED.	THU.	FRI.	SAT.
11–5	9–9	9–9	9–9	9–9	9–9	9–5

SAVINGS: 20%–50% off (in stock); 10%–25% off (special orders)
BRAND NAMES: Galaxy, Brite Star, Armstrong, Horizon, Signatures, Monticello
PARKING: street, meters
PAYMENT: cash, checks (amount of purchase only, no personal checks), MasterCard,
  VISA, American Express

Delfast Corporation Factory Outlet
   See listing under *Automotive* in Chicago, Illinois.

Polk Brothers Outlet
   See listing under *Appliances* in Chicago, Illinois.

ARLINGTON HEIGHTS, IL

Towel Factory Outlet Center
   See listing under *Linens* in Arlington Heights, Illinois.

Carpet Values of Chicago, 2406 E. Oakton Street, Arlington Heights, IL 60005; (312)
   228-5160
   This outlet sells most major brands of carpeting. Installed savings are at least 25%
off retail price, with best buys on imperfects, ends and pieces, surplus, overstocks, and
last year's lines.

SUN.	MON.	TUE.	WED.	THU.	FRI.	SAT.
11–4	9:30–9	9:30–5	9:30–5	9:30–9	9:30–9	9–5

SAVINGS: at least 25% off
PARKING: street
PAYMENT: cash, checks, MasterCard, VISA (financing available)

BARRINGTON, IL

Carpet Mill Outlet, 122 W. Northwest Highway, Barrington, IL 60010; (312) 381-6171
   This outlet sells carpeting from most major mills, at discounts from 40%–60% off
retail price. Best buys are mill ends, overstocks, overruns, last year's lines, end-of-
season, discontinued, and closeouts.

SUN.	MON.	TUE.	WED.	THU.	FRI.	SAT.
10–5	9–9	9–9	9–9	9–9	9–9	9–5

SAVINGS: 40%–60% off
BRAND NAMES: Galaxy, Burlington, Philadelphia, Salem, Coronet, Queens, Horizon,
  Hardwick
PARKING: lot
PAYMENT: cash, checks (amount of purchase only, with proper I.D.), MasterCard, VISA

Carpet Wholesalers, 7108 Cermak Road, Berwyn, IL 60402; (312) 484-8994
See listing in Chicago, Illinois.

SUN.	MON.	TUE.	WED.	THU.	FRI.	SAT.
11–5	9–9	9–9	9–9	9–9	9–9	9–5

SAVINGS: 10%–50% off
BRAND NAMES: Galaxy, World, Philadelphia, Armstrong, Domco
PARKING: lot
PAYMENT: cash, checks (with proper I.D.), MasterCard, VISA, American Express

Towel Factory Outlet Center
See listing under *Linens* in Downers Grove, Illinois.

Carpet Wholesalers, 502 Northwest Highway, Fox River Grove, IL 60021; (312) 639-0017
See listing in Chicago, Illinois.

SUN.	MON.	TUE.	WED.	THU.	FRI.	SAT.
11–5	9–9	9–9	9–9	9–9	9–9	9–5

SAVINGS: 10%–50% off   *All First Quality*
BRAND NAMES: Galaxy, Monticello, World, Philadelphia, Armstrong, Domco
PARKING: lot
PAYMENT: cash, checks, MasterCard, VISA

Ozite Mill Outlet Store, 1755 Butterfield Road, Libertyville, IL 60048; (312) 362-8214
This is the outlet for Ozite and Philadelphia. They sell carpeting, oriental design rugs, and some kitchen prints and wall coverings. Savings begin at 40% off retail price, and can go as high as 60% on some seconds on wall coverings and mill end carpeting.

SUN.	MON.	TUE.	WED.	THU.	FRI.	SAT.
noon–4	closed	9–5	9–5	9–5	9–5	9–4

SAVINGS: 40%–60% off
BRAND NAMES: Ozite, Philadelphia, Queen, Cumberland, Richmond
SALE DAYS: monthly
ANNUAL SALES: anniversary sale
PARKING: lot
PAYMENT: cash, checks

Carpet Wholesalers, 55 E. Roosevelt Road, Lombard, IL 60148; (312) 932-4844
See listing in Chicago, Illinois.

SUN.	MON.	TUE.	WED.	THU.	FRI.	SAT.
11–5	9–9	9–9	9–9	9–9	9–9	9–5

SAVINGS: 10%–50% off
BRAND NAMES: Galaxy, World, Monticello, Philadelphia, Armstrong, Domco
PARKING: lot
PAYMENT: cash, checks (with proper I.D.), MasterCard, VISA, American Express

Carpet Wholesalers, 5708 W. Dempster Avenue, Morton Grove, IL 60053; (312) 966-0877
See listing in Chicago, Illinois.

SUN.	MON.	TUE.	WED.	THU.	FRI.	SAT.
11–5	9–9	9–9	9–9	9–9	9–9	9–5

SAVINGS: 20%–50% off
BRAND NAMES: Galaxy, Monticello, Philadelphia, World, Armstrong, Domco
PARKING: lot
PAYMENT: cash, checks (amount of purchase only, with proper I.D.), MasterCard, VISA, American Express

NILES, IL

Towel Factory Outlet—Revere Mills
See listing under *Linens* in Niles, Illinois.

OAK LAWN, IL

Carpet Wholesalers, 5163 W. 95th Street, Oak Lawn, IL 60653; (312) 423-8052
See listing in Chicago, Illinois.

SUN.	MON.	TUE.	WED.	THU.	FRI.	SAT.
11–5	9–9	9–9	9–9	9–9	9–9	9–5

SAVINGS: 10%–50% off
BRAND NAMES: Galaxy, Monticello, Philadelphia, World, Armstrong, Domco
PARKING: lot
PAYMENT: cash, checks (with proper I.D.), MasterCard, VISA

SCHAUMBURG, IL

Carpet Wholesalers, 1228 N. Roselle Road, Schaumburg, IL 60172; (312) 843-0310
See listing in Chicago, Illinois.

SUN.	MON.	TUE.	WED.	THU.	FRI.	SAT.
11–5	9–9	9–9	9–9	9–9	9–9	9–5

SAVINGS: 10%–50% off
BRAND NAMES: Galaxy, Monticello, Philadelphia, Armstong, Domco
PARKING: lot
PAYMENT: cash, checks (amount of purchase only, with proper I.D.), MasterCard, VISA, American Express

WAUKEGAN, IL

Carpet World, 3200 W. Belvedere Road, Waukegan, IL 60085; (312) 662-4080
This is an outlet for most major carpet mills. Best buys are on surplus, discontinued, closeouts, and last year's lines.

SUN.	MON.	TUE.	WED.	THU.	FRI.	SAT.
10–5	8–9	8–9	8–9	8–9	8–9	8–5

SAVINGS: 30%–50% off
SPECIAL DISCOUNTS: military, 10% off
PARKING: lot
PAYMENT: cash, checks (amount of purchase only, with proper I.D., no out-of-state checks), MasterCard, VISA

INDIANA

GARY, IN

Brady's This Is It—Factory Outlet Store—Furniture
See listing under *Furniture* in Gary, Indiana.

Royal Belgium Rug Outlet, Century Consumer Mall, 8275 Broadway, Merrillville, IN 46410; (312) 736-9092

This store sells all kinds of oriental and other rugs at savings that can go as high as 70% off retail price.

SUN.	MON.	TUE.	WED.	THU.	FRI.	SAT.
11-5	10-9	10-9	10-9	10-9	10-9	10-9

SAVINGS: 30%-70% off   *All First Quality*
PARKING: lot
PAYMENT: cash, checks (amount of purchase only, with proper I.D.), MasterCard, VISA

Regal Rug Outlet, 100 Madison Street, North Vernon, IN 47265; (812) 346-1555

This outlet sells Canterbury House area rugs and bathroom rugs. Savings are greatest on seconds, overruns, overstocks, discontinued, and closeouts.

SUN.	MON.	TUE.	WED.	THU.	FRI.	SAT.
closed	closed	10-5	10-5	10-5	10-5	10-5

SAVINGS: up to 50% off
BRAND NAMES: Canterbury House
PARKING: lot
PAYMENT: cash, checks, (amount of purchase only, with proper I.D.), MasterCard, VISA

6
CERAMICS

The few outlets listed here had large selections of ceramics. Look for more in Chapter 14, *Gift Items*; Chapter 15, *Housewares*; Chapter 17, *Lamps and Lighting*; and Chapter 24, *Plates, Glassware, and Tableware*.

Savings were generally very good on first quality merchandise. Best buys were on seconds (look closely, so you can decide which seconds will not affect your use of an item) and on discontinued or closeout merchandise.

ILLINOIS
CHICAGO, IL

Keller's 2nd Place, 2614 N. Lakewood Avenue, Chicago, IL 60614; (312) 281-7259

Although first quality merchandise is at normal retail price, savings can run as high as 50% off retail on seconds and closeouts of pottery and potted plants.

SUN.	MON.	TUE.	WED.	THU.	FRI.	SAT.
11–4	9–4	9–4	9–4	9–4	9–4	11–4

SAVINGS: 50% off   *Mailing List*
PARKING: street, can be difficult
PAYMENT: cash, checks

EAST DUNDEE, IL

Haeger Potteries—Factory Outlet Complex, 7 Maiden Lane, Van Buren Street, East Dundee, IL 60118; (312) 426-3441

This is the factory outlet for Haeger pottery. They sell various kinds of housewares, bird baths, water coolers, candles, candle holders, designer floral arrangements, vases, planters, ashtrays, bowls, decorative accessories, lamps, and shades. Free factory tours are available Monday-Friday (call ahead). Savings average 25%-30% off retail on items that they do not manufacture, and their 3-for-1 pricing policy (on items manufactured at the plant) brings savings to 66%. Some items are seconds, samples, test runs, surplus, overruns, overstock, last year's lines, discontinued, and closeout merchandise.

SUN.	MON.	TUE.	WED.	THU.	FRI.	SAT.
10–4:30	8–4:30	8–4:30	8–4:30	8–4:30	8–4:30	10–4:30

SAVINGS: 25%–66% off
BRAND NAMES: Haeger
ANNUAL SALES: first two weeks of July, and last two weeks of October
PARKING: lot
PAYMENT: cash, checks (amount of purchase only, with proper I.D.), MasterCard, VISA

ROLLING MEADOWS, IL

Waccamaw Pottery
   See listing under *Housewares* in Rolling Meadows, Illinois.

INDIANA

GARY, IN

Brady's This Is It—Factory Outlet Store—Home and Auto
   See listing under *Plates, Glassware, and Tableware* in Gary, Indiana.

7
CLOTHING

This chapter was one of the most difficult to research and organize. Many stores sell mostly one type of clothing, but there is a lot of overlapping. I have categorized stores by the majority of merchandise they sell. The categories are: Accessories, Activewear, Babies', Children's, Family, Footwear, Large Sizes, Lingerie, Maternity, Men's, Outerwear, Sportswear, Women's, and Miscellaneous. Start by looking under the heading for the items you need, then look in related categories. Also look in Chapter 10, *Department Stores*; Chapter 16, *Jewelry*; and Chapter 25, *Sewing Supplies and Equipment*, for additional merchandise.

Plan ahead and be prepared. Before you go to an outlet, write down the sizes of all members of your family. Make notes on color and style preferences. Do your homework: know the brand names and retail prices of the items you need; you want to be able to recognize a bargain when you see it. Although most outlets in malls have dressing room facilities, some of the factory outlets do not. Call ahead, or ask the clerk about return or exchange policies; they vary.

Savings are usually greatest on seconds and irregular merchandise. They are also usually very good on end of season and closeout merchandise. If you can plan your shopping at times when they are clearing one season's merchandise, you will make the best buys.

Look closely at all merchandise. Most outlets clearly mark seconds or irregular merchandise, and many put seconds on a separate rack or table, but you will want to decide if the flaw in a garment is worth the difference in money you will save.

CLOTHING—ACCESSORIES
This chapter includes stores which sell mostly accessories. You will find gloves, mittens, hats, earmuffs, scarves, mufflers, ties, socks and leg warmers, purses and handbags, tote bags, wallets and billfolds, key cases, belts, rainwear and umbrellas, and other knit or leather accessories in this chapter. You will also want to look in this chapter under *Activewear*, *Sportswear*, *Children's*, *Men's*, *Women's*, and in Chapter 19, *Luggage*. Many of these stores sell accessories along with other merchandise.

Savings were usually best on seconds and irregulars, but excellent savings were usually available at the end of the season, when the stores were clearing merchandise for their new shipments. If you can plan your winter shopping in the spring, you will usually find savings beginning at 50% off retail prices.

ILLINOIS

CHICAGO, IL

B.J. Handbag Outlet, 610 W. Adams Street, Chicago, IL 60606; (312) 263-1311
See listing under National Handbag Outlet Store in Chicago, Illinois.

SUN.	MON.	TUE.	WED.	THU.	FRI.	SAT.
closed*	10–5:30	10–5:30	10–5:30	10–5:30	10–3	closed

SAVINGS: 40%–90%   *Mailing List*
BRAND NAMES: B.J. Handbag
SPECIAL SALES: Sunday
ANNUAL SALES: ends-of-seasons
PARKING: street, meters, can be difficult
PAYMENT: cash, checks (with proper I.D.), MasterCard, VISA, American Express

----

*They are open Sunday during special sales.

Besley's Tie Shop, 121 S. Franklin Street, Chicago, IL 60606; (312) 726-4238
This manufacturer's outlet sells Besley neckwear: ties for men, scarves for women, at savings averaging 20%–40% off retail price. They also sell Cambridge Hall button-down oxford shirts for men and women at 20% off retail price.

SUN.	MON.	TUE.	WED.	THU.	FRI.	SAT.
closed	7:30–5	7:30–5	7:30–5	7:30–5	7:30–5	closed

SAVINGS: 20%–40% off   *All First Quality*
BRAND NAMES: Besley, Cambridge Hall
PARKING: street
PAYMENT: cash, checks (amount of purchase only, with proper I.D.)

Clothing Clearance Center
See two listings under *Clothing—Men's* in Chicago, Illinois.

Ideal Fashions, 1923 N. Halsted Street, Chicago, IL 60614; (312) 751-0050
This outlet sells leather accessories and clothes. Savings average 40%–80% off normal retail prices.

SUN.	MON.	TUE.	WED.	THU.	FRI.	SAT.
closed	9–4	9–4	9–4	9–4	9–4	9–4

SAVINGS: 40%–80% off   *All First Quality*
PARKING: street
PAYMENT: cash, checks (amount of purchase only, with proper I.D., no out-of-state checks), MasterCard, VISA, American Express

The Leather Shop
See listing under *Luggage* in Chicago, Illinois.

Leo's Advance Theatrical Company
See listing under *Clothing—Activewear* in Chicago, Illinois.

Morris & Sons
See listing under *Clothing—Men's* in Chicago, Illinois.

National Handbag Outlet Store, 1036 W. Van Buren Street, Chicago, IL 60607; (312) 421-4589

This factory outlet sells leather handbags, luggage, belts, and wallets. Savings begin at 40% off retail price, and quickly go as high as 75% on overstocks and closeout merchandise. There is another store, called B.J. Handbag Outlet, in Chicago.

SUN.	MON.	TUE.	WED.	THU.	FRI.	SAT.
*	9–5	9–5	9–5	9–5	9–3	closed

SAVINGS: 40%–75% off   *Mailing List*
BRAND NAMES: B.J. Handbags, Tamex, National Wallet
SALE DAYS: Sunday
ANNUAL SALES: November–Christmas
SPECIAL DISCOUNTS: senior citizens, 20% off, minimum $20.00
PARKING: lot
PAYMENT: checks (with proper I.D.), MasterCard, VISA

---

*During holiday seasons, and for special sales, Sunday hours are 8:30–4.

Royal Knitting Mills, 2007 S. California Avenue, Chicago, IL 60608; (312) 247-6300
This factory outlet sells hats, gloves, and sweaters. Savings begin at 30% off retail price on first quality, and go as high as 50% on seconds, samples, overstocks, surplus, last year's lines, and discontinued merchandise.

SUN.	MON.	TUE.	WED.	THU.	FRI.	SAT.
closed	9:30–3:30	9:30–3:30	9:30–3:30	9:30–3:30	9:30–3:30	closed

SAVINGS: 30%–50% off
BRAND NAMES: Land's End, Eddie Bauer
SALE DAYS: vary
PARKING: lot
PAYMENT: cash, checks (amount of purchase only, with proper I.D.), MasterCard, VISA

ARLINGTON HEIGHTS, IL

Tony Lama Boots
See listing under *Clothing—Footwear* in Arlington Heights, Illinois.

CHICAGO RIDGE, IL

Tony Lama Boots
See listing under *Clothing—Footwear* in Chicago Ridge, Illinois.

DEERFIELD, IL

The Kaehler Outlet
See listing under *Luggage* in Deerfield, Illinois.

DOWNERS GROVE, IL

Tony Lama Boots
See listing under *Clothing—Footwear* in Downers Grove, Illinois.

EAST DUNDEE, IL

Winona Knits, Haeger Pottery Factory Outlet Complex, 7 Maiden Lane, East Dundee, IL 60118; (312) 426-4623
This is an outlet for Winona Knitting Mills. They sell hats, gloves, blankets, sweaters, and other sportwear and activewear for men and women. Savings begin at 20% off retail price on first quality, and can go as high as 70% on seconds, overruns, overstocks, discontinued, and last year's lines. There is one wall of nothing but clearance items. They also have stores in Green Bay, Kenosha, Plover, Sister Bay, and West Bend, Wisconsin.

SUN.	MON.	TUE.	WED.	THU.	FRI.	SAT.
10–5	8:30–5	closed	closed	closed	closed	10–5

SAVINGS: up to 70% off
BRAND NAMES: Winona
ANNUAL SALES: June
PARKING: lot
PAYMENT: cash, checks (amount of purchase only, with proper I.D.), MasterCard, VISA

ELK GROVE VILLAGE, IL

Lebo's Factory Shoe Outlet
See listing under *Clothing—Footwear* in Elk Grove Village, Illinois.

HIGHLAND PARK, IL

Clothing Clearance Center
See listing under *Clothing—Men's* in Highland Park, Illinois.

LOMBARD, IL

Clothing Clearance Center
See listing under *Clothing—Men's* in Lombard, Illinois.

LOVES PARK, IL

VIP Yarn and Craft Center, Knit Pikker, Gloray Knitting Mills
See listing under *Crafts* in Loves Park, Illinois.

MATTESON, IL

Hamilton Luggage and Handbags
See listing under *Luggage* in Matteson, Illinois.

Tony Lama Boots
See listing under *Clothing—Footwear* in Matteson, Illinois.

MORTON GROVE, IL

Front Row, 1163 E. Ogden Avenue, Morton Grove, IL 60053; (312) 967-0220
This store sells many brands of men's, women's, and children's clothing and accessories. Savings average 30% off retail price. Best buys are on some overstocks and end-of-season items. They also have stores in Naperville, Illinois, and Indianapolis, Indiana.

SUN.	MON.	TUE.	WED.	THU.	FRI.	SAT.
11-5	9:30-9:30	9:30-9:30	9:30-9:30	9:30-9:30	9:30-9:30	9:30-9:30

SAVINGS: average 30% off
PARKING: lot
PAYMENT: cash, checks (amount of purchase only, with proper I.D.), MasterCard, VISA

Clothing Clearance Center
See listing under *Clothing—Men's* in Morton Grove, Illinois.

NAPERVILLE, IL

Tony Lama Boots
See listing under *Clothing—Footwear* in Naperville, Illinois.

Front Row, Dempster Street and Waukegan Road, Naperville, IL 60540; (312) 357-5660
See listing in Morton Grove, Illinois.

SUN.	MON.	TUE.	WED.	THU.	FRI.	SAT.
11-5	9:30-9:30	9:30-9:30	9:30-9:30	9:30-9:30	9:30-9:30	9:30-9:30

SAVINGS: at least 30% off
PARKING: lot
PAYMENT: cash, checks (amount of purchase only, with proper I.D.), MasterCard, VISA

NILES, IL

Gloves Factory Outlet, Lawrencewood Shopping Center, 370 W. Oakton Road, Niles,
IL 60648; (312) 967-7008
 This is the factory outlet for the Wells Lamont Corporation. They sell Wells Lamont
socks and several brands of gloves. Savings begin at 20% off retail price on first
quality, and can go to 50% on seconds, samples, test runs, overruns, overstocks, last
year's lines, and closeouts.

SUN.	MON.	TUE.	WED.	THU.	FRI.	SAT.
closed	closed	10–5	closed	10–5	closed	10–3:30

SAVINGS: 20%–50% off
BRAND NAMES: Wells Lamont
SPECIAL DISCOUNTS: summer coupons on garden gloves
PARKING: lot
PAYMENT: cash, checks (amount of purchase only, with proper I.D., maximum $200)

ORLAND PARK, IL

Clothing Clearance Center
 See listing under *Clothing—Men's* in Orland Park, Illinois.

SCHAUMBURG, IL

Clothing Clearance Center
 See listing under *Clothing—Men's* in Schaumburg, Illinois.

Tony Lama Boots
 See listing under *Clothing—Footwear* in Schaumburg, Illinois.

SKOKIE, IL

Tony Lama Boots
 See listing under *Clothing—Footwear* in Skokie, Illinois.

TINLEY PARK, IL

Lebo's Factory Shoe Outlet
 See listing under *Clothing—Footwear* in Tinley Park, Illinois.

WHEELING, IL

Factory Outlet Gloves, 847 W. Dundee Road, Wheeling, IL 60090; (312) 541-8420
 This is the factory outlet for Wells Lamont. They sell gloves, ski hats, tennis socks,
and athletic socks. Savings begin at 25% off retail price, and can go higher on some
seconds, irregulars, samples, test runs, overruns, overstocks, last year's lines, end-of-
season, and closeout merchandise.

SUN.	MON.	TUE.	WED.	THU.	FRI.	SAT.
closed	closed	10–5	closed	10–5	closed	10–5

SAVINGS: 25%–50% off
BRAND NAMES: Wells Lamont
PARKING: lot
PAYMENT: cash, checks (amount of purchase only, with proper I.D.), MasterCard, VISA

INDIANA

INDIANAPOLIS, IN

The Front Row, Eastgate Consumer Mall, 7150 E. Washington Street, Indianapolis, IN 46201; (317) 353-1114
See listing in Morton Grove, Illinois.

SUN.	MON.	TUE.	WED.	THU.	FRI.	SAT.
noon-5	10-9	10-9	10-9	10-9	10-9	10-9

SAVINGS: 10%–50% off   *Mailing List*
ANNUAL SALES: January, July
PARKING: lot
PAYMENT: cash, checks (with proper I.D.), MasterCard, VISA

Kuppenheimer Men's Clothing
See two listings under Clothing Clearance Center under *Clothing—Men's* in Indianapolis, Indiana.

JASPER, IN

Jasper Glove Company Outlet Store, W. 7th Street, Jasper, IN 47546; (812) 482-4473
This factory outlet sells Jasper work gloves and leather aprons. Savings begin at 20% off retail price, and can go higher on some seconds, irregulars, overruns, discontinued, closeouts, and "as is" merchandise.

SUN.	MON.	TUE.	WED.	THU.	FRI.	SAT.
closed	7-3:30	7-3:30	7-3:30	7-3:30	7-3:30	closed

SAVINGS: 20%–30% off
PARKING: street
PAYMENT: cash, checks (amount of purchase only, with proper I.D.)

MERRILLVILLE, IN

Sole Hole Shoes
See listing under *Clothing—Footwear* in Merrillville, Indiana.

Tony Lama Boots
See listing under *Clothing—Footwear* in Merrillville, Indiana.

MICHIGAN CITY, IN

Burnham Glove Outlet, 1608 Tennessee Street, Michigan City, IN 46360; (219) 874-5205
This outlet offers the greatest savings on seconds, irregulars, and closeout merchandise, although they also carry some first quality gloves.

SUN.	MON.	TUE.	WED.	THU.	FRI.	SAT.
closed	9-4	9-4	9-4	9-4	9-4	9-noon

SAVINGS: 35%–75% off
PARKING: lot
PAYMENT: cash, checks

MISHAWAKA, IN

Bags Plus, Buyer's Marketplace, 5901 N. Grape Road, Mishawaka, IN 46545; (219) 277-0474
This store is full of their own brand of leather bags, suitcases, and handbags at savings that begin at 30% off retail price. A rack in the middle of the store saves you an additional 20%.

SUN.	MON.	TUE.	WED.	THU.	FRI.	SAT.
noon–5	9:30–9	9:30–9	9:30–9	9:30–9	9:30–9	9:30–9

SAVINGS: 30%–50% off   ***Mailing List***   ***All First Quality***
ANNUAL SALES: January, Mother's Day, Memorial Day
PARKING: lot
PAYMENT: cash, checks (amount of purchase only, with proper I.D.), MasterCard, VISA

Socks Galore and More, Buyer's Marketplace, 5901 N. Grape Road, Mishawaka, IN
    46545; (219) 227-8692
    This store sells a wide variety of socks. Prices start at 20% off retail price on first
quality, and can go as high as 80% on slightly defective irregulars, overstocks,
overruns, and discontinued items. They also sell Leroy baby sleepers. They have
another store in Kenosha, Wisconsin.

SUN.	MON.	TUE.	WED.	THU.	FRI.	SAT.
noon–5	9:30–9	9:30–9	9:30–9	9:30–9	9:30–9	9:30–9

SAVINGS: 20%–80% off
BRAND NAMES: Leroy, P.S., Dior, Green Tree
SALE DAYS: Tuesday
ANNUAL SALES: May
PARKING: lot
PAYMENT: cash, checks (amount of purchase only, with proper I.D., no out-of-state
    checks), MasterCard, VISA

The Wallet Works, Buyer's Marketplace, 5901 N. Grape Road, Mishawaka, IN 46545;
    (219) 277-0487
    This is the factory outlet for Amity leather products. Savings start at 25% off retail
price on wallets, billfolds, key cases, clutches, and french purses, and can go as high
as 75% on irregulars, samples, test runs, surplus, overruns, overstocks, last year's line,
end-of-season, discontinued, and closeout merchandise. They also sell other brands of
handbags, luggage, briefcases, belts, and travel and garment bags. Ask to be put on
their mailing list at each location so you will know of their special sales. They also
have stores in Kenosha, Madison, and Sister Bay, Wisconsin, and in West Bend,
Wisconsin, where they are called Amity Leather Products.

SUN.	MON.	TUE.	WED.	THU.	FRI.	SAT.
noon–5	9:30–9	9:30–9	9:30–9	9:30–9	9:30–9	9:30–9

SAVINGS: 25%–75% off   ***Mailing List***
SALE DAYS: Tuesday
ANNUAL SALES: major holidays
SPECIAL DISCOUNTS: senior citizens, 10% off one Tuesday each month
PARKING: lot
PAYMENT: cash, checks (amount of purchase only, with proper I.D.), MasterCard, VISA

SEYMOUR, IN

Excello Factory Store
    See listing under *Clothing—Men's* in Seymour, Indiana.

WISCONSIN

APPLETON, WI

Knit Pikker, 306 N. Richmond Street, Appleton, WI 54915; (414) 733-1711
    This is one of several outlets for the Zwicker Knitting Mills. Savings are greatest on
Zwicker knit hats, scarves, and mittens, especially on irregulars, discontinued,
closeout, samples, and overstocks. They also sell OshKosh B'Gosh and Curity boys'
underwear, children's apparel, and sportswear for the whole family. They have other
stores in Kenosha, Waupaca, West Allis, and West Bend, Wisconsin, and another in
Appleton called Zwicker.

SUN.	MON.	TUE.	WED.	THU.	FRI.	SAT.
closed	9:30–5	9:30–5	9:30–5	9:30–5	9:30–5	9:30–4

SAVINGS: at least 50% off
BRAND NAMES: OshKosh B'Gosh, Wrangler, Eagle Knit
PARKING: lot
PAYMENT: cash, checks (amount of purchase only, with proper I.D.), MasterCard, VISA

Zwicker Knitting Mills, 410 N. Richmond Street, Appleton, WI 54913; (414) 731-7000
See listing under Knit Pikker above.

SUN.	MON.	TUE.	WED.	THU.	FRI.	SAT.
closed	9:30–5	9:30–5	9:30–5	9:30–5	9:30–5	9:30–4

SAVINGS: 25% off   *Mailing List*
BRAND NAMES: Zwicker, OshKosh B'Gosh, Health-Tex, Curity
SPECIAL SALES: monthly sales
PARKING: lot
PAYMENT: cash, checks (amount of purchase only, with proper I.D.), MasterCard, VISA

BERLIN, WI

Mid-Western Sport Togs, 150 N. Franklin Street, Berlin, WI 54923; (414) 361-2555
This is the outlet for Deerwear leather gloves, jackets, moccasins, and mittens. Savings begin at 25% off retail price and quickly go to 50% on seconds, irregulars, surplus, overruns, overstocks, discontinued, and closeout merchandise.

SUN.	MON.	TUE.	WED.	THU.	FRI.	SAT.
closed*	8–5	8–5	8–5	8–5	8–5	8–noon*

SAVINGS: 25%–50% off
BRAND NAMES: Deerwear
ANNUAL SALES: end of September
PARKING: lot
PAYMENT: cash, checks (amount of purchase only, with proper I.D.), MasterCard, VISA

---

*From Labor Day to Memorial Day, Saturday hours are 8:00–3:00; from Thanksgiving to Christmas, Sunday hours are 10:00–4:00.

GRAFTON, WI

Grafton Yarn Company Outlet Store, 1300 Fourteenth Avenue, Grafton, WI 53024; (414) 377-0344
This mill outlet sells Wigwam socks, hats, scarves, and mittens. They also sell mill-end yarns and craft supplies. First quality merchandise starts at 20% off retail price, and can go as high as 50% on some irregulars and mill ends.

SUN.	MON.	TUE.	WED.	THU.	FRI.	SAT.
closed	9–4:30	9–4:30	9–4:30	9–4:30	9–4:30	9–3

SAVINGS: 20%–50% off   *Mailing List*
BRAND NAMES: Wigwam
ANNUAL SALES: spring, fall, winter
PARKING: lot
PAYMENT: cash, checks, MasterCard, VISA

GREEN BAY, WI

The Leather Shop, 1514 Morrow Street, Green Bay, WI 54302; (414) 437-4935
See Saranac Factory Store in Marinette, Wisconsin.

SUN.	MON.	TUE.	WED.	THU.	FRI.	SAT.
closed	10–5*	10–5*	10–5*	10–5*	10–5*	10–5*

SAVINGS: 25%–50% off   *Mailing List*
BRAND NAMES: Saranac, Scan, Minnetonka
ANNUAL SALES: July
PARKING: lot
PAYMENT: cash, checks (amount of purchase only, with proper I.D.), MasterCard,
  VISA, American Express

*From September through May, store hours are: Monday through Friday, 9:00–6:00 and Saturday 9:00–5:00.

Winona Knits, 2017 Port Plaza Mall, Green Bay, WI 54301; (414) 437-4143
  See listing in East Dundee, Illinois.

SUN.	MON.	TUE.	WED.	THU.	FRI.	SAT.
noon–5	10–9	10–9	10–9	10–9	10–9	10–5:30

SAVINGS: 25%–60% off
BRAND NAMES: Winona
PARKING: lot
PAYMENT: cash, checks (amount of purchase only, with proper I.D.), MasterCard, VISA

HINGHAM, WI

Whitewater Glove Company, 216 Main Street, Hingham, WI 53031; (414) 564-2674
  This factory outlet sells an unbelievable assortment of gloves. They also sell some belts, purses, hats, and other accessories. Best savings are on seconds, overruns, overstocks, and closeout merchandise. They also have stores in Kenosha and Sheboygan, Wisconsin.

SUN.	MON.	TUE.	WED.	THU.	FRI.	SAT.
closed	8–5	8–5	8–5	8–5	8–5	8–5

SAVINGS: 40%–50% off
PARKING: lot
PAYMENT: cash, checks (with proper I.D.)

KENOSHA, WI

The Brandwagon, Factory Outlet Centre, 7700 120th Avenue, Kenosha, WI 53142; (414) 857-7977
  This is the outlet for Brills men's wear. They sell outerwear, rainwear, and accessories at discounts ranging from 25%–60% off retail. They have another store in Madison, Wisconsin.

SUN.	MON.	TUE.	WED.	THU.	FRI.	SAT.
noon–5	9:30–9	9:30–9	9:30–9	9:30–9	9:30–9	9:30–6

SAVINGS: 25%–60% off   *Mailing List*   *All First Quality*
BRAND NAMES: Eagle Knit, Etienne, Caron, Polo, Witty Brothers, Pierre Cardin
SPECIAL SALES: two-for-one sales four times a year
PARKING: lot
PAYMENT: cash, checks (amount of purchase only, with proper I.D.), MasterCard,
  VISA, American Express

Knit Pikker, Factory Outlet Centre, 7700 120th Avenue, Kenosha, WI 53142; (414) 857-2213
  See listing in Appleton, Wisconsin.

SUN.	MON.	TUE.	WED.	THU.	FRI.	SAT.
noon–5	9:30–9	9:30–9	9:30–9	9:30–9	9:30–9	9:30–5

SAVINGS: 15%–50% off   *Mailing List*
BRAND NAMES: Eagle Knit, OshKosh B'Gosh, Zwicker, Wrangler, Health-Tex, Curity
PARKING: lot
PAYMENT: cash, checks (amount of purchase only, with proper I.D.), MasterCard, VISA

Leading Labels, Factory Outlet Centre, 7700 120th Avenue, Kenosha, WI 53142; (414) 857-7454

This is an outlet for L'Eggs, Haines, and Valley hosiery. They also sell some Haines knitwear. Most merchandise is irregular, overruns, overstocks, and closeouts.

SUN.	MON.	TUE.	WED.	THU.	FRI.	SAT.
11-5	9:30-9	9:30-9	9:30-9	9:30-9	9:30-9	9:30-6

SAVINGS: 35%-75% off
BRAND NAMES: L'Eggs, Haines, Valley
SPECIAL SALES: monthly
PARKING: lot
PAYMENT: cash, checks (amount of purchase only, with proper I.D.), MasterCard, VISA

Midwest Hosiery Company—The Sock Market, 8716 36th Avenue, Kenosha, WI 53142; (414) 857-2627

This store sells several major manufacturers' brands of socks for men, women, and children. They also sell infants' tights and footies, and women's and children's tights. Savings begin at 30% off retail price for first quality, and can go as high as 80% off seconds, irregulars, samples, test runs, surplus, overstocks, last year's lines, end-of-season, discontinued, and closeout merchandise. They have another outlet (called The Sock Market) in West Bend, Wisconsin.

SUN.	MON.	TUE.	WED.	THU.	FRI.	SAT.
noon-5	9:30-9	9:30-9	9:30-9	9:30-9	9:30-9	9:30-6

SAVINGS: 30%-80% off
BRAND NAMES: Puma, Izod, Wigwam, Champion, Trimfit, Eagle Knit, Gold Bug, Hanover
SPECIAL SALES: buy six, get one free
SPECIAL DISCOUNTS: senior citizens, 10% off Wednesday
PARKING: lot
PAYMENT: cash, checks, MasterCard, VISA

Mitchell Outlet, Factory Outlet Centre, 7700 120th Avenue, Kenosha, WI 53142; (414) 857-7675

This is the factory outlet for Mitchell handbags. They also sell major brands of luggage, briefcases, Swinging Set sportswear, and tennis and golf accessories. Best savings are on seconds, discontinued, and closeout merchandise. They have another store in Milwaukee, Wisconsin.

SUN.	MON.	TUE.	WED.	THU.	FRI.	SAT.
11-5	9:30-9	9:30-9	9:30-9	9:30-9	9:30-9	9:30-6

SAVINGS: 50% off
BRAND NAMES: Mitchell, Swinging Set
SALE DAYS: vary
SPECIAL DISCOUNTS: senior citizens, 20% off handbags on Wednesday
PARKING: lot
PAYMENT: cash, checks (amount of purchase only)

Socks Galore and More, Factory Outlet Centre, 7700 120th Avenue, Kenosha, WI 53142; (414) 857-7600

See listing in Mishawaka, Indiana.

SUN.	MON.	TUE.	WED.	THU.	FRI.	SAT.
11-5	9:30-9	9:30-9	9:30-9	9:30-9	9:30-9	9:30-9

SAVINGS: 20%-80% off   *Mailing List*
PARKING: lot
PAYMENT: cash, checks (amount of purchase only, with proper I.D.), MasterCard, VISA

The Wallet Works, Factory Outlet Centre, 7700 120th Avenue, Kenosha, WI 53142; (414) 857-9028

See listing in Mishawaka, Indiana.

SUN.	MON.	TUE.	WED.	THU.	FRI.	SAT.
11–5	9:30–9	9:30–6	9:30–6	9:30–6	9:30–6	9:30–6

SAVINGS: 20%–40% off *Mailing List*
BRAND NAMES: Amity, Rolf's, Wins, Elizabeth, Frank Saliba, Stone Mountain, Airway, London Fog, Oleg Cassini
SPECIAL SALES: before holidays
SPECIAL DISCOUNTS: senior citizens, 10% off
PARKING: lot
PAYMENT: cash, checks (with proper I.D.), MasterCard, VISA

Whitewater Glove Company, Factory Outlet Centre, 7700 120th Avenue, Kenosha, WI 53142; (414) 857-7003
See listing in Hingham, Wisconsin.

SUN.	MON.	TUE.	WED.	THU.	FRI.	SAT.
11–5	9:30–9	9:30–9	9:30–9	9:30–9	9:30–9	9:30–6

SAVINGS: 40%–50% off
SALE DAYS: Tuesday
SPECIAL DISCOUNTS: senior citizens, 10% off
PARKING: lot
PAYMENT: cash, checks (amount of purchase only, with proper I.D.), MasterCard, VISA

Winona Knits, Factory Outlet Centre, 7700 120th Avenue, Kenosha, WI 53142; (414) 857-2921
See listing in East Dundee, Illinois.

SUN.	MON.	TUE.	WED.	THU.	FRI.	SAT.
11–5	9:30–9	9:30–9	9:30–9	9:30–9	9:30–9	9:30–5

SAVINGS: 25%–60% off
BRAND NAMES: Winona
PARKING: lot
PAYMENT: cash, checks (amount of purchase only, with proper I.D.), MasterCard, VISA

MADISON, WI

The Brandwagon, 4302 E. Washington Avenue, Madison, WI 53704; (608) 241-8780
See listing in Kenosha, Wisconsin.

SUN.	MON.	TUE.	WED.	THU.	FRI.	SAT.
noon–5	9:30–9	9:30–9	9:30–9	9:30–9	9:30–9	9:30–6

SAVINGS: 25%–60% off *Mailing List* *All First Quality*
BRAND NAMES: Brills
SPECIAL DISCOUNTS: two-for-one sale with another person
PARKING: lot
PAYMENT: cash, checks (with proper I.D.), MasterCard, VISA, American Express

VIP Mill Store—Knit Pikker
See listing under *Crafts* (look under VIP Yarn and Craft Center, Knit Pikker, Gloray Knitting Mills in Loves Park, Illinois) in Madison, Wisconsin.

The Wallet Works, Factory Outlet Centre, 4609 Verona Road, Madison, WI 53711; (608) 273-3713
See listing in Mishawaka, Indiana.

SUN.	MON.	TUE.	WED.	THU.	FRI.	SAT.
noon–5	9:30–9	9:30–9	9:30–9	9:30–9	9:30–9	9:30–6

SAVINGS: 40%–60% off
BRAND NAMES: Amity, London Fog, Oleg Cassini, Rolf's
ANNUAL SALES: Father's Day

SPECIAL DISCOUNTS: senior citizens, 10% off Wednesday
PARKING: lot
PAYMENT: cash, checks, MasterCard, VISA

MANITOWOC, WI

Right Step Factory Shoe Outlet
See listing under *Clothing—Footwear* in Manitowoc, Wisconsin.

MARINETTE, WI

Saranac Factory Store, 1316 Marinette Avenue, Marinette, WI 54143; (715) 732-2385
This is the factory outlet for Saranac gloves. They also sell women's designer clothes, outerwear, moccasins, boots and shoes, and accessories.

SUN.	MON.	TUE.	WED.	THU.	FRI.	SAT.
1–4	10–5	10–5	10–5	10–8	10–5	10–5

SAVINGS: about 50% off   *Mailing List*
BRAND NAMES: Saranac, Minnetonka
PARKING: lot
PAYMENT: cash, checks (amount of purchase only, with proper I.D.), MasterCard,
   VISA, American Express

MILWAUKEE, WI

Allen D. Everitt Knitting Company—Outlet Store, 234 W. Florida Street,
   Milwaukee, WI 53204; (414) 276-4647
This factory outlet store has savings on hats, mittens, fabrics, and yarns that average 25%–50% off retail prices. Some merchandise is first quality, the rest is seconds, irregulars, imperfects, end of seasons, and discontinued. Savings are even greater during their January and July sales.

SUN.	MON.	TUE.	WED.	THU.	FRI.	SAT.
closed	10–4	10–4	10–4	10–4	10–4	closed

SAVINGS: 25%–50% off
ANNUAL SALES: January, July
PARKING: street
PAYMENT: cash, checks (no out-of-state checks)

Mitchell Handbags, 226 N. Water Street, Milwaukee, WI 53202; (414) 272-5942
See listing in Kenosha, Wisconsin.

SUN.	MON.	TUE.	WED.	THU.	FRI.	SAT.
closed	9–3:30	9–3:30	9–3:30	9–3:30	9–3:30	10–3

SAVINGS: 30%–60% off   *Mailing List*
BRAND NAMES: M/M Verdi, Skyway, Amelia Earhart, Winn, Pegasus
PARKING: meters
PAYMENT: cash, checks (amount of purchase only, with proper I.D.), MasterCard, VISA

Odds 'N' Ends Shop, 231 E. Chicago Street, Milwaukee, WI 53202; (414) 272-5084
This is the outlet for Reliable of Milwaukee. They sell knit caps, scarves, knee socks, leg warmers, gloves and mittens, and also Foot Lights slippers, Mukluks slippers, and some yarn and knit novelties. Best buys are on irregulars, samples, test runs, overruns, discontinued, closeouts, and odd lots.

SUN.	MON.	TUE.	WED.	THU.	FRI.	SAT.
closed*	9–4	9–4	9–4	9–4	9–4	9–noon

SAVINGS: 50% off   *Mailing List*
BRAND NAMES: Foot Lights, Mukluks
ANNUAL SALES: January

SPECIAL DISCOUNTS: senior citizens, 20% off
PARKING: street, meters
PAYMENT: cash, checks

---

*Closed from February 1st to September 1st.

Jersild Store, 318 First Street, Neenah, WI 54956; (414) 722-7751
    This factory outlet sells men's, women's, and children's scarves, caps, mittens, socks, blankets, and other related knitwear. Savings start at 40% off retail price and go even higher on seconds, irregulars, and overstocks. They also conduct factory tours between Memorial Day and Labor Day. Call ahead for information.

SUN.	MON.	TUE.	WED.	THU.	FRI.	SAT.
closed	10–5	10–5	10–5	10–5	10–5	10–4

SAVINGS: at least 40%   *Mailing List*
BRAND NAMES: Jersild
ANNUAL SALES: January, August
SPECIAL DISCOUNTS: senior citizens, 10% off Wednesday
PARKING: lot
PAYMENT: cash, checks (amount of purchase only, with proper I.D.), MasterCard, VISA

Winona Glove Company, Manufacturers Direct Mall, 101 Plover Road, Plover, WI 54467; (715) 341-8833
    This outlet sells Conroy and Dolphin ski gloves, Icelandic hats, and Ream Leather and ADR handbags. Savings begin at 10% off retail price on first quality merchandise and go up to 50% on seconds, samples, discontinued, overstocks, closeouts, odd lots, and end-of-season items. Some merchandise, left over from the last year's lines, can be 90% off retail price.

SUN.	MON.	TUE.	WED.	THU.	FRI.	SAT.
11–6	9:30–9	9:30–9	9:30–9	9:30–9	9:30–9	9:30–6

SAVINGS: 10%–90% off
BRAND NAMES: Ream Leather, Conroy, Dolphin, Icelandic, ADR
PARKING: lot
PAYMENT: cash, checks (amount of purchase only, with proper I.D.), MasterCard, VISA

Winona Knits, Manufacturers Direct Mall, 101 Plover Road, Plover, WI 54467; (715) 344-6299
    See listing in East Dundee, Illinois.

SUN.	MON.	TUE.	WED.	THU.	FRI.	SAT.
11–6	9:30–9	9:30–9	9:30–9	9:30–9	9:30–9	9:30–6*

SAVINGS: 25%–60% off
BRAND NAMES: Winona
PARKING: lot
PAYMENT: cash, checks (amount of purchase only, with proper I.D.), MasterCard, VISA

---

*From Thanksgiving to Christmas Saturday hours are 9:30–9:00.

Fox River Glove Factory Outlet Store
    See listing under *Clothing—Outerwear* in Ripon, Wisconsin.

Right Step Factory Shoe Outlet
    See listing under *Clothing—Footwear* in Sheboygan, Wisconsin.

Whitewater Glove Company, I-43 & County Junction "**V**" Sheboygan, WI 53081; (414) 457-6827
See listing in Hingham, Wisconsin.

SUN.	MON.	TUE.	WED.	THU.	FRI.	SAT.
closed	9–9	9–9	9–9	9–9	9–9	9–5

SAVINGS: 40%–50% off
PARKING: lot
PAYMENT: cash, checks (amount of purchase only, with proper I.D.)

SISTER BAY, WI

The Wallet Works, Country Walk Shops, Highway 42, Sister Bay, WI 54234; (414) 854-5544
See listing in Mishawaka, Indiana.

SUN.	MON.	TUE.	WED.	THU.	FRI.	SAT.
10–5	10–5	10–5	10–5	10–5	10–5	10–5

SAVINGS: 40%–60% off   *Mailing List*
BRAND NAMES: Rolf's, Amity, Wins, Elizabeth, Frank Saliba, Stone Mountain, Airway, London Fog, Oleg Cassini
PARKING: lot
PAYMENT: cash, checks (amount of purchase only, with proper I.D.), MasterCard, VISA

Winona Knits, Country Walk Mall, Highway 42, Sister Bay, WI 54234; (414) 854-4743
See listing in East Dundee, Illinois.

SUN.	MON.	TUE.	WED.	THU.	FRI.	SAT.
10–8	10–8	10–8	10–8	10–8	10–8	10–8

SAVINGS: 25%–40% off
BRAND NAMES: Winona Knits
PARKING: lot
PAYMENT: cash, checks (amount of purchase only, with proper I.D.), MasterCard, VISA

WAUPACA, WI

Knit Pikker, 810 N. Churchill Street, Waupaca, WI 54981; (715) 258-5616
See listing in Appleton, Wisconsin.

SUN.	MON.	TUE.	WED.	THU.	FRI.	SAT.
closed	10–4	10–4	10–4	10–4	10–4	9–noon

SAVINGS: 15%–50% off   *Mailing List*
BRAND NAMES: Zwicker, OshKosh B'Gosh, Health-Tex, Curity
SALE DAYS: monthly sales, dates vary
PARKING: lot
PAYMENT: cash, checks (amount of purchase only, with proper I.D.), MasterCard, VISA

WEST ALLIS, WI

Knit Pikker, 2942 S. 108th Street, West Allis, WI 53227; (414) 733-1711
See listing in Appleton, Wisconsin.

SUN.	MON.	TUE.	WED.	THU.	FRI.	SAT.
closed	9–5	9–8	9–5	9–8	9–8	9–4

SAVINGS: 15%–50% off   *Mailing List*
BRAND NAMES: Zwicker, OshKosh B'Gosh, Health-Tex, Curity
SALE DAYS: monthly sales, dates vary
PARKING: lot
PAYMENT: cash, checks (amount of purchase only, with proper I.D.), MasterCard, VISA

Amity Leather Products—Factory Outlet Store, 505 Rolfs Road (at Highway 33 East), West Bend, WI 53095; (414) 338-6505
See listing under Wallet Works in Mishawaka, Indiana.

SUN.	MON.	TUE.	WED.	THU.	FRI.	SAT.
closed	8–4:30	8–4:30	8–4:30	8–4:30	8–4:30	8–1

SAVINGS: 25%–75% off _Mailing List_
BRAND NAMES: Amity, Rolf's
ANNUAL SALES: spring, fall
PARKING: lot
PAYMENT: cash, checks (amount of purchase only, with proper I.D.), MasterCard, VISA

E K Outlet, 151 Wisconsin Street, West Bend, WI 53095; (414) 334-3455
This is the factory outlet for Enger Kress. They sell many kinds of leather accessories. The outlet also sells several major brands of cookware and small appliances manufactured in Wisconsin. Savings begin at 30% off retail prices for first quality, and can go as high as 50% on seconds, test runs, overstocks, last year's lines, end-of-season, discontinued, closeout, and "as is" merchandise.

SUN.	MON.	TUE.	WED.	THU.	FRI.	SAT.
11–5	8–5	8–5	8–5	8–5	8–5	8–5

SAVINGS: 30%–75% off
BRAND NAMES: Enger Kress, Heritage, Regal Ware, Oster, Presto, Mirro, Vollrath
ANNUAL SALES: Christmas
SPECIAL DISCOUNTS: senior citizens, 10% off
PARKING: lot
PAYMENT: cash, checks (amount of purchase only, with proper I.D.), MasterCard, VISA, American Express

General Shoe (Factory To You)
See listing under _Clothing—Footwear_ in West Bend, Wisconsin.

Handbag Factory Outlet, West Bend Outlet Mall, 180 Island Avenue, West Bend, WI 53095; (414) 338-2929
This outlet sells handbags and other women's accessories. Savings can go as high as 70% off retail price on all first quality merchandise.

SUN.	MON.	TUE.	WED.	THU.	FRI.	SAT.
11–6	9:30–9	9:30–9	9:30–9	9:30–9	9:30–9	9:30–6

SAVINGS: 30%–70% off _All First Quality_
SPECIAL SALES: seasonal
ANNUAL SALES: February, August
PARKING: lot
PAYMENT: cash, checks (amount of purchase only, with proper I.D.), MasterCard, VISA

Just Accessories, West Bend Factory Outlet Mall, 180 Island Avenue, West Bend, WI 53095; (414) 338-2929
This outlet sells purses, hats, bags, gloves and mittens, and other accessories at savings of 40%–80% off retail price.

SUN.	MON.	TUE.	WED.	THU.	FRI.	SAT.
11–6	9:30–9	9:30–9	9:30–9	9:30–9	9:30–9	9:30–6

SAVINGS: 40%–80% off _All First Quality_
ANNUAL SALES: spring, summer, fall, winter
PARKING: lot
PAYMENT: cash, checks (amount of purchase only, with proper I.D.), MasterCard, VISA

Knit Pikker, West Bend Outlet Mall, 180 Island Avenue, West Bend, WI 53095; (414) 334-5167
   See listing in Appleton, Wisconsin.

SUN.	MON.	TUE.	WED.	THU.	FRI.	SAT.
noon-5	9:30-5	9:30-5	9:30-5	9:30-5	9:30-8	9:30-5

SAVINGS: 15%-50% off   *Mailing List*
BRAND NAMES: Zwicker, OshKosh B'Gosh, Health-Tex, Curity
SALE DAYS: vary
PARKING: lot
PAYMENT: cash, checks (amount of purchase only, with proper I.D.), MasterCard, VISA

The Sock Market, West Bend Outlet Mall, 180 Island Avenue, West Bend, WI 53095; (414) 338-8869
   See Midwest Hosiery Company in Kenosha, Wisconsin.

SUN.	MON.	TUE.	WED.	THU.	FRI.	SAT.
11-5	9:30-6	9:30-6	9:30-6	9:30-6	9:30-8	9:30-5

SAVINGS: 30%-70% off
BRAND NAMES: Izod, Wigwam, Puma
ANNUAL SALES: back-to-school, Christmas
SPECIAL DISCOUNTS: senior citizens, 10% off
PARKING: lot
PAYMENT: cash, checks (amount of purchase only, with proper I.D.), MasterCard, VISA

Winona Knits, West Bend Outlet Mall, 180 Island Avenue, West Bend, WI 53095; (414) 338-2545
   See listing in East Dundee, Illinois.

·SUN.	MON.	TUE.	WED.	THU.	FRI.	SAT.
noon-5	9:30-5	9:30-5	9:30-5	9:30-5	9:30-8	9:30-5

SAVINGS: 25%-40% off
BRAND NAMES: Winona Knits
PARKING: lot
PAYMENT: cash, checks (amount of purchase only, with proper I.D.), MasterCard, VISA

CLOTHING—ACTIVEWEAR

Activewear includes clothing associated with most sports and physical activities. Only a few stores specialize in activewear, but many sell activewear along with other clothes. Look also in this chapter under *Sportswear*, *Women's*, and *Men's*. If you are familiar with brands and retail prices before you go shopping, you will make the best buys. Feel free to ask to have irregularities pointed out if you are buying seconds.

Before you go shopping make a list of sizes for each member of your family. Although outlets in the malls have dressing rooms and usually make refunds or exchanges, many outlets at the factory lack these amenities. Ask about returns and exchanges before making your purchases.

ILLINOIS

CHICAGO, IL

Land's End Outlet, 2241 N. Elston Avenue, Chicago, IL 60614; (312) 276-2232
   This is the men's outlet (the women's outlet is down the street, look below) for the

Land's End catalog merchandise. They sell clothing and equipment for most sports and lots of sports-related merchandise. Almost everything that was or is in the catalog is on sale here, along with some irregulars, imperfects, last year's line, discontinued, closeouts, and overstocks. Savings average 20%–70% off retail price, with the greatest savings on irregulars and closeouts. They have other stores in Deerfield, Lombard, Morton Grove, and Schaumburg, Illinois.

SUN.	MON.	TUE.	WED.	THU.	FRI.	SAT.
11–5	10–5:30	10–5:30	10–5:30	10–5:30	10–5:30	10–5:30

SAVINGS: 20%–70% off
BRAND NAMES: Land's End
SALE DAYS: weekly
ANNUAL SALES: January, July
PARKING: lot
PAYMENT: cash, checks (with proper I.D.), MasterCard, VISA, American Express

Land's End Outlet, 2317 N. Elston Avenue, Chicago, IL 60614; (312) 384-4170
This is the women's outlet for the Land's End catalog. See listing above.

SUN.	MON.	TUE.	WED.	THU.	FRI.	SAT.
11–5	10–9	10–9	10–9	10–9	10–9	11–5

SAVINGS: 20%–60% off
BRAND NAMES: Land's End
PARKING: lot
PAYMENT: cash, checks (amount of purchase only, with proper I.D.), MasterCard, VISA, American Express

Leo's Advance Theatrical Company, 1900 N. Narragansett Avenue, Chicago, IL 60647; (312) 889-7700
This outlet sells Leo's brand of dancewear, shoes, leotards, and tights. They also sell other major brands. Although some merchandise is at retail prices, savings average 10%–20% on a few seconds, last year's lines, end-of-season, discontinued, and overstocked merchandise.

SUN.	MON.	TUE.	WED.	THU.	FRI.	SAT.
closed	10–5	10–5	10–5	10–5	10–5	10–2*

SAVINGS: 10%–40% off   *Mailing List*
BRAND NAMES: Leo's, Danskin
SALE DAYS: vary
PARKING: street
PAYMENT: cash, MasterCard, VISA

---

*Not open on Saturday during the summer from Memorial Day to Labor Day.

DEERFIELD, IL

Land's End Outlet, 405 Lake Cook Road, Deerfield, IL 60015; (312) 564-0955
See listing in Chicago, Illinois.

SUN.	MON.	TUE.	WED.	THU.	FRI.	SAT.
11–5	10–9	10–9	10–9	10–9	10–9	10–6

SAVINGS: about 20% off   *Mailing List*
BRAND NAMES: Land's End
SPECIAL SALES: weekly
PARKING: lot
PAYMENT: cash, checks (with proper I.D.), MasterCard, VISA, American Express

Golfer's Outlet
See listing under *Sporting Goods* in Elmwood Park, Illinois.

Land's End Outlet, #20 Yorktown Convenience Center, Lombard, IL 60148; (312) 953-8855
See listing in Chicago, Illinois.

SUN.	MON.	TUE.	WED.	THU.	FRI.	SAT.
11–5	10–9	10–9	10–9	10–9	10–9	10–6

SAVINGS: 20%–40% off
BRAND NAMES: Land's End
SALE DAYS: vary
PARKING: lot
PAYMENT: cash, checks (amount of purchase only, with proper I.D.), MasterCard, VISA, American Express

Land's End Outlet, 6131 W. Dempster, Morton Grove, IL 60053; (312) 470-0320
See listing in Chicago, Illinois.

SUN.	MON.	TUE.	WED.	THU.	FRI.	SAT.
11–5	10–9	10–9	10–9	10–9	10–9	10–6

SAVINGS: 20%–40% off
BRAND NAMES: Land's End
PARKING: lot
PAYMENT: cash, checks (amount of purchase only, with proper I.D.), MasterCard, VISA, American Express

Strictly Golf of Naperville
See listing under *Sporting Goods* in Naperville, Illinois.

The Wear House
See listing under *Clothing—Children's* in Niles, Illinois.

Sneakee Feet
See listing under *Clothing—Footwear* in Rolling Meadows, Illinois.

Land's End Outlet, 251 W. Golf Road, Schaumburg, IL 60074; (312) 884-1900
See listing in Chicago, Illinois.

SUN.	MON.	TUE.	WED.	THU.	FRI.	SAT.
11–5	10–9	10–9	10–9	10–9	10–9	10–6

SAVINGS: 20%–40% off
BRAND NAMES: Land's End
SPECIAL SALES: weekly
ANNUAL SALES: January, July
PARKING: lot
PAYMENT: cash, checks (amount of purchase only, with proper I.D.), MasterCard, VISA, American Express

Gossard's Factory Outlet, 401 Fourth Street, Huntingburg, IN 47542; (812) 683-2426

This is the factory outlet for the Gossard Company. They make men's baseball shirts, T-shirts, sweatshirts, and jogging shorts. They also sell men's sweaters, ladies' lingerie, and men's and boys' underwear. Savings begin at 15% off retail price on first quality, and can go as high as 60% on some irregulars, last year's lines, discontinued, overstocks, and end-of-season merchandise. They also have a store in Logansport, Indiana.

SUN.	MON.	TUE.	WED.	THU.	FRI.	SAT.
closed	9–5	9–5	9–5	9–5	9–5	9–5

SAVINGS: 15%–60% off   *Mailing List*
BRAND NAMES: Signal, Heritage, Playtex, Von Furstenberg, Dixie Belle
SALE DAYS: vary
PARKING: street, can be difficult
PAYMENT: cash, checks (amount of purchase only, with proper I.D.), MasterCard, VISA

Gossard's Factory Outlet, Eastgate Plaza, U.S. 24 East, Logansport, IN 46947; (219) 753-2808

See listing in Huntingburg, Indiana.

SUN.	MON.	TUE.	WED.	THU.	FRI.	SAT.
closed	9–6	9–6	9–6	9–6	9–6	9–6

SAVINGS: 15%–60% off   *Mailing List*
BRAND NAMES: Signal, Heritage, Pinehurst, Carole, Von Furstenberg, Playtex
ANNUAL SALES: holidays
PARKING: lot
PAYMENT: cash, checks (amount of purchase only, with proper I.D., no out-of-state checks), MasterCard, VISA

AAA Sports

See listing under *Sporting Goods* in Janesville, Wisconsin.

Midwest Hosiery Company—The Sock Market

See listing under *Clothing—Accessories* in Kenosha, Wisconsin.

Mitchell Outlet

See listing under *Clothing—Accessories* in Kenosha, Wisconsin.

Nike Factory Outlet

See listing under *Clothing—Footwear* in Kenosha, Wisconsin.

AAA Sports

See listing under *Sporting Goods* in La Crosse, Wisconsin.

AAA Sports

See listing under *Sporting Goods* in Madison, Wisconsin.

Formfit

See listing under *Clothing—Lingerie* in Madison, Wisconsin.

Mitchell Handbags
See listing under *Clothing—Accessories* in Milwaukee, Wisconsin.

West Bend Woolen Mills
See listing under *Clothing—Sportswear* in West Bend, Wisconsin.

CLOTHING—BABIES'

The outlets listed here primarily sell clothing for infants and toddlers, although there is much overlapping in the clothing division, and many also sell children's clothing. Look in Chapter 3, *Baby Accessories*, because many of those outlets also sell baby clothes, and look in this chapter under *Children's* and *Family* for more outlets that sell baby clothes.

You probably won't think twice about buying seconds or irregular diapers, undershirts, rubber pants, or sleepers. Most of the dresses, shirts, pants, rompers, etc., I saw in seconds had only minor flaws, and, considering the rough use, frequent washings, and short time they'll fit your baby, can be excellent buys. End-of-season savings are excellent, but remember to buy for the size your baby will be when that season rolls around again, or buy a few extra things to give as gifts in the seasons to come.

ILLINOIS

CHICAGO, IL

Rubens Baby Factory, 2340 N. Racine Avenue, Chicago, IL 60614; (312) 348-6200
This factory outlet sells baby underwear: kimonos, bibs, pants, shirts, diapers, and crib sheets. They also sell cribs and bassinets. Most items sold at the factory are seconds, irregulars, imperfect, samples, or discontinued merchandise.

SUN.	MON.	TUE.	WED.	THU.	FRI.	SAT.
closed	9–3:30	9–3:30	9–3:30	9–3:30	9–3:30	closed

SAVINGS: 25%–50% off
BRAND NAMES: Rubens
PARKING: street
PAYMENT: cash, checks

SCHAUMBURG, IL

The Children's Outlet, 175 W. Golf Road, Schaumburg, IL 60195; (312) 884-6170
This is the outlet for the Federated Department Store chain. They sell major brands of infants' and children's clothing, including Health-Tex and OshKosh B'Gosh. Most merchandise is seconds, irregulars, last year's lines, end-of-season, discontinued, and closeouts, which provide the best savings. They have other stores in Indianapolis, Indiana; and La Crosse, Wisconsin.

SUN.	MON.	TUE.	WED.	THU.	FRI.	SAT.
11–5	10–9	10–9	10–9	10–9	10–9	10–6

SAVINGS: 10%–50% off
BRAND NAMES: Health-Tex, OshKosh B'Gosh, Carter
PARKING: lot

PAYMENT: cash, checks (amount of purchase only, with proper I.D.), MasterCard, VISA, American Express

INDIANA
FRANKLIN, IN

Carter's Factory Outlet, Northwood Plaza Shopping Center, U.S. Route 31, Franklin, IN 46131; (317) 736-8667
    This is the factory outlet for Carter's underwear and pajamas in infant and children's sizes. They also sell other brands at lesser savings. Greatest savings are on seconds, irregulars, overstocks, last year's lines, and closeout merchandise. They have other stores in Kenosha and Plover, Wisconsin.

SUN.	MON.	TUE.	WED.	THU.	FRI.	SAT.
noon-5	10-5	10-5	10-5	10-5	10-5	10-5

SAVINGS: 20%–50% off
BRAND NAMES: Carter
SALE DAYS: vary
PARKING: lot
PAYMENT: cash, checks (amount of purchase only, with proper I.D.)

GARY, IN

Brady's This Is It—Factory Outlet Store—Clothing
    See listing under *Clothing—Family* in Gary, Indiana.

INDIANAPOLIS, IN

The Children's Outlet, Eastgate Consumer Mall, 7150 E. Washington Street, Indianapolis, IN 46201; (317) 359-2021
    See listing in Schaumburg, Illinois.

SUN.	MON.	TUE.	WED.	THU.	FRI.	SAT.
noon-5	10-9	10-9	10-9	10-9	10-9	10-9

SAVINGS: 10%–50% off
BRAND NAMES: Lee
PARKING: lot
PAYMENT: cash, checks (amount of purchase only, with proper I.D.), MasterCard, VISA, American Express

Les Kids
    See listing under *Clothing—Children's* in Indianapolis, Indiana.

MERRILLVILLE, IN

Kid's Ca'pers
    See listing under *Clothing—Children's* in Merrillville, Indiana.

MIDDLEBURY, IN

Gohn Brothers Manufacturing Company
    See listing under *Fabrics* in Middlebury, Indiana.

MISHAWAKA, IN

Kid's Ca'pers
    See listing under *Clothing—Children's* in Mishawaka, Indiana.

Socks Galore and More
    See listing under *Clothing—Accessories* in Mishawaka, Indiana.

Carter's Factory Outlet, Factory Outlet Centre, 7700 120th Avenue, Kenosha, WI 53142; (414) 857-2049
See listing in Franklin, Indiana.

SUN.	MON.	TUE.	WED.	THU.	FRI.	SAT.
11–5	9:30–9	9:30–9	9:30–9	9:30–9	9:30–9	9:30–6

SAVINGS: 20%–50% off
BRAND NAMES: Carter's
PARKING: lot
PAYMENT: cash, checks (with proper I.D.)

Kid's Ca'pers, Factory Outlet Centre, 7700 120th Avenue, Kenosha, WI 53142; (414) 857-2287
See listing in Mishawaka, Indiana.

SUN.	MON.	TUE.	WED.	THU.	FRI.	SAT.
11–5	9:30–9	9:30–9	9:30–9	9:30–9	9:30–9	9:30–6

SAVINGS: 25%–75% off   *Mailing List*
BRAND NAMES: Kid's Ca'pers
SALE DAYS: vary
PARKING: lot
PAYMENT: cash, checks (with proper I.D.), MasterCard, VISA

Socks Galore and More
See listing under *Clothing—Accessories* in Kenosha, Wisconsin.

Children's Outlet, La Crosse Factory Outlet Mall, 301 Sky Harbor Drive, La Crosse, WI 54601; (608) 783-7440
See listing in Schaumburg, Illinois.

SUN.	MON.	TUE.	WED.	THU.	FRI.	SAT.
11–5	10–9	10–9	10–9	10–9	10–9	9–6

SAVINGS: 10%–50% off   *Mailing List*
BRAND NAMES: Britanna, OshKosh B'Gosh, Petite Ami, Wrangler
ANNUAL SALES: winter clearance
PARKING: lot
PAYMENT: cash, checks (amount of purchase only, with proper I.D.), MasterCard, VISA .

Kid's Ca'pers
See listing under *Clothing—Children's* in Madison, Wisconsin.

Carter's Factory Outlet, Manufacturers Direct Mall, 101 Plover Road, Plover, WI 54467; (715) 344-2193
See listing in Franklin, Indiana.

SUN.	MON.	TUE.	WED.	THU.	FRI.	SAT.
11–6	9:30–9	9:30–9	9:30–9	9:30–9	9:30–9	9:30–6

SAVINGS: 20%–50% off
BRAND NAMES: Carter's, Lawrence, Pixie Playmates, Billy the Kid, Ronna
ANNUAL SALES: twice a year
PARKING: lot
PAYMENT: cash, checks ($300 maximum)

CLOTHING—CHILDREN'S

Since the lines between baby clothes and children's clothes are slim, look in this chapter under *Babies'*; also look in this chapter under *Family* for more outlets that sell children's clothing.

Savings on seconds and irregulars can be excellent. When buying closeout or discontinued merchandise or end-of-season items, keep in mind what size your child will be when the clothes are again in season.

ILLINOIS

CHICAGO, IL

The Children's Outlet
See listing under *Clothing—Babies'* in Schaumburg, Illinois.

Cut-Rate Toys
See listing under *Toys* in Chicago, Illinois.

Meystel
See listing under *Clothing—Family* in Chicago, Illinois.

CICERO, IL

Kids Things, Guinta's Factory Outlet Mall, 1800 S. Cicero Avenue, Cicero, IL 60650; (312) 852-6962
This outlet sells infants' and children's clothing at savings that begin at 30% off retail price.

SUN.	MON.	TUE.	WED.	THU.	FRI.	SAT.
10–6	10–8	closed	10–8	10–8	10–8	10–6

SAVINGS: at least 30% off
PARKING: lot
PAYMENT: cash, checks (amount of purchase only, with proper I.D.), MasterCard, VISA

DOWNERS GROVE, IL

Clothes-Outs, 2752 Maple Avenue, Downers Grove, IL 60515; (312) 963-8890
This shop sells major brands of children's clothing: shirts, jeans, pants, underwear, and socks. Savings are greatest on irregulars.

SUN.	MON.	TUE.	WED.	THU.	FRI.	SAT.
11–4	10–5:30	10–5:30	10–5:30	10–8:30	10–5:30	10–5

SAVINGS: 15%–25% off
SALE DAYS: vary
PARKING: lot
PAYMENT: cash, checks (amount of purchase only, with proper I.D.), MasterCard, VISA

EVANSTON, IL

Good Children Street, 914 Chicago Avenue, Evanston, IL 60201; (312) 869-5980
This shop makes their own children's clothing. It was very difficult to determine the savings compared to mass-produced, comparable clothing, but the quality seems excellent.

SUN.	MON.	TUE.	WED.	THU.	FRI.	SAT.
closed	11–5:30	11–5:30	11–5:30	11–5:30	11–5:30	11–4

SAVINGS: 10%–20% off   *All First Quality*
PARKING: street, meters
PAYMENT: cash, checks, MasterCard, VISA

The Wear House, 6101 Gross Point Road, Niles, IL 60648; (312) 647-1211
This factory manufactures many major brands of snowsuits, ski vests and pants, sweaters, knit tops, sportwear, jackets, and swimsuits. Most merchandise is for children, but some ladies' clothing is available. Savings begin at 50% off retail price on first quality, and climb to 70% on seconds, irregulars, samples, surplus, overruns, last year's lines, end-of-season, discontinued, closeout, and some "as is" merchandise.

SUN.	MON.	TUE.	WED.	THU.	FRI.	SAT.
closed	10–4:30	10–4:30	10–4:30	10–4:30	10–4:30	10–3

SAVINGS: 50%–70% off   *Mailing List*
PARKING: lot
PAYMENT: cash and travelers' checks only

The Children's Outlet
See listing under *Clothing—Babies'* in Schaumburg, Illinois.

Chocolate Soup, 602 Green Bay Road, Winnetka, IL 60093; (312) 446-8951
This outlet sells children's clothing, in infants' and boys' sizes to 6 and girls' sizes to 12, at discounts up to 70% off retail prices on last year's lines, end-of-season, and discontinued merchandise.

SUN.	MON.	TUE.	WED.	THU.	FRI.	SAT.
closed	10:30–5:30	10–5:30	10:30–5:30	10–5:30	10–5:30	10–5:30

SAVINGS: 10%–70% off   *Mailing List*
BRAND NAMES: CS
ANNUAL SALES: back-to-school, Christmas, January
PARKING: lot
PAYMENT: cash, checks (with proper I.D.), MasterCard, VISA

Kid and Kaboodle, 1048 Gage Street, Winnetka, IL 60093; (312) 441-6640
This is a children's resale shop, but look for samples and overruns in Billy the Kid children's shirts, Season snowsuits, OshKosh B'Gosh jeans and overalls, and Donmoor shirts, shorts, and coveralls. Savings run 33%–50% off normal retail prices.

SUN.	MON.	TUE.	WED.	THU.	FRI.	SAT.
closed	closed	10–4	10–4	10–4	10–4	10–4

SAVINGS: 33%–50% off   *Mailing List*
BRAND NAMES: Billy the Kid, OshKosh B'Gosh, Season, Donmoor
ANNUAL SALES: January, March, July, August
PARKING: lot
PAYMENT: cash, checks

Carter's Factory Outlet
See listing under *Clothing—Babies'* in Franklin, Indiana.

The Children's Outlet
See listing under *Clothing—Babies'*, in Indianapolis, Indiana.

Les Kids, Nora Plaza Shopping Center, 1300 E. 86th Street, Indianapolis, IN 46240; (317) 844-4498
This is a sample shop offering mostly one-of-a-kind clothing for boys and girls, infants through preteens. They carry many major brands.

SUN.	MON.	TUE.	WED.	THU.	FRI.	SAT.
closed	10-6	10-6	10-6	10-6	10-6	10-5

SAVINGS: 25%–40% off
BRAND NAMES: London Fog, Bryan, Head, Tidykins, Baby Bliss, Youngland, Cinderella
ANNUAL SALES: January, July
PARKING: lot
PAYMENT: cash, checks (amount of purchase only, with proper I.D.), MasterCard, VISA

MERRILLVILLE, IN

Kid's Ca'pers, Century Consumer Mall, 8275 Broadway, Merrillville, IN 46410; (219) 769-2459

This is the outlet of Jolene children's dresses. They also sell Garanimals and Stone babies' and children's clothing. Greatest savings are on seconds, which are clearly marked. They have other stores in Mishawaka, Indiana; and Kenosha and Madison Wisconsin.

SUN.	MON.	TUE.	WED.	THU.	FRI.	SAT.
11-5	10-9	10-9	10-9	10-9	10-9	10-9

SAVINGS: 20%–70% off   *Mailing List*
SPECIAL SALES: most holidays
ANNUAL SALES: January, June
PARKING: lot
PAYMENT: cash, checks (amount of purchase only, with proper I.D.), MasterCard, VISA

Kid's Warehouse, 7239 Taft Street, Merrillville, IN 46410; (219) 769-5034

This is an outlet for OshKosh B'Gosh and many other national brands of boys' and girls' clothing. Boys' clothing runs to size 7; girls' clothing runs to size 14. They also sell girls' underwear. Savings average 20% off retail price, but are greater on overstocks, discontinued, and closeout items.

SUN.	MON.	TUE.	WED.	THU.	FRI.	SAT.
closed	10-6	10-6	10-6	10-6	10-6	10-6

SAVINGS: average 20% off
BRAND NAMES: OshKosh B'Gosh
ANNUAL SALES: July
PARKING: lot
PAYMENT: cash, checks, MasterCard, VISA

MISHAWAKA, IN

Kid's Ca'pers, Buyer's Marketplace, 5901 N. Grape Road, Mishawaka, IN 46545; (219) 277-2940

See listing in Merrillville, Indiana.

SUN.	MON.	TUE.	WED.	THU.	FRI.	SAT.
noon-5	9:30-9	9:30-9	9:30-9	9:30-9	9:30-9	9:30-9

SAVINGS: about 50% off   *Mailing List*
BRAND NAMES: Jolene, Garanimals, Stone
SALE DAYS: Tuesday
ANNUAL SALES: back-to-school, baby sale four times a year
PARKING: lot
PAYMENT: cash, checks (amount of purchase only, with proper I.D.), MasterCard, VISA

WISCONSIN
APPLETON, WI

Knit Pikker
See listing under *Clothing—Accessories* in Appleton, Wisconsin.

Zwicker Knitting Mills
See listing under *Clothing—Accessories* in Appleton, Wisconsin.

Florence Eiseman, Inc., 631 S. Hickory Street, Fond du Lac, WI 54935; (414)
922-0030
This factory outlet is open only twice a year, for two weekends in April and two weekends in October. Savings run from 50% off retail price on first quality to 75% off retail price on overruns and overstocks of children's clothing. Ask to be put on their mailing list so you will know when the sales are scheduled. They have another outlet in Milwaukee, Wisconsin.

SUN.	MON.	TUE.	WED.	THU.	FRI.	SAT.
*	closed	closed	closed	closed	closed	*

SAVINGS: 50%–75% off   *Mailing List*
ANNUAL SALES: April, October
PARKING: lot
PAYMENT: cash, checks (amount of purchase only, with proper I.D.), MasterCard, VISA

---

*First Saturday: 7:00–5:00; second Saturday: 9:00–4:00; both Sundays: 10:00–4:00.

Carter's Factory Outlet
See listing under *Clothing—Babies'* in Kenosha, Wisconsin.

Kid's Ca'pers
See listing under *Clothing—Babies'* in Kenosha, Wisconsin.

Knit Pikker
See listing under *Clothing—Accessories* in Kenosha, Wisconsin.

Children's Outlet
See listing under *Clothing—Babies'* in La Crosse, Wisconsin.

Kid's Ca'pers, Factory Outlet Centre, 4609 Verona Road, Madison, WI 53704; (608)
273-8877
See listing in Merrillville, Indiana

SUN.	MON.	TUE.	WED.	THU.	FRI.	SAT.
noon-5	9:30-9	9:30-9	9:30-9	9:30-9	9:30-9	9:30-6

SAVINGS: 20%–50% off   *Mailing List*
SALE DAYS: vary
PARKING: lot
PAYMENT: cash, checks (amount of purchase only, with proper I.D.), MasterCard, VISA

Florence Eiseman, Inc., 301 N. Water Street, Milwaukee, WI 53202; (414) 271-3222
See listing in Fond du Lac, Wisconsin.

SUN.	MON.	TUE.	WED.	THU.	FRI.	SAT.
*	closed	closed	closed	closed	closed	*

SAVINGS: 50%–75% off   *Mailing List*
ANNUAL SALES: April, October
PARKING: lot

PAYMENT: cash, checks (amount of purchase only, with proper I.D.), MasterCard, VISA
_____
*First Saturday: 7:00–5:00; second Saturday: 9:00–4:00; both Sundays: 10:00–4:00.

Carter's Factory Outlet
See listing under *Clothing—Babies'* in Plover, Wisconsin.

Knit Pikker
See listing under *Clothing—Accessories* in Waupaca, Wisconsin.

Knit Pikker
See listing under *Clothing—Accessories* in West Allis, Wisconsin.

Knit Pikker
See listing under *Clothing—Accessories* in West Bend, Wisconsin.

CLOTHING—FAMILY

This chapter includes outlets that sell clothing for every member of the family. Also look in all of the other clothing chapters for specific family members or clothing items and in Chapter 10, *Department Stores*.

Burlington Coat Factory
See listing under *Clothing—Outerwear* in Chicago, Illinois.

Meystel, 1222 S. Wabash Avenue, Chicago, IL 60605; (312) 922-5930
This store sells many brands of men's, women's, and children's clothing. Savings average about 50% off retail price on seconds and irregulars. They occasionally have last year's lines.

SUN.	MON.	TUE.	WED.	THU.	FRI.	SAT.
10-4	8-5	8-5	8-5	8-5	8-5	closed

SAVINGS: about 50% off
ANNUAL SALES: January/February, July
PARKING: lot
PAYMENT: cash, checks (amount of purchase only, with proper I.D.), MasterCard, VISA

Burlington Coat Factory Warehouse
See listing under *Clothing—Outerwear* in Arlington Heights, Illinois.

Gossard's Factory Outlet
See listing under *Clothing—Activewear* in Batavia, Illinois.

Burlington Coat Factory Warehouse
See listing under *Clothing—Outerwear* in Libertyville, Illinois.

VIP Yarn and Craft Center, Knit Pikker, Gloray Knitting Mills
See listing under *Crafts* in Loves Park, Illinois.

Front Row
See listing under *Clothing—Accessories* in Morton Grove, Illinois.

Front Row
See listing under *Clothing—Accessories* in Naperville, Illinois.

Burlington Coat Factory
See listing under *Clothing—Outerwear* in Villa Park, Illinois.

Ashley's Outlet Store, 607 Diamond Avenue, Evansville, IN 47711; (812) 423-0353
This is one of several outlets selling major brands of men's and women's clothing, as well as bedspreads, towels, curtains, and comforters. Although 80% of the merchandise is first quality, savings on seconds and irregulars can go as high as 75% off retail price. They have other stores in Evansville, Mount Vernon, and Tell City, Indiana.

SUN.	MON.	TUE.	WED.	THU.	FRI.	SAT.
1–5	10–8	10–8	10–8	10–8	10–8	9:30–5:30

SAVINGS: up to 75% off   *Mailing List*
ANNUAL SALES: back-to-school, Christmas
SPECIAL DISCOUNTS: senior citizens, 10% off Monday through Thursday
PARKING: lot
PAYMENT: cash, checks (amount of purchase only, with proper I.D.), MasterCard, VISA

Ashley's Outlet Store, South Lane Shopping Center, 2606 S. Kentucky Avenue, Evansville, IN 47714; (812) 423-9732
See listing above.

SUN.	MON.	TUE.	WED.	THU.	FRI.	SAT.
1–5	10–8	10–8	10–8	10–8	10–8	9:30–5:30

SAVINGS: up to 75% off   *Mailing List*
ANNUAL SALES: back-to-school, Christmas
SPECIAL DISCOUNTS: senior citizens, 10% off Monday through Thursday
PARKING: lot
PAYMENT: cash, checks (amount of purchase only, with proper I.D.), MasterCard, VISA

Ashley's Outlet Store, 1412 S. Green River Road, Evansville, IN 47714; (812) 473-4401
See listing above.

SUN.	MON.	TUE.	WED.	THU.	FRI.	SAT.
1–5	10–8	10–8	10–8	10–8	10–8	9:30–5:30

SAVINGS: up to 75% off   *Mailing List*
ANNUAL SALES: back-to-school, Christmas
SPECAL DISCOUNTS: senior citizens, 10% off Monday through Thursday
PARKING: lot
PAYMENT: cash, checks (amount of purchase only, with proper I.D.), MasterCard, VISA

Brady's This Is It—Factory Outlet Store—Clothing, 5306 W. 25th Avenue, Gary,
IN 46406; (219) 844-1130
　　This store sells clothing for men, women, and children. They also sell men's work
shoes and children's underwear. Savings begin at 20% off retail price, and can go as
high as 45% off retail price on some seconds and discontinued merchandise. See other
Brady's stores (p.000–000).

SUN.	MON.	TUE.	WED.	THU.	FRI.	SAT.
10-6	10-9	10-9	10-9	10-9	10-9	10-9

SAVINGS: 20%–45% off
BRAND NAMES: BB Walker, Spencer, Union, Fruit of the Loom
PARKING: lot
PAYMENT: cash, MasterCard, VISA

Burlington Coat Factory
　　See listing under *Clothing—Outerwear* in Indianapolis, Indiana.

C J's Company Store, Eastgate Consumer Mall, 7150 E. Washington Street,
Indianapolis, IN 64610; (317) 359-9720
　　This outlet sells mostly women's and children's clothing, although there are some
men's. Savings average 30%–50% off retail price on all first quality merchandise.

SUN.	MON.	TUE.	WED.	THU.	FRI.	SAT.
noon-5	10-9	10-9	10-9	10-9	10-9	10-9

SAVINGS: 30%–50% off　　　　　　　　　*Mailing List*　　　*All First Quality*
SPECIAL SALES: vary
ANNUAL SALES: August, November, Christmas
PARKING: lot
PAYMENT: cash, checks (amount of purchase only, with proper I.D.), MasterCard, VISA

The Front Row
　　See listing under *Clothing—Accessories* in Indianapolis, Indiana.

Ashley's Outlet Store, 3 D Shopping Center, Highway 231, Jasper, IN 47546; (812)
634-9400
　　See listing in Evansville, Indiana.

SUN.	MON.	TUE.	WED.	THU.	FRI.	SAT.
1-5	10-8	10-6	10-6	10-6	10-8	9:30-5:30

SAVINGS: up to 75% off　　　　　　　　　　　　　　　　　*Mailing List*
ANNUAL SALES: back-to-school, Christmas
SPECIAL DISCOUNTS: senior citizens, 10% off Monday through Thursday
PARKING: lot
PAYMENT: cash, checks (amount of purchase only, with proper I.D.), MasterCard, VISA

Burlington Coat Factory
　　See listing under *Clothing—Outerwear* in Merrillville, Indiana.

Ashley's Outlet Store, Southwinds Shopping Center, Highway 62 East, Mount
Vernon, IN 47620; (812) 838-2251
    See listing in Evansville, Indiana.

SUN.	MON.	TUE.	WED.	THU.	FRI.	SAT.
1-5	10-8	10-6	10-6	10-6	10-8	9:30-5:30

SAVINGS: up to 75% off   *Mailing List*
ANNUAL SALES: back-to-school, Christmas
SPECIAL DISCOUNTS: senior citizens, 10% off Monday through Thursday
PARKING: lot
PAYMENT: cash, checks (amount of purchase only, with proper I.D.), MasterCard, VISA

Ashley's Outlet Store, 114 E. Highway 66 South, Tell City, IN 47586; (812) 547-8025
    See listing in Evansville, Indiana.

SUN.	MON.	TUE.	WED.	THU.	FRI.	SAT.
1-5	10-8	10-6	10-6	10-6	10-8	9:30-5:30

SAVINGS: up to 75% off   *Mailing List*
ANNUAL SALES: back-to-school, Christmas
SPECIAL DISCOUNTS: senior citizens, 10% off Monday through Thursday
PARKING: lot
PAYMENT: cash, checks (amount of purchase only, with proper I.D.), MasterCard, VISA

The Genuine Article, Factory Outlet Centre, 7700 120th Avenue, Kenosha, WI 53142;
    (414) 857-9224
    This is the outlet for OshKosh B'Gosh clothing. They sell clothing for infants,
toddlers, children, teens, and adults, as well as some sportswear and men's workwear.
They started with bib overalls; their new line is Oh M'Gosh maternity clothes. Savings
are greatest on some irregulars, last year's line, discontinued, and closeout
merchandise. They also have outlets in Oshkosh, Plover, and West Bend, Wisconsin.

SUN.	MON.	TUE.	WED.	THU.	FRI.	SAT.
11-5	9:30-9	9:30-9	9:30-9	9:30-9	9:30-9	9:30-6

SAVINGS: 20%-50% off   *Mailing List*
BRAND NAMES: OshKosh B'Gosh, Oh M'Gosh
PARKING: lot
PAYMENT: cash, checks (amount of purchase only, with proper I.D.), MasterCard, VISA

Wag's Family Outlet, La Crosse Factory Outlet Mall, 301 Sky Harbor Drive, La
    Crosse, WI 54601; (608) 783-7633
    This outlet sells sportswear for all members of the family. Savings begin about
20% off retail price on first quality, and can reach 50% on irregulars, samples, last
year's lines, discontinued, and closeout merchandise.

SUN.	MON.	TUE.	WED.	THU.	FRI.	SAT.
11-5	10-9	10-9	10-9	10-9	10-9	10-6

SAVINGS: 20%-50% off
SALE DAYS: vary
SPECIAL DISCOUNTS: senior citizens, 10% off
PARKING: lot
PAYMENT: cash, checks (amount of purchase only, with proper I.D.), MasterCard, VISA

Burlington Coat Factory
See listing under *Clothing—Outerwear* in Madison, Wisconsin.

Branovan Outlet Store, 6555 W. Mill Road, Milwaukee, WI 53218; (414) 353-6900
This store sells several major brands of clothing and shoes. Most pairs of shoes are $5.00 off retail price.

SUN.	MON.	TUE.	WED.	THU.	FRI.	SAT.
closed	9–5	9–5	9–5	9–6	9–6	9–5

SAVINGS: 10%–30% off   *Mailing List*   *All First Quality*
SALE DAYS: vary
PARKING: lot
PAYMENT: cash, checks (amount of purchase only, with proper I.D., no out-of-state checks), MasterCard, VISA, American Express

Burlington Coat Factory
See two listings under *Clothing—Outerwear* in Milwaukee, Wisconsin.

The Genuine Article, 206 State Street, Oshkosh, WI 54901; (414) 426-5817
See listing in Kenosha, Wisconsin.

SUN.	MON.	TUE.	WED.	THU.	FRI.	SAT.
11–4	9:30–5	9:30–5	9:30–5	9:30–5	9:30–8	9:30–5

SAVINGS: 20%–50% off   *Mailing List*
BRAND NAMES: OshKosh B'Gosh, Oh M'Gosh
PARKING: lot
PAYMENT: cash, checks (amount of purchase only, with proper I.D.), MasterCard, VISA

C. J. Sports and T-Shirts, Manufacturers Direct Mall, 101 Plover Road, Plover, WI 54467; (715) 341-9292
This store sells T-shirts; they also sell socks and sports jackets. Savings average about 20% off retail price. At the time I was there they were selling a dozen custom-made T-shirts for $25.00.

SUN.	MON.	TUE.	WED.	THU.	FRI.	SAT.
9:30–6	9:30–9	9:30–9	9:30–9	9:30–9	9:30–9	9:30–6

SAVINGS: 20% off   *All First Quality*
PARKING: lot
PAYMENT: cash, checks, MasterCard, VISA

The Genuine Article, Factory Direct Mall, 101 Plover Road, Plover, WI 54467; (715) 344-0175
See listing in Kenosha, Wisconsin.

SUN.	MON.	TUE.	WED.	THU.	FRI.	SAT.
11–6	9:30–9	9:30–9	9:30–9	9:30–9	9:30–9	9:30–6

SAVINGS: 20%–50% off   *Mailing List*
BRAND NAMES: OshKosh B'Gosh, Oh M'Gosh
SPECIAL SALES: end-of-season
PARKING: lot
PAYMENT: cash, checks (amount of purchase only, with proper I.D.), MasterCard, VISA

The Genuine Article, West Bend Outlet Mall, 180 Island Avenue, West Bend, WI 53095; (414) 334-1121
See listing in Kenosha, Wisconsin.

SUN.	MON.	TUE.	WED.	THU.	FRI.	SAT.
11-5	9:30-6	9:30-6	9:30-6	9:30-6	9:30-6	9:30-5

SAVINGS: 20%-50% off   *Mailing List*
BRAND NAMES: OshKosh B'Gosh, Oh M'Gosh
ANNUAL SALES: spring, summer, fall, winter
PARKING: lot
PAYMENT: cash, checks (amount of purchase only, with proper I.D.), MasterCard, VISA

CLOTHING—FOOTWEAR

These outlets sell mostly shoes, although many of them also sell clothing accessories. Also look in other clothing sections, since many other stores sell shoes along with other clothing, and in Chapter 10, *Department Stores.*

Savings were excellent on seconds, but look closely and be sure to try on both shoes. This is not a category where I would recommend bringing along sizes for other members of your family. Return policies vary, so it is safer for each person to try on the shoes at the store.

ILLINOIS

CHICAGO, IL

Adams Factory Shoe Outlet, 3655 W. Irving Park Road, Chicago, IL 60618; (312) 539-4120
They say they are not allowed to specify for which "major brands" they are an outlet. Savings run 10%-25% off retail price on first quality, and up to 50% on irregulars, samples, and closeouts of men's, women's, and children's shoes.

SUN.	MON.	TUE.	WED.	THU.	FRI.	SAT.
10-4:30	9-9	9-6	9-6	9-9	9-9	9-6

SAVINGS: 10%-50% off   *Mailing List*
PARKING: lot
PAYMENT: cash, checks (amount of purchase only, with proper I.D.), MasterCard, VISA

Chicago Shoe Outlet, 4020 N. Lincoln Avenue, Chicago, IL 60618; (312) 528-9333
This store sells major brands of men's, women's, and children's shoes. Best savings are on irregulars, discontinued, closeouts, and last year's lines.

SUN.	MON.	TUE.	WED.	THU.	FRI.	SAT.
11:30-5:30	10-8	10-7	10-7	10-8	10-8	9:30-7

SAVINGS: 20%-25% off
BRAND NAMES: Barclay, Nike, Energetics, Mellow-Mate, Mother Goose
ANNUAL SALES: July
PARKING: street, meter, can be difficult
PAYMENT: cash, checks (amount of purchase only, with proper I.D.), MasterCard, VISA, American Express

General Jobbing Corporation Warehouse
See listing under *Clothing—Men's* in Chicago, Illinois.

ARLINGTON HEIGHTS, IL

Tony Lama Boots, 456 E. Rand Road, Arlington Heights, IL 60004; (312) 392-7722
This is one of several outlets for Tony Lama boots. Savings begin at 20% off on

first quality, and can run as high as 40% on a few irregulars, last year's line, and end-of-season merchandise. They also sell socks, belts, purses, and accessories. They have other stores in Chicago Ridge, Downers Grove, Matteson, Naperville, Schaumburg, and Skokie, Illinois; and in Merrillville, Indiana.

SUN.	MON.	TUE.	WED.	THU.	FRI.	SAT.
11-5	10-9	10-9	10-9	10-9	10-9	9:30-6

SAVINGS: about 30% off   *Mailing List*
BRAND NAMES: Tony Lama, Zodiac, Bingo
PARKING: lot
PAYMENT: cash, checks (amount of purchase only, with proper I.D.), MasterCard,
    VISA, American Express, Diners Club

CHAMPAIGN, IL

Bass Shoe Factory Outlet, 503 S. Mattis Street, Champaign, IL 61820; (217)
    359-7359
    This is an outlet for Bass Shoes. Savings start at 20% off on first quality and go higher on irregulars, surplus, overruns, last year's line, end-of-season, discontinued, and closeouts. They even take $5.00 off the price of Nike tennis shoes. See listing below.

SUN.	MON.	TUE.	WED.	THU.	FRI.	SAT.
10-6	9-9	9-9	9-9	9-9	9-9	9-9

SAVINGS: 20%-50% off
BRAND NAMES: Bass, Nike
SALE DAYS: vary
PARKING: lot
PAYMENT: cash, checks (amount of purchase only, with proper I.D.), MasterCard,
    VISA, American Express

Bass Shoe Factory Outlet, 1901 N. Market Street, Champaign, IL 61820; (217)
    398-0068
    See listing above.

SUN.	MON.	TUE.	WED.	THU.	FRI.	SAT.
noon-5	10-9	10-9	10-9	10-9	10-9	10-9

SAVINGS: 20%-50% off
BRAND NAMES: Bass, Weejuns
PARKING: lot
PAYMENT: cash, checks (with proper I.D.), MasterCard, VISA, American Express

CHICAGO RIDGE, IL

Tony Lama Boots, 100 Chicago Ridge Mall, Chicago Ridge, IL 60415; (312) 424-9669
    See listing in Arlington Heights, Illinois.

SUN.	MON.	TUE.	WED.	THU.	FRI.	SAT.
11-5	10-9	10-9	10-9	10-9	10-9	9:30-6

SAVINGS: about 30% off   *Mailing List*
BRAND NAMES: Tony Lama, Zodiac, Dingos
PARKING: lot
PAYMENT: cash, checks (amount of purchase only, with proper I.D.), MasterCard,
    VISA, American Express, Diners Club

DOWNERS GROVE, IL

The Outletters
    See listing under *Clothing—Outerwear* in Downers Grove, Illinois.

Tony Lama Boots, 1304 Butterfield Road, Downers Grove, IL 60515; (312) 629-8220
  See listing in Arlington Heights, Illinois.

SUN.	MON.	TUE.	WED.	THU.	FRI.	SAT.
noon-5	10-9	10-9	10-9	10-9	10-9	10-6

SAVINGS: 25%–40% off
BRAND NAMES: Tony Lama
PARKING: lot
PAYMENT: cash, checks (amount of purchase only, with proper I.D.), MasterCard,
  VISA, American Express

ELK GROVE VILLAGE, IL

Lebo's Factory Shoe Outlet, 1440 S. Busse Road, Elk Grove Village, IL 60007; (312)
  640-7004
    This store sell major brands of shoes, handbags, and socks at savings of 20%–50%
off retail price. Best buys are on overruns, end-of-season merchandise, discontinued,
and closeouts. They occasionally have some seconds, which are clearly marked. They
have another store in Tinley Park, Illinois.

SUN.	MON.	TUE.	WED.	THU.	FRI.	SAT.
10-5	9:30-9	9:30-9	9:30-9	9:30-9	9:30-9	9:30-6

SAVINGS: 20%–50% off   *Mailing List*
BRAND NAMES: Nike, Adidas, Hush Puppies
PARKING: lot
PAYMENT: cash, checks (amount of purchase only, with proper I.D.), MasterCard, VISA

FRANKLIN PARK, IL

Todd's Factory Outlet Store, 2727 N. Mannheim Road, Franklin Park, IL 60131; (312)
  451-0024
    This is the factory outlet for Frye boots. Savings on men's and women's shoes and
boots, and some handbags and accessories, begin at 30% off retail price on first
quality and can go as high as 70% on some seconds, irregulars, overstocks, and last
year's lines.

SUN.	MON.	TUE.	WED.	THU.	FRI.	SAT.
noon-5	10-6	10-6	10-8	10-8	10-8	10-6

SAVINGS: 40%–60% off
BRAND NAMES: Frye
SALE DAYS: vary
PARKING: lot
PAYMENT: cash, checks (amount of purchase only, with proper I.D.), MasterCard,
  VISA, American Express

LOVES PARK, IL

Bass Shoe Factory Outlet, Park Plaza Outlet Mart, 6411 N. 2nd Street, Loves Park,
  IL 61111; (815) 654-3130
    See listing in Champaign, Illinois.

SUN.	MON.	TUE.	WED.	THU.	FRI.	SAT.
11-5	9:30-9	9:30-9	9:30-9	9:30-9	9:30-9	9:30-6

SAVINGS: 20%–70% off
BRAND NAMES: Bass, Beartraps
PARKING: lot
PAYMENT: cash, checks, MasterCard, VISA, American Express

MATTESON, IL

Tony Lama Boots, 130 Town Center Plaza, Matteson, IL 60443; (312) 748-2808
  See listing in Arlington Heights, Illinois.

SUN.	MON.	TUE.	WED.	THU.	FRI.	SAT.
noon-5	10-9	10-9	10-9	10-9	10-9	10-6

SAVINGS: 25%–40% off
BRAND NAMES: Tony Lama
PARKING: lot
PAYMENT: cash, checks (amount of purchase only, with proper I.D.), MasterCard, VISA, American Express

NAPERVILLE, IL

Tony Lama Boots, 1163 E. Ogden Avenue, Naperville, IL 60540; (312) 355-9737
See listing in Arlington Heights, Illinois.

SUN.	MON.	TUE.	WED.	THU.	FRI.	SAT.
11-5	10-9	10-9	10-9	10-9	10-9	10-6

SAVINGS: 25%–40% off
BRAND NAMES: Tony Lama
ANNUAL SALES: August
PARKING: lot
PAYMENT: cash, checks (amount of purchase only, with proper I.D.), MasterCard, VISA, American Express

ROLLING MEADOWS, IL

Sneakee Feet, 1400 E. Golf Road, Rolling Meadows, IL 60008; (312) 439-1118
This is an outlet for Athlete's Foot stores. They sell sports shoes, some sports clothing, and some sports equipment at savings that begin at 20% off retail price on first quality and can go up to 60% on some seconds, surplus, discontinued, closeouts, and last year's lines.

SUN.	MON.	TUE.	WED.	THU.	FRI.	SAT.
11-5	10-9:30	10-9:30	10-9:30	10-9:30	10-9:30	10-6

SAVINGS: 20%–60% off
ANNUAL SALES: October
PARKING: lot
PAYMENT: cash, checks (amount of purchase only, with proper I.D.), MasterCard, VISA, American Express, Diners Club, Discover, Choice

SCHAUMBURG, IL

Famous Footwear, 159 W. Golf Road, Schaumburg, IL 60195; (312) 885-9899
This outlet sells many major brands of shoes for the entire family. Savings begin at approximately 20% off retail price, and can go as high as 40% on some overstocked merchandise. They have other stores in Indianapolis, Merrillville, and Mishawaka, Indiana.

SUN.	MON.	TUE.	WED.	THU.	FRI.	SAT.
noon-5	10-9	10-9	10-9	10-9	10-9	10-6

SAVINGS: 20%–40% off   *All First Quality*
PARKING: lot
PAYMENT: cash, checks (amount of purchase only, with proper I.D.), MasterCard, VISA

Tony Lama Boots, 235 W. Golf Road, Schaumburg, IL 60194; (312) 885-3930
See listing in Arlington Heights, Illinois.

SUN.	MON.	TUE.	WED.	THU.	FRI.	SAT.
noon-5	10-9	10-9	10-9	10-9	10-9	10-6

SAVINGS: 20%–40% off
BRAND NAMES: Tony Lama, Zodiac, Dingos
PARKING: lot
PAYMENT: cash, checks (amount of purchase only, with proper I.D.), MasterCard, VISA, American Express, Diners Club

Tony Lama Boots, 9412 N. Skokie Boulevard, Skokie, IL 60077; (312) 679-3970
See listing in Arlington Heights, Illinois.

SUN.	MON.	TUE.	WED.	THU.	FRI.	SAT.
noon-8	10-9	10-9	10-9	10-9	10-9	10-6

SAVINGS: 20%-40% off
BRAND NAMES: Tony Lama, Zodiac, Dingos
PARKING: lot
PAYMENT: cash, checks (amount of purchase only, with proper I.D.), MasterCard,
VISA, American Express

Lebo's Factory Shoe Outlet, 16037 S. Harlem Avenue, Tinley Park, IL 60477; (312)
429-5040
See listing in Elk Grove Village, Illinois.

SUN.	MON.	TUE.	WED.	THU.	FRI.	SAT.
11-5	10-9	10-9	10-9	10-9	10-9	10-6

SAVINGS: 30%-50% off   *Mailing List*
BRAND NAMES: Nike, Adidas, Hush Puppies, L'Eggs
PARKING: lot
PAYMENT: cash, checks (amount of purchase only, with proper I.D.), MasterCard, VISA

Little Red Shoe House, 1011-A W. 7th Street, Auburn, IN 46706; (219) 925-0060
This is one of many outlets for Wolverine Worldwide shoes. Savings begin at 25%
off and quickly go to 75% off retail price on seconds, irregulars, and some last year's
lines, end-of-season, surplus, discontinued, overstocks, and closeout merchandise.
They also have stores in Mishawaka and Plymouth, Indiana; and in Kenosha, La
Crosse, Madison, Plover, and West Bend, Wisconsin.

SUN.	MON.	TUE.	WED.	THU.	FRI.	SAT.
noon-5	9:30-8	9:30-8	9:30-8	9:30-8	9:30-8	9:30-8

SAVINGS: 10%-50% off   *All First Quality*
PARKING: lot
PAYMENT: cash, checks (amount of purchase only, with proper I.D.), MasterCard,
VISA, American Express

El-Bee Shoes, 1201 College Mall Road, Bloomington, IN 47401; (812) 333-8998
This store sells major brands of men's and women's athletic and dress shoes.
Savings begin at 50% off retail price on first quality, and can go as high as 70% off on
last year's lines. They have other stores in Evansville, three in Indianapolis, Lafayette,
Mishawaka, Muncie, and Richmond, Indiana.

SUN.	MON.	TUE.	WED.	THU.	FRI.	SAT.
noon-5:30	10-9	10-9	10-9	10-9	10-9	10-9

SAVINGS: 50%-70% off
BRAND NAMES: Nunn-Bush, Florsheim, Adidas, Joyce, Puma, Converse
PARKING: lot
PAYMENT: cash, checks (amount of purchase only, with proper I.D.), MasterCard,
VISA, American Express

El-Bee Shoes, 3842 N. First Avenue, Evansville, IN 47710; (812) 423-8815
See listing in Bloomington, Indiana.

SUN.	MON.	TUE.	WED.	THU.	FRI.	SAT.
noon–5	10–9	10–9	10–9	10–9	10–9	10–9

SAVINGS: 50%–70% off   *All First Quality*
BRAND NAMES: Nunn-Bush, Florsheim, Adidas, Joyce, Puma, Converse
PARKING: lot
PAYMENT: cash, checks (amount of purchase only, with proper I.D.), MasterCard,
  VISA, American Express

GARY, IN

Brady's This Is It—Factory Outlet Store—Clothing
See listing under *Clothing—Family* in Gary, Indiana.

INDIANAPOLIS, IN

El-Bee Shoes, Nora Plaza Shopping Center, 1300 E. 86th Street, Indianapolis, IN
  46240; (317) 848-4029
  See listing in Bloomington, Indiana.

SUN.	MON.	TUE.	WED.	THU.	FRI.	SAT.
noon–5:30	10–9	10–9	10–9	10–9	10–9	10–9

SAVINGS: 50%–70% off
BRAND NAMES: Nunn-Bush, Florsheim, Adidas, Puma, Converse, Joyce
PARKING: lot
PAYMENT: cash, checks (amount of purchase only, with proper I.D.), MasterCard,
  VISA, American Express

El-Bee Shoes, Eastgate Consumer Mall, 7150 E. Washington Street, Indianapolis, IN
  46201; (317) 353-2911
  See listing in Bloomington, Indiana.

SUN.	MON.	TUE.	WED.	THU.	FRI.	SAT.
noon–5	10–9	10–9	10–9	10–9	10–9	10–9

SAVINGS 50%–70% off
BRAND NAMES: Nunn-Bush, Florsheim, Adidas, Joyce, Puma, Converse
PARKING: lot
PAYMENT: cash, checks (amount of purchase only, with proper I.D.), MasterCard,
  VISA, American Express

El-Bee Shoes, 10030 E. Washington Street, Washington Plaza Shopping Center,
  Indianapolis, IN 46229; (317) 899-1576
  See listing in Bloomington, Indiana.

SUN.	MON.	TUE.	WED.	THU.	FRI.	SAT.
noon–5:30	10–9	10–9	10–9	10–9	10–9	10–9

SAVINGS: 20%–60% off   *Mailing List*
BRAND NAMES: Nunn-Bush, Florsheim, Adidas, Puma
SALE DAYS: Wednesday, Sunday
PARKING: lot
PAYMENT: cash, checks (amount of purchase only, with proper I.D.), MasterCard,
  VISA, American Express

Famous Footwear, Eastgate Consumer Mall, 7150 E. Washington Street, Indianapolis,
  IN 46201; (317) 356-5513
  See listing in Schaumburg, Illinois.

SUN.	MON.	TUE.	WED.	THU.	FRI.	SAT.
noon–5	10–9	10–9	10–9	10–9	10–9	10–9

SAVINGS: 25%–50% off   *Mailing List*
BRAND NAMES: Nunn-Bush, Hang Ten, Tretorn, Roadster, Etonic

PARKING: lot
PAYMENT: cash, checks (amount of purchase only, with proper I.D.), MasterCard, VISA

LAFAYETTE, IN

El-Bee Shoes, 311 Sagamore Parkway North, Lafayette, IN 47904; (317) 448-1242
See listing in Bloomington, Indiana.

SUN.	MON.	TUE.	WED.	THU.	FRI.	SAT.
noon–5:30	10–9	10–9	noon–9	10–9	10–9	10–9

SAVINGS: 50%–70% off   *All First Quality*
BRAND NAMES: Nunn-Bush, Florsheim, Adidas, Joyce, Puma, Converse
PARKING: lot
PAYMENT: cash, checks (amount of purchase only, with proper I.D.), MasterCard,
VISA, American Express

MERRILLVILLE, IN

Famous Footwear, Century Consumer Mall, 8275 Broadway, Merrillville, IN 46410;
(219) 736-1181
See listing in Schaumburg, Illinois.

SUN.	MON.	TUE.	WED.	THU.	FRI.	SAT.
11–5	10–9	10–9	10–9	10–9	10–9	10–9

SAVINGS: 25%–50% off   *Mailing List*
PARKING: lot
PAYMENT: cash, checks (amount of purchase only, with proper I.D.), MasterCard, VISA

Frugal Frank's, Century Consumer Mall, 8275 Broadway, Merrillville, IN 46410; (219)
736-6806
This is the outlet for Kinney Shoes. They sell major brands of shoes and boots
with best savings on some irregular and overrun merchandise. They also have stores in
Kenosha and Madison, Wisconsin.

SUN.	MON.	TUE.	WED.	THU.	FRI.	SAT.
11–5	10–9	10–9	10–9	10–9	10–9	10–9

SAVINGS: 10%–30% off
BRAND NAMES: Nike, 9 West, Georgia Boot
PARKING: lot
PAYMENT: cash, checks (amount of purchase only, with proper I.D.), MasterCard,
VISA, American Express

Sole Hole Shoes, Century Consumer Mall, 8275 Broadway, Merrillville, IN 46410;
(219) 738-1790
This is an outlet for Butler women's shoes. They also sell handbags and hosiery.
Greatest savings are on some last year's lines.

SUN.	MON.	TUE.	WED.	THU.	FRI.	SAT.
11–6	10–9	10–9	10–9	10–9	10–9	10–9

SAVINGS: up to 20% off
BRAND NAMES: Butler, Imperial, Gold-Magic
SPECIAL SALES: all holidays
PARKING: lot
PAYMENT: cash, checks (amount of purchase only, with proper I.D., no out-of-state
checks), MasterCard, VISA

Tony Lama Boots, Century Consumer Mall, 8275 Broadway, Merrillville, IN 46410;
(219) 238-3263
See listing in Arlington Heights, Illinois.

SUN.	MON.	TUE.	WED.	THU.	FRI.	SAT.
11–5	10–9	10–9	10–9	10–9	10–9	10–9

SAVINGS: 25%–40% off
BRAND NAMES: Tony Lama
PARKING: lot
PAYMENT: cash, checks (amount of purchase only, with proper I.D.), MasterCard,
   VISA, American Express

MIDDLEBURY, IN

Gohn Brothers Manufacturing Company
   See listing under *Fabrics* in Middlebury, Indiana.

MISHAWAKA, IN

El-Bee Shoes, Buyer's Marketplace, 5901 N. Grape Road, Mishawaka, IN 46545; (219)
   277-6793
   See listing in Bloomington, Indiana.

SUN.	MON.	TUE.	WED.	THU.	FRI.	SAT.
noon–5	9:30–9	9:30–9	9:30–9	9:30–9	9:30–9	9:30–9

SAVINGS: 20%–60% off   *Mailing List*
SPECIAL SALES: weekly
PARKING: lot
PAYMENT: cash, checks (amount of purchase only, with proper I.D.), MasterCard, VISA

Famous Footwear, Buyer's Marketplace, 5901 N. Grape Road, Mishawaka, IN 46545;
   (219) 277-0801
   See listing in Schaumburg, Illinois.

SUN.	MON.	TUE.	WED.	THU.	FRI.	SAT.
noon–5	9:30–9	9:30–9	9:30–9	9:30–9	9:30–9	9:30–9

SAVINGS: 10%–40% off   *Mailing List*
BRAND NAMES: Nike, Adidas, Converse, Nunn-Bush, Kangaroos
PARKING: lot
PAYMENT: cash, checks (amount of purchase only, with proper I.D.), MasterCard, VISA

Little Red Shoe House, Buyer's Marketplace, 5901 N. Grape Road, Mishawaka, IN
   46545; (219) 277-0432
   See listing in Auburn, Indiana.

SUN.	MON.	TUE.	WED.	THU.	FRI.	SAT.
noon–5	9:30–9	9:30–9	9:30–9	9:30–9	9:30–9	9:30–9

SAVINGS: 20%–75% off
SALE DAYS: Tuesday
SPECIAL DISCOUNTS: senior citizens, 10% off
PARKING: lot
PAYMENT: cash, checks (amount of purchase only, with proper I.D.), MasterCard, VISA

MUNCIE, IN

El-Bee Shoes, Northwest Shopping Center, 1605 W. McGalliard Road, Muncie, IN
   47305; (317) 284-2170
   See listing in Bloomington, Indiana.

SUN.	MON.	TUE.	WED.	THU.	FRI.	SAT.
noon–5:30	10–9	10–9	10–9	10–9	10–9	10–9

SAVINGS: 50%–70% off
BRAND NAMES: Nunn-Bush, Florsheim, Adidas, Joyce, Puma, Converse
PARKING: lot
PAYMENT: cash, checks (amount of purchase only, with proper I.D.), MasterCard,
   VISA, American Express

Little Red Shoe House, 113 E. Washington Street, Plymouth, IN 46563; (219) 935-5204

See listing in Auburn, Indiana.

SUN.	MON.	TUE.	WED.	THU.	FRI.	SAT.
noon–5	9:30–8	9:30–8	9:30–8	9:30–8	9:30–8	9:30–8

SAVINGS: 10%–50% off
PARKING: lot
PAYMENT: cash, checks (amount of purchase only, with proper I.D.), MasterCard, VISA, American Express

El-Bee Shoes, Gateway Shopping Center, 4633 E. Main Street, Richmond, IN 47374; (317) 966-9533

See listing in Bloomington, Indiana.

SUN.	MON.	TUE.	WED.	THU.	FRI.	SAT.
noon–5:30	10–9	10–9	10–9	10–9	10–9	10–9

SAVINGS: 50%–70% off
BRAND NAMES: Nunn-Bush, Florsheim, Adidas, Joyce, Puma, Converse
PARKING: lot
PAYMENT: cash, checks (amount of purchase only, with proper I.D.), MasterCard, VISA, American Express

M.G. Grundman & Sons, 906 N. 7th Street, Vincennes, IN 47591; (812) 882-4770

This is the factory outlet for Grundman shoes and boots. They sell boots for adults and shoes for children. Savings average 20% off retail price, and can go higher on some discontinued items.

SUN.	MON.	TUE.	WED.	THU.	FRI.	SAT.
closed	8–5	8–5	8–5	8–5	8–5	8–5

SAVINGS: average 20% off   *Mailing List*
BRAND NAMES: Grundman
SPECIAL DISCOUNTS: senior citizens and organizations
PARKING: lot
PAYMENT: cash, checks (with proper I.D.)

Weinbrenner Factory Shoe Outlet, Highway 45 North, Antigo, WI 54409; (715) 623-4705

This factory outlet sells Weinbrenner work shoes and other brands of casual, dress, and athletic shoes. Savings begin at 25% off retail on first quality, and can go as high as 75% on some seconds, discontinued, and closeout merchandise. They have other stores in Marshfield and Merrill, Wisconsin.

SUN.	MON.	TUE.	WED.	THU.	FRI.	SAT.
noon–5	9–5	9–5	9–5	9–5	9–9	9–5

SAVINGS: 25%–75% off
BRAND NAMES: Weinbrenner, Kangaroos
ANNUAL SALES: Christmas
PARKING: lot
PAYMENT: cash, checks (amount of purchase only, with proper I.D.), MasterCard, VISA

BELGIUM, WI

The Shoe Bank, 775 Main Street, Belgium, WI 53004; (414) 285-3481
This is the factory outlet for the Allen-Edmonds Shoe Corporation. Savings on men's dress shoes begin at 35% off retail price, and go higher on some seconds, samples, discontinued, overstocks, and closeout merchandise.

SUN.	MON.	TUE.	WED.	THU.	FRI.	SAT.
noon-5	9-5	9-5	9-9	9-5	9-9	9-5

SAVINGS: 35%–40% off
BRAND NAMES: Allen-Edmonds
ANNUAL SALES: February, 4th of July
PARKING: street
PAYMENT: cash, checks (amount of purchase only), MasterCard, VISA, American Express

BELOIT, WI

Freeman Outlet Store, Freeman Outlet Mall, 5 Freeman Lane, Beloit, WI 53511; (608) 364-1334
This outlet is across the street from the factory. They sell several brands of shoes manufactured by the Freeman Company. Savings can go as high as 50% off retail price on some seconds, irregulars, surplus, overruns, overstocks, last year's lines, end-of-season, closeouts, discontinued merchandise, and factory-damaged shoes. They have other stores in Wisconsin Dells and Wisconsin Rapids, Wisconsin.

SUN.	MON.	TUE.	WED.	THU.	FRI.	SAT.
11-6	9-9	9-9	9-9	9-9	9-9	9-6

SAVINGS: 25%–50% off   *Mailing List*
BRAND NAMES: Nettleton, Freeman, Bill Blass, Florsheim, Clark
PARKING: lot
PAYMENT: cash, checks (amount of purchase only, with proper I.D.), MasterCard, VISA, American Express

BERLIN, WI

Mid-Western Sport Togs
See listing under *Clothing—Accessories* in Berlin, Wisconsin.

CHIPPEWA FALLS, WI

Mason Shoe Store, 307 N. Bridge Street, Chippewa Falls, WI 54729; (715) 723-4323
This is the outlet for the Mason Shoe Company. Savings start at 20% on first quality and go as high as 60% off retail price on some seconds, irregulars, samples, closeouts, and discontinued merchandise.

SUN.	MON.	TUE.	WED.	THU.	FRI.	SAT.
closed	9-5	9-5	9-5	9-5	9-5	9-5

SAVINGS: 20%–60% off
BRAND NAMES: Mason
PARKING: lot
PAYMENT: cash, checks, MasterCard, VISA

GREEN BAY, WI

The Leather Shop
See listing under *Clothing—Accessories* in Green Bay, Wisconsin.

KENOSHA, WI

The Athletic Shoe Outlet, Factory Outlet Centre, 7700 120th Avenue, Kenosha, WI 53142; (414) 857-2709

This is an outlet for Kinney shoes. Prices start at 15% off on first quality, and go to about 30% off retail price on some seconds.

SUN.	MON.	TUE.	WED.	THU.	FRI.	SAT.
11–5	9:30–9	9:30–9	9:30–9	9:30–9	9:30–9	9:30–6

SAVINGS: 15%–30% off
SALE DAYS: weekends
PARKING: lot
PAYMENT: cash, checks (amount of purchase only, with proper I.D.), MasterCard, VISA

Frugal Frank's, Factory Outlet Centre, 7700 120th Avenue, Kenosha, WI 53142; (414) 857-7170
See listing in Merrillville, Indiana.

SUN.	MON.	TUE.	WED.	THU.	FRI.	SAT.
11–5	9:30–9	9:30–9	9:30–9	9:30–9	9:30–9	9:30–6

SAVINGS: 10%–30% off
ANNUAL SALES: January, July
SPECIAL DISCOUNTS: senior citizens, 10% off
PARKING: lot
PAYMENT: cash, checks (amount of purchase only, with proper I.D.), MasterCard, VISA, American Express

The Little Red Shoe House, Factory Outlet Centre, 7700 120th Avenue, Kenosha, WI 53142; (414) 857-7344
See listing in Auburn, Indiana.

SUN.	MON.	TUE.	WED.	THU.	FRI.	SAT.
11–5	9:30–9	9:30–9	9:30–9	9:30–9	9:30–9	9:30–6

SAVINGS: 25%–70% off
BRAND NAMES: Wolverine
ANNUAL SALES: summer, winter
SPECIAL DISCOUNTS: senior citizens, 10% off
PARKING: lot
PAYMENT: cash, checks (amount of purchase only, with proper I.D.), MasterCard, VISA, American Express

Mid-American Shoe Factory Outlet, Factory Outlet Centre, 7700 120th Avenue, Kenosha, WI 53142; (414) 857-2920
This factory outlet sells major brands of shoes and boots. Savings begin at 25% off retail price on first quality, and can go as high as 75% on some seconds, irregulars, last year's lines, end-of-season, discontinued, and closeout merchandise. They have another store in Madison, Wisconsin.

SUN.	MON.	TUE.	WED.	THU.	FRI.	SAT.
11–5	9:30–9	9:30–9	9:30–9	9:30–9	9:30–9	9:30–6

SAVINGS: 25%–75% off
BRAND NAMES: Rogan Shoes
PARKING: lot
PAYMENT: cash, checks (with proper I.D.), MasterCard

Nike Factory Outlet, 5999 E. 120th Avenue, Kenosha, WI 53142; (414) 857-7333
This factory outlet sells all Nike running shoes and other activewear at savings that begin at 40% off retail price on first quality merchandise and go up to 80% on seconds (marked B-grade), samples, surplus, overruns, overstocks, last year's lines, end-of-season, discontinued, and closeout merchandise.

SUN.	MON.	TUE.	WED.	THU.	FRI.	SAT.
11–6	10–8	10–8	10–8	10–8	10–8	10–6

SAVINGS: 40%–80% off   *Mailing List*
BRAND NAMES: Nike
SPECIAL SALES: weekly specials
PARKING: lot
PAYMENT: cash, checks (amount of purchase only, with proper I.D., Telecheck),
  MasterCard, VISA

KIEL, WI

Sheboygan Footwear, Highway 32 North, Kiel, WI 53042; (414) 894-2355
  This factory outlet sells mostly work shoes, boots, and some socks. Savings begin
at 10% off retail price on first quality and can go as high as 60% on selected seconds.
They have another store (called Shoe Factory Outlet) in Sheboygan, Wisconsin.

SUN.	MON.	TUE.	WED.	THU.	FRI.	SAT.
closed	9-5	9-5	9-5	9-5	9-8	9-noon

SAVINGS: 10%–60% off
BRAND NAMES: Sheboygan Shoes
SALE DAYS: weekly
PARKING: lot
PAYMENT: cash, checks (amount of purchase only, with proper I.D.), MasterCard, VISA

LA CROSSE, WI

Little Red Shoe House, La Crosse Factory Outlet Center, 301 Sky Harbor Drive, La
  Crosse, WI 54467; (608) 783-3388
    See listing in Auburn, Indiana.

SUN.	MON.	TUE.	WED.	THU.	FRI.	SAT.
11-6	10-9	10-9	10-9	10-9	10-9	9-6

SAVINGS: 60% off
BRAND NAMES: Adidas, Puma, Nunn-Bush
PARKING: lot
PAYMENT: cash, checks (amount of purchase only, with proper I.D.), MasterCard, VISA

MADISON, WI

Frugal Frank's, Factory Outlet Centre, 4609 Verona Road, Madison, WI 53711; (608)
  273-4071
    See listing in Merrillville, Indiana.

SUN.	MON.	TUE.	WED.	THU.	FRI.	SAT.
9-5	9:30-9	9:30-9	9:30-9	9:30-9	9:30-9	9:30-6

SAVINGS: 10%–30% off
BRAND NAMES: Nike, Pony, Puma, British Walker, 9 West, Air Step, Cherokee
SPECIAL SALES: month-end clearance
ANNUAL SALES: after Christmas
SPECIAL DISCOUNTS: senior citizens, 10% off Wednesday
PARKING: lot
PAYMENT: cash, checks (amount of purchase only, with proper I.D.)

Little Red Shoe House, Factory Outlet Centre, 4609 Verona Road, Madison, WI
  53711; (608) 274-8747
    See listing in Auburn, Indiana.

SUN.	MON.	TUE.	WED.	THU.	FRI.	SAT.
noon-5	9:30-9	9:30-9	9:30-9	9:30-9	9:30-9	9:30-6

SAVINGS: 10%–50% off
SPECIAL DISCOUNTS: senior citizens
PARKING: lot
PAYMENT: cash, checks (amount of purchase only, with proper I.D.), MasterCard,
  VISA, American Express

Mid-American Shoe Factory Outlet, Factory Outlet Centre, 4609 Verona Road, Madison, WI 53711; (608) 273-4840
See listing in Kenosha, Wisconsin.

SUN.	MON.	TUE.	WED.	THU.	FRI.	SAT.
noon–5	9:30–9	9:30–9	9:30–9	9:30–9	9:30–9	9:30–6

SAVINGS: 25%–75% off
PARKING: lot
PAYMENT: cash, checks (amount of purchase only, with proper I.D.), MasterCard, VISA

MANITOWOC, WI

Right Step Factory Shoe Outlet, 919 E. Franklin Street, Manitowoc, WI 54220; (414) 682-6021
This factory outlet sells several major brands of men's and women's shoes. They also sell handbags. Savings begin at 30% off retail price for first quality, and can go as high as 60% on some seconds, irregulars, last year's lines, discontinued, and close-out merchandise. They have another outlet in Sheboygan, Wisconsin.

SUN.	MON.	TUE.	WED.	THU.	FRI.	SAT.
closed	9–8	9–5	9–5	9–5	9–8	9–5

SAVINGS: 50%–60% off
ANNUAL SALES: December
PARKING: lot
PAYMENT: cash, checks (amount of purchase only, with proper I.D.), MasterCard, VISA

MARINETTE, WI

Saranac Factory Store
See listing under *Clothing—Accessories* in Marinette, WI.

MARSHFIELD, WI

Weinbrenner Factory Shoe Outlet, Highway 13 North, Marshfield, WI 54449; (715) 387-6125
See listing in Antigo, Wisconsin.

SUN.	MON.	TUE.	WED.	THU.	FRI.	SAT.
noon–5	9–5	9–5	9–5	9–5	9–9	9–5

SAVINGS: 50%–60% off
ANNUAL SALES: December
PARKING: lot
PAYMENT: cash, checks (amount of purchase only, with proper I.D.), MasterCard, VISA

MERRILL, WI

Weinbrenner Factory Shoe Outlet, Highway 64 at Highway 51, Merrill, WI 54452; (715) 536-5559
See listing in Antigo, Wisconsin.

SUN.	MON.	TUE.	WED.	THU.	FRI.	SAT.
noon–5	9–5	9–5	9–5	9–5	9–9	9–5

SAVINGS: 25%–75% off
ANNUAL SALES: Christmas
PARKING: lot
PAYMENT: cash, checks (amount of purchase only, with proper I.D.), MasterCard, VISA

MILWAUKEE, WI

Branovan Outlet Store
See listing under *Clothing—Family* in Milwaukee, Wisconsin.

The Odd Lot Shoe Store, 1007 N. 3rd Street, Milwaukee, WI 53203; (414) 271-1964
This store sells all styles of major brands of men's shoes. Savings begin at 10% off retail price on first quality, and can go as high as 60% on some seconds, closeouts, last year's lines, and discontinued merchandise.

SUN.	MON.	TUE.	WED.	THU.	FRI.	SAT.
closed*	10-5	10-5	10-5	10-5	10-5	10-5

SAVINGS: 10%–60% off
BRAND NAMES: Nunn-Bush, Dexter, Stacy-Adams
SALE DAYS: weekly sales
ANNUAL SALES: summer, winter
PARKING: street, can be difficult
PAYMENT: cash, MasterCard, VISA, American Express

---

*Summer hours: Monday–Saturday, 10:00–9:00; Sunday, noon–5.

The Odd Lot Shoe Store, 6542 N. 76th Street, Milwaukee, WI 53223; (414) 353-0540
See listing above.

SUN.	MON.	TUE.	WED.	THU.	FRI.	SAT.
noon-5	10-9	10-9	10-9	10-9	10-9	9:30-6

SAVINGS: 10%–60% off
BRAND NAMES: Nunn-Bush, Dexter, Stacy-Adams
ANNUAL SALES: summer, winter
PARKING: lot
PAYMENT: cash, MasterCard, VISA, American Express

The Odd Lot Shoe Store, 2944 S. 108th Street, Milwaukee, WI 53227; (414) 327-7776
See listing above.

SUN.	MON.	TUE.	WED.	THU.	FRI.	SAT.
noon-5	10-9	10-9	10-9	10-9	10-9	9:30-6

SAVINGS: 10%–60% off
BRAND NAMES: Nunn-Bush, Dexter, Stacy-Adams
SPECIAL SALES: weekly
ANNUAL SALES: summer, winter
PARKING: lot
PAYMENT: cash, checks, MasterCard, VISA, American Express

The Odd Lot Shoe Store, 8779 N. Port Washington Road, Milwaukee, WI 53217; (414) 352-2563
See listing above.

SUN.	MON.	TUE.	WED.	THU.	FRI.	SAT.
noon-5	10-9	10-9	10-9	10-9	10-9	9:30-6

SAVINGS: 10%–60% off
BRAND NAMES: Nunn-Bush, Dexter, Stacy-Adams
ANNUAL SALES: summer, winter
PARKING: lot
PAYMENT: cash, MasterCard, VISA, American Express

The Odd Lot Shoe Store, 3400 S. 27th Street, Milwaukee, WI 53221; (414) 672-2711
See listing above.

SUN.	MON.	TUE.	WED.	THU.	FRI.	SAT.
noon-5	10-9	10-9	10-9	10-9	10-9	9:30-6

SAVINGS: 10%–60% off
BRAND NAMES: Nunn-Bush, Dexter, Stacy-Adams
SPECIAL SALES: weekly
ANNUAL SALES: summer, winter

PARKING: lot
PAYMENT: cash, MasterCard, VISA, American Express

OCONOMOWOC, WI

Musbeck Shoes, 803 W. Westover Road, Oconomowoc, WI 53066; (414) 567-5564
This is the outlet for Musbeck shoes. Savings are greatest on surplus, overruns, overstocks, and discontinued items.

SUN.	MON.	TUE.	WED.	THU.	FRI.	SAT.
closed	7:30–4:30	7:30–4:30	7:30–4:30	7:30–4:30	7:30–4:30	9–4:30

SAVINGS: 20%–40% off   *Mailing List*
BRAND NAMES: Musbeck
PARKING: lot
PAYMENT: cash, checks (with proper I.D.)

OSHKOSH, WI

Mondl Boots and Shoes, 111 Otter Avenue, Oshkosh, WI 54901; (414) 231-2226
This is the factory outlet for Mondl boots and shoes. They also sell moccasins, slippers, and some winter boots. Savings begin at 30% off retail price on first quality, and can go as high as 50% on seconds, overruns, overstocks, and discontinued merchandise.

SUN.	MON.	TUE.	WED.	THU.	FRI.	SAT.
closed	9:30–5	9:30–5	9:30–5	9:30–5	9:30–5	9:30–5

SAVINGS: up to 50% off
ANNUAL SALES: last week of July, first week of August
PARKING: street, meters
PAYMENT: cash, checks (amount of purchase only, with proper I.D.), MasterCard, VISA

PLOVER, WI

Little Red Shoe House, Manufacturers Direct Mall, 101 Plover Road, Plover, WI 54467; (715) 344-5366
See listing in Auburn, Indiana.

SUN.	MON.	TUE.	WED.	THU.	FRI.	SAT.
11–6	9:30–9	9:30–9	9:30–9	9:30–9	9:30–9	9:30–6

SAVINGS: 25%–70% off
ANNUAL SALES: spring, fall
SPECIAL DISCOUNTS: senior citizens, 10% off
PARKING: lot
PAYMENT: cash, checks (amount of purchase only, with proper I.D.), MasterCard, VISA

Norman's Shoes, Manufacturers Direct Mall, 101 Plover Road, Plover, WI 54467; (715) 344-1444
This is an outlet for Wolverine. They sell Naturalizer shoes and handbags. Discounts run from 20% off first quality, and as high as 75% on irregulars, last year's lines, and overstocks.

SUN.	MON.	TUE.	WED.	THU.	FRI.	SAT.
11–6	9:30–9	9:30–9	9:30–9	9:30–9	9:30–9	9:30–6

SAVINGS: 20%–75% off
BRAND NAMES: Naturalizer, Wolverine
PARKING: lot
PAYMENT: cash, checks (amount of purchase only, with proper I.D.), MasterCard, VISA

SHEBOYGAN, WI

Right Step Factory Shoe Outlet, 1211 Indiana Avenue, Sheboygan, WI 53081; (414) 452-8506
See listing in Manitowoc, Wisconsin.

SUN.	MON.	TUE.	WED.	THU.	FRI.	SAT.
closed	9–8	9–5	9–5	9–8	9–8	9–5

SAVINGS: 30%–60% off
SPECIAL DISCOUNTS: senior citizens, 10% off with I.D.
PARKING: lot
PAYMENT: cash, checks (amount of purchase only, with proper I.D.), MasterCard, VISA

Shoe Factory Outlet, 620 S. 8th Street, Sheboygan, WI 53081; (414) 458-1008
See listing under Sheboygan Footwear in Kiel, Wisconsin.

SUN.	MON.	TUE.	WED.	THU.	FRI.	SAT.
closed	10–6	10–6	10–6	10–6	10–8	9–5

SAVINGS: 10%–30% off   *Mailing List*
ANNUAL SALES: August
PARKING: lot
PAYMENT: cash, checks (amount of purchase only, with proper I.D.), MasterCard, VISA

WEST BEND, WI

General Shoe (Factory To You), West Bend Outlet Mall, 180 Island Avenue, West
Bend, WI 53095; (414) 338-2558
This is the outlet for Genesco Shoes. They sell several major brands of shoes,
boots, and accessories. Savings begin at 40% off retail price on first quality
merchandise, and can go as high as 70% on some seconds, irregulars, and overrun
merchandise.

SUN.	MON.	TUE.	WED.	THU.	FRI.	SAT.
11–5	9:30–6	9:30–6	9:30–6	9:30–6	9:30–8	9:30–5

SAVINGS: 25%–70% off   *Mailing List*
SALE DAYS: spring, fall
SPECIAL DISCOUNTS: senior citizens, 10% off Wednesday
PARKING: lot
PAYMENT: cash, checks (with proper I.D.), MasterCard, VISA

Little Red Shoe House, West Bend Island Avenue, 180 Island Avenue, West Bend, WI
53095; (414) 334-3112
See listing in Auburn, Indiana.

SUN.	MON.	TUE.	WED.	THU.	FRI.	SAT.
noon–5	9:30–5	9:30–5	9:30–5	9:30–5	9:30–9	9:30–5

SAVINGS: 25%–70% off
ANNUAL SALES: spring, fall
SPECIAL DISCOUNTS: senior citizens
PARKING: lot
PAYMENT: cash, checks (with proper I.D.), MasterCard, VISA

WISCONSIN DELLS, WI

Freeman Outlet Store, 321 Broadway, Wisconsin Dells, WI 53965; (608) 254-2233
See listing in Beloit, Wisconsin.

SUN.	MON.	TUE.	WED.	THU.	FRI.	SAT.
10–6	9–10	9–10	9–10	9–10	closed	9–10

SAVINGS: up to 50% off   *Mailing List*
BRAND NAMES: Freeman, French Shriner, Bill Blass, Members Only, Nike, Puma, New
Balance, Etonic, Converse, Adidas, Reebok, Candies, Capezio, Red Cross, Sporto,
Joyce, Cobbies, Pappagallo, Selby
PARKING: street, meters
PAYMENT: cash, checks (amount of purchase only, with proper I.D.), MasterCard,
VISA, American Express

Freeman Outlet Store, 1000 E. Riverview Expressway, Wisconsin Rapids, WI 54494; (715) 424-3210

See listing in Beloit, Wisconsin.

SUN.	MON.	TUE.	WED.	THU.	FRI.	SAT.
noon–5	10–9	10–9	10–9	10–9	10–9	10–9

SAVINGS: up to 50% off   *All First Quality*
BRAND NAMES: Freeman, Bill Blass, Nike, Puma, Pappagallo, Red Cross, Candies
PARKING: lot
PAYMENT: cash, checks (amount of purchase only, with proper I.D., no out-of-state checks), MasterCard, VISA

CLOTHING—LARGE SIZES

The outlets listed here specialize in large sizes. Also look in the other clothing sections, since several of the outlets carry some large sizes.

ILLINOIS

CHICAGO, IL

Al's Men's Wear—Big & Tall, 4701 N. Milwaukee Avenue, Chicago, IL 60630; (312) 283-1551

This store carries Jaymar-Ruby shirts, dress slacks, sports coats, and suits at 40%–50% off retail price. They also carry Cliftex sport coats, Glen Eagle raincoats, Enro shirts, and Sergio Valente jackets, pants, and shirts for men in large sizes. There is some first quality merchandise; the rest is samples, irregulars, imperfect, test runs, surplus, overruns, overstocks, and end-of-season. Ask to be put on their mailing list so you won't miss their February and August sales when all prices are halved. They carry sizes to 64.

SUN.	MON.	TUE.	WED.	THU.	FRI.	SAT.
noon–4	10–6	10–6	10–6	10–6	10–6	10–5:30

SAVINGS: 40%–70% off   *Mailing List*
BRAND NAMES: Cliftex, Glen Eagle, Jaymar-Ruby, Enro, Sergio Valente
ANNUAL SALES: February and August
PARKING: lot
PAYMENT: cash, checks (no out-of-state checks), MasterCard, VISA

Sizes Unlimited, 16 S. Wabash Avenue, Chicago, IL 60603; (312) 346-4226

This store sells large sizes of women's clothing at savings that begin at 20% off retail price on first quality and can go as high as 70% on overruns, overstocks, and end-of-season merchandise. They have two other stores in Merrillville, Indiana.

SUN.	MON.	TUE.	WED.	THU.	FRI.	SAT.
noon–5	10–7	10–6	10–6	10–7	10–7	10–6

SAVINGS: 20%–70% off
PARKING: street, meters
PAYMENT: cash, checks, (amount of purchase only, with proper I.D.), MasterCard, VISA

CICERO, IL

Plus Size Fashion Outlet, Guinta's Factory Outlet Mall, 1800 S. Cicero Avenue, Cicero, IL 60650; (312) 652-9898

This store sells large women's clothing and outerwear. Savings can go up to 75% off retail price on some seconds, surplus, overruns, overstocks, last year's lines, and discontinued merchandise.

SUN.	MON.	TUE.	WED.	THU.	FRI.	SAT.
10–6	10–8	closed	10–8	10–8	10–8	10–6

SAVINGS: up to 75% off
PARKING: lot
PAYMENT: cash only

ROLLING MEADOWS, IL

Classic Lady, 1400 E. Golf Road, Rolling Meadows, IL 60008; (312) 956-1910
This stores sells large sizes in women's clothing. Savings begin at 30% off retail price and can reach 80% on some items.

SUN.	MON.	TUE.	WED.	THU.	FRI.	SAT.
11–5	10–9	10–9	10–9	10–9	10–9	10–6

SAVINGS: 30%–80% off   *Mailing List*   *All First Quality*
PARKING: lot
PAYMENT: cash, checks (amount of purchase only, with proper I.D., no out-of-state checks), MasterCard, VISA

INDIANA
INDIANAPOLIS, IN

Donlevy's Back Room
See two listings under *Clothing—Women's* in Indianapolis, Indiana.

MERRILLVILLE, IN

Sizes Unlimited, Century Consumer Mall, 8275 Broadway, Merrillville, IN 46410; (219) 769-7154
See listing in Chicago, Illinois.

SUN.	MON.	TUE.	WED.	THU.	FRI.	SAT.
11–5	10–9	10–9	10–9	10–9	10–9	10–9

SAVINGS: 20%–70% off   *Mailing List*
PARKING: lot
PAYMENT: cash, checks (amount of purchase only, with proper I.D.), MasterCard, VISA

Sizes Unlimited, 251 W. Lincoln Highway, Merrillville, IN 46360; (219) 736-0310
See listing in Chicago, Illinois

SUN.	MON.	TUE.	WED.	THU.	FRI.	SAT.
noon–5	10–9	10–9	10–9	10–9	10–9	10–6

SAVINGS: 20%–70% off   *Mailing List*
PARKING: lot
PAYMENT: cash, checks (amount of purchase only, with proper I.D.), MasterCard, VISA

WISCONSIN
KENOSHA, WI

Large Size Outlet, Factory Outlet Centre, 7700 120th Avenue, Kenosha, WI 53142; (414) 857-7740
This outlet sells large size women's clothing at savings that average 40%–60% off retail price on all first quality merchandise.

SUN.	MON.	TUE.	WED.	THU.	FRI.	SAT.
11–5	9:30–9	9:30–9	9:30–9	9:30–9	9:30–9	9:30–6

SAVINGS: 40%–60% off   *All First Quality*
BRAND NAMES: Jordache, Devon, Shaker Sports, Lucky Me, Peggy Lu

SALE DAYS: Tuesday
SPECIAL DISCOUNTS: senior citizens, 10% off Wednesday
PARKING: lot
PAYMENT: cash, checks (amount of purchase only, with proper I.D.), MasterCard, VISA

PLOVER, WI

House of Large Sizes, Manufacturers Direct Mall, 101 Plover Road, Plover, WI 54467; (715) 345-0717
This store sells large sizes in women's clothing. Savings begin at 25% off retail price on first quality merchandise and can reach 75% on some end-of-season and last year's lines.

SUN.	MON.	TUE.	WED.	THU.	FRI.	SAT.
11-5	9:30-9	9:30-9	9:30-9	9:30-9	9:30-9	9:30-6

SAVINGS: 25%-75% off   *Mailing List*   *All First Quality*
SALE DAYS: vary
SPECIAL DISCOUNTS: guests at a local motel, 15% off (ask)
PARKING: lot
PAYMENT: cash, checks (amount of purchase only, with proper I.D.), MasterCard, VISA, Discover

WEST BEND, WI

West Bend Woolen Mills
See listing under *Clothing—Sportswear* in West Bend, Wisconsin.

CLOTHING—LINGERIE

The outlets listed here sell lingerie, and some also sell hosiery, sleepwear, and exercisewear. Also look in this chapter under *Activewear*, *Family*, *Large Sizes*, *Maternity*, *Sportswear*, and *Women's* for other outlets that sell lingerie.

ILLINOIS

CHICAGO, IL

Lorraine Lingerie Outlet Store, 4220 W. Belmont Avenue, Chicago, IL 60641; (312) 283-3000
This is the outlet for O'Brien Brothers. They sell lingerie, robes, and loungewear at discounts up to 60% off retail prices. Best buys are on seconds, samples, end-of-season, and discontinued merchandise.

SUN.	MON.	TUE.	WED.	THU.	FRI.	SAT.
closed	9-5	9-5	9-5	9-5	9-5	9-5

SAVINGS: 40%-60% off   *Mailing List*
BRAND NAMES: Lorraine
ANNUAL SALES: February, August
PARKING: lot, street
PAYMENT: cash, checks (with proper I.D.)

CICERO, IL

Under Things Unlimited, Guinta's Factory Outlet Mall, 1800 S. Cicero Avenue, Cicero, IL 60650; (312) 652-6962
This store sells major brands of lingerie and hosiery. Savings are greatest on surplus and overruns.

SUN.	MON.	TUE.	WED.	THU.	FRI.	SAT.
10–6	10–8	closed	10–8	10–8	10–8	10–6

SAVINGS: at least 30% off
PARKING: lot
PAYMENT: cash only

INDIANA
HUNTINGBURG, IN

Gossard's Factory Outlet
See listing under *Clothing—Activewear* in Huntingburg, Indiana.

LOGANSPORT, IN

Gossard's Factory Outlet
See listing under *Clothing—Activewear* in Logansport, Indiana.

MISHAWAKA, IN

Candlelight Fashions, Buyer's Marketplace, 5901 Grape Road, Mishawaka, IN 46545; (219) 277-0930
This outlet sells lingerie and intimate apparel. Savings average 40% off retail price on first quality merchandise, and can go to 60% on some seconds, overstocks, closeouts, and last year's lines.

SUN.	MON.	TUE.	WED.	THU.	FRI.	SAT.
11–5	9:30–9	9:30–9	9:30–9	9:30–9	9:30–9	9:30–9

SAVINGS: 40%–60% off   *Mailing List*
BRAND NAMES: Katsy, Futureform
ANNUAL SALES: seasonal, most holidays
PARKING: lot
PAYMENT: cash, checks (amount of purchase only, with proper I.D., Telecheck), MasterCard, VISA

WISCONSIN
KENOSHA, WI

Bare Essentials, Factory Outlet Centre, 7700 120th Avenue, Kenosha, WI 53142; (414) 857-7565
This outlet has a large assortment of Seroma and Jansen swimwear and Bali lingerie. Savings start at 50% off retail, and go higher on last year's lines, discontinued, overruns, closeouts, and odd lots.

SUN.	MON.	TUE.	WED.	THU.	FRI.	SAT.
11–5	9:30–9	9:30–9	9:30–9	9:30–9	9:30–9	9:30–6

SAVINGS: at least 50% off
BRAND NAMES: Seroma, Jansen, Bali
SPECIAL DISCOUNTS: senior citizens, 10% off Wednesday
PARKING: lot
PAYMENT: cash, checks (amount of purchase only, with proper I.D.), MasterCard, VISA

Munsingwear Factory Outlet
See listing under *Clothing—Sportswear* in Kenosha, Wisconsin.

MADISON, WI

Formfit, Factory Outlet Centre, 4609 Verona Road, Madison, WI 53711; (608) 273-1866
This factory outlet sells women's lingerie and exercisewear. Savings begin at 30% off retail price on first quality and can go as high as 70% on some irregular merchandise.

SUN.	MON.	TUE.	WED.	THU.	FRI.	SAT.
9-5	9:30-9	9:30-9	9:30-9	9:30-9	9:30-9	9:30-6

SAVINGS: 30%–70% off
BRAND NAMES: Pierre Cardin, Danskin, Formfit
ANNUAL SALES: July
SPECIAL DISCOUNTS: senior citizens, 10% off Wednesday
PARKING: lot
PAYMENT: cash, checks (amount of purchase only, with proper I.D.), MasterCard, VISA, travelers' checks

CLOTHING—MATERNITY

Maternity clothes present a new problem in an attempt to save money. Savings are excellent on seconds and irregular merchandise, but savings on end-of-season and closeout merchandise are negated by the fact that you will no longer be pregnant when the clothes come into season again.

ILLINOIS

CHICAGO, IL

Dan Howard's Maternity Factory Outlet, 710 W. Jackson Boulevard, Chicago, IL 60606; (312) 263-6700
This is the factory outlet for Dan Howard maternity clothing. Savings range from 25% off retail price for first quality to 50% on irregulars. They also sell some seconds, discontinued, last year's lines, and overstocks. They occasionally sell some sample and test-run items. There are other stores in Downers Grove, Homewood, Niles, North Riverside, Orland Park, Schaumburg, Vernon Hills, and Wilmette, Illinois; two in Indianapolis, Indiana; another in West Allis, Wisconsin.

SUN.	MON.	TUE.	WED.	THU.	FRI.	SAT.
noon-5	9-5	9-5	9-5	9-5	9-5	10-5

SAVINGS: 25%–50% off   *Mailing List*
BRAND NAMES: Dan Howard, Leading Lady
SALE DAYS: vary, twice a month
PARKING: lot
PAYMENT: cash, checks (amount of purchase only, with proper I.D., no out-of-state checks), MasterCard, VISA, American Express

Lady Madonna Maternity Outlet, 300 W. Grand Avenue, Chicago, IL 60610; (312) 329-0771
This is the outlet for Lady Madonna maternity clothes. Savings average 30%–50% off retail prices, and are greatest on irregulars, last year's lines, and discontinued merchandise.

SUN.	MON.	TUE.	WED.	THU.	FRI.	SAT.
11-5	10-6	10-6	10-6	10-6	10-6	10-5

SAVINGS: 30%–50% off   *Mailing List*
BRAND NAMES: Lady Madonna
ANNUAL SALES: vary
PARKING: street, meters
PAYMENT: cash, checks (amount of purchase only, with proper I.D., no out-of-state checks), MasterCard, VISA

DOWNERS GROVE, IL

Dan Howard's Maternity Factory Outlet, 2019 Ogden Avenue, Downers Grove, IL 60532; (312) 969-4666
   See listing in Chicago, Illinois.

SUN.	MON.	TUE.	WED.	THU.	FRI.	SAT.
noon–5	10–9	10–6	10–6	10–9	10–6	10–5

SAVINGS: 25%–50% off   *Mailing List*
BRAND NAMES: Dan Howard
PARKING: lot
PAYMENT: cash, checks (amount of purchase only, with proper I.D.), MasterCard,
   VISA, American Express

HOMEWOOD, IL

Dan Howard's Maternity Factory Outlet, 17932 S. Halsted Street, Homewood, IL 60430; (312) 798-4347
   See listing in Chicago, Illinois.

SUN.	MON.	TUE.	WED.	THU.	FRI.	SAT.
noon–4	10–9	10–6	10–6	10–9	10–6	10–5

SAVINGS: 25%–50% off   *Mailing List*
BRAND NAMES: Dan Howard
PARKING: lot
PAYMENT: cash, checks (amount of purchase only, with proper I.D.), MasterCard,
   VISA, American Express

NILES, IL

Dan Howard's Maternity Factory Outlet, 9026 Milwaukee Avenue, Niles, IL 60648;
(312) 299-2800
   See listing in Chicago, Illinois.

SUN.	MON.	TUE.	WED.	THU.	FRI.	SAT.
noon–5	10–9	10–6	10–6	10–5	10–6	10–6

SAVINGS: 25%–50% off   *Mailing List*
BRAND NAMES: Dan Howard
PARKING: lot
PAYMENT: cash, checks (amount of purchase only, with proper I.D.), MasterCard,
   VISA, American Express

NORTH RIVERSIDE, IL

Dan Howard's Maternity Factory Outlet, 7305 W. 25th Street, North Riverside, IL 60546; (312) 447-2772
   See listing in Chicago, Illinois.

SUN.	MON.	TUE.	WED.	THU.	FRI.	SAT.
noon–5	10–9	10–6	10–6	10–9	10–6	10–5

SAVINGS: 25%–50% off   *Mailing List*
BRAND NAMES: Dan Howard
PARKING: lot
PAYMENT: cash, checks (with proper I.D.), MasterCard, VISA, American Express

ORLAND PARK, IL

Dan Howard's Maternity Factory Outlet, 15024 LaGrange Road, Orland Park, IL 60462; (312) 460-8778
   See listing in Chicago, Illinois.

SUN.	MON.	TUE.	WED.	THU.	FRI.	SAT.
noon–5	10–9	10–6	10–6	10–9	10–6	10–5

SAVINGS: 25%–50% off   *Mailing List*
BRAND NAMES: Dan Howard
PARKING: lot
PAYMENT: cash, checks (amount of purchase only, with proper I.D.), MasterCard, VISA

SCHAUMBURG, IL

Dan Howard's Maternity Factory Outlet, 215 W. Golf Road, Schaumburg, IL 60172;
(312) 884-8990
See listing in Chicago, Illinois.

SUN.	MON.	TUE.	WED.	THU.	FRI.	SAT.
noon-5	10-9	10-6	10-6	10-9	10-6	10-5

SAVINGS: 25%–50% off   *Mailing List*
BRAND NAMES: Dan Howard
PARKING: lot
PAYMENT: cash, checks (amount of purchase only, with proper I.D.), MasterCard,
VISA, American Express

VERNON HILLS, IL

Dan Howard's Maternity Factory Outlet, 115 Town Line Road, Vernon Hills, IL
60061; (312) 680-1200
See listing in Chicago, Illinois.

SUN.	MON.	TUE.	WED.	THU.	FRI.	SAT.
noon-5	10-9	10-6	10-6	10-9	10-6	10-5

SAVINGS: 25%–50% off   *Mailing List*
BRAND NAMES: Dan Howard
PARKING: lot
PAYMENT: cash, checks (amount of purchase only, with proper I.D.), MasterCard,
VISA, American Express

WILMETTE, IL

Dan Howard's Maternity Factory Outlet, 3217 Lake Avenue, Wilmette, IL 60091;
(312) 251-3303
See listing in Chicago, Illinois.

SUN.	MON.	TUE.	WED.	THU.	FRI.	SAT.
noon-5	10-9	10-6	10-6	10-9	10-6	10-5

SAVINGS: 25%–50% off   *Mailing List*
BRAND NAMES: Dan Howard
PARKING: lot
PAYMENT: cash, checks (amount of purchase only, with proper I.D.), MasterCard,
VISA, American Express

INDIANA
INDIANAPOLIS, IN

Dan Howard's Maternity Factory Outlet, 5372 W. 38th Street, Indianapolis, IN
46254; (317) 293-2600
See listing in Chicago, Illinois.

SUN.	MON.	TUE.	WED.	THU.	FRI.	SAT.
noon-5	10-8	10-8	10-8	10-8	10-8	10-6

SAVINGS: 25%–50% off
BRAND NAMES: Dan Howard, Leading Lady
ANNUAL SALES: Memorial Day, end-of-season
SPECIAL DISCOUNTS: Cradle Club members, one time only
PARKING: lot

PAYMENT: cash, checks (amount of purchase only, with proper I.D.), MasterCard, VISA, American Express

Dan Howard's Maternity Factory Outlet, 8314 Castleton Corner Drive, Indianapolis, IN 46250; (317) 842-9123
    See listing in Chicago, Illinois.

SUN.	MON.	TUE.	WED.	THU.	FRI.	SAT.
noon–5	10–9	10–9	10–9	10–9	10–9	10–6

SAVINGS: 25%–50% off   *Mailing List*   *All First Quality*
PARKING: lot
PAYMENT: cash, checks (with proper I.D.), MasterCard, VISA

WISCONSIN
KENOSHA, WI

The Genuine Article
    See listing under *Clothing—Family* in Kenosha, Wisconsin.

OSHKOSH, WI

The Genuine Article
    See listing under *Clothing—Family* in Oshkosh, Wisconsin.

PLOVER, WI

The Genuine Article
    See listing under *Clothing—Family* in Plover, Wisconsin.

WEST ALLIS, WI

Dan Howard's Maternity Factory Outlet, 2755 S. 108th Street, West Allis, WI 53227; (414) 327-7799
    See listing in Chicago, Illinois.

SUN.	MON.	TUE.	WED.	THU.	FRI.	SAT.
noon–5	10–9	10–6	10–9	10–6	10–6	10–6

SAVINGS: 25%–50% off   *Mailing List*   *All First Quality*
BRAND NAMES: Dan Howard
SALE DAYS: every other month
PARKING: lot
PAYMENT: cash, checks (with proper I.D.), MasterCard, VISA, American Express

WEST BEND, WI

The Genuine Article
    See listing under *Clothing—Family* in West Bend, Wisconsin.

CLOTHING—MEN'S

The outlets listed here sell mostly men's clothing. Also look in this chapter under *Activewear, Family, Large Sizes, Outerwear, Sportswear,* and *Women's* for other outlets that sell men's clothing.

Savings are excellent on seconds and irregular merchandise, but look closely to see if the irregularity will make a difference in your use of the item. Savings on end-of-season and closeout merchandise will be most beneficial to you if you can buy an item at great savings, then put it away until the next year. Dressing rooms and return policies vary, so shop carefully and make sure of sizes before making a purchase.

ILLINOIS
CHICAGO, IL

Clothing Clearance Center, 3161 N. Clark Street, Chicago, IL 60657; (312) 929-0100
   This is one of several stores that carries men's clothing, sportswear, suits, and accessories. Savings begin at 20% off retail price for first quality, but the real savings are on last year's lines where savings average 50% off retail price. They have other stores in Chicago, Lombard, Morton Grove, Orland Park, and Schaumburg, Illinois; and two stores (called Kuppenheimer's) in Indianapolis, Indiana.

SUN.	MON.	TUE.	WED.	THU.	FRI.	SAT.
10-5	10-9	10-9	10-9	10-9	10-9	10-6

SAVINGS: 20%–50% off   *Mailing List*   *All First Quality*
ANNUAL SALES: two-for-one (end of each season)
PARKING: street, meters, can be difficult
PAYMENT: cash, checks (with proper I.D.), MasterCard, VISA, American Express

Clothing Clearance Center, 1006 S. Michigan Avenue, Chicago, IL 60605; (312) 663-4170
   See listing above.

SUN.	MON.	TUE.	WED.	THU.	FRI.	SAT.
11-5	10-9	10-9	10-9	10-9	10-9	10-6

SAVINGS: 20%–50% off   *Mailing List*
BRAND NAMES: Arrow, Manhattan, Dior
ANNUAL SALES: two-for-one sales (end of each season)
PARKING: lot
PAYMENT: cash, checks (amount of purchase only, with proper I.D.), MasterCard,
   VISA, American Express

County Seat Outlet, 7983 S. Cicero Avenue, Chicago, IL 60652; (312) 767-6633
   This store sells major brands of men's and women's clothing. Savings are greatest on overstocks, overruns, and closeout merchandise.

SUN.	MON.	TUE.	WED.	THU.	FRI.	SAT.
11-5	10-9	10-9	10-9	10-9	10-9	10-6

SAVINGS: at least 10% off
BRAND NAMES: General, St. Cruz, Levi's, Esprit
PARKING: lot
PAYMENT: cash, checks (amount of purchase only, with proper I.D.), MasterCard, VISA

General Jobbing Corporation Warehouse, 5547 W. Belmont Avenue, Chicago, IL 60641; (312) 282-4130
   This is the outlet for the liquidations of several companies. Savings begin at 60% off retail price for first quality, and can go as high as 95% off retail price on some irregulars, overruns, overstocks, last year's lines, end-of-season, discontinued, closeouts, and odd lots of men's and women's clothing and shoes.

SUN.	MON.	TUE.	WED.	THU.	FRI.	SAT.
9-5	9-7	9-6	9-6	9-7	9-7	9-6

SAVINGS: 60%–95% off
BRAND NAMES: J.G. Hook, Bally, Newman, Ralph Lauren, Stuart McGuire, Lee, Levi's
SPECIAL DISCOUNTS: volume discounts only
PARKING: lot
PAYMENT: cash, MasterCard, VISA

Joseph A. Bank Clothiers, 25 E. Washington Street, Chicago, IL 60602; (312) 782-4432
   This outlet sells their own label of men's and women's clothing, business apparel,

and men's shoes at savings of 20%–40% on all first quality merchandise. They have another store in Wilmette, Illinois.

SUN.	MON.	TUE.	WED.	THU.	FRI.	SAT.
closed	8:30-7	8:30-6	8:30-6	8:30-7	8:30-6	9-5:30

SAVINGS: 20%–40% off   *Mailing List*   *All First Quality*
BRAND NAMES: Joseph A. Bank
ANNUAL SALES: July 4th, Christmas
PARKING: street, meters, very difficult
PAYMENT: cash, checks (amount of purchase only, with proper I.D.), MasterCard, VISA, American Express

Karol's Men's Fashions—Men's Clothing Warehouse, 3201 W. 63rd Street, Chicago, IL 60629; (312) 476-9581
    This is the outlet for the Karol's retail shops. Savings begin at 20% off retail price on first quality merchandise, and run as high as 60% on last year's line, end-of-season, and overstocks of men's clothing and accessories.

SUN.	MON.	TUE.	WED.	THU.	FRI.	SAT.
9-5	9-5	9-5	9-5	9-5	9-5	9-5

SAVINGS: 40%–60% off   *Mailing List*   *All First Quality*
BRAND NAMES: Palm Beach, London Fog, Jaymar, Hager, Manhattan, Levi's, Wrangler
PARKING: street, meters
PAYMENT: cash, checks (amount of purchase only, with proper I.D.), MasterCard, VISA, American Express, Karol's charge

Karol's Men's Fashions—Men's Clothing Warehouse, 1400 S. Clinton Street, Chicago, IL 60607; (312) 226-9859
    See listing above.

SUN.	MON.	TUE.	WED.	THU.	FRI.	SAT.
9-5	9-5	9-5	9-5	9-5	9-5	9-5

SAVINGS: 20%–60% off   *Mailing List*
BRAND NAMES: London Fog, Cassini, Palm Beach, Manhattan, Members Only, Sasson
PARKING: lot
PAYMENT: cash, checks (amount of purchase only, with proper I.D.), MasterCard, VISA, American Express

Land's End Outlet
    See listing under *Clothing—Activewear* in Chicago, Illinois.

Meystel
    See listing under *Clothing—Family* in Chicago, Illinois.

Morris & Sons, 555 W. Roosevelt Road (2nd floor), Chicago, IL 60607; (312) 243-5635
    This store sells several Italian brands of men's and women's apparel and accessories. In order to be on their mailing list and to be invited to their private sales, you must spend $200 at one time.

SUN.	MON.	TUE.	WED.	THU.	FRI.	SAT.
9-4	9-5:30	9-5:30	9-5:30	closed	closed	9-5:30

SAVINGS: 30%–70% off   *Mailing List*   *All First Quality*
SALE DAYS: private sales for special customers
PARKING: lot
PAYMENT: cash, checks, MasterCard, VISA, American Express

Rottapel Clothes, 531 W. Roosevelt Road, Chicago, IL 60607;(312) 942-0816
    This store sells major brands of men's sportswear, dress shirts, suits, and accessories. They also sell Gloria Vanderbilt women's jeans and blouses. Savings start at 20% off on first quality, and go as high as 60% on surplus and overruns.

SUN.	MON.	TUE.	WED.	THU.	FRI.	SAT.
9:30-4	9:30-5	9:30-5	9:30-5	9:30-5	9:30-5	9:30-5

SAVINGS: 20%-60% off
BRAND NAMES: Eagle, Geoffrey Beene, Society, Arrow, Johnny Carson, Christian Dior, Gloria Vanderbilt, Manhattan
SPECIAL DISCOUNTS: they say they would "consider negotiating" with senior citizens and charity groups (ask)
PARKING: street, can be difficult
PAYMENT: cash, checks (amount of purchase only, with proper I.D.)

Sid's Discount Clothing and University Shop, 609 W. Roosevelt Road, Chicago, IL 60607; (312) 421-3332
This store sells several major brands of men's sportswear, shirts, ties, and belts

SUN.	MON.	TUE.	WED.	THU.	FRI.	SAT.
9-5	9-5	9-5	9-5	9-5	9-5	9-5

SAVINGS: 15%-20% off   *All First Quality*
BRAND NAMES: Kangol, Hager
ANNUAL SALES: January, April, end of August
PARKING: lot
PAYMENT: cash, MasterCard, VISA, American Express

Textile Discount Outlet
See listing under *Fabrics* in Chicago, Illinois.

BUFFALO GROVE, IL

Van Heusen Factory Outlet Store, 1275 W. Dundee Avenue, Buffalo Grove, IL 60090; (312) 577-5186
This is the factory outlet for Van Heusen shirts. They also sell women's shirts and blouses, and some sports jackets and accessories. Savings begin at about 30% off retail price on mostly first quality, in-season merchandise. A single table of irregulars is clearly marked. Savings can go as high as 75% off retail price on end-of-season, discontinued, and closeout merchandise. Although exchanges are possible, refunds are not. They have other stores in Lombard, Niles, and Schaumburg, Illinois; Merrillville, Indiana; and Beloit, Wisconsin.

SUN.	MON.	TUE.	WED.	THU.	FRI.	SAT.
noon-5	10-6	10-6	10-6	10-9	10-9	10-6

SAVINGS: 30%-75% off
BRAND NAMES: Van Heusen, Players, Windbreaker
ANNUAL SALES: January, July
PARKING: lot
PAYMENT: cash, checks (amount of purchase only, with proper I.D.), MasterCard, VISA

CICERO, IL

Waveland International Imports, Guinta's Factory Outlet Mall, 1800 S. Cicero Avenue, Cicero, IL 60650; (312) 656-3375
This store sells several major brands of men's and women's clothing. Discounts begin at 30% off retail price for first quality, and can run as high as 70% off on last year's lines, end-of-season, and unlabeled merchandise.

SUN.	MON.	TUE.	WED.	THU.	FRI.	SAT.
11-8	10-8	closed	10-8	10-8	10-8	10-8

SAVINGS: 30%-70% off   *Mailing List*
PARKING: lot
PAYMENT: cash, MasterCard, VISA

Clothing Clearance Center, 800 E. Roosevelt Road, Lombard, IL 60148; (312) 627-0050
    See listing in Chicago, Illinois.

SUN.	MON.	TUE.	WED.	THU.	FRI.	SAT.
11–5	10–9	10–9	10–9	10–9	10–9	10–6

SAVINGS: 20%–50% off   *Mailing List*
BRAND NAMES: Arrow, Manhattan, Dior
SPECIAL SALES: two-for-one (end of each season)
PARKING: lot
PAYMENT: cash, checks (amount of purchase only, with proper I.D., Compucheck),
    MasterCard, VISA, American Express

Van Heusen Factory Outlet Store, 1111 S. Main Street, Lombard, IL 60148; (312) 629-5062
    See listing in Buffalo Grove, Illinois.

SUN.	MON.	TUE.	WED.	THU.	FRI.	SAT.
noon–5	10–9	10–9	10–9	10–9	10–9	10–6

SAVINGS: 30%–60% off
BRAND NAMES: Van Heusen, Players, Windbreaker
ANNUAL SALES: Father's Day, 4th of July, back-to-school, Christmas
PARKING: lot
PAYMENT: cash, checks (amount of purchase only, with proper I.D.), MasterCard, VISA

The Factory Outlet Store, 300 Rowan Drive, McLeansboro, IL 62859; (618) 643-3011
    This is the factory outlet for Elders clothing. Most merchandise is for men and
boys, but they do sell some women's clothing. They also sell Levi's and Lee jeans.
Savings can go up to 75% off retail price on some irregulars.

SUN.	MON.	TUE.	WED.	THU.	FRI.	SAT.
closed	9:30–5	9:30–5	9:30–5	9:30–5	9:30–5	9:30–5

SAVINGS: up to 50% off
BRAND NAMES: Elders, Levi's, Lee
ANNUAL SALES: Easter, Father's Day
PARKING: lot
PAYMENT: cash, checks (amount of purchase only, with proper I.D.), MasterCard, VISA

Clothing Clearance Center, 6717 W. Dempster Street, Morton Grove, IL 60053; (312) 967-8840
    See listing in Chicago, Illinois.

SUN.	MON.	TUE.	WED.	THU.	FRI.	SAT.
11–5	10–9	10–9	10–9	10–9	10–9	10–6

SAVINGS: 20%–50% off   *Mailing List*
BRAND NAMES: Arrow, Manhattan, Dior
ANNUAL SALES: two-for-one (end of each season)
PARKING: lot
PAYMENT: cash, checks (amount of purchase only, with proper I.D.), MasterCard,
    VISA, American Express

Aparacor Outlet Store
    See listing under *Clothing—Women's* in Niles, Illinois.

Van Heusen Factory Outlet Store, 8474 W. Golf Road, Niles, IL 60648; (312) 966-2205

See listing in Buffalo Grove, Illinois.

SUN.	MON.	TUE.	WED.	THU.	FRI.	SAT.
noon–5	10–9	10–9	10–9	10–9	10–9	10–6

SAVINGS: 40%–60% off
BRAND NAMES: Van Heusen, Players, Windbreaker
PARKING: lot
PAYMENT: cash, checks (amount of purchase only, with proper I.D.), MasterCard, VISA

ORLAND PARK, IL

Clothing Clearance Center, 15645 S. 71st Court, Orland Park, IL 60462; (312)
532-1424
See listing in Chicago, Illinois.

SUN.	MON.	TUE.	WED.	THU.	FRI.	SAT.
11–5	10–9	10–9	10–9	10–9	10–9	10–6

SAVINGS: 20%–50% off   *Mailing List*
BRAND NAMES: Arrow, Manhattan, Dior
ANNUAL SALES: two-for-one (end of each season)
PARKING: lot
PAYMENT: cash, checks (amount of purchase only, with proper I.D.), MasterCard,
VISA, American Express

SCHAUMBURG, IL

Clothing Clearance Center, 830 E. Golf Road, Schaumburg, IL 60195; (312)
882-7466
See listing in Chicago, Illinois.

SUN.	MON.	TUE.	WED.	THU.	FRI.	SAT.
11–5	10–9	10–9	10–9	10–9	10–9	10–6

SAVINGS: 20%–50% off   *Mailing List*
BRAND NAMES: Arrow, Manhattan, Dior
ANNUAL SALES: two-for-one (end of each season)
PARKING: lot
PAYMENT: cash, checks (amount of purchase only, with proper I.D.), MasterCard,
VISA, American Express

Van Heusen Factory Outlet Store, 243 W. Golf Road, Schaumburg, IL 60194; (312)
882-5750
See listing in Buffalo Grove, Illinois.

SUN.	MON.	TUE.	WED.	THU.	FRI.	SAT.
noon–5	10–9	10–9	10–9	10–9	10–9	10–6

SAVINGS: 40%–60% off
BRAND NAMES: Van Heusen, Players, Windbreaker
PARKING: lot
PAYMENT: cash, checks (amount of purchase only, with proper I.D.), MasterCard, VISA

WILMETTE, IL

Joseph A. Bank Clothiers, Edens Plaza, 1101 Skokie Boulevard, Wilmette, IL 60091;
(312) 256-5124
See listing in Chicago, Illinois.

SUN.	MON.	TUE.	WED.	THU.	FRI.	SAT.
noon–5	10–9	10–9	10–9	10–9	10–9	9-5:30

SAVINGS: 20%–40% off   *Mailing List*   *All First Quality*
BRAND NAMES: Joseph A. Bank
SALE DAYS: vary
PARKING: lot
PAYMENT: cash, checks (amount of purchase only, with proper I.D.), MasterCard, VISA

Kuppenheimer Men's Clothing, 5439 U.S. 31 South, Indianapolis, IN 46227; (317) 783-9396
   See listing under Clothing Clearance Center in Chicago, Illinois.

SUN.	MON.	TUE.	WED.	THU.	FRI.	SAT.
noon–5:30	10–9	10–9	10–9	10–9	10–9	10–6

SAVINGS: 40% off   *Mailing List*
BRAND NAMES: Kuppenheimer
SPECIAL DISCOUNTS: charitable groups
PARKING: lot
PAYMENT: cash, checks (amount of purchase only, with proper I.D.), MasterCard,
   VISA, American Express

Kuppenheimer Men's Clothing, 5621 W. 85th Street, Indianapolis, IN 46278; (317) 872-8325
   See listing under Clothing Clearance Center in Chicago, Illinois.

SUN.	MON.	TUE.	WED.	THU.	FRI.	SAT.
noon–5:30	10–9	10–9	10–9	10–9	10–9	10–6

SAVINGS: about 40% off   *Mailing List*   *All First Quality*
BRAND NAMES: Kuppenheimer
ANNUAL SALES: spring
PARKING: lot
PAYMENT: cash, checks (amount of purchase only, with proper I.D.), MasterCard, VISA

Van Heusen Factory Store, Century Consumer Mall, 8275 Broadway, Merrillville, IN 46410; (219) 738-1959
   See listing in Buffalo Grove, Illinois.

SUN.	MON.	TUE.	WED.	THU.	FRI.	SAT.
11–5	10–9	10–9	10–9	10–9	10–9	10–9

SAVINGS: 30%–50% off
BRAND NAMES: Van Heusen, Geoffrey Beene
PARKING: lot
PAYMENT: cash, checks (amount of purchase only, with proper I.D.), MasterCard, VISA

Jaymar Slacks—Factory Outlet Store, 209 W. Michigan Boulevard, Michigan City, IN 46360; (219) 879-7341
   This factory outlet sells Sansabelt slacks, suits, and sportswear at savings up to 50% off retail price on first quality, and as high as 75% off on seconds, samples, surplus, overruns, overstocks, end-of-season, discontinued, closeouts, and odd lots. They also sell Pierre Cardin slacks at savings up to 50% off retail prices.

SUN.	MON.	TUE.	WED.	THU.	FRI.	SAT.
10–5	10–5	10–5	10–5	10–5	10–5	10–5

SAVINGS: 30%–70% off   *Mailing List*
BRAND NAMES: Sansabelt, Sansabelt Sport, Jaymar, Pierre Cardin
ANNUAL SALES: January, June
PARKING: lot
PAYMENT: cash, checks (amount of purchase only, with proper I.D.), MasterCard,
   VISA, American Express

Excello Factory Store, 400 S. Airport Road, Seymour, IN 47274; (812) 522-1176

This is the factory outlet for Excello men's dress shirts. They also sell socks, pants, and ties. Savings begin at 40% on first quality, and can go higher on some seconds, irregulars, last year's line, and discontinued items.

SUN.	MON.	TUE.	WED.	THU.	FRI.	SAT.
closed	8:30–4:30	8:30–4:30	8:30–4:30	8:30–4:30	8:30–4:30	9:30–4:30

SAVINGS: at least 40% off
BRAND NAMES: Excello, Interwoven, Champion
PARKING: lot
PAYMENT: cash, checks (amount of purchase only, with proper I.D.)

WISCONSIN

BELOIT, WI

Manhattan Factory Outlet, Freeman Outlet Mall, 5 Freeman Lane, Beloit, WI 53511; (608) 365-5584

This is an outlet for Manhattan. They sell men's shirts, sportswear, and pants, and Vira ties and accessories. They also sell Peter Ashley blouses and Lady John Henry blouses, pants, some dresses and skirts, and Revlon cosmetics for women. Savings begin at 25% off retail prices. They also sell some seconds and last year's lines, where savings can be as high as 60%. They have other stores in Kenosha, Madison, Plover, and West Bend, Wisconsin.

SUN.	MON.	TUE.	WED.	THU.	FRI.	SAT.
11–5	9–9	9–9	9–9	9–9	9–9	9–6

SAVINGS: 25%–60% off   *Mailing List*
BRAND NAMES: Manhattan, Henry Grethel, Lucinda Rhodes, Lady John Henry, Perry
    Ellis, Anne Klein
PARKING: lot
PAYMENT: cash, checks (amount of purchase only, with proper I.D.), MasterCard,
    VISA, American Express

Van Heusen Factory Outlet Store, Freeman Outlet Mall, 5 Freeman Lane, Beloit, WI
    53511; (608) 362-1700
    See listing in Buffalo Grove, Illinois.

SUN.	MON.	TUE.	WED.	THU.	FRI.	SAT.
11–6	9–9	9–9	9–9	9–9	9–9	9–6

SAVINGS: 30%–60% off   *Mailing List*
BRAND NAMES: Van Heusen
PARKING: lot
PAYMENT: cash, checks (amount of purchase only, with proper I.D.), MasterCard, VISA

EAU CLAIRE, WI

Clothing Factory Outlet, 1408 S. Hastings Way, Eau Claire, WI 54701; (715)
    834-3624
    This outlet sells men's shirts, slacks, and outerwear at savings of 30%–50% off
retail prices.

SUN.	MON.	TUE.	WED.	THU.	FRI.	SAT.
closed	9–9	9–9	9–9	9–9	9–9	9–5:30

SAVINGS: 30%–50% off   *Mailing List*   *All First Quality*
BRAND NAMES: Eagle, Middishade, Browning King, College Hall
PARKING: lot
PAYMENT: cash, checks, MasterCard, VISA

Bottom Line Outlet
See listing under *Clothing—Women's* in Green Bay, Wisconsin.

The Brandwagon
See listing under *Clothing—Accessories* in Kenosha, Wisconsin.

C.J. Chips
See listing under *Clothing—Sportswear* in Kenosha, Wisconsin.

Fashions For Less
See listing under *Clothing—Women's* in Kenosha, Wisconsin.

Gentlemen's Wear House, Factory Outlet Centre, 7700 120th Avenue, Kenosha, WI
53142; (414) 857-2250
This outlet sells their own brand of men's suits, sport coats, pants, shirts,
sweaters, and ties. Savings average 40%–60% off retail price on all first quality
merchandise.

SUN.	MON.	TUE.	WED.	THU.	FRI.	SAT.
noon–5	9:30–9	9:30–9	9:30–9	9:30–9	9.30–9	9:30–6

SAVINGS: 40%–60% off   *Mailing List*   *All First Quality*
ANNUAL SALES: end of each season
SPECIAL DISCOUNTS: senior citizens, 10% off Wednesday
PARKING: lot
PAYMENT: cash, checks (amount of purchase only, with proper I.D.), MasterCard,
VISA, American Express

Jockey Men's Wear—Factory Outlet, 4200 N. 39th Avenue, Kenosha, WI 53142;
(414) 654-5737
This factory outlet sells Jockey men's underwear, sportswear, shirts, and slacks.
Savings average 50% off retail, with the best buys being on seconds, last year's lines,
discontinued, end-of-season, closeouts, and odd lots.

SUN.	MON.	TUE.	WED.	THU.	FRI.	SAT.
closed	10–5	10–5	10–5	10–5	10–5	10–5

SAVINGS: 50% off   *Mailing List*
BRAND NAMES: Jockey
ANNUAL SALES: summer, Christmas
PARKING: lot
PAYMENT: cash, checks (amount of purchase only, with proper I.D.), MasterCard, VISA

Manhattan Factory Outlet, Factory Outlet Centre, 7700 120th Avenue, Kenosha, WI
53142; (414) 857-7993
See listing in Beloit, Wisconsin.

SUN.	MON.	TUE.	WED.	THU.	FRI.	SAT.
11–5	9:30–9	9:30–9	9:30–9	9:30–9	9:30–9	9:30–6

SAVINGS: 50%–70% off   *Mailing List*
BRAND NAMES: Manhattan, Lady Manhattan, John Henry, Lady John Henry, Peter
Ashley
SPECIAL SALES: shirt-of-the-month
SPECIAL DISCOUNTS: senior citizens, 10% off Wednesday
PARKING: lot
PAYMENT: cash, checks (amount of purchase only, with proper I.D.), MasterCard,
VISA, American Express

The Brandwagon
See listing under *Clothing—Accessories* in Madison, Wisconsin.

Manhattan Factory Outlet, Factory Outlet Centre, 4609 Verona Road, Madison, WI 53711; (608) 273-4004
See listing in Beloit, Wisconsin.

SUN.	MON.	TUE.	WED.	THU.	FRI.	SAT.
noon-5	9:30-9	9:30-9	9:30-9	9:30-9	9:30-9	9:30-6

SAVINGS: 25%-60% off   *Mailing List*
BRAND NAMES: Manhattan, Lady Manhattan
SALE DAYS: Tuesday
SPECIAL DISCOUNTS: senior citizens, 10% off Wednesday
PARKING: lot
PAYMENT: cash, checks (amount of purchase only, with proper I.D.), MasterCard, VISA, American Express

Melco Clothing Company, 200 S. Water Street, Milwaukee, WI 53202; (414) 273-6682
This store sells major brands of men's sportswear, suits, rainwear, outerwear, and accessories.

SUN.	MON.	TUE.	WED.	THU.	FRI.	SAT.
closed	9-5	9-5	9-5	9-5	9-5	9-4

SAVINGS: at least 10% off   *Mailing List*
PARKING: lot
PAYMENT: cash, checks, MasterCard, VISA

Manhattan Factory Outlet, Manufacturers Direct Mall, 101 Plover Road, Plover, WI 54467; (715) 344-2241
See listing in Beloit, Wisconsin.

SUN.	MON.	TUE.	WED.	THU.	FRI.	SAT.
11-6	9:30-9	9:30-9	9:30-9	9:30-9	9:30-9	9:30-6

SAVINGS: 25%-60% off   *Mailing List*
BRAND NAMES: Manhattan, Vira, Peter Ashley, Lady John Henry
ANNUAL SALES: October
SPECIAL DISCOUNTS: senior citizens, 10% off
PARKING: lot
PAYMENT: cash, checks (amount of purchase only, with proper I.D.), MasterCard, VISA, American Express

Van Heusen Factory Outlet Store, Manufacturers Direct Mall, 101 Plover Road, Plover, WI 54467; (715) 344-4456
See listing in Buffalo Grove, Illinois.

SUN.	MON.	TUE.	WED.	THU.	FRI.	SAT.
11-5	9:30-9	9:30-9	9:30-9	9:30-9	9:30-9	9:30-6

SAVINGS: 30%-60% off
BRAND NAMES: Van Heusen
PARKING: lot
PAYMENT: cash, checks (amount of purchase only, with proper I.D.), MasterCard, VISA

Mill City Outlet, 410 S. Main Street, Racine, WI 53403; (414) 633-0515
This store sells mostly men's clothing, but they do have a small section for women. Greatest savings are on seconds, irregulars, overruns, discontinued, and closeouts. Their store in Kenosha, Wisconsin, sells mostly women's clothing.

SUN.	MON.	TUE.	WED.	THU.	FRI.	SAT.
closed	9–5:30	9–5:30	9–5:30	9–5:30	9–5:30	9–5:30

SAVINGS: 20%–50% off
BRAND NAMES: Lee
PARKING: lot
PAYMENT: cash, checks (amount of purchase only, with proper I.D., Telecheck), MasterCard, VISA

The Bottom Line
See listing under *Clothing—Women's* in Sister Bay, Wisconsin.

Manhattan Factory Outlet, West Bend Outlet Mall, 180 Island Avenue, West Bend, WI 53095; (414) 338-3636
See listing in Beloit, Wisconsin.

SUN.	MON.	TUE.	WED.	THU.	FRI.	SAT.
11–5	9:30–6	9:30–6	9:30–6	9:30–6	9:30–8	9:30–5

SAVINGS: 25%–60% off   *Mailing List*
BRAND NAMES: Manhattan, Henry Grethel, Lucinda Rhodes, John Henry, Perry Ellis, Anne Klein
PARKING: lot
PAYMENT: cash, checks (amount of purchase only, with proper I.D.), MasterCard, VISA, American Express

CLOTHING—OUTERWEAR

The outlets listed here sell mostly outerwear, although some sell other merchandise as well. Also look in this chapter under *Activewear, Babies', Children's, Family, Large Sizes, Maternity, Men's,* and *Sportswear* for other outlets that carry outerwear.

Savings on seconds and irregular merchandise can be excellent, but look closely to see the flaws, so you can judge whether they matter to you. End-of-season and closeout merchandise also offers great savings, if you can put the garment away until next year.

Burlington Coat Factory, 7340 W. Foster Avenue, Chicago, IL 60656; (312) 763-6006
This outlet has a huge selection of coats for every member of the family. They also have an extensive assortment of sportswear and shoes, and there is even a small selection of linens. Most merchandise is first quality, with savings ranging from 25%–60% off retail price. Be sure to check the clearance section where end-of-season merchandise is discounted even further. They have other stores in Arlington Heights, Libertyville, and Villa Park, Illinois; Indianapolis and Merrillville, Indiana; and Madison and two in Milwaukee, Wisconsin.

SUN.	MON.	TUE.	WED.	THU.	FRI.	SAT.
11–5	10–9	10–9	10–9	10–9	10–9	10–9

SAVINGS: 25%–65% off
BRAND NAMES: Burlington, Panther, Villager, Maidenform, Jack Winter, Act III,
   Warner, Nickels, Capezio, Marimekko, J.P. Stevens
PARKING: lot
PAYMENT: cash, checks (amount of purchase only, with proper I.D.), MasterCard, VISA
   (minimum $25)

Ideal Fashions
   See listing under *Clothing—Accessories* in Chicago, Illinois.

ARLINGTON HEIGHTS, IL

Burlington Coat Factory Warehouse, 30 W. Rand Road, Arlington Heights, IL
   60004; (312) 577-7878
   See listing in Chicago, Illinois.

SUN.	MON.	TUE.	WED.	THU.	FRI.	SAT.
11–5	10–9	10–9	10–9	10–9	10–9	10–9

SAVINGS: 25%–60% off
PARKING: lot
PAYMENT: cash, checks (amount of purchase only, with proper I.D.), MasterCard, VISA

CICERO, IL

Simandl Garment Company, 2506 S. Laramie Avenue, Cicero, IL 60650; (312)
   863-2718
   This manufacturer custom makes ladies' 100% wool coats, with or without fur
collars, at discounts 30%–50% off retail price. Customers can select fabrics, colors, and
styles.

SUN.	MON.	TUE.	WED.	THU.	FRI.	SAT.
closed	9–7	9–4:30	9–4:30	9–4:30	9–4:30	9–4

SAVINGS: 30%–50% off   *All First Quality*
PARKING: street
PAYMENT: cash, checks (amount of purchase only, with proper I.D.), MasterCard, VISA

DOWNERS GROVE, IL

The Outletters, 1300 E. Butterfield Road, Downers Grove, IL 60515; (312) 953-1629
   This store sells men's and women's outerwear and men's shoes. Discounts begin at
30% off retail price on first quality, and quickly jump to 50% on surplus, overstocks,
and last year's lines.

SUN.	MON.	TUE.	WED.	THU.	FRI.	SAT.
noon–5	10–9	10–9	10–9	10–9	10–9	10–6

SAVINGS: 30%–50% off
PARKING: lot
PAYMENT: cash, checks (amount of purchase only, with proper I.D.), MasterCard,
   VISA, American Express

LIBERTYVILLE, IL

Burlington Coat Factory Warehouse, 920 S. Milwaukee Avenue, Libertyville, IL
   60048; (312) 680-8150
   See listing in Chicago, Illinois.

SUN.	MON.	TUE.	WED.	THU.	FRI.	SAT.
11–5	10–9	10–9	10–9	10–9	10–9	10–9

SAVINGS: 25%–75%
BRAND NAMES: Calvin Klein, Botany 500, Carol Little
ANNUAL SALES: January
PARKING: lot
PAYMENT: cash, checks (amount of purchase only, with proper I.D.), MasterCard, VISA

Burlington Coat Factory, 174 W. Roosevelt Road, Villa Park, IL 60181; (312) 832-4500
　　See listing in Chicago, Illinois

SUN.	MON.	TUE.	WED.	THU.	FRI.	SAT.
11–5	10–9	10–9	10–9	10–9	10–9	10–9

SAVINGS: 20%–60% off　　　　　　　　　　　　　　　　　*All First Quality*
PARKING: lot
PAYMENT: cash, checks (amount of purchase only, with proper I.D.), MasterCard, VISA

Value Center
　　See listing under *Clothing—Sportswear* in Elkhart, Indiana

Burlington Coat Factory, Eastgate Consumer Mall, 7150 E. Washington Street, Indianapolis, IN 46201; (317) 352-9166
　　See listing in Chicago, Illinois.

SUN.	MON.	TUE.	WED.	THU.	FRI.	SAT.
11–5	10–9	10–9	10–9	10–9	10–9	10–9

SAVINGS: 25%–60% off
BRAND NAMES: Burlington
SALE DAYS: vary
PARKING: street
PAYMENT: cash, checks, MasterCard, VISA

The Company Store, 1465 W. 86th Street, Indianapolis, IN 46268; (317) 875-5030
　　This outlet sells Company Store down-filled items, such as comforters, down-filled jackets, and pillows. Some items carry the Bill Blass label. Savings are greatest on seconds, irregulars, discontinued, end-of-season, last year's lines, overruns, and overstocks. They also do mail order business. Ask to be put on their mailing list to receive a catalog. They have other stores in Eau Claire, Kenosha, two in La Crosse, Oshkosh, Plover, and Redwing, Wisconsin.

SUN.	MON.	TUE.	WED.	THU.	FRI.	SAT.
noon–5	10–9	10–9	10–9	10–9	10–9	10–6

SAVINGS: 20%–60% off　　　　　　　　　　　　　　　　　*Mailing List*
PARKING: lot
PAYMENT: cash, checks (amount of purchase only, with proper I.D.), MasterCard, VISA, American Express

Burlington Coat Factory, Century Consumer Mall, 8275 Broadway, Merrillville, IN 46410; (219) 736-0636
　　See listing in Chicago, Illinois.

SUN.	MON.	TUE.	WED.	THU.	FRI.	SAT.
11–5	10–9	10–9	10–9	10–9	10–9	10–9

SAVINGS: 25%–60% off
BRAND NAMES: Burlington
SALE DAYS: vary
PARKING: street
PAYMENT: cash, checks, MasterCard, VISA

Gohn Brothers Manufacturing Company
See listing under *Fabrics* in Middlebury, Indiana.

Londontown—Factory Outlet Store, Richmond Mall Square, 3801 East National
Road (U.S. Route 40), Richmond, IN 47374; (317) 966-1021
This is the outlet for London Fog outerwear. The entire stock of jackets, coats, leathers, and raincoats for men, women, and children is priced at half the regular retail price. All merchandise is seconds, irregulars, samples, overruns, and closeouts. There are no refunds and no exchanges.

SUN.	MON.	TUE.	WED.	THU.	FRI.	SAT.
noon–5	10–9	10–9	10–9	10–9	10–9	10–9

SAVINGS: 50% off   *Mailing List*
BRAND NAMES: London Fog
ANNUAL SALES: year-end inventory sale; MAILING LIST
PARKING: lot
PAYMENT: cash, checks (amount of purchase only, with proper I.D.), MasterCard, VISA

Mid-Western Sport Togs
See listing under *Clothing—Accessories* in Berlin, Wisconsin.

The Company Store, 1811 S. Hasting Way, Eau Claire, WI 54720; (715) 836-9265
See listing in Indianapolis, Indiana.

SUN.	MON.	TUE.	WED.	THU.	FRI.	SAT.
noon–5	9:30–5:30	9:30–5:30	9:30–5:30	9:30–5:30	9:30–5:30	9:30–5:30

SAVINGS: at least 50% off
BRAND NAMES: Company Store
PARKING: lot
PAYMENT: cash, checks (amount of purchase only, with proper I.D.), MasterCard, VISA

The Leather Shop
See listing under *Clothing—Accessories* in Green Bay, Wisconsin.

North Trail Sportswear, 129 S. Washington Street, Green Bay, WI 54301; (414)
435-6500
This factory outlet sells North Trail outerwear and sportswear. They also sell zippers and buttons. Savings run 40%–60% off normal retail price.

SUN.	MON.	TUE.	WED.	THU.	FRI.	SAT.
closed	7–5	7–5	7–5	7–5	7–5	10–3*

SAVINGS: 40%–60% off   *All First Quality*
PARKING: street
PAYMENT: cash, checks (amount of purchase only, with proper I.D.)

---

*They are closed on Saturday between Memorial Day and Labor Day.

The Brandwagon
See listing under *Clothing—Accessories* in Kenosha, Wisconsin.

The Company Store, Factory Outlet Centre, 7700 120th Avenue, Kenosha, WI 53142; (414) 857-7027
   See listing in Indianapolis, Indiana.

SUN.	MON.	TUE.	WED.	THU.	FRI.	SAT.
11–5	9:30–9	9:30–9	9:30–9	9:30–9	9:30–9	9:30–6

SAVINGS: about 50% off   *Mailing List*
SPECIAL DISCOUNTS: senior citizens, 10% off Wednesday
PARKING: lot
PAYMENT: cash, checks (amount of purchase only, with proper I.D.), MasterCard, VISA

LA CROSSE, WI

The Company Store, 1205 S. 7th Street, La Crosse, WI 54601; (608) 784-9522
   See listing in Indianapolis, Indiana.

SUN.	MON.	TUE.	WED.	THU.	FRI.	SAT.
noon–5	9–5	9–5	9–5	9–5	9–5	9–5

SAVINGS: at least 50% off
BRAND NAMES: Company Store
PARKING: lot
PAYMENT: cash, checks (amount of purchase only, with proper I.D.), MasterCard

The Company Store, La Crosse Factory Outlet Mall, 301 Sky Harbor Drive, La Crosse, WI 54601; (608) 783-4171
   See listing in Indianapolis, Indiana.

SUN.	MON.	TUE.	WED.	THU.	FRI.	SAT.
11–5	10–9	10–9	10–9	10–9	10–9	9–6

SAVINGS: at least 50% off
BRAND NAMES: Company Store
PARKING: lot
PAYMENT: cash, checks (amount of purchase only, with proper I.D.), MasterCard, VISA

MADISON, WI

The Brandwagon
   See listing under *Clothing—Accessories* in Madison, Wisconsin.

Burlington Coat Factory, 1810 W. Beltline Highway, Madison, WI 53713; (608) 257-6505
   See listing in Chicago, Illinois.

SUN.	MON.	TUE.	WED.	THU.	FRI.	SAT.
11–5	10–9	10–9	10–9	10–9	10–9	10–9

SAVINGS: 40%–70% off
BRAND NAMES: Evan-Picone, Liz Claiborne, Pierre Cardin
PARKING: lot
PAYMENT: cash, checks (amount of purchase only, with proper I.D.), MasterCard, VISA

MILWAUKEE, WI

Burlington Coat Factory, 1501 W. Jewel Street, Milwaukee, WI 53221; (414) 764-2774
   See listing in Chicago, Illinois.

SUN.	MON.	TUE.	WED.	THU.	FRI.	SAT.
11–5	10–9	10–9	10–9	10–9	10–9	10–9

SAVINGS: 20%–50% off   *All First Quality*
PARKING: lot
PAYMENT: cash, checks (amount of purchase only, with proper I.D.), MasterCard, VISA

Burlington Coat Factory, 6554 N. 76th Street, Milwaukee, WI 53223; (414) 385-0500
See listing in Chicago, Illinois.

SUN.	MON.	TUE.	WED.	THU.	FRI.	SAT.
11–5	10–9	10–9	10–9	10–9	10–9	10–9

SAVINGS: 20%–50% off
BRAND NAMES: Burlington   *All First Quality*
ANNUAL SALES: January, February
PARKING: lot
PAYMENT: cash, checks (amount of purchase only, with proper I.D.), MasterCard, VISA

OSHKOSH, WI

The Company Store, 901 S. Main Street, Oshkosh, WI 54901; (414) 426-1443
See listing in Indianapolis, Indiana.

SUN.	MON.	TUE.	WED.	THU.	FRI.	SAT.
noon–4	10–5	10–5	10–5	10–5	10–5	10–5

SAVINGS: about 50% off   *Mailing List*
BRAND NAMES: Company Store
ANNUAL SALES: July, August
SPECIAL DISCOUNTS: guests at a local motel get 10% off
PARKING: street
PAYMENT: cash, checks (amount of purchase only, with proper I.D.), MasterCard, VISA

PLOVER, WI

The Company Store, Manufacturers Direct Mall, 101 Plover Road, Plover, WI 54467;
(715) 344-5656
See listing in Indianapolis, Indiana.

SUN.	MON.	TUE.	WED.	THU.	FRI.	SAT.
11–6	9:30–9	9:30–9	9:30–9	9:30–9	9:30–9	9:30–6

SAVINGS: at least 50% off   *Mailing List*
BRAND NAMES: Company Store
PARKING: lot
PAYMENT: cash, checks (amount of purchase only, with proper I.D.), MasterCard, VISA

REDWING, WI

The Company Store, 2000 Old West Main, Redwing, WI 55066; (612) 388-9555
See listing in Indianapolis, Indiana.

SUN.	MON.	TUE.	WED.	THU.	FRI.	SAT.
9–6	9–8	9–8	9–8	9–8	9–8	10–6

SAVINGS: about 50% off
BRAND NAMES: Company Store
PARKING: lot
PAYMENT: cash, checks (amount of purchase only, with proper I.D.), MasterCard, VISA

RIPON, WI

Fox River Glove Factory Outlet Store, 113 W. Fond Du Lac Street, Ripon, WI
54971; (414) 748-5845
This is the factory outlet for Fox River Glove Company They sell gloves and other
leather goods, including jackets and bags, made in the factory on the premises. They
also sell several other brands of socks, moccasins, jeans, and Weber knit caps, scarves,
mittens, and gloves. The moccasins are first quality; most other merchandise is
seconds, irregulars, end-of-season, surplus, overruns, discontinued, closeouts, and odd
lots.

SUN.	MON.	TUE.	WED.	THU.	FRI.	SAT.
noon–4	9–5	9–5	9–5	9–5	9–9	9–5

SAVINGS: 33%–50% off
BRAND NAMES: Wigwam, Minnetonka, Grandoe, Chic, Levi's, Weber Knits, Fabrico
ANNUAL SALES: January, June, August, September
SPECIAL DISCOUNTS: senior citizens, 10% off
PARKING: lot
PAYMENT: cash, checks (with proper I.D.)

WEST BEND, WI

West Bend Woolen Mills
 See listing under *Clothing—Sportswear* in West Bend, Wisconsin.

CLOTHING—SPORTSWEAR

This chapter section includes outlets which sell mostly casual clothes. Look at this chapter under *Accessories, Activewear, Children's, Family, Men's*, and *Women's*, for more outlets that also sell sportswear.

Know the retail prices of the items you are buying. It will help you recognize a bargain when you see it. Seconds are usually marked, but feel free to ask to have the irregularity pointed out to you before you buy.

Before you go shopping, remember to make a list of sizes of the members of your family. Although outlets in the malls have dressing rooms and usually make refunds or exchanges, many outlets at the factory lack these amenities. Ask about returns and exchanges before making your purchases.

ILLINOIS
CHICAGO, IL

Ideal Fashions
 See listing under *Clothing—Accessories* in Chicago, Illinois.

Land's End Outlet
 See two listings under *Clothing—Activewear* in Chicago, Illinois.

Rottapel Clothes
 See listing under *Clothing—Men's* in Chicago, Illinois.

DEERFIELD, IL

Land's End Outlet
 See listing under *Clothing—Activewear* in Deerfield, Illinois.

EAST DUNDEE, IL

Winona Knits
 See listing under *Clothing—Accessories* in East Dundee, Illinois.

LOMBARD, IL

Land's End Outlet
 See listing under *Clothing—Activewear* in Lombard, Illinois.

MORTON GROVE, IL

Land's End Outlet
 See listing under *Clothing—Activewear* in Morton Grove, Illinois.

Land's End Outlet
See listing under *Clothing—Activewear* in Schaumburg, Illinois.

A & S Factory Clothing Outlet, 1517 N. Lewis Avenue, Waukegan, IL 60085; (312) 249-2233
This outlet store sells surplus, irregular, and closeout merchandise for famous name manufacturers. They carry men's, women's, and children's jeans and Sergio Valente and Jordache jeans, tops, and jackets. Savings begin at 20% off retail price for first quality, and go up to 70% off seconds, irregulars, imperfects, overruns, and closeouts. Ask to be put on their mailing list, so you will be informed of their special bargains.

SUN.	MON.	TUE.	WED.	THU.	FRI.	SAT.
11-4	10-8	10-8	10-8	10-8	10-8	9-5

SAVINGS: 20%-70% off   *Mailing List*
BRAND NAMES: Levi's, Lee, Wrangler, Jordache, Sergio Valente
PARKING: lot
PAYMENT: cash, checks (amount of purchase only, with proper I.D.), MasterCard, VISA

Price Tag, 216 N. Gables Boulevard, Wheaton, IL 60187; (312) 682-1820
This is an outlet for better quality sportswear. Savings start at 50% off retail price on first quality, and go even higher on imperfect and overstocked items.

SUN.	MON.	TUE.	WED.	THU.	FRI.	SAT.
closed	9-5	9-5	9-5	9-noon	9-5	9-4

SAVINGS: 50%-70% off   *Mailing List*
PARKING: lot
PAYMENT: cash, checks (amount of purchase only, with proper I.D.)

Value Center, 1333 S. Nattanee Street, Elkhart, IN 46516; (219) 293-0111
This store sells major brands of sportswear, jeans, swimwear, winter coats, and sweaters. Check the bargain basement where savings on select imperfect merchandise and closeouts can run as high as 70% off retail price.

SUN.	MON.	TUE.	WED.	THU.	FRI.	SAT.
closed	10-8	10-8	10-8	10-8	10-8	10-8

SAVINGS: 30%-70% off
BRAND NAMES: Wrangler, Lee, Calvin Klein
PARKING: lot
PAYMENT: cash, MasterCard, VISA

Gossard's Factory Outlet
See listing under *Clothing—Activewear* in Huntingburg, Indiana.

Old Mill Ladies Sportswear Factory Outlet, Eastgate Consumer Mall, 7150 E. Washington Street, Indianapolis, IN 46201; (317) 352-9170
This is the outlet for Country Mills women's sportswear. Savings begin at 20% off

retail for first quality, and quickly go as high as 70% on last year's lines, end-of-season, and discontinued merchandise. They have another store in Plover, Wisconsin.

SUN.	MON.	TUE.	WED.	THU.	FRI.	SAT.
noon–5	10–9	10–9	10–9	10–9	10–9	10–9

SAVINGS: about 20% off   *Mailing List*
BRAND NAMES: Country Suburban, Weatherlane, Handmacher
SPECIAL SALES: weekly
ANNUAL SALES: end-of-season
PARKING: lot
PAYMENT: cash, checks (amount of purchase only, with proper I.D.), MasterCard, VISA, American Express

LOGANSPORT, IN

Gossard's Factory Outlet
See listing under *Clothing—Activewear* in Logansport, Indiana.

MISHAWAKA, IN

Cornerstone, Buyer's Marketplace, 5901 N. Grape Road, Mishawaka, IN 46545; (219) 277-6957
This outlet sells men's and women's sportswear at savings up to 50% off retail price.

SUN.	MON.	TUE.	WED.	THU.	FRI.	SAT.
noon–5	9:30–9	9:30–9	9:30–9	9:30–9	9:30–9	9:30–9

SAVINGS: 20%–50% off   *All First Quality*
BRAND NAMES: Levi's, Wrangler
SALE DAYS: Tuesday
PARKING: lot
PAYMENT: cash, checks (amount of purchase only, with proper I.D.), MasterCard, VISA

Newport Sportswear, Buyer's Marketplace, 5901 N. Grape Road, Mishawaka, IN 46545; (219) 277-7615
This outlet sells men's and women's sportswear. Most merchandise is first quality, but they do sell a few seconds which are clearly marked. They have other stores in Kenosha, Plover, and West Bend, Wisconsin.

SUN.	MON.	TUE.	WED.	THU.	FRI.	SAT.
noon–5	9:30–9	9:30–9	9:30–9	9:30–9	9:30–9	9:30–9

SAVINGS: about 25% off
BRAND NAMES: Pace, Jordache, Newport, Clearcreek
PARKING: lot
PAYMENT: cash, checks (amount of purchase only, with proper I.D.), MasterCard, VISA

WISCONSIN
APPLETON, WI

Knit Pikker
See listing under *Clothing—Accessories* in Appleton, Wisconsin.

Zwicker Knitting Mills
See listing under *Clothing—Accessories* in Appleton, Wisconsin.

GREEN BAY, WI

North Trail Sportswear
See listing under *Clothing—Outerwear* in Green Bay, Wisconsin.

Winona Knits
See listing under *Clothing—Accessories* in Green Bay, Wisconsin.

C.J. Chips, Factory Outlet Centre, 7700 120th Avenue, Kenosha, WI 53142; (414) 857-7973

This store sells major brands of men's and women's sportswear and businesswear.

SUN.	MON.	TUE.	WED.	THU.	FRI.	SAT.
11-5	9:30-9	9:30-9	9:30-9	9:30-9	9:30-9	9:30-6

SAVINGS: 20%-45% off   *Mailing List*   *All First Quality*
BRAND NAMES: Villager, Aileen, Damon
SALE DAYS: Tuesday
SPECIAL DISCOUNTS: senior citizens, 10% off Wednesday
PARKING: lot
PAYMENT: cash, checks (amount of purchase only, with proper I.D.), MasterCard, VISA

Fashion Rack, Factory Outlet Centre, 7700 120th Avenue, Kenosha, WI 53142; (414) 857-7935

This shop sells women's sportswear. Savings can go as high as 80% off retail price.

SUN.	MON.	TUE.	WED.	THU.	FRI.	SAT.
11-5	9:30-9	9:30-9	9:30-9	9:30-9	9:30-9	9:30-9

SAVINGS: 35%-80% off   *All First Quality*
PARKING: lot
PAYMENT: cash, checks (amount of purchase only, with proper I.D.), MasterCard, VISA

Knit Pikker
See listing under *Clothing—Accessories* in Kenosha, Wisconsin.

Munsingwear Factory Outlet, Factory Outlet Centre, 7700 120th Avenue, Kenosha, WI 53142; (414) 857-7991

This is the factory outlet for Munsingwear. They sell men's and women's sportswear, and some women's lingerie and sleepwear. Greatest savings are on seconds, irregulars, surplus, and end-of-season items.

SUN.	MON.	TUE.	WED.	THU.	FRI.	SAT.
11-5	9:30-9	9:30-9	9:30-9	9:30-9	9:30-9	9:30-6

SAVINGS: 50% off
BRAND NAMES: Munsingwear, Vassarette
SPECIAL DISCOUNTS: senior citizens, 10% off Wednesday
PARKING: lot
PAYMENT: cash, checks (amount of purchase only, with proper I.D.), MasterCard, VISA, American Express

Newport Sportswear, Factory Outlet Centre, 7700 120th Avenue, Kenosha, WI 53142; (414) 857-9217

See listing in Mishawaka, Indiana.

SUN.	MON.	TUE.	WED.	THU.	FRI.	SAT.
11-5	9:30-9	9:30-9	9:30-9	9:30-9	9:30-9	9:30-6

SAVINGS: 25% off
SPECIAL DISCOUNTS: senior citizens, 10% off Wednesday
PARKING: lot
PAYMENT: cash, checks (amount of purchase only, with proper I.D.), MasterCard, VISA

Winona Knits
See listing under *Clothing—Accessories* in Kenosha, Wisconsin.

Jean's Sample Shop
See listing under *Clothing—Women's* in Milwaukee, Wisconsin.

Newport Sportswear, Manufacturers Direct Mall, 101 Plover Road, Plover, WI 54467;
(715) 341-3455
See listing in Mishawaka, Indiana.

SUN.	MON.	TUE.	WED.	THU.	FRI.	SAT.
11–6	9:30–9	9:30–9	9:30–9	9:30–9	9:30–9	9:30–6

SAVINGS: 25% off
PARKING: lot
PAYMENT: cash, checks (amount of purchase only, with proper I.D.), MasterCard, VISA

Old Mill Ladies Sportswear Factory Outlet, Factory Direct Mall, 101 Plover Road,
Plover, WI 54467; (715) 345-2900
See listing in Indianapolis, Indiana.

SUN.	MON.	TUE.	WED.	THU.·	FRI.	SAT.
11–6	9:30–9	9:30–9	9:30–9	9:30–9	9:30–9	9:30–6

SAVINGS: 25%–70% off   *Mailing List*   *All First Quality*
PARKING: lot
PAYMENT: cash, checks (with proper I.D.), MasterCard, VISA, American Express

Winona Glove Company
See listing under *Clothing—Accessories* in Plover, Wisconsin.

Winona Knits
See listing under *Clothing—Accessories* in Plover, Wisconsin.

Fox River Glove Factory Outlet Store
See listing under *Clothing—Outerwear* in Ripon, Wisconsin.

Winona Knits
See listing under *Clothing—Accessories* in Sister Bay, Wisconsin.

Knit Pikker
See listing under *Clothing—Accessories* in Waupaca, Wisconsin.

Knit Pikker
See listing under *Clothing—Accessories* in West Allis, Wisconsin.

Knit Pikker
See listing under *Clothing—Accessories* in West Bend, Wisconsin.

Newport Sportswear, West Bend Outlet Mall, 180 Island Avenue, West Bend, WI
53095; (414) 334-4711
See listing in Mishawaka, Indiana.

SUN.	MON.	TUE.	WED.	THU.	FRI.	SAT.
11–5	9:30–6	9:30–6	9:30–6	9:30–6	9:30–8	9:30–5

SAVINGS: 25% off
ANNUAL SALES: July
PARKING: lot
PAYMENT: cash, checks, MasterCard, VISA

West Bend Woolen Mills, 1125 E. Washington Street, West Bend, WI 53095; (414) 334-7052
This factory outlet sells jeans, jackets, shirts, sweatshirts, underwear, pants, and outerwear. They also sell big and tall sizes. Savings are greatest on seconds, irregulars, discontinued, overstocks, and closeout merchandise.

SUN.	MON.	TUE.	WED.	THU.	FRI.	SAT.
12:30–4:30	9–9	9–5:30	9–5:30	9–5:30	9–9	9–5

SAVINGS: 10%–60% off
BRAND NAMES: Lee, Health Knit, Dee Cee, Walls
PARKING: lot
PAYMENT: cash, checks (amount of purchase only, with proper I.D.)

Winona Knits
See listing under *Clothing—Accessories* in West Bend, Wisconsin.

CLOTHING—WOMEN'S

The outlets listed here sell mostly women's clothing, although some also sell men's clothing. Also look in this chapter under *Activewear*, *Family*, *Large Sizes*, *Lingerie*, *Maternity*, *Men's* (some outlets sell women's clothing as well), *Outerwear*, and *Sportswear*, and Chapter 10, *Department Stores* for other outlets that sell women's clothing.

Not all outlets have dressing rooms, and return policies vary, so ask ahead of time. Savings are generally much better on seconds and irregular merchandise. Look closely at the item before you buy. End-of-season and closeout merchandise can also save a lot of money if you can shop when the prices are low, and put away the item until the season comes around again.

ILLINOIS

CHICAGO, IL

B.G. Chicago, 4745 N. Ravenswood Avenue, Chicago, IL 60640; (312) 334-1800
This is the factory outlet for the Bender Glickman Company. Discounts start at 30% off retail on first quality sportswear and separates, and climb to 75% on irregulars, samples, overruns, and closeouts. They also have stores in Kenosha and Plover, Wisconsin.

SUN.	MON.	TUE.	WED.	THU.	FRI.	SAT.
closed	10–4	10–4	10–4	10–4	10–4	9–noon

SAVINGS: 15%–70% off   *Mailing List*
BRAND NAMES: Robbie Sport, Terry III
SALE DAYS: vary
SPECIAL DISCOUNTS: senior citizens, 10% off
PARKING: lot
PAYMENT: cash, checks (amount of purchase only, with proper I.D.), MasterCard, VISA (minimum $10)

County Seat
See listing under *Clothing—Men's* in Chicago, Illinois.

General Jobbing Corporation Warehouse
See listing under *Clothing—Men's* in Chicago, Illinois.

International Boutique—Outlet Store at the Apparel Center, 170 Apparel
Center, 350 Orleans Street, Chicago, IL 60654; (312) 836-4477
   This outlet sells over a hundred major brands of women's suits, jackets, sweaters,
dresses, and blouses at savings that average 40%–60% off retail price. Much of the
merchandise is samples. Best savings are on surplus, overruns, and overstocked items.

SUN.	MON.	TUE.	WED.	THU.	FRI.	SAT.
closed	9:30-6	9.30-6	9:30-6	9:30-6	9:30-6	*

SAVINGS: 40%–60% off   *Mailing List*
PARKING: street, meters, can be difficult
PAYMENT: cash, checks (amount of purchase only, with proper I.D., no out-of-state
   checks), MasterCard, VISA

―――――――
*Open Saturday by appointment only.

Joseph A. Bank Clothiers
   See listing under *Clothing—Men's* in Chicago, Illinois

Land's End Outlet
   See listing under *Clothing—Activewear* in Chicago, Illinois.

Lisel's Sample Shop, 6952 N. Glenwood Avenue, Chicago, IL 60640; (312) 764-1130
   This shop sells mostly one-of-a-kind dresses and other sample items from many
major manufacturers. Savings average 30%–50% off regular retail price.

SUN.	MON.	TUE.	WED.	THU.	FRI.	SAT.
closed	closed	11-6	11-6	11-6	11-6	10-5

SAVINGS: 30%–50% off   *All First Quality*
BRAND NAMES: Max, Gill Ambez, Warren L., Sterling, Choon
PARKING: street, meters
PAYMENT: cash, checks (amount of purchase only, with proper I.D.), MasterCard,
   VISA

Mary Walter, 300 W. Grand Avenue, Chicago, IL 60601; (312) 661-1094
   This store has a back room which is the outlet for the other Mary Walter stores.
Savings on end-of-season, last year's lines, discontinued, and closeout merchandise
can go as high as 80% off retail price. They sell stylish women's clothing and
accessories, everything from sportswear to executive clothing and outerwear.

SUN.	MON.	TUE.	WED.	THU.	FRI.	SAT.
closed	10-6	10-6	10-6	10-6	10-6	10-5

SAVINGS: 50%–80% off   *Mailing List*
BRAND NAMES: Mary Walter
ANNUAL SALES: January, July
PARKING: street, meters, can be difficult
PAYMENT: cash, checks (amount of purchase only, with proper I.D.), MasterCard, VISA

Meystel
   See listing under *Clothing—Family* in Chicago, Illinois.

Morris & Sons
   See listing under *Clothing—Men's* in Chicago, Illinois.

Page One Outlet, 11101 S. Kedzie Avenue, Chicago, IL 60655; (312) 238-8989
   This store sells women's clothing. Discounts begin at 20% off retail price on first
quality, and quickly jump to 60% on irregulars, overruns, overstocks, last year's lines,
end-of-season, and discontinued merchandise.

SUN.	MON.	TUE.	WED.	THU.	FRI.	SAT.
closed	9:30-5:30	9-6	9-5:30	9-5:30	9-6	9-5:30

SAVINGS: 20%–60% off
PARKING: street
PAYMENT: cash, checks (amount of purchase only, with proper I.D., no out-of-state checks), MasterCard, VISA, American Express

Rottapel Clothes
See listing under *Clothing—Men's* in Chicago, Illinois.

Smoler Brothers Fashion Factory Outlet, 2300 W. Wabansia Avenue, Chicago, IL 60647; (312) 384-1200
This is the factory outlet for Smoler Brothers ladies' fashions. All of the labels have been removed. Savings begin at 20% off retail price on first quality, and can go as high as 50% on seconds, samples, test runs, surplus, discontinued, closeouts, and last year's line. They also sell bolt-end fabrics.

SUN.	MON.	TUE.	WED.	THU.	FRI.	SAT.
closed	9–4	9–4	9–4	9–9	9–4	9–3

SAVINGS: 20%–50% off   *Mailing List*
SALE DAYS: Tuesday
ANNUAL SALES: before Easter
PARKING: lot
PAYMENT: cash, checks (with proper I.D.)

Textile Discount Outlet
See listing under *Fabrics* in Chicago, Illinois.

AURORA, IL

Prevue Fashions, 908 N. Lake Street, Aurora, IL 60505; (312) 892-7200
This is the outlet for R.M. Coffman. They sell Cricket Lane blazers and slacks and Vicky Vaughn dresses. They also sell some bolt-end fabrics. Some merchandise is first quality, but best buys are on irregulars, samples, and end-of-season merchandise. They have another store in Naperville, Illinois.

SUN.	MON.	TUE.	WED.	THU.	FRI.	SAT.
noon–5	9:30–9	9:30–9	9:30–9	9:30–9	9:30–9	9:30–5:30

SAVINGS: 50% off   *Mailing List*
BRAND NAMES: Vicky Vaughn, Lady Laura
PARKING: lot
PAYMENT: cash, checks (amount of purchase only, with proper I.D., no out-of-state checks), MasterCard, VISA

BUFFALO GROVE, IL

Van Heusen Factory Outlet Store
See listing under *Clothing—Men's* in Buffalo Grove, Illinois.

CICERO, IL

Waveland International Imports
See listing under *Clothing—Men's* in Cicero, Illinois.

LINCOLN, IL

Lincoln Garment Company Outlet Store, 220 N. Chicago Street, Lincoln, IL 62656; (217) 732-3104
This is an outlet for Smoler Brothers clothing. Savings on women's blouses, dresses, slacks, and skirts average 20% off retail price with best buys on seconds, irregulars, last year's lines, and end-of-season clothing.

SUN.	MON.	TUE.	WED.	THU.	FRI.	SAT.
closed	9:30–4:30	9:30–4:30	9:30–4:30	9:30–4:30	9:30–4:30	9:30–4:30

SAVINGS: 30% off
BRAND NAMES: Smoler Brothers
PARKING: street
PAYMENT: cash, checks (amount of purchase only, with proper I.D.), MasterCard, VISA

LOMBARD, IL

Van Heusen Factory Outlet Store
See listing under *Clothing—Men's* in Lombard, Illinois.

McLEANSBORO, IL

The Factory Outlet Store
See listing under *Clothing—Men's* in McLeansboro, Illinois.

NAPERVILLE, IL

Prevue Fashions, 1263 E. Ogden Avenue, Naperville, IL 60540; (312) 369-9049
See listing in Aurora, Illinois.

SUN.	MON.	TUE.	WED.	THU.	FRI.	SAT.
noon–5	9:30–9	9:30–9	9:30–9	9:30–9	9:30–9	9:30–5:30

SAVINGS: 30% off   *Mailing List*
BRAND NAMES: Cricket Lane, Vicky Vaughn, Sprouts, Tony Todd
SPECIAL DISCOUNTS: teachers, 10% off
PARKING: lot
PAYMENT: cash, checks (with proper I.D.), MasterCard, VISA

NILES, IL

Aparacor Outlet Store, 6412 Vapor Lane, Niles, IL 60648; (312) 965-4222
This is the outlet for Aparacor clothing manufacturers. Savings on Queensway men's and women's apparel start about 60% off retail price. They sell Career Guild dresses, shoes, and skirts, and Fashion Find shoes. Most merchandise is irregular, with some first quality, last year's lines, end-of-season, and overstocks. The best buys are up to 80% off retail on irregular.

SUN.	MON.	TUE.	WED.	THU.	FRI.	SAT.
closed	closed	closed	11–4:30	11–4:30	11–6	10–4

SAVINGS: 60%–80% off   *Mailing List*
BRAND NAMES: Queensway, Career Guild, Fashion Find
SPECIAL SALES: every 6–8 weeks
PARKING: lot
PAYMENT: cash, checks (amount of purchase only, with proper I.D.), MasterCard, VISA

Van Heusen Factory Outlet Store
See listing under *Clothing—Men's* in Niles, Illinois.

SCHAUMBURG, IL

Van Heusen Factory Outlet Store
See listing under *Clothing—Men's* in Schaumburg, Illinois.

WILMETTE, IL

Joseph A. Bank Clothiers
See listing under *Clothing—Men's* in Wilmette, Illinois.

ZION, IL

Sewing Factory Outlet Store, 3280 S. Sheridan Road, Zion, IL 60099; (312) 872-8988

This factory outlet sells Sewing Factory women's apparel. They also sell some fabrics. Savings are greatest on seconds, last year's lines, end-of-season, and discontinued merchandise. They also sell some bolt-end fabrics.

SUN.	MON.	TUE.	WED.	THU.	FRI.	SAT.
9-5	9-5	9-5	9-5	9-5	9-5	9-5

SAVINGS: 35%–75% off
BRAND NAMES: Sewing Factory
ANNUAL SALES: January, July
PARKING: lot
PAYMENT: cash, checks (amount of purchase only, with proper I.D.), MasterCard, VISA

INDIANA

INDIANAPOLIS, IN

Donlevy's Back Room, 4233 N. Lafayette Road, Indianapolis, IN 46254; (317) 297-0522

This store sells major designer brands of women's, juniors', half sizes, and petite clothing of coats and suits. Savings begin at 10% off retail price on first quality, and can go as high as 70% on some irregulars and end-of-season merchandise.

SUN.	MON.	TUE.	WED.	THU.	FRI.	SAT.
noon–5	9:30–9:30	9:30–9:30	9:30–9:30	9:30–9:30	9:30–9:30	9:30–9:30

SAVINGS: 10%–70% off   *Mailing List*
SPECIAL SALES: every week
PARKING: lot
PAYMENT: cash, checks, MasterCard, VISA

Donlevy's Back Room, 2505 E. 65th Street, Indianapolis, IN 46220; (317) 253-6725
See listing above.

SUN.	MON.	TUE.	WED.	THU.	FRI.	SAT.
noon–5	9:30–9:30	9:30–9:30	9:30–9:30	9:30–9:30	9:30–9:30	9:30–9:30

SAVINGS: about 40% off
BRAND NAMES: Harvé Benard, Gloria Bernard
ANNUAL SALES: end of February, end of July
PARKING: lot
PAYMENT: cash, checks (amount of purchase only, with proper I.D.), MasterCard, VISA

MERRILLVILLE, IN

Van Heusen Factory Store
See listing under *Clothing—Men's* in Merrillville, Indiana.

MISHAWAKA, IN

Can'da Fashions, Buyer's Marketplace, 5901 N. Grape Road, Mishawaka, IN 46545; (219) 277-2875

This is one of several outlets for Can'da Fashions. Most items are first quality, but they do sell some irregulars, some last year's lines, end-of-season, discontinued, overstocks, closeouts, and odd lots. They also have stores in Kenosha, Plover, Madison, and West Bend, Wisconsin.

SUN.	MON.	TUE.	WED.	THU.	FRI.	SAT.
noon–5	9:30–9	9:30–9	9:30–9	9:30–9	9:30–9	9:30–9

SAVINGS: 30%–70% off   *Mailing List*
SALE DAYS: Tuesday
ANNUAL SALES: seasonal sales
PARKING: lot
PAYMENT: cash, checks (amount of purchase only, with proper I.D.), MasterCard, VISA

Mandy's Sample Shop, 321 Pearl Street, New Albany, IN 47150; (812) 945-9448
This sample shop sells major brands of women's dresses, skirts, jackets, coats, blouses, and lingerie. Most merchandise is first quality samples, but there is some test-run and end-of-season merchandise.

SUN.	MON.	TUE.	WED.	THU.	FRI.	SAT.
closed	10-5	10-5	10-5	10-5	10-5	10-5

SAVINGS: 10%–20% off   *Mailing List*
PARKING: lot
PAYMENT: cash, checks (amount of purchase only, with proper I.D., no out-of-state checks), MasterCard, VISA, American Express

WISCONSIN

Clothesworks, Freeman Outlet Mall, 5 Freeman Lane, Beloit, WI 53511; (608) 365-9992
This is an outlet for Jack Winter contemporary women's sportswear, although they do sell some other brands. Most merchandise is first quality, but savings are greater on seconds, last year's lines, samples, end-of-season, discontinued, closeouts, and odd lots. Check a rack in the back of the store for the best buys. They have other stores in Kenosha, La Crosse, and Milwaukee, Wisconsin.

SUN.	MON.	TUE.	WED.	THU.	FRI.	SAT.
11-5	9-9	9-9	9-9	9-9	9-9	9-9

SAVINGS: 20%–60% off   *Mailing List*
BRAND NAMES: Jack Winter
SPECIAL SALES: occasionally 20% off
PARKING: lot
PAYMENT: cash, checks (amount of purchase only, with proper I.D.), MasterCard, VISA

Manhattan Factory Outlet
See listing under *Clothing—Men's* in Beloit, Wisconsin.

Van Heusen Factory Outlet Store
See listing under *Clothing—Men's* in Beloit, Wisconsin.

J. H. Collectibles, 314 E. Wall Street, Eagle River, WI 54521; (715) 479-2355
This is one of several outlets for Junior House Collectibles. They sell business suits and casual wear for the career woman. Savings begin at 20% off retail price on first quality and can run as high as 60% on some samples, surplus, overruns, last year's lines, end-of-season, and closeouts. They also have stores in Ephraim, Janesville, Lake Geneva, and Milwaukee (called Junior House), Wisconsin.

SUN.	MON.	TUE.	WED.	THU.	FRI.	SAT.
noon-4	10-5	10-5	10-5	10-5	10-5	10-5

SAVINGS: 20%–60% off
BRAND NAMES: Junior House
SALE DAYS: August, end of season
PARKING: lot, street, meters
PAYMENT: cash, checks (amount of purchase only, with proper I.D.), MasterCard, VISA

J. H. Collectibles Factory Outlet, 315 Water Street North, Ephraim, WI 54211; (414) 854-2380
See listing in Eagle River, Wisconsin.

SUN.	MON.	TUE.	WED.	THU.	FRI.	SAT.
10-5	10-5	10-5	10-5	10-5	10-5	10-5

SAVINGS: 20%–60% off
BRAND NAMES: Junior House
PARKING: lot
PAYMENT: cash, checks (amount of purchase only, with proper I.D.), MasterCard, VISA

GERMANTOWN, WI

Outlets Unlimited, Washington Square Mall, N 122 W 15800 Mequon Road,
Germantown, WI 53022; (414) 255-9098
This is an unusual store: not quite a mall, more than an outlet. They are the outlet for six manufacturers. All the women's clothing is first quality, with some samples and overstocks, occasional surplus, and some end-of-season merchandise in the Hang Ten line. They have another store in Oshkosh, Wisconsin.

SUN.	MON.	TUE.	WED.	THU.	FRI.	SAT.
noon-5	10-8	10-8	10-8	10-8	10-8	10-5

SAVINGS: at least 50% off   *Mailing List*   *All First Quality*
BRAND NAMES: Jack Winter
ANNUAL SALES: winter
PARKING: lot
PAYMENT: cash, checks (with proper I.D.), MasterCard, VISA

GREEN BAY, WI

Bottom Line Outlet, 151 N. 3rd Street, Green Bay, WI 54235; (414) 743-9605
This store sells several brands of women's clothing. They also sell a few items of men's clothing. Savings begin at 20% off retail price, and go higher on some seconds, irregulars, last year's lines, end-of-season, overruns, overstocks, and closeouts. They have another store in Sister Bay, Wisconsin

SUN.	MON.	TUE.	WED.	THU.	FRI.	SAT.
closed	9-5	9-5	9-5	9-5	9-5	9-5

SAVINGS: 20%–30% off
BRAND NAMES: Marvin, College Point, Sweet Tree
PARKING: street
PAYMENT: cash, checks (amount of purchase only, with proper I.D.), MasterCard, VISA

The Leather Shop
See listing under *Clothing—Accessories* in Green Bay, Wisconsin.

JANESVILLE, WI

J. H. Collectibles, 31 S. Main Street, Janesville, WI 53545; (608) 752-3120
See listing in Eagle River, Wisconsin

SUN.	MON.	TUE.	WED.	THU.	FRI.	SAT.
closed	9:30-5	9:30-5	9:30-5	9:30-5	9:30-5	9:30-4

SAVINGS: 30%–60% off
BRAND NAMES: Junior House
PARKING: street
PAYMENT: cash, checks (amount of purchase only, with proper I.D.), MasterCard, VISA

KENOSHA, WI

B. G. Chicago, Factory Outlet Centre, 7700 120th Avenue, Kenosha, WI 53142; (414) 857-2858
See listing in Chicago, Illinois.

SUN.	MON.	TUE.	WED.	THU.	FRI.	SAT.
11-5	9:30-9	9:30-9	9:30-9	9:30-9	9:30-9	9:30-6

SAVINGS: 30%-70% off   *Mailing List*
BRAND NAMES: Terry, Robbie Sport
SPECIAL DISCOUNT: senior citizens, 10% off Wednesday
PARKING: lot
PAYMENT: cash, checks (amount of purchase only, with proper I.D.), MasterCard, VISA

C. J. Chips
See listing under *Clothing—Sportswear* in Kenosha, Wisconsin.

Can'da Fashions, Factory Outlet Centre, 7700 120th Avenue, Kenosha, WI 53142; (414) 857-7553
See listing in Mishawaka, Indiana.

SUN.	MON.	TUE.	WED.	THU.	FRI.	SAT.
11-5	9:30-9	9:30-9	9:30-9	9:30-9	9:30-9	9:30-6

SAVINGS: 30%-70% off   *Mailing List*
BRAND NAMES: Brian David, Mulberry Street, Plumtree, Nanci, Jennifer,
   Complements
SPECIAL DISCOUNTS: senior citizens, 10% off Wednesday
PARKING: lot
PAYMENT: cash, checks (amount of purchase only, with proper I.D.), MasterCard, VISA

Clothesworks, Factory Outlet Centre, 7700 120th Avenue, Kenosha, WI 53142; (414) 857-2326
See listing in Beloit, Wisconsin.

SUN.	MON.	TUE.	WED.	THU.	FRI.	SAT.
11-5	9:30-9	9:30-9	9:30-9	9:30-9	9:30-9	9:30-6

SAVINGS: 30%-70% off   *Mailing List*
BRAND NAMES: Jack Winter
SPECIAL DISCOUNTS: senior citizens, 10% off
PARKING: lot
PAYMENT: cash, checks (amount of purchase only, with proper I.D.), MasterCard, VISA

Fashion Rack
See listing under *Clothing—Sportswear* in Kenosha, Wisconsin.

Fashions For Less, Factory Outlet Centre, 7700 120th Avenue, Kenosha, WI 53142; (414) 857-2037
This is the outlet for National Fashions. They sell several major brands of men's and women's clothing at discounts that average 25% off retail price. Best buys are on surplus, overstocks, last year's line, end-of-season, and discontinued merchandise.

SUN.	MON.	TUE.	WED.	THU.	FRI.	SAT.
11-5:30	9:30-9	9:30-9	9:30-9	9:30-9	9:30-9	9-5:30

SAVINGS: 35%-50% off   *Mailing List*
BRAND NAMES: Bill Blass, Ellen Tracy, Headsports
SPECIAL SALES: seasonal clearance
ANNUAL SALES: November
SPECIAL DISCOUNTS: senior citizens, 10% off Wednesday
PARKING: lot
PAYMENT: cash, checks (with proper I.D.), MasterCard, VISA

Manhattan Factory Outlet
See listing under *Clothing—Men's* in Kenosha, Wisconsin.

Mill City Outlet, Factory Outlet Centre, 7700 120th Avenue, Kenosha, WI 53142; (414) 857-2055

This store sells mostly junior sizes of women's clothing. Best savings are on seconds, irregulars, overruns, discontinued, and closeout merchandise. Their store in Racine, Wisconsin, sells mostly men's clothing.

SUN.	MON.	TUE.	WED.	THU.	FRI.	SAT.
11-5	9:30-9	9:30-9	9:30-9	9:30-9	9:30-9	9:30-6

SAVINGS: 20%-50% off
BRAND NAMES: Lee
SPECIAL DISCOUNTS: senior citizens, 10% off Wednesday
PARKING: lot
PAYMENT: cash, checks (amount of purchase only, with proper I.D.), MasterCard, VISA

LA CROSSE, WI

Clothesworks, La Crosse Factory Outlet Mall, 301 Sky Harbor Drive, La Crosse, WI 54601; (608) 783-7077
See listing in Beloit, Wisconsin.

SUN.	MON.	TUE.	WED.	THU.	FRI.	SAT.
11-5	10-9	10-9	10-9	10-9	10-9	10-6

SAVINGS: 20%-60% off   *Mailing List*
BRAND NAMES: Jack Winter
SPECIAL SALES: 20% off
PARKING: lot
PAYMENT: cash, checks (amount of purchase only, with proper I.D.), MasterCard, VISA

Jack Winter Outlet, 2325 Enterprise Avenue, La Crosse, WI 54601; (608) 781-0780
This is the outlet for Jack Winter women's clothing. They sell sportswear, career clothes, casual wear, slacks, suits, jeans, and dresses. Savings begin at 30% off retail price for first quality, and can go as high as 50% on last year's lines and end-of-season merchandise.

SUN.	MON.	TUE.	WED.	THU.	FRI.	SAT.
noon-5	10-5:30	10-5:30	10-5:30	10-5:30	10-8:30	9-5:30

SAVINGS: 30%-50% off   *Mailing List*
BRAND NAMES: Jack Winter
SALE DAYS: weekends
PARKING: lot
PAYMENT: cash, checks (amount of purchase only, with proper I.D.), MasterCard, VISA

LAKE GENEVA, WI

J. H. Collectibles Factory Outlet, 830 Main Street, Lake Geneva, WI 53147; (414) 248-1151
See listing in Eagle River, Wisconsin.

SUN.	MON.	TUE.	WED.	THU.	FRI.	SAT.
11-5	10-5	10-5	10-5	10-5	10-5	10-5

SAVINGS: 20%-60% off
BRAND NAMES: Junior House
PARKING: meters
PAYMENT: cash, checks (amount of purchase only, with proper I.D.), MasterCard, VISA

MADISON, WI

Can'da Fashions, 426 Westgate Mall, Madison, WI 53711; (608) 273-3227
See listing in Mishawaka, Indiana.

SUN.	MON.	TUE.	WED.	THU.	FRI.	SAT.
noon-5	10-9	10-9	10-9	10-9	10-9	10-5

SAVINGS: 30%–70% off   *Mailing List*
BRAND NAMES: Brian David, Mulberry, Plumtree, Nanci, Jennifer
ANNUAL SALES: January, July
PARKING: lot
PAYMENT: cash, checks (amount of purchase only, with proper I.D.), MasterCard, VISA

Manhattan Factory Outlet
See listing under *Clothing—Men's* in Madison, Wisconsin.

MARINETTE, WI

Saranac Factory Store
See listing under *Clothing—Accessories* in Marinette, Wisconsin.

MILWAUKEE, WI

(The Original) Clothes Rack, 250 N. Water Street, Milwaukee, WI 53202; (414) 224-4951
     This outlet sells merchandise from manufacturers with the labels removed. Best buys are on private-label suits, skirts, and blazers, at savings up to 50% off retail price. They also sell fabric mill ends.

SUN.	MON.	TUE.	WED.	THU.	FRI.	SAT.
closed	10–6*	10–6*	10–6*	10–6*	10–6*	9–3

SAVINGS: 30%–50% off   *Mailing List*
BRAND NAMES: John Meyer, Villager, Bill Blass, Anne Klein, Bonnie & Bill, Decouve, Crazy Horse, Act I, Kollection, Outlander
ANNUAL SALES: twice yearly
SPECIAL DISCOUNTS: gift certificates, fashion shows, fashion clubs
PARKING: lot
PAYMENT: cash, checks (amount of purchase only, with proper I.D.), MasterCard, VISA

*Winter hours:

SUN.	MON.	TUE.	WED.	THU.	FRI.	SAT.
closed	10–5	10–5	10–5	10–5	10–5	9–3

Clothesworks, 8100 N. Teutonia Avenue, Milwaukee, WI 53209; (414) 357-4888
     See listing in Beloit, Wisconsin.

SUN.	MON.	TUE.	WED.	THU.	FRI.	SAT.
closed	10–5:30	10–5:30	10–5:30	10–5:30	10–5:30	9–5:30

SAVINGS: 20%–60% off   *Mailing List*
BRAND NAMES: Jack Winter
SPECIAL SALES: 20% off
PARKING: lot
PAYMENT: cash, checks (amount of purchase only, with proper I.D.), MasterCard, VISA

Jean's Sample Shop, 3301 W. Lincoln Avenue, Milwaukee, WI 53215; (414) 645-1021
     This sample shop sells women's clothing and sportswear. Prices average 30%–60% off retail price on all first quality merchandise.

SUN.	MON.	TUE.	WED.	THU.	FRI.	SAT.
11–4	10–5	10–5	10–5	10–5	10–8	10–5

SAVINGS: 30%–60% off   *All First Quality*
BRAND NAMES: Russ, White Stag, Jansen, Harbor, Personal, Country Suburban, Ilene, Shapely
PARKING: street
PAYMENT: cash, checks (amount of purchase only, with proper I.D.), MasterCard, VISA, American Express

Junior House Company Outlet Store, 710 S. 3rd Street, Milwaukee, WI 53240; (414) 744-5080
See listing under J. H. Collectibles in Eagle River, Wisconsin.

SUN.	MON.	TUE.	WED.	THU.	FRI.	SAT.
closed	9:30–5	9:30–5	9:30–5	9:30–5	9:30–5	9:30–4:30

SAVINGS: 20%–50% off   ***Mailing List***   ***All First Quality***
ANNUAL SALES: warehouse sale four times a year
PARKING: lot
PAYMENT: cash, checks (amount of purchase only, with proper I.D.), MasterCard, VISA, American Express

Stuart Manufacturing Company, 201 N. Water Avenue, Milwaukee, WI 53201; (414) 271-4650
This factory outlet sells several major brands of women's sportswear. They also sell some costume jewelry. Savings begin at 30% off retail price.

SUN.	MON.	TUE.	WED.	THU.	FRI.	SAT.
closed	10–5	10–5	10–5	10–5	10–5	9–3

SAVINGS: at least 30% off   ***Mailing List***
BRAND NAMES: Liz Claiborne, Emily, Lady Manhattan, Anne Klein, Outlander, Villager, John Meyer
ANNUAL SALES: summer, winter
SPECIAL DISCOUNTS: charity organizations
PARKING: lot
PAYMENT: cash, checks (amount of purchase only, with proper I.D.), MasterCard, VISA

OSHKOSH, WI

King Industries Outlet Store, 913 S. Main Street, Oshkosh, WI 54901; (414) 233-1995
This is the factory outlet for King Industries; the factory is upstairs. They sell major brands of women's clothes at discounts up to 50% off retail price on first quality. Savings can run as high as 80% on seconds, irregulars, and imperfects. They also sell some samples and test runs.

SUN.	MON.	TUE.	WED.	THU.	FRI.	SAT.
noon–4	10–5	10–5	10–5	10–5	10–5	10–5

SAVINGS: 30%–80% off
BRAND NAMES: Bill Blass, Calvin Klein, Gloria Vanderbilt
ANNUAL SALES: end of season, Christmas
SPECIAL DISCOUNTS: senior citizens, 15% off; if you stay at a particular local motel, 10% off (call for information)
PARKING: street in front
PAYMENT: cash, checks (amount of purchase only, with proper I.D.), MasterCard, VISA

Outlets Unlimited, 605 S. Main Street, Oshkosh, WI 54901; (414) 233-6780
See listing in Germantown, Wisconsin.

SUN.	MON.	TUE.	WED.	THU.	FRI.	SAT.
noon–4	10–5	10–5	10–5	10–5	10–5	10–5

SAVINGS: at least 50% off   ***Mailing List***
BRAND NAMES: Jack Winter, Personal, Hang Ten, Ocean Pacific, Bon Jour, Cambridge
SPECIAL DISCOUNTS: if you stay at a particular local motel, 10% off (call for information)
PARKING: lot
PAYMENT: cash, checks (amount of purchase only, with proper I.D.), MasterCard, VISA

B. G. Chicago, Manufacturers Direct Mall, 101 Plover Road, Plover, WI 54467; (715) 341-8850
See listing in Chicago, Illinois.

SUN.	MON.	TUE.	WED.	THU.	FRI.	SAT.
11–6	9:30–9	9:30–9	9:30–9	9:30–9	9:30–9	9:30–6

SAVINGS: 25%–75% off   *Mailing List*
BRAND NAMES: Bender Glick, Robbie Sport, Terry
ANNUAL SALES: end of season
SPECIAL DISCOUNTS: senior citizens, 10% off Tuesday
PARKING: lot
PAYMENT: cash, checks (amount of purchase only, with proper I.D.), MasterCard, VISA

Can'da Fashions, Manufacturers Direct Mall, 101 Plover Road, Plover, WI 54467; (715) 344-4423
See listing in Mishawaka, Indiana.

SUN.	MON.	TUE.	WED.	THU.	FRI.	SAT.
11–5	9:30–9	9:30–9	9:30–9	9:30–9	9:30–9	9:30–6

SAVINGS: 30%–70% off   *Mailing List*
BRAND NAMES: Plumtree, Nanci, Jennifer, Brian David
SPECIAL SALES: occasionally; buy one, get one free
PARKING: lot
PAYMENT: cash, checks (amount of purchase only, with proper I.D.), MasterCard, VISA

Clothesworks, Manufacturers Direct Mall, 101 Plover Road, Plover, WI 54467; (715) 341-8331
See listing in Beloit, Wisconsin.

SUN.	MON.	TUE.	WED.	THU.	FRI.	SAT.
closed	10–5:30	10–5:30	10–5:30	10–5:30	10–5:30	9–5:30

SAVINGS: 20%–60% off   *Mailing List*
BRAND NAMES: Jack Winter
SPECIAL SALES: 20% off
PARKING: lot
PAYMENT: cash, checks (amount of purchase only, with proper I.D.), MasterCard, VISA

Manhattan Factory Outlet
See listing under *Clothing—Men's* in Plover, Wisconsin.

Van Heusen Factory Outlet Store
See listing under *Clothing—Men's* in Plover, Wisconsin.

The Bottom Line, 529 Bayshore Drive, Sister Bay, WI 54234; (414) 854-4460
See listing in Green Bay, Wisconsin.

SUN.	MON.	TUE.	WED.	THU.	FRI.	SAT.
closed	9–5	9–5	9–5	9–5	9–5	9–5

SAVINGS: 20%–30% off
BRAND NAMES: OshKosh B'Gosh, Dee Cee, Washington, College Point, Dominion, Sweet Tree, Winona
SPECIAL SALES: sidewalk sales
PARKING: street
PAYMENT: cash, checks (amount of purchase only, with proper I.D.), MasterCard, VISA

Can'da Fashions, West Bend Outlet Mall, 180 Island Avenue, West Bend, WI 53095; (414) 338-1998
See listing in Mishawaka, Indiana.

SUN.	MON.	TUE.	WED.	THU.	FRI.	SAT.
noon-5	9:30-5	9:30-5	9:30-5	9:30-5	9:30-8	9:30-5

SAVINGS: about 40% off   *Mailing List*   *All First Quality*
BRAND NAMES: Brian David, Plumtree, Mulberry Street
SPECIAL SALES: twice a year
PARKING: lot
PAYMENT: cash, checks (amount of purchase only, with proper I.D.), MasterCard, VISA

Manhattan Factory Outlet
See listing under *Clothing—Men's* in West Bend, Wisconsin.

CLOTHING—MISCELLANEOUS

This section has all clothing items that didn't fit in the other clothing categories. Look here for uniforms, formalwear, team jackets and cheerleading sweaters, coveralls and work clothing, and horseback-riding attire. Also look in Chapter 28, *Miscellaneous*.

Advance Uniform Company, 1132 S. Wabash Avenue, Chicago, IL 60605; (312) 922-1797
You can save 20%-30% off retail prices on El Beco and Conqueror uniform shirts, Nurse Maids uniform shoes, White Swan nurses' uniforms, and various brands of police uniforms and uniform accessories. Ask to be put on their mailing list so you can take advantage of their special sales. Parking in their lot is free with a purchase. They will do custom work—shorten your pants while you wait; they will even custom-make a uniform for you.

SUN.	MON.	TUE.	WED.	THU.	FRI.	SAT.
closed	8-5:30	8-5:30	8-5:30	8-5:30	8-5:30	8-3

SAVINGS: 20%-30% off   *Mailing List*   *All First Quality*
BRAND NAMES: El Beco, Nurse Maids, White Swan, Conqueror
SALE DAYS: dates vary (ask)
PARKING: lot
PAYMENT: cash, checks (from police personnel only), MasterCard, VISA

Buy-A-Tux, 545 W. Roosevelt Road, Chicago, IL 60607; (312) 243-5465
This store sells major brands of men's formalwear. Savings are greatest on used, formerly rental, clothing.

SUN.	MON.	TUE.	WED.	THU.	FRI.	SAT.
10-3	10-6	10-6	10-6	10-6	10-6	10-6

SAVINGS: 30%-60% off
BRAND NAMES: Oscar De La Renta, Pierre Cardin, Versailles, Lion of Troy
SPECIAL DISCOUNTS: senior citizens, groups, theaters, 10% off
PARKING: lot
PAYMENT: cash, MasterCard, VISA

Chicago Knitting Mills, 3344 W. Montrose Avenue, Chicago, IL 60618; (312) 463-1464

This outlet sells high school team jackets, emblems, and cheerleading sweaters. Although their primary business is with the schools, they are open to the public. Savings are up to 50% off retail price. Ask to see the seconds; there are very few, but they are the best buys.

SUN.	MON.	TUE.	WED.	THU.	FRI.	SAT.
closed	8-4:30	8-4:30	8-4:30	8-4:30	8-4:30	9-4

SAVINGS: up to 50% off
SPECIAL DISCOUNTS: discounts for groups subject to negotiation (ask)
PARKING: street
PAYMENT: cash, checks (amount of purchase only, with proper I.D., no out-of-state checks)

Gingiss Formalwear Warehouse, 555 W. 14th Place, Chicago, IL 60607; (312) 829-0001

This is the outlet for Gingiss Formalwear rentals. Savings on some seconds, irregulars, samples, discontinued, and closeout merchandise can go as high as 60% off regular retail prices.

SUN.	MON.	TUE.	WED.	THU.	FRI.	SAT.
closed	9:30-5	9:30-5	9:30-5	9:30-5	9:30-5	9:30-5

SAVINGS: 10%-50% off   *Mailing List*
ANNUAL SALES: dates vary (ask)
SPECIAL DISCOUNTS: musicians or waiters (with union card), 10% off
PARKING: lot
PAYMENT: cash, checks (with proper I.D.)

INDIANA
BERNE, IN

Berco, 104 E. Main Street, Berne, IN 46711; (219) 589-3136

This outlet offers Big Bear coveralls at 15% off retail price for first quality and 25% on seconds.

SUN.	MON.	TUE.	WED.	THU.	FRI.	SAT.
closed	8-5	8-5	8-5	8-5	8-5	closed

SAVINGS: 15%-25% off
BRAND NAMES: Big Bear
PARKING: lot
PAYMENT: cash only

ROCHESTER, IN

Work Clothing Outlet Store, 501 Main Street, Rochester, IN 46975; (219) 223-4311

This is the factory outlet for Edmonton, Elin uniforms, and Topps manufacturing company. They sell pants, shirts, jackets, quilted windbreakers, coveralls, jumpsuits, smocks, vests, aprons, and T-shirts.

SUN.	MON.	TUE.	WED.	THU.	FRI.	SAT.
closed	8-4	8-4	8-4	8-4	8-4	closed

SAVINGS: 25%-30% off   *All First Quality*
BRAND NAMES: Toppmaster
PARKING: street
PAYMENT: cash, checks (with proper I.D.), MasterCard, VISA

Bare Essentials
For bathing suits, see listing under *Clothing—Lingerie* in Kenosha, Wisconsin.

H & J Outfitters
For English and western horseback-riding clothes, see listing under *Miscellaneous* in Plymouth, Wisconsin.

8
CRAFTS

The outlets listed here sell mostly craft items. Listed here are yarns and supplies for knitting and crocheting, needlepoint, weaving, and other crafts. Also look in Chapter 11, *Fabrics*, and Chapter 25, *Sewing Supplies and Equipment*, for other craft materials.

Savings on damaged kits and goods can be excellent, and if you have leftovers from previous projects, you may be able to make use of a damaged kit. The most consistent savings can be had by buying closeout items at the end of a holiday season; you will have nearly a year to complete your projects for the following year.

ILLINOIS

LOVES PARK, IL

VIP Yarn and Craft Center, Knit Pikker, Gloray Knitting Mills, Park Plaza Outlet Mart, 6415 N. 2nd Street, Loves Park, IL 61111; (815) 633-2966

This is the outlet for Caron yarns. They sell yarn, yarn kits, and craft items. Most merchandise is first quality, but they do sell some seconds, imperfects, irregulars, discontinued, closeouts, last year's lines, and test runs. They also sell some mill-end yarn. They have other stores in Mendota, Oregon, and Rochelle, Illinois; Mishawaka, Indiana; and Kenosha, Madison, and Plover, Wisconsin. They also are an outlet for Knit Pikker and Gloray Knitting Mills. Savings on sweaters and knit accessories average 50%–70% off retail price.

SUN.	MON.	TUE.	WED.	THU.	FRI.	SAT.
noon–5	9:30–9	9:30–9	9:30–9	9:30–9	9:30–9	9:30–5

SAVINGS: 50%–70% off
BRAND NAMES: Caron
SPECIAL DISCOUNTS: senior citizens, 10% off Tuesday
PARKING: lot
PAYMENT: cash, checks (amount of purchase only, with proper I.D.), MasterCard, VISA

MENDOTA, IL

VIP Yarn and Craft Center, Highway 51 North, Mendota, IL 61342; (815) 538-3171
See listing in Loves Park, Illinois.

SUN.	MON.	TUE.	WED.	THU.	FRI.	SAT.
closed	9–5	9–5	9–5	9–5	9–5	9–4:30

SAVINGS: 10%–50% off   *Mailing List*
BRAND NAMES: Caron
ANNUAL SALES: four times a year
PARKING: lot
PAYMENT: cash, checks

VIP Yarn and Craft Center, White Pines Road, Oregon, IL 61061; (815) 732-2007
See listing in Loves Park, Illinois.

SUN.	MON.	TUE.	WED.	THU.	FRI.	SAT.
closed	8:30–4:30	8:30–4:30	8:30–4:30	8:30–4:30	8:30–4:30	8:30–4:30

SAVINGS: about 15% off   *Mailing List*
SALE DAYS: monthly specials
SPECIAL DISCOUNTS: senior citizens, 10% off Tuesday
PARKING: lot
PAYMENT: cash, checks (amount of purchase only, with proper I.D.), MasterCard, VISA

VIP Yarn and Craft Center, 224 4th Avenue, Rochelle, IL 61068; (815) 562-5900
See listing in Loves Park, Illinois.

SUN.	MON.	TUE.	WED.	THU.	FRI.	SAT.
noon–4:30	9–5	9–5	9–5	9–5	9–5	9–4:30

SAVINGS: 15%–50% off   *Mailing List*
BRAND NAMES: Caron, Susan Bates
SPECIAL DISCOUNTS: senior citizens, 10% off Tuesday
PARKING: street
PAYMENT: cash, checks (amount of purchase only, with proper I.D.), MasterCard,
   VISA, American Express

VIP Yarn and Craft Center, Buyer's Marketplace, 5901 N. Grape Road, Mishawaka,
   IN 46545; (219) 277-0491
See listing in Loves Park, Illinois.

SUN.	MON.	TUE.	WED.	THU.	FRI.	SAT.
noon–5	9:30–9	9:30–9	9:30–9	9:30–9	9:30–9	9:30–9

SAVINGS: 40%–70% off   *Mailing List*
BRAND NAMES: Caron
SPECIAL DISCOUNTS: senior citizens, 10% off Tuesday
PARKING: lot
PAYMENT: cash, checks (amount of purchase only, with proper I.D.), MasterCard, VISA

Grafton Yarn Company Outlet Store
See listing under *Clothing—Accessories* in Grafton, Wisconsin.

VIP Yarn and Craft Center, Factory Outlet Centre, 7700 120th Avenue, Kenosha, WI
   53142; (414) 857-7393
See listing in Loves Park, Illinois.

SUN.	MON.	TUE.	WED.	THU.	FRI.	SAT.
11–5	9:30–9	9:30–9	9:30–9	9:30–9	9:30–9	9:30–6

SAVINGS: 40%–80% off   *Mailing List*
BRAND NAMES: Caron
ANNUAL SALES: anniversary sale
SPECIAL DISCOUNTS: senior citizens, 10% off Wednesday
PARKING: lot

PAYMENT: cash, checks (with proper I.D.), MasterCard, VISA ($5 minimum on credit cards)

MADISON, WI

VIP Mill Store—Knit Pikker, Factory Outlet Centre, 4609 Verona Road, Madison, WI 53711; (608) 271-6357
    See VIP Yarn and Craft Center in Loves Park, Illinois, and/or Knit Pikker in Kenosha, Wisconsin.

SUN.	MON.	TUE.	WED.	THU.	FRI.	SAT.
noon-5	9:30-9	9:30-9	9:30-9	9:30-9	9:30-9	9:30-6

SAVINGS: 15%–50% off   *Mailing List*
BRAND NAMES: Caron, Zwicker, OshKosh B'Gosh, Health-Tex, Curity
ANNUAL SALES: holidays
SPECIAL DISCOUNTS: senior citizens, 10% off
PARKING: lot
PAYMENT: cash, checks (amount of purchase only, with proper I.D.), MasterCard, VISA, American Express

PLOVER, WI

VIP Yarn and Craft Center, Factory Direct Mall, 101 Plover Road, Plover, WI 54467; (715) 344-6062
    See listing in Loves Park, Illinois.

SUN.	MON.	TUE.	WED.	THU.	FRI.	SAT.
11-6	9:30-9	9:30-9	9:30-9	9:30-9	9:30-9	9:30-6

SAVINGS: 40%–80% off   *Mailing List*
BRAND NAMES: Caron
SPECIAL DISCOUNTS: senior citizens, 10% off Tuesday
PARKING: lot
PAYMENT: cash, checks (amount of purchase only, with proper I.D.), MasterCard, VISA

STEVENS POINT, WI

Herrschner's, Inc., Hoover Road, Stevens Point, WI 54481; (715) 341-0560
    This is the factory outlet for Herrschner's craft and supply items. They also sell some other brands. Savings average 20% off on first quality, and can go higher on some damaged goods.

SUN.	MON.	TUE.	WED.	THU.	FRI.	SAT.
closed	9-5	9-5	9-5	9-5	9-5	9-5

SAVINGS: up to 20% off   *Mailing List*
SPECIAL DISCOUNTS: senior citizens, 10% off with card
PARKING: lot
PAYMENT: cash, checks (amount of purchase only, with proper I.D.), MasterCard, VISA, American Express

WAUPUN, WI

Nasco-Handcrafters, 1 W. Brown Street, Waupun, WI 53963; (414) 324-2031
    This outlet sells arts and crafts supplies, and Peacock weaving looms. Savings on first quality are 10%, but quickly rise to 33%–50% off retail price on seconds. They also sell some surplus, overstocks, discontinued, and closeout merchandise.

SUN.	MON.	TUE.	WED.	THU.	FRI.	SAT.
closed	9-3	9-3	closed	9-3	9-3	closed

SAVINGS: 10%–50% off
BRAND NAMES: Nasco, Peacock
ANNUAL SALES: twice a year
PARKING: lot
PAYMENT: cash, checks

9
DECORATING

The outlets listed here are very different, but united by the theme of decorating. Listed here are various window treatments like blinds, shades, draperies, and curtains; paint and painting supplies; wallpaper and other wall treatments; wall units and other storage systems, which are more a part of decorating than of furniture; tiles; kitchen and bath decorating accessories; shelving; building supplies; and hardware.

Also look in Chapter 5, *Carpeting, Rugs, and Floor Coverings*; Chapter 6, *Ceramics*; Chapter 11, *Fabrics*; Chapter 13, *Furniture*; Chapter 14, *Gift Items*; Chapter 18, *Linens*; and Chapter 24, *Plates, Glassware, and Tableware*; for other outlets that sell decorating accessories. If you are a do-it-yourselfer, you are already trying to save money as you decorate your house. These outlets should help your projects.

For the best savings, measure carefully before you go shopping, and bring samples of colors to be matched. Look for custom-made items that have been made wrong and returned, test runs of colors or patterns, and discontinued merchandise. Some carefully chosen seconds will also help you save money.

ILLINOIS

CHICAGO, IL

Deesigned Trees, 3100 W. Grand Avenue, Chicago, IL 60622; (312) 722-7300
This store sells artificial trees and floral arrangements. First quality merchandise is at retail price, but there are savings on discontinued merchandise.

SUN.	MON.	TUE.	WED.	THU.	FRI.	SAT.
closed	8-4:30	8-4:30	8-4	8-4:30	8-4:30	closed

SAVINGS: at least 30% off
PARKING: lot
PAYMENT: cash, checks (amount of purchase only, with proper I.D.)

Design Interiors, 226 W. Ontario Street, Chicago, IL 60610; (312) 943-6150
This outlet store sells custom-made, laminated formica furniture from kitchen cabinets to bedroom and living room wall systems. They also sell most major brands of furniture at discounts of 30% off retail price. Savings can run as high as 40% on custom-designed work. They have another store in Downers Grove, Illinois.

SUN.	MON.	TUE.	WED.	THU.	FRI.	SAT.
closed	9-5	9-5	9-5	9-5	9-5	closed

SAVINGS: 20%–30% off   *Mailing List*   *All First Quality*
BRAND NAMES: Design Interiors
ANNUAL SALES: twice a year (up to 50% off)
PARKING: lot
PAYMENT: cash, checks (with proper I.D.), MasterCard, VISA, American Express

Fernchar Textiles—The Window-Wear Warehouse, 222 W. Ontario Street,
   Chicago, IL 60610; (312) 321-1510
   This store sells window furnishings and blinds. Savings average 40%–50% off on
first quality and some overruns.

SUN.	MON.	TUE.	WED.	THU.	FRI.	SAT.
closed	9:30–5:30	9:30–5:30	9:30–5:30	9:30–5:30	9:30–5:30	10–4:30

SAVINGS: 40%–50% off   *Mailing List*
BRAND NAMES: Bally, Levelor
PARKING: street, meters
PAYMENT: cash, checks (with proper I.D.), MasterCard, VISA, American Express

Glover Shade Company, 617 N. Wells Street, Chicago, IL 60610; (312) 787-1825
   This factory produces vertical blinds. Savings on window blinds, window shades,
and vertical blinds average 35%–50% off retail price on first quality merchandise, and
some discontinued lines.

SUN.	MON.	TUE.	WED.	THU.	FRI.	SAT.
closed	8–6	8–6	8–6	8–6	8–6	9–6

SAVINGS: 30%–50% off
BRAND NAMES: Levelor, Louverdrape, Joanna Western, Glover
ANNUAL SALES: spring, fall
SPECIAL DISCOUNTS: quantity or commercial jobs
PARKING: street, meters; it is difficult
PAYMENT: cash, checks, MasterCard, VISA, American Express

Linker's New York Textiles
   See listing under *Fabrics* in Chicago, Illinois.

Tile Outlet Company, 2434 W. Fullerton Avenue, Chicago, IL 60647; (312) 276-2662
   This outlet sells Sunbeam, Armstrong, and Majestic tiles. Savings average
approximately 30% off retail price. Some merchandise is irregular and surplus.

SUN.	MON.	TUE.	WED.	THU.	FRI.	SAT.
10–6	9–9	9–6	9–6	9–9	9–6	9–6

SAVINGS: up to 30% off
BRAND NAMES: Sunbeam, Armstrong, Majestic
PARKING: lot
PAYMENT: cash, checks, MasterCard, VISA

UCI Paint Factory Outlet, 2601 W. Barry Street, Chicago, IL 60618; (312) 583-3700
   This is the factory outlet for United Coatings. Savings on paint begin at 40% off
retail price on first quality, and can go as high as 60% on some test runs, surplus,
discontinued, and closeout items. They also sell brushes, rollers, and other painting
accessories.

SUN.	MON.	TUE.	WED.	THU.	FRI.	SAT.
closed	8–4	8–4	8–4	8–4	8–4	9–1

SAVINGS: 45%–60% off   *Mailing List*
SALE DAYS: vary
PARKING: street
PAYMENT: cash, checks (amount of purchase only, with proper I.D.), MasterCard, VISA

Wallstreet
See listing under *Fabrics* in Chicago, Illinois.

Western Textile Outlet Store
See listing under *Fabrics* in Chicago, Illinois.

ALGONQUIN, IL

Story Design and Manufacturing
See listing under *Linens* in Algonquin, Illinois.

ARLINGTON HEIGHTS, IL

Gift Outlet
See listing under *Gift Items* in Arlington Heights, Illinois

CARY, IL

Harvey Manufacturing Company, 1122 N. Silver Lake Road, Cary, IL 60013; (312)
639-2166
This is the factory outlet for Harvey hampers and bath accessories. They also sell
tissue boxes, wastebaskets, and wall shelving. Savings go up to 75% off retail price on
seconds, irregulars, and imperfect merchandise.

SUN.	MON.	TUE.	WED.	THU.	FRI.	SAT.
closed	8-3	8-3	8-3	8-3	closed	closed

SAVINGS: up to 75% off
BRAND NAMES: Harvey
SALE DAYS: vary
PARKING: lot
PAYMENT: cash only

DOWNERS GROVE, IL

Design Interiors of Downers Grove, 1404 Butterfield Road, Downers Grove, IL
60515; (312) 953-8383
See listing in Chicago, Illinois.

SUN.	MON.	TUE.	WED.	THU.	FRI.	SAT.
noon-5	10-9	10-9	10-9	10-9	10-9	10-6

SAVINGS: 20%-40% off   *Mailing List*   *All First Quality*
PARKING: lot
PAYMENT: cash, checks (amount of purchase only, with proper I.D.), MasterCard,
VISA, American Express

EAST DUNDEE, IL

Haeger Potteries—Factory Outlet Complex
See listing under *Ceramics* in East Dundee, Illinois.

HINSDALE, IL

Calico Corners
See listing under *Fabrics* in Hinsdale, Illinois.

LAKE FOREST, IL

Calico Corners
See listing under *Fabrics* in Lake Forest, Illinois.

LIBERTYVILLE, IL

Berggren Trayner Corporation
See listing under *Plates, Glassware, and Tableware* in Libertyville, Illinois.

Ozite Mill Outlet Store
See listing under *Carpeting, Rugs, and Floor Coverings* in Libertyville, Illinois.

ORLAND PARK, IL

Just Wallpaper, 15609 S. 71st Court, Orland Park, IL 60462; (312) 532-9050
This shop sells most major brands of wallpaper at savings up to 50% on overstocks and discontinued patterns.

SUN.	MON.	TUE.	WED.	THU.	FRI.	SAT.
noon-5*	9-6	9-6	9-6	9-6	9-6	9-5

SAVINGS: 20%–50% off
ANNUAL SALES: twice a year, dates vary
PARKING: lot
PAYMENT: cash, checks (amount of purchase only, with proper I.D.)

---

*They are closed on Sunday between July 4th and Labor Day.

ROLLING MEADOWS, IL

Loomcraft, 1400 E. Golf Road, Rolling Meadows, IL 60008; (312) 640-8878
See listing under *Fabrics* in Chicago, Illinois.

SUN.	MON.	TUE.	WED.	THU.	FRI.	SAT.
11-5	10-9:30	10-9:30	10-9:30	10-9:30	10-9:30	10-6

SAVINGS: 50%–75% off   *Mailing List*
BRAND NAMES: Loomcraft
SPECIAL SALES: vary
ANNUAL SALES: January
SPECIAL DISCOUNTS: to the trade, 10%–20% off
PARKING: lot
PAYMENT: cash, checks (amount of purchase only, with proper I.D., no out-of-state checks), MasterCard, VISA

SKOKIE, IL

Gift Outlet
See listing under *Gift Items* in Skokie, Illinois.

SOUTH CHICAGO HEIGHTS, IL

Stead Textile Company Outlet, 18 E. Sauk Trail, South Chicago Heights, IL 60411; (312) 754-9252
This factory outlet sells many types of draperies and upholstery fabrics. They also sell drapery hardware, bedspreads, and pillows. Savings begin at 50% off retail price on first quality, and can go as high as 80% on irregulars, discontinued, closeouts, overstocks, and last year's lines. They also sell some customer returns of made-to-order merchandise.

SUN.	MON.	TUE.	WED.	THU.	FRI.	SAT.
closed	10-5	10-5	10-5	10-5	10-5	10-5

SAVINGS: 50%–80% off   *Mailing List*
PARKING: lot
PAYMENT: cash, checks, (amount of purchase only, with proper I.D.), MasterCard, VISA

WHEELING, IL

Aero Drapery Company—Division of Minnesota Fabrics
See listing under *Fabrics* in Wheeling, Illinois.

Calico Corners
See listing under *Fabrics* in Wilmette, Illinois.

Creative Surfaces, 474 A North Central Avenue, Wooddale, IL 60007; (312) 595-3030
    This store has a large selection of ceramic tiles. Savings average 25% off retail price depending on what merchandise you buy, and on the quantity.

SUN.	MON.	TUE.	WED.	THU.	FRI.	SAT.
closed	8–4:30	8–4:30	8–4:30	8–4:30	8–4:30	closed

SAVINGS: about 25% off   *All First Quality*
PARKING: lot
PAYMENT: cash, checks (amount of purchase only, with proper I.D.)

Allee Drapes and Curtains, Century Consumer Mall, 8275 Broadway, Merrillville, IN 46410; (219) 769-5393
    This store sells custom-made draperies. They also sell curtains, bedspreads, blinds, related hardware, and towels. Savings begin at 30% off retail price on first quality, and can go as high as 70% on some seconds, last year's lines, end-of-season, discontinued, and closeout merchandise.

SUN.	MON.	TUE.	WED.	THU.	FRI.	SAT.
11–5	10–9	10–9	10–9	10–9	10–9	10–9

SAVINGS: 30%–70% off
ANNUAL SALES: January, June
PARKING: lot
PAYMENT: cash, checks (amount of purchase only, with proper I.D.), MasterCard, VISA

Kemper Factory Outlet, 633 S. "H" Street, Richmond, IN 47374; (317) 966-3875
    This factory outlet sells Kemper kitchen and bathroom cabinets. They also sell Richwood bathroom vanities. Savings can go as high as 70% off retail price on some seconds and "bruised" merchandise.

SUN.	MON.	TUE.	WED.	THU.	FRI.	SAT.
closed	closed	8–8	8–5	8–5	8–5	9–1

SAVINGS: 60%–70% off
BRAND NAMES: Kemper, Richwood
PARKING: lot
PAYMENT: cash, checks (amount of purchase only, with proper I.D.)

Zuern Building Products, 426 Railroad Street, Allenton, WI 53002; (414) 629-5551
    Savings on lumber and building products begin at 10% off retail price.

SUN.	MON.	TUE.	WED.	THU.	FRI.	SAT.
closed	8:30–5:30	8:30–5:30	8:30–5:30	8:30–5:30	8:30–5:30	8:30–3:30

SAVINGS: at least 10% off   *All First Quality*
PARKING: lot
PAYMENT: cash, checks (amount of purchase only, with proper I.D.), MasterCard, VISA

Home Textile Outlet, 1402 S. Hastings Way, Eau Claire, WI 54701; (715) 839-9000
    This store sells bed and bath draperies and curtains. Savings average 20% off retail price on first quality, and quickly go to 60% on seconds, last year's lines, discontinued, and closeout merchandise.

SUN.	MON.	TUE.	WED.	THU.	FRI.	SAT.
noon–5	9:30–9	9:30–6	9:30–6	9:30–9	9:30–6	9:30–5

SAVINGS: 20%–60% off   *Mailing List*
ANNUAL SALES: July
PARKING: lot
PAYMENT: cash, checks (amount of purchase only, with proper I.D.), MasterCard, VISA

Outlet 9, 1300 S. Industrial Road, Hudson, WI 54016; (715) 386-8318
    This outlet sells made-to-measure drapes at savings that begin at 20% off retail price. They also sell some irregulars, overstocks, overruns, and discontinued items at discounts up to 50% off retail price.

SUN.	MON.	TUE.	WED.	THU.	FRI.	SAT.
closed	9–4	9–4	9–4	9–4	9–4	9–4

SAVINGS: 20%–50% off
PARKING: lot
PAYMENT: cash, checks (amount of purchase only, with proper I.D.), MasterCard, VISA

Schweiger Fabric Outlet
    See listing under *Fabrics* in Jefferson, Wisconsin.

Draperies, Etc., Factory Outlet Centre, 7700 120th Avenue, Kenosha, WI 53142; (414) 857-2006
    This is an outlet for Robertson Factories. Savings start at 35% on made-to-measure draperies. They sell some irregulars, and they also have a complete line of domestics, hardware for draperies, and bathroom accessories.

SUN.	MON.	TUE.	WED.	THU.	FRI.	SAT.
11–5	9:30–9	9:30–9	9:30–9	9:30–9	9:30–9	9:30–6

SAVINGS: 35% off
SALE DAYS: Tuesday
SPECIAL DISCOUNTS: senior citizens, 10% off Wednesday
PARKING: lot
PAYMENT: cash, checks (amount of purchase only, with proper I.D.), MasterCard, VISA

Buckstaff—Authentic Factory Outlet
    See listing under *Furniture* in Oshkosh, Wisconsin.

Calico Corners
    See listing under *Fabrics* in Waukesha, Wisconsin.

10
DEPARTMENT STORES

The outlets listed here sell a wide assortment of different items. Some are outlets for large chains, and some buy large lots (broken or damaged in shipment) of assorted merchandise.

This is a category in which repeat visits to a store will be necessary to find the best bargains. Most merchandise changes often, so you may have to make a quick decision and buy an item when you see it, then return to see what new merchandise has arrived. You will see a lot of one-of-a-kind items, and a lot of floor samples and damaged merchandise. Look carefully at all items, so you can decide if the savings compensate for any flaws.

ILLINOIS

CHICAGO, IL

Marshall Field Warehouse, 4000 W. Diversey Avenue, Chicago, IL 60639; (312) 282-9000

This is the outlet for the Marshall Field retail stores. It is usually open to the public about three times a year, at which time savings can run as high as 80% off usual retail prices on seconds, irregulars, imperfects, last year's lines, discontinued, overstocks, closeouts, and "as is" items. Call ahead to find out when sales are. They have another store in Itasca, Illinois, called Marshall Field's Commercial Interiors, which sells commercial furniture and accessories.

SUN.	MON.	TUE.	WED.	THU.	FRI.	SAT.
*	*	*	*	*	*	*

SAVINGS: up to 80% off
ANNUAL SALES: July
PARKING: lot
PAYMENT: cash, checks, MasterCard, VISA, American Express, Marshall Field charge card

---

*Call for their hours during special sales.

Sears Catalog Surplus Store, 5555 S. Archer Avenue, Chicago, IL 60638; (312) 284-3200

This is an outlet for Sears catalog merchandise. Savings begin at 10% off retail prices and climb quickly to at least 50% on some floor samples, surplus, discontinued, last year's lines, closeouts, and overstocked merchandise. They have several other outlets, for both catalog and store merchandise, in Addison, Aurora, Carol Stream, Melrose Park, Waukegan, and Wheeling, Illinois; Highland and Indianapolis, Indiana; and Manitowoc and West Allis, Wisconsin.

SUN.	MON.	TUE.	WED.	THU.	FRI.	SAT.
11–5	9:30–9	9:30–9	9:30–9	9:30–9	9:30–9	9:30–5:30

SAVINGS: 10%–50% off
SALE DAYS: vary
PARKING: lot
PAYMENT: checks (amount of purchase only, with proper I.D.), Sears charge card

Spiegel Outlet Store, 1105 W. 35th Street, Chicago, IL 60609; (312) 890-9690
This is one of several outlets for the Spiegel catalog. Savings begin at 30% off on first quality merchandise, but can go as high as 70% on overstocks, last year's lines, end-of-season, and discontinued merchandise. They have other stores in Arlington Heights, Countryside, Deerfield, Downers Grove, Matteson, Naperville, and Villa Park, Illinois.

SUN.	MON.	TUE.	WED.	THU.	FRI.	SAT.
10–5	10–5	10–5	10–7:30	10–7:30	10–7:30	9–5

SAVINGS: 40%–70% off   *Mailing List*
SALE DAYS: Wednesday, Friday, Sunday
PARKING: lot
PAYMENT: cash, checks (with proper I.D.), MasterCard, VISA, American Express, Diners Club

ADDISON, IL

The Garage Sale Store, 513 W. Lake Street, Addison, IL 60101; (312) 628-6290
This store sells just about anything. There were a lot of clothes, appliances, and housewares. Most merchandise is first quality, but some of the clothes are seconds and irregulars. Savings begin about 20% off retail price and can go as high as 80% off retail price.

SUN.	MON.	TUE.	WED.	THU.	FRI.	SAT.
10:30–5	9–8:30	9–8:30	9–8:30	9–8:30	9–8:30	9–6

SAVINGS: 20%–80% off
SALE DAYS: weekly sales
SPECIAL DISCOUNTS: will negotiate
PARKING: lot
PAYMENT: cash, checks (amount of purchase only, with proper I.D., no out-of-state checks), MasterCard, VISA

Sears Surplus Store, 110 W. Lake Street, Addison, IL 60101; (312) 543-1756
See listing in Chicago, Illinois.

SUN.	MON.	TUE.	WED.	THU.	FRI.	SAT.
11–5	9:30–9	9:30–9	9:30–9	9:30–9	9:30–9	9:30–5

SAVINGS: 40%–50% off
ANNUAL SALES: Christmas toy sale
PARKING: lot
PAYMENT: cash, checks (amount of purchase only, with proper I.D., no out-of-state checks), Sears charge card

ARLINGTON HEIGHTS, IL

Spiegel Outlet Store, 310 E. Rand Road, Arlington Heights, IL 60004; (312) 577-5971
See listing in Chicago, Illinois

SUN.	MON.	TUE.	WED.	THU.	FRI.	SAT.
11–5	10–9	10–9	10–9	10–9	10–9	10–5

SAVINGS: 40%–70% off   *Mailing List*
SALE DAYS: Wednesday, Friday, Sunday
PARKING: lot

PAYMENT: cash, checks (with proper I.D.), MasterCard, VISA, American Express, Diners Club

AURORA, IL

Sears Surplus Store, 930 N. Lake Street, Aurora, IL 60507; (312) 859-2400
See listing in Chicago, Illinois

SUN.	MON.	TUE.	WED.	THU.	FRI.	SAT.
11–5	9:30–9	9:30–9	9:30–9	9:30–9	9:30–9	9:30–5

SAVINGS: 20%–80% off
PARKING: lot
PAYMENT: cash, checks (amount of purchase only, with proper I.D.), Sears charge card

CAROL STREAM, IL

Sears Catalog Surplus Store, 455 S. Schmale Road, Carol Stream, IL 60187; (312) 690-7200
See listing in Chicago, Illinois.

SUN.	MON.	TUE.	WED.	THU.	FRI.	SAT.
11–5	9:30–9	9:30–9	9:30–9	9:30–9	9:30–9	9:30–5:30

SAVINGS: 30%–50% off
SALE DAYS: coupon days
SPECIAL DISCOUNTS: senior citizens, 10% off
PARKING: lot
PAYMENT: cash, checks (with proper I.D.), Sears charge card

COUNTRYSIDE, IL

Spiegel Outlet Store, 9950 Joliet Road (Route 66), Countryside, IL 60525; (312) 352-3370
See listing in Chicago, Illinois.

SUN.	MON.	TUE.	WED.	THU.	FRI.	SAT.
11–5	10–9	10–9	10–9	10–9	10–9	10–5

SAVINGS: 40%–70% off   *Mailing List*
SALE DAYS: Wednesday, Friday, Sunday
PARKING: lot
PAYMENT: cash, checks (with proper I.D.), MasterCard, VISA, American Express, Diners Club

CRYSTAL LAKE, IL

Merchandise Clearance Center, 301 W. Virginia Street, Crystal Lake, IL 60014; (815) 455-0333
This is the outlet for J. T.'s General Stores. They sell their own brand of clothing. They also sell Fisher Price toys, domestics, West Bend and Revere Ware housewares, groceries, and some furniture. Most merchandise is first quality, but greatest savings are on samples, overruns, overstocks, last year's lines, discontinued, and closeouts. They have another store in Wauconda, Illinois.

SUN.	MON.	TUE.	WED.	THU.	FRI.	SAT.
10–3	9–5	9–5	9–8	9–8	9–8	9–5

SAVINGS: 40%–50% off
PARKING: lot
PAYMENT: cash, checks (amount of purchase only, with proper I.D. and their check cashing card), MasterCard, VISA

DEERFIELD, IL

Spiegel Outlet Store, 220 S. Waukegan Road, Deerfield, IL 60015; (312) 564-8370
See listing in Chicago, Illinois.

SUN.	MON.	TUE.	WED.	THU.	FRI.	SAT.
10-5	10-9	10-9	10-9	10-9	10-9	10-5

SAVINGS: 40%–70% off
PARKING: lot
PAYMENT: cash, checks, MasterCard, VISA, American Express, Diners Club

DES PLAINES, IL

Econo Outlet, 1637 Oakton Place, Des Plaines, IL 60018; (312) 827-0022
This store sells all kinds of general merchandise. Savings begin at 20% off first quality, and can go as high as 70% on irregulars, overstocks, last year's lines, and discontinued merchandise. They have other stores in Prospect Heights and Rolling Meadows, Illinois.

SUN.	MON.	TUE.	WED.	THU.	FRI.	SAT.
10-5	10-8	10-8	10-8	10-8	10-8	10-6

SAVINGS: 20%–70% off
PARKING: lot
PAYMENT: cash, checks (amount of purchase only, with proper I.D., no out-of-state checks), MasterCard, VISA

DOWNERS GROVE, IL

Spiegel Outlet Store, 1432 Butterfield Road, Downers Grove, IL 60532; (312) 620-5030
See listing in Chicago, Illinois.

SUN.	MON.	TUE.	WED.	THU.	FRI.	SAT.
11-5	10-9	10-9	10-9	10-9	10-9	10-5

SAVINGS: 40%–70% off　　　　　　　　　　　　　　　　　　*Mailing List*
SALE DAYS: Wednesday, Friday, Sunday
PARKING: lot
PAYMENT: cash, checks (with proper I.D.), MasterCard, VISA, American Express, Diners Club

FRANKLIN PARK, IL

Montgomery Ward Budget Store, 10601 W. Seymour Avenue, Franklin Park, IL 60131; (312) 678-8813
This is the outlet for Montgomery Ward's catalog and stores. Most merchandise is overstock or discontinued, with some customer returns, damaged, seconds, closeouts, and last year's lines. They have most items available in the catalog, including appliances, furniture, building supplies, and more. There is another store in Villa Park, Illinois.

SUN.	MON.	TUE.	WED.	THU.	FRI.	SAT.
11-5	9-5	9-5	9-9	9-9	9-9	9-5

SAVINGS: 50% off
PARKING: lot
PAYMENT: cash, checks (amount of purchase only, with proper I.D., no out-of-state checks), MasterCard, VISA, Montgomery Ward charge card

KEWANEE, IL

Insurance Liquidators, 206 N. Tremont Street, Kewanee, IL 61443; (309) 852-2238
This unusual store sells just about anything you might need. Most merchandise is from insurance liquidations, and, although much of the merchandise is first quality,

most is last year's line, end-of-season, discontinued, closeouts, and odd lots, and there are many seconds, irregulars, bruised, and damaged items. Savings average 40%–60% off retail prices. They have other stores in Peru, two in Rockford, and Sterling, Illinois; and two in Madison and another in Milwaukee, Wisconsin.

SUN.	MON.	TUE.	WED.	THU.	FRI.	SAT.
noon–5	9–9	9–9	9–9	9–9	9–9	9–9

SAVINGS: 40%–60% off
PARKING: lot
PAYMENT: cash, checks (amount of purchase only, with proper I.D. and place of employment), MasterCard, VISA

LOMBARD, IL

The Garage Sale Outlet Store, 837 S. Westmore Avenue, Lombard, IL 60148; (312) 620-0129
See listing in Addison, Illinois.

SUN.	MON.	TUE.	WED.	THU.	FRI.	SAT.
10–4	9–6	9–6	9–8	9–8	9–6	9–6

SAVINGS: 20%–80% off
SPECIAL DISCOUNTS: senior citizens, charity groups (ask)
PARKING: lot
PAYMENT: cash, checks (amount of purchase only, with proper I.D., no out-of-state checks), MasterCard, VISA

MATTESON, IL

Spiegel Outlet Store, Loehmann's Center, 184 Town Center, Matteson, IL 60443; (312) 747-6930
See listing in Chicago, Illinois.

SUN.	MON.	TUE.	WED.	THU.	FRI.	SAT.
11–5	10–9	10–9	10–9	10–9	10–9	10–5

SAVINGS: 40%–70% off   *Mailing List*
SALE DAYS: Wednesday, Friday, Sunday
PARKING: lot
PAYMENT: cash, checks (amount of purchase only, with proper I.D.), MasterCard, VISA, American Express, Diners Club

MELROSE PARK, IL

Sears Warehouse Outlet Store, 2065 N. George Street, Melrose Park, IL 60160; (312) 865-4408
See Sears Catalog Surplus Store in Chicago, Illinois.

SUN.	MON.	TUE.	WED.	THU.	FRI.	SAT.
closed	9–5:30	9–5:30	9–5:30	9–5:30	9–5:30	9–5:30

SAVINGS: up to 85% off
BRAND NAMES: Kenmore
SALE DAYS: vary
PARKING: lot
PAYMENT: cash, checks (amount of purchase only, with proper I.D.), Sears charge card

NAPERVILLE, IL

Spiegel Outlet Store, 540 S. Route 59, Naperville, IL 60540; (312) 961-4980
See listing in Chicago, Illinois.

SUN.	MON.	TUE.	WED.	THU.	FRI.	SAT.
11–5	10–9	10–9	10–9	10–9	10–9	10–5:30

SAVINGS: 40%–70% off   *Mailing List*
PARKING: lot
PAYMENT: cash, checks (with proper I.D.), MasterCard, VISA, American Express,
   Diners Club

PERU, IL

Insurance Liquidators, 1010 Shooting Park Road, Peru, IL 60110; (815) 224-3937
   See listing in Kewanee, Illinois.

SUN.	MON.	TUE.	WED.	THU.	FRI.	SAT.
noon–5	9–9	9–9	9–9	9–9	9–9	9–9

SAVINGS: 40%–60% off
PARKING: lot
PAYMENT: cash, checks (amount of purchase only, with proper I.D. and place of
   employment), MasterCard, VISA

PROSPECT HEIGHTS, IL

Econo Outlet, 672 W. Milwaukee Avenue, Prospect Heights, IL 60070; (312) 459-6710
   See listing in Des Plaines, Illinois.

SUN.	MON.	TUE.	WED.	THU.	FRI.	SAT.
closed	10–8	10–8	10–8	10–8	10–8	10–7

SAVINGS: 20%–70% off
PARKING: lot
PAYMENT: cash, checks (amount of purchase only, with proper I.D., no out-of-state
   checks), MasterCard, VISA

ROCKFORD, IL

Insurance Liquidators, 1233 Sandy Hollow Road, Rockford, IL 61109; (815) 398-6835
   See listing in Kewanee, Illinois.

SUN.	MON.	TUE.	WED.	THU.	FRI.	SAT.
noon–5	9–9	9–9	9–9	9–9	9–9	9–9

SAVINGS: 40%–60% off
PARKING: lot
PAYMENT: cash, checks (amount of purchase only, with proper I.D., place of
   employment), MasterCard, VISA

Insurance Liquidators, 3921 E. State Street, Rockford, IL 61108; (815) 397-0732
   See listing in Kewanee, Illinois.

SUN.	MON.	TUE.	WED.	THU.	FRI.	SAT.
noon–5	9–9	9–9	9–9	9–9	9–9	9–9

SAVINGS: 40%–60% off
PARKING: lot
PAYMENT: cash, checks (amount of purchase only, with proper I.D., and place of
   employment), MasterCard, VISA

ROLLING MEADOWS, IL

Econo Outlet, 2206 W. Algonquin Road, Rolling Meadows, IL 60008; (312) 577-6920
   See listing in Des Plaines, Illinois.

SUN.	MON.	TUE.	WED.	THU.	FRI.	SAT.
closed	10–8	10–8	10–8	10–8	10–8	10–7

SAVINGS: 20%–70% off
PARKING: lot
PAYMENT: cash, checks (amount of purchase only, with proper I.D.), MasterCard, VISA

Insurance Liquidators, 1403 W. 4th Street, Sterling, IL 61081; (815) 625-0972
See listing in Kewanee, Illinois.

SUN.	MON.	TUE.	WED.	THU.	FRI.	SAT.
noon-5	9-9	9-9	9-9	9-9	9-9	9-9

SAVINGS: 40%-60% off
PARKING: lot
PAYMENT: cash, checks (amount of purchase only, with proper I.D. and place of
employment), MasterCard, VISA

J. C. Penney Catalog Outlet Store, 250 W. North Avenue, Villa Park, IL 60181;
(312) 279-1700
This is the outlet for the J. C. Penney stores and catalog merchandise. Savings
begin at about 25% off retail price on first quality and can go as high as 50% on last
year's lines, end-of-season, discontinued, closeout, and overstocked merchandise.
They also have stores in Cudahy and Milwaukee, Wisconsin.

SUN.	MON.	TUE.	WED.	THU.	FRI.	SAT.
10-5	9:30-9	9:30-9	9:30-9	9:30-9	9:30-9	9:30-6

SAVINGS: 25%-50% off
PARKING: lot
PAYMENT: cash, checks (amount of purchase only, with proper I.D., no out-of-state
checks), MasterCard, VISA, American Express, J. C. Penney charge card

Montgomery Ward Catalog Store, 701 W. North Avenue, Villa Park, IL 60181; (312)
834-9860
See Montgomery Ward Budget Store in Franklin Park, Illinois.

SUN.	MON.	TUE.	WED.	THU.	FRI.	SAT.
10-5	9:30-9	9:30-9	9:30-9	9:30-9	9:30-9	9:30-6

SAVINGS: 10%-50% off
SALE DAYS: occasional specials
PARKING: lot
PAYMENT: cash, checks (amount of purchase only, with proper I.D.), MasterCard,
VISA, Montgomery Ward charge card

Spiegel Outlet Store, 200 E. North Avenue, Villa Park, IL 60181; (312) 833-0400
See listing in Chicago, Illinois.

SUN.	MON.	TUE.	WED.	THU.	FRI.	SAT.
11-5	10-9	10-9	10-9	10-9	10-9	10-5

SAVINGS: 30%-60% off
SALE DAYS: Wednesday, Friday, Sunday
PARKING: lot
PAYMENT: cash, checks (with proper I.D.), MasterCard, VISA, American Express

Merchandise Clearance Center, 476 W. Liberty (Route 176), Wauconda, IL 60084;
(312) 526-2247
See listing in Crystal Lake, Illinois.

SUN.	MON.	TUE.	WED.	THU.	FRI.	SAT.
9-3	9-5	9-5	9-8	9-8	9-8	9-5

SAVINGS: 40%-50% off
BRAND NAMES: Fisher, West Bend, Revere Ware, Park (Jewel)
SALE DAYS: Wednesday

SPECIAL DISCOUNTS: senior citizens, 30% off any item not already on sale on
  Monday
PARKING: lot
PAYMENT: cash, checks (amount of purchase only, with proper I.D.), MasterCard, VISA

WAUKEGAN, IL

Sears Surplus Store, 1535 N. Lewis Street, Waukegan, IL 60085; (312) 249-5320
  See Sears Catalog Surplus Store in Chicago, Illinois.

SUN.	MON.	TUE.	WED.	THU.	FRI.	SAT.
noon–5	10–9	10–9	10–9	10–9	10–9	10–5

SAVINGS: 20%–70% off
SALE DAYS: Tuesday, weekends
PARKING: lot
PAYMENT: cash, checks (amount of purchase only, proper I.D.), Sears charge card

WHEELING, IL

Sears Catalog Surplus Store, 903 W. Dundee Road, Wheeling, IL 60090; (312)
  541-2910
  See listing in Chicago, Illinois.

SUN.	MON.	TUE.	WED.	THU.	FRI.	SAT.
11–5	9–9	9–9	9–9	9–9	9–9	9:30–5:30

SAVINGS: 25%–70% off
SALE DAYS: Tuesday 6:00–9:00 p.m.
PARKING: lot
PAYMENT: cash, checks (amount of purchase only, with proper I.D.), Sears charge
  card

INDIANA
HIGHLAND, IN

Sears Surplus Store, 8401 N. Indianapolis Boulevard, Highland, IN 46322; (219)
  972-0202
  See Sears Catalog Surplus Store in Chicago, Illinois.

SUN.	MON.	TUE.	WED.	THU.	FRI.	SAT.
11–5	9–9	9–9	9–9	9–9	9–9	9–5

SAVINGS: 20%–50% off
PARKING: lot
PAYMENT: cash, checks (amount of purchase only, with proper I.D.), Sears charge
  card

INDIANAPOLIS, IN

Big and Small Lots, Eastgate Consumer Mall, 7150 E. Washington Street,
  Indianapolis, IN 46201; (317) 356-9611
  This store sells a wide assortment of merchandise at remarkable savings. They buy
lots of general merchandise, and, although their stock varies, savings are usually
substantial. They have another store, called Big Lots, in Mishawaka, Indiana.

SUN.	MON.	TUE.	WED.	THU.	FRI.	SAT.
noon–5	10–9	10–9	10–9	10–9	10–9	10–9

SAVINGS: 50%–80% off
SPECIAL SALES: monthly
PARKING: lot
PAYMENT: cash, checks (amount of purchase only, with proper I.D., no out-of-state
  checks), MasterCard, VISA

Sears Surplus Store, 2829 S. Madison Avenue, Indianapolis, IN 46225; (317) 783-1742

See Sears Catalog Surplus Store in Chicago, Illinois.

SUN.	MON.	TUE.	WED.	THU.	FRI.	SAT.
noon–5	9:30–9	9:30–9	9:30–9	9:30–9	9:30–9	9:30–5

SAVINGS: 30%–50% off
PARKING: lot
PAYMENT: cash, checks (amount of purchase only, with proper I.D., no out-of-state checks), Sears charge card

MISHAWAKA, IN

Big Lots, Buyer's Marketplace, 5901 Grape Road, Mishawaka, IN 46545; (219) 277-2664

See listing under Big and Small Lots in Indianapolis, Indiana.

SUN.	MON.	TUE.	WED.	THU.	FRI.	SAT.
11–5	9:30–9	9:30–9	9:30–9	9:30–9	9:30–9	9:30–9

SAVINGS: 25%–70% off
PARKING: lot
PAYMENT: cash, checks (amount of purchase only, with proper I.D.), MasterCard, VISA

WISCONSIN
CUDAHY, WI

J. C. Penney Catalog Outlet Store, 5656 S. Packard Avenue, Cudahy, WI 53110; (414) 769-6210

See listing in Villa Park, Illinois.

SUN.	MON.	TUE.	WED.	THU.	FRI.	SAT.
11–5	9–9	9–9	9–9	9–9	9–9	9–5

SAVINGS: 40% to 50% off
PARKING: lot
PAYMENT: cash, checks (amount of purchase only, with proper I.D.), MasterCard, VISA, J. C. Penney charge card

LA CROSSE, WI

C.O.M.B., La Crosse Factory Outlet Mall, 301 Sky Harbor Drive, La Crosse, WI 54607; (608) 783-6464

This store has a bit of everything, all carefully labeled as seconds, overstocks, name brands, etc. Savings average 50%–75% off retail. The name stands for Close Out Merchandise Buyers. One of my researchers paid $2.00 for a *quart* of name brand shampoo (probably packaged for beauty shops).

SUN.	MON.	TUE.	WED.	THU.	FRI.	SAT.
11–5	10–9	10–9	10–9	10–9	10–9	9–6

SAVINGS: 50%–75% off
PARKING: lot
PAYMENT: cash, checks (amount of purchase only, with proper I.D.), MasterCard, VISA

MADISON, WI

Insurance Liquidators, 125 W. Beltline Highway, Madison, WI 53711; (608) 274-9740

See listing in Kewanee, Illinois.

SUN.	MON.	TUE.	WED.	THU.	FRI.	SAT.
noon–5	9–9	9–9	9–9	9–9	9–9	9–9

SAVINGS: 40%–60% off
PARKING: lot

PAYMENT: cash, checks (amount of purchase only, with proper I.D. and place of
employment), MasterCard, VISA

Insurance Liquidators, 2825 E. Washington Avenue, Madison, WI 53704; (608)
249-8483
See listing in Kewanee, Illinois.

SUN.	MON.	TUE.	WED.	THU.	FRI.	SAT.
noon-5	9-9	9-9	9-9	9-9	9-9	9-9

SAVINGS: 40%-60% off
PARKING: lot
PAYMENT: cash, checks (amount of purchase only, with proper I.D. and place of
employment), MasterCard, VISA

MANITOWOC, WI

Sears Surplus Store, 700 E. Magnolia Street, Manitowoc, WI 54220; (414) 682-8831
See Sears Catalog Surplus Store in Chicago, Illinois.

SUN.	MON.	TUE.	WED.	THU.	FRI.	SAT.
noon-4	10-8	10-8	10-8	10-8	10-8	9:30-5

SAVINGS: 30%-50% off
PARKING: lot
PAYMENT: cash, checks (amount of purchase only, with proper I.D.), Sears charge
card

MILWAUKEE, WI

Insurance Liquidators, 3305 W. Forest Home Avenue, Milwaukee, WI 53215; (414)
643-8678
See listing in Kewanee, Illinois.

SUN.	MON.	TUE.	WED.	THU.	FRI.	SAT.
noon-5	9-9	9-9	9-9	9-9	9-9	9-9

SAVINGS: 40%-60% off
PARKING: lot
PAYMENT: cash, checks (amount of purchase only, with proper I.D. and place of
employment), MasterCard, VISA

J. C. Penney Catalog Outlet Store, 10332 W. Silver Spring Road, Milwaukee, WI
53225; (414) 464-1111
See listing in Villa Park, Illinois.

SUN.	MON.	TUE.	WED.	THU.	FRI.	SAT.
11-5	9-9	9-9	9-9	9-9	9-9	9-5

SAVINGS: up to 50% off
PARKING: lot
PAYMENT: cash, checks (amount of purchase only, with proper I.D.), MasterCard,
VISA, J. C. Penney charge card

PLOVER, WI

The Discounter, Manufacturer's Direct Mall, 101 Plover Road, Plover, WI 54467; (715)
344-4771
This store had a bit of everything, stacked or stuffed, with no particular order. If
you can find what you need, you'll probably save 50%-90% off retail price. They say
they carry the full glossary of this book's terms—except "first quality."

SUN.	MON.	TUE.	WED.	THU.	FRI.	SAT.
11-6	9:30-9	9:30-9	9:30-9	9:30-9	9:30-9	9:30-9

SAVINGS: 50%–90% off
PARKING: lot
PAYMENT: cash, checks (amount of purchase only, with proper I.D.), MasterCard, VISA

WEST ALLIS, WI

Sears Surplus Store, 10635 W. Greenfield Avenue, West Allis, WI 53214; (414) 259-0033
See Sears Catalog Surplus Store in Chicago, Illinois.

SUN.	MON.	TUE.	WED.	THU.	FRI.	SAT.
noon–4	10–8	10–8	10–8	10–8	10–8	10–5

SAVINGS: 30%–50% off
PARKING: lot
PAYMENT: cash, checks (amount of purchase only, with proper I.D.), Sears charge card

11
FABRICS

The outlets listed here sell a variety of fabrics. Their uses range from sewing projects to upholstery, drapery, and designer wall treatments. Several outlets sell related supplies for upholstery.

Many other outlets sell remnants left from the manufacture of other goods; also look in Chapter 7, *Clothing—Women's*; Chapter 8, *Crafts*; Chapter 9, *Decorating*; Chapter 13, *Furniture*; Chapter 18, *Linens*; and Chapter 25, *Sewing Supplies and Equipment*.

On the whole, savings were best on remnants, mill ends, and bolt-end pieces, and I saw many pieces large enough for a major project at give-away prices. Also look at discontinued colors and patterns, and closeout merchandise for excellent savings.

ILLINOIS

CHICAGO, IL

Elco Supply Company
See listing under *Furniture* in Chicago, Illinois.

Fishman's Fabric Outlet, 628 W. Roosevelt Road, Chicago, IL 60607; (312) 922-4170
This is the outlet for Fishman Fabrics (around the corner). Savings start at 50% off retail price and some remarkable bargains can be found. All silks (values to $50/yard) are $4–5/yard; zippers are 50¢. Be sure to check the dollar bin. They say—the longer the merchandise stays the lower the price. There are some bolt ends and remnants at 95% off. They also sharpen scissors.

SUN.	MON.	TUE.	WED.	THU.	FRI.	SAT.
9:30–4:30	9:30–5:30	9:30–5:30	9:30–5:30	9–5	9:30–5:30	9:30–5:30

SAVINGS: 50%–95% off   *Mailing List*
SPECIAL DISCOUNTS: senior citizens (ask; they were planning at this writing)
PARKING: lot (in back, near the retail store)
PAYMENT: cash, checks (amount of purchase only, with proper I.D.), MasterCard, VISA

Linker's New York Textiles, 556 W. Roosevelt Road, Chicago, IL 60607; (312) 427-5441
This shop sells many major brands of fabrics, some embroidered, and lace at savings of 15%–20% off retail price on first quality merchandise. They also sell some Waverly wallpaper.

SUN.	MON.	TUE.	WED.	THU.	FRI.	SAT.
9–4	9–5:15	9–5:15	9–5:15	9–5:15	9–5:15	closed

SAVINGS: 15%–20% off   *Mailing List*   *All First Quality*
BRAND NAMES: Waverly

ANNUAL SALES: February, March
PARKING: lot
PAYMENT: cash, checks (amount of purchase only, with proper I.D.), MasterCard, VISA

Loomcraft Textiles, 4892 N. Clark Street, Chicago, IL 60640; (312) 275-1414
This outlet sells all kinds of fabrics, including drapery and upholstery fabrics, and supplies for do-it-yourself upholstery. Greatest savings are on seconds, irregulars, imperfects, samples, mill-ends, bolt-ends, and overruns. They have another store in Kenosha, Wisconsin.

SUN.	MON.	TUE.	WED.	THU.	FRI.	SAT.
10-5	9:30-9	9:30-9	9:30-9	9:30-9	9:30-9	9:30-6

SAVINGS: 50%-75% off
PARKING: lot, street
PAYMENT: cash, checks, MasterCard, VISA

Smoler Brothers Fashion Factory Outlet
See listing under *Clothing—Women's* in Chicago, Illinois.

Textile Discount Outlet, 2126 W. 21st Place, Chicago, IL 60608; (312) 847-0572
This outlet sells all kinds of fabrics and notions at savings that begin at 10% off retail price, but can go as high as 70% on some irregulars, bolt-ends, surplus, overruns, overstocks, last year's lines, discount, and close-out items. They also sell linens and towels, and some ready-to-wear items for men and women. At this writing, they were planning a new made-to-order department, including the services of a designer.

SUN.	MON.	TUE.	WED.	THU.	FRI.	SAT.
10-4	9:30-5	9:30-5	9:30-5	9:30-5	9:30-5	closed

SAVINGS: 10%-70% off   *Mailing List*
SPECIAL SALES: weekly
SPECIAL DISCOUNTS: quantity, groups, 10% (ask)
PARKING: street
PAYMENT: cash, checks (amount of purchase only, with proper I.D.)

Wallstreet, Ford City Shopping Center, 7601 S. Cicero Avenue, Chicago, IL 60652; (312) 581-3311
This store sells wallpaper and fabrics for decorating needs. Savings are greatest on bolt-ends, discontinued, overstocks, and closeout items.

SUN.	MON.	TUE.	WED.	THU.	FRI.	SAT.
noon-5	10-9	10-9	10-9	10-9	10-9	10-5:30

SAVINGS: 25%-50% off
BRAND NAMES: Kaufman's, Kinney, Waverly
ANNUAL SALES: February
PARKING: lot
PAYMENT: cash, checks (amount of purchase only, with proper I.D.), MasterCard, VISA, American Express

Western Textile Outlet Store, 419 W. Erie Street, Chicago, IL 60610; (312) 751-0600
This factory outlet sells draperies and drapery linings. Savings are greatest on seconds, irregulars, discontinued, overstocks, and closeout merchandise.

SUN.	MON.	TUE.	WED.	THU.	FRI.	SAT.
closed	9-3	9-3	9-3	9-3	closed	closed

SAVINGS: 40%-65% off
BRAND NAMES: Western Textile
PARKING: lot
PAYMENT: cash only

Towel Factory Outlet Center
See listing under *Linens* in Arlington Heights, Illinois.

Prevue Fashions
See listing under *Clothing—Women's* in Aurora, Illinois.

Grist "Mill Ends" & Things, 39 E. Main Street, Carpentersville, IL 60110; (312)
426-6455
This is an outlet for Collin & Aikman and Robert Allen fabrics. Savings average
20% off retail price on first quality, but check the second floor where there are
occasional test runs, bolt-ends, and remnants at greater savings.

SUN.	MON.	TUE.	WED.	THU.	FRI.	SAT.
closed	9-5	9-5	9-5	9-5	9-5	9:30-3:30

SAVINGS: average 20% off
BRAND NAMES: Collin & Aikman, Robert Allen
SPECIAL DISCOUNTS: senior citizens, 10% off
PARKING: lot
PAYMENT: cash, checks (amount of purchase only, with proper I.D.), MasterCard, VISA

Towel Factory Outlet Center
See listing under *Linens* in Downers Grove, Illinois.

Calico Corners, 777 N. York Road, Hinsdale, IL 60521; (312) 920-1955
This outlet specializes in draperies, slipcovers, and upholstery fabrics. Savings
average 30%–60% off because all of the merchandise is carefully selected seconds.
They also do custom-made upholstery. Some merchandise are mill ends, bolt-ends,
discounted designs, and imperfect dye lots. They also have stores in Lake Forest and
Wilmette, Illinois; Zionsville, Indiana; and Waukesha, Wisconsin.

SUN.	MON.	TUE.	WED.	THU.	FRI.	SAT.
closed	9:30-8:30	9:30-5:30	9:30-5:30	9:30-5:30	9:30-5:30	9:30-5:30

SAVINGS: 30%–60% off   *Mailing List*
PARKING: lot
PAYMENT: cash, checks (amount of purchase only, with proper I.D.), MasterCard, VISA

Calico Corners, 896 S. Waukegan Road, Lake Forest, IL 60045; (312) 234-6800
See listing in Hinsdale, Illinois.

SUN.	MON.	TUE.	WED.	THU.	FRI.	SAT.
closed	9:30-8:30	9:30-5:30	9:30-5:30	9:30-5:30	9:30-5:30	9:30-5:30

SAVINGS: 30%–60% off
ANNUAL SALES: second week in August
PARKING: lot
PAYMENT: cash, checks (amount of purchase only, with proper I.D.), MasterCard, VISA

Prevue Fashions
See listing under *Clothing—Women's* in Naperville. Illinois.

JJ's Bedding & Furniture Discount
See listing under *Beds, Mattresses, and Box Springs* in Niles, Illinois.

Towel Factory Outlet—Revere Mills
See listing under *Linens* in Niles, Illinois.

Oops, We Goofed, 18 E. Sauk Trail, South Chicago Heights, IL 60411; (312) 754-5250
This is the outlet for Stead Textiles. Savings begin at 50% off retail price on first quality merchandise, and quickly jump as high as 80% on custom-made draperies, curtains, and bedspreads that had been made the wrong size. They also sell some seconds, samples, mill- and bolt-end fabrics, surplus, and discontinued items.

SUN.	MON.	TUE.	WED.	THU.	FRI.	SAT.
closed	10-5	10-5	10-5	10-5	10-5	10-5

SAVINGS: 40%–75% off   *Mailing List*
SALE DAYS: vary
SPECIAL DISCOUNTS: will negotiate with charity groups
PARKING: lot
PAYMENT: cash, checks (amount of purchase only, with proper I.D.), MasterCard, VISA

Stead Textile Company Outlet
See listing under *Decorating* in South Chicago Heights, Illinois.

Aero Drapery Company—Division of Minnesota Fabrics, 122 Messner Drive, Wheeling, IL 60090; (312) 520-2680
This is the outlet for Minnesota Fabrics. Savings range from 50% off retail price on custom draperies and bedspreads, to 60% off on drapery and upholstery fabric ends, and up to 75% off blinds. They sell mostly first quality merchandise with some imperfects, bolt-ends, and "as is" merchandise.

SUN.	MON.	TUE.	WED.	THU.	FRI.	SAT.
closed	8-5	8-5	8-5	8-5	8-5	closed

SAVINGS: 50%–75% off
BRAND NAMES: Aero
PARKING: lot
PAYMENT: cash, checks (amount of purchase only, with proper I.D.), MasterCard, VISA

Calico Corners, 105 S. Green Bay Road, Wilmette, IL 60091; (312) 256-1500
See listing in Hinsdale, Illinois.

SUN.	MON.	TUE.	WED.	THU.	FRI.	SAT.
closed	9:30–8:30	9:30–5:30	9:30–5:30	9:30–5:30	9:30–5:30	9:30–5:30

SAVINGS: 30%–60% off
ANNUAL SALES: second week in August
PARKING: lot
PAYMENT: cash, checks (amount of purchase only, with proper I.D.), MasterCard, VISA

Sewing Factory Outlet Store
See listing under *Clothing—Women's* in Zion, Illinois.

Farmhouse Studio, 2215 East 350 North, LaPorte, IN 46350; (219) 326-5255
This is the outlet for Elenhank and Farmhouse Studios. They produce printed fabric yardage and panels. The retail price usually runs $50–$75/yard, but here they sell from $1–$10/yard. Some items are first quality; the rest are seconds, samples, test runs, mill-ends, bolt-ends, surplus, overruns, last year's lines, discontinued, and closeout merchandise.

SUN.	MON.	TUE.	WED.	THU.	FRI.	SAT.
*	*	*	*	*	*	*

SAVINGS: 50%–98% off   *Mailing List*
BRAND NAMES: Elenhank, Farmhouse Studios
PARKING: lot
PAYMENT: cash, MasterCard, VISA

—————
*Hours are by appointment only.

Gohn Brothers Manufacturing Company, 105 S. Main Street, Box 111,
Middlebury, IN 46540; (219) 825-2400
This outlet sells Spring Mills broadcloth, Red Wing shoes, Gerber baby clothing, and coats. They also sell printed fabric, rubber footwear, and sewing accessories. Savings average 20%–50% off retail price on all first quality merchandise.

SUN.	MON.	TUE.	WED.	THU.	FRI.	SAT.
closed	8–6	8–6	8–6	8–6	8–6	8–6

SAVINGS: 20%–50% off   *Mailing List*   *All First Quality*
BRAND NAMES: Spring Mill, Red Wing, VIP, La Crosse
PARKING: lot
PAYMENT: cash, checks only

Calico Corners, 165 W. Sycamore, Zionsville, IN 46077; (317) 873-3347
See listing in Hinsdale, Illinois.

SUN.	MON.	TUE.	WED.	THU.	FRI.	SAT.
closed	9:30–5:30	9:30–5:30	9:30–5:30	9:30–5:30	9:30–8:30	9:30–5:30

SAVINGS: 30%–60% off
PARKING: lot
PAYMENT: cash, checks (amount of purchase only, with proper I.D.), MasterCard, VISA

McArthur Towels
See listing under *Linens* in Baraboo, Wisconsin.

Grafton Yarn Company Outlet Store
See listing under *Clothing—Accessories* in Grafton, Wisconsin.

Monterey Mills Outlet Store, 1725 E. Delavan Drive, Janesville, WI 53545; (608) 754-8309
This mill outlet sells Monterey fake fur fabrics at discount up to 75% off retail

price. Savings are greatest on seconds, samples, ends and pieces, overruns, overstocks, discontinued, and closeout merchandise.

SUN.	MON.	TUE.	WED.	THU.	FRI.	SAT.
closed	9–4	9–4	9–4	9–4	9–4	8–noon

SAVINGS: 40%–75% off *Mailing List*
BRAND NAMES: Monterey Mills
PARKING: lot
PAYMENT: cash, checks (with proper I.D.)

Norwood Mills Outlet Store, 2101 Kennedy Road, Janesville, WI 53545; (608) 756-0321
This is the outlet for Norwood Mills, which manufactures imitation fur fabrics. They sell a variety of items like bathroom tank sets, bathroom carpet throw rugs, pillows, stuffed toys, hospital pads, fur fabrics, scraps, and car seat covers. Best buys are on seconds, samples, test runs, mill-ends, overruns, last year's lines, discontinued, and closeout merchandise.

SUN.	MON.	TUE.	WED.	THU.	FRI.	SAT.
closed	9–4	9–4	9–4	9–4	9–4	9–noon

SAVINGS: 30%–50% off
BRAND NAMES: Norwood Mills
PARKING: street
PAYMENT: cash, checks (amount of purchase only, with proper I.D.)

JEFFERSON, WI

Fur the Fun of It, 105 S. Center Avenue, Jefferson, WI 53549; (414) 674-2744
This factory outlet sells "fun fur" fabrics, custom-made pillows, custom-made bedspreads, and stuffed animals. They also sell pillow fillings. Best buys are on seconds, remnants, and surplus merchandise.

SUN.	MON.	TUE.	WED.	THU.	FRI.	SAT.
closed	9–5	9–5	9–5	9–5	9–8	9–4

SAVINGS: 20%–40% off *Mailing List*
BRAND NAMES: Borg
PARKING: lot
PAYMENT: cash, checks (amount of purchase only, with proper I.D.), MasterCard, VISA

Schweiger Fabric Outlet, 111 Landing Avenue, Jefferson, WI 53549; (414) 674-2330
Savings here begin at 50% off on first quality and rise quickly on bolt-ends, remnants, and overstocked merchandise. Check the back room for a large stock of wood, hardware, mirrors, and glass at large discounts. They also sell pillows, cushions, fiberfill, poly foam, and other upholstering supplies.

SUN.	MON.	TUE.	WED.	THU.	FRI.	SAT.
closed	9–5	9–5	9–5	9–5	9–5	9–noon

SAVINGS: 50%–70% off
PARKING: street
PAYMENT: cash, MasterCard, VISA

KENOSHA, WI

Loomcraft Textiles, Factory Outlet Centre, 7700 120th Avenue, Kenosha, WI 53142: (414) 857-2100
See listing in Chicago, Illinois.

SUN.	MON.	TUE.	WED.	THU.	FRI.	SAT.
11–5	9:30–9	9:30–9	9:30–9	9:30–9	9:30–9	9:30–6

SAVINGS: 50%–75% off *Mailing List*

BRAND NAMES: Quaker, Burlington, Rassville, Kaufman's, Roc-Lon, Collin & Aikman, La France, J. P. Martin
SPECIAL DISCOUNTS: senior citizens, Wednesday (on request)
PARKING: lot
PAYMENT: cash, checks (amount of purchase only, with proper I.D.), MasterCard, VISA

MILWAUKEE, WI

(The Original) Clothes Rack
See listing under *Clothing—Women's* in Milwaukee, Wisconsin.

NEW GLARUS, WI

Swiss Miss Textile Mart, 1101 Highway 69 South, New Glarus, WI 53574; (608) 527-2514
This is the factory outlet for Upright Swiss embroideries. They sell Swiss Miss fabrics, pillowcases, embroidery fabrics, laces, and flounces. They also sell place mats and aprons.

SUN.	MON.	TUE.	WED.	THU.	FRI.	SAT.
noon-5	9-5	9-5	9-5	9-5	9-5	9-5

SAVINGS: 10%–50% off   *All First Quality*
BRAND NAMES: Swiss Miss
ANNUAL SALES: July, and Thanksgiving through Christmas
PARKING: lot
PAYMENT: cash, checks (amount of purchase only, with proper I.D.), travelers' checks, money orders

WAUKESHA, WI

Bazaar Factory Outlet Store, W. 220 N. 1560 Jerico Center, Waukesha, WI 53186; (414) 549-1171
This store sells major brands of upholstery and drapery fabric. Best savings are on surplus, overruns, overstocks, discontinued, and closeout merchandise.

SUN.	MON.	TUE.	WED.	THU.	FRI.	SAT.
closed	closed	9-5	9-5	9-5	9-5	9-5

SAVINGS: 10%–50% off
ANNUAL SALES: spring, fall
PARKING: lot
PAYMENT: cash, checks (amount of purchase only, with proper I.D.), MasterCard, VISA

Calico Corners, 275 Regency Court, Town of Brookfield, Waukesha, WI 53186; (414) 786-4646
See listing in Hinsdale, Illinois.

SUN.	MON.	TUE.	WED.	THU.	FRI.	SAT.
closed	9:30-8:30	9:30-5:30	9:30-5:30	9:30-5:30	9:30-5:30	9:30-5:30

SAVINGS: 50%–60% off   *Mailing List*
ANNUAL SALES: August
PARKING: lot
PAYMENT: cash, checks (amount of purchase only, with proper I.D.), MasterCard, VISA

12
FOOD

Savings on food varied greatly. Listed here are outlets for manufacturers. You are probably aware of several chains that sell groceries at discount prices. They are not included, but check your local telephone directory for locations. Food categories are: *Bakery*; *Candy, Nuts, and Dried Fruit*; *Canned*; *Cheese*; *Meat and Sausage*; and *Miscellaneous*.

Savings are greatest on seconds and irregulars (although terms vary). The flaw is usually in packaging or in appearance, and does not affect the quality of the food. If you plan to freeze the bread, pay 35¢ instead of $1.09 for the loaf. If you don't mind a broken crust on a $3.29 quiche, or a cracked top on the cheesecake, you'll pay $1.50. If you can remember the unlabeled cans of tomatoes are in one box and the unlabeled beans are in another, you'll save about 50% off retail price.

FOOD—BAKERY

There is a bakery outlet in almost every community in the Chicago-land area. Most bread manufacturers have outlets where they sell "day-old" items. This term usually means that the bread was not sold on the delivery route, so it is brought to the outlet. Also listed in this chapter are outlets that sell cookies, cakes, pies, snack cakes, and other baked goods.

The majority of outlets here are for one manufacturer. Savings on items they manufacture are usually between 33% and 50% off retail price. Look closely at other items they sell. I noticed that they were often at retail price or at small savings. Look for the bargain day(s). If you can stock up once a week or once a month, savings frequently go to 75% off retail price.

ILLINOIS
CHICAGO, IL

Atlas Baking Company, 1429 W. Grand Avenue, Chicago, IL 60622; (312) 421-5726
This small bakery makes wonderful french bread. They also sell pizza slices, sandwiches, and terrific bread crumbs. Savings average 20% off retail price.

SUN.	MON.	TUE.	WED.	THU.	FRI.	SAT.
7–1	6–4	6–4	6–4	6–4	6–4	6–4

SAVINGS: 10%–20% off
PARKING: street
PAYMENT: cash only

143

Baltic Bakery, 4627 S. Hermitage Avenue, Chicago, IL 60609; (312) 523-1510
A two-pound loaf of bread which retails for $1.69, here is $1.15, and day-old is 85¢.
They also sell rolls, coffee cakes, candy, and cookies. See listing below.

SUN.	MON.	TUE.	WED.	THU.	FRI.	SAT.
6–7	6–7	6–7	6–7	6–7	6–7	6–6

SAVINGS: 20%–50% off
PARKING: lot
PAYMENT: cash only

Baltic Bakery, 2616 W. 69th Street, Chicago, IL 60629; (312) 737-6784
See listing above.

SUN.	MON.	TUE.	WED.	THU.	FRI.	SAT.
8–2	8:30–7	8:30–7	8:30–7	8:30–7	8:30–7	8–6

SAVINGS: 20%–50% off
PARKING: street
PAYMENT: cash, checks (amount of purchase only, with proper I.D.)

Buttermaid Bakeries Thrift Store, 2925 W. Montrose Avenue, Chicago, IL 60618;
(312) 463-9750
This is one of many outlets for Buttermaid bread, Butternut bread, and Dolly
Madison snack cakes. They also sell Vitners chips, Milbrook stuffing mix, and Beatrice
bread crumbs at savings up to 50% off retail price on overstocks, day-old, and surplus
merchandise. They have other stores in Chicago, Hillside, Kankakee, Mundelein, and
Tinley Park, Illinois; and in Highland, Indiana.

SUN.	MON.	TUE.	WED.	THU.	FRI.	SAT.
10–3	9–7	9–7	9–7	9–7	9–7	9–6

SAVINGS: up to 50% off
BRAND NAMES: Buttermaid, Dolly Madison, Butternut
PARKING: lot
PAYMENT: cash, food stamps

Buttermaid Bakeries Thrift Store, 7816 S. Vincennes Avenue, Chicago, IL 60620;
(312) 483-8387
See listing above.

SUN.	MON.	TUE.	WED.	THU.	FRI.	SAT.
closed	8–6	8–6	8–6	8–6	8–6	8–6

SAVINGS: up to 50% off
BRAND NAMES: Buttermaid, Dolly Madison, Butternut, Vitners
SALE DAYS: Wednesday, extra 10% off
SPECIAL DISCOUNTS: senior citizens, 10% off
PARKING: street
PAYMENT: cash, checks (amount of purchase only, with proper I.D.)

Butternut Bread Thrift Store, 40 E. Garfield Boulevard, Chicago, IL 60615; (312)
536-7700
This is one of many outlets for Butternut bread, Hostess snack cakes, and Vitners
chips. Some of the outlets also carry Dolly Madison products, Roman Meal bread, and
Sun-Maid raisin bread. Savings average 30%–50% off retail price, and go as high as
75% on day-old items. They also have stores in Arlington Heights, Calumet City, Elgin,
Joliet, Lansing, Lombard, Markham, Naperville, Northlake, Rockford, Schaumburg,
Waukegan, and Woodstock, Illinois; and one in Gary, Indiana.

SUN.	MON.	TUE.	WED.	THU.	FRI.	SAT.
9–5	7:30–8	7:30–8	7:30–8	7:30–8	7:30–8	7:30–8

SAVINGS: 10%–75% off
BRAND NAMES: Butternut, Hostess, Vitners

SPECIAL DISCOUNTS: senior citizens, 10% off
PARKING: lot
PAYMENT: cash only

The Cookie Jar, 4474 N. Harlem Avenue, Chicago, IL 60656; (312) 456-6500
This is the outlet for Maurice Lenell cookies. Discounts are up to 50% off retail price on 1½-pound ($2.30–$2.55) and 2-pound ($2.99–$3.15) boxes of cookies. Assorted buckets are even less. Bags of broken cookies are $1.25/lb. Most items are first quality, but some seconds, broken pieces, and test runs are occasionally available. Enjoy the free samples on the counter.

SUN.	MON.	TUE.	WED.	THU.	FRI.	SAT.
9-5	8-9:30	8-9:30	8-9:30	8-9:30	8-9:30	8-6

SAVINGS: up to 25% off
BRAND NAMES: Maurice Lenell
PARKING: lot
PAYMENT: cash, checks (amount of purchase only, with proper I.D.)

Delicious Cookie Company Thrift Store, 1001 W. North Avenue, Chicago, IL 60622; (312) 664-5900
This small factory outlet offers cookies and crackers at about 40% off retail price. They also sell broken pieces at even greater savings, and empty cookie tins.

SUN.	MON.	TUE.	WED.	THU.	FRI.	SAT.
closed	9-5:30	9-5:30	9-5:30	9-5:30	9-5:30	closed

SAVINGS: 40%–50% off
BRAND NAMES: Delicious, Hearthside
SPECIAL SALES: weekly
SPECIAL DISCOUNTS: charity organizations get additional discount in quantity
PARKING: lot
PAYMENT: cash, checks (with proper I.D. and major credit card, no out-of-state checks)

Dolly Madison Cakes Outlet, 2925 W. Montrose Avenue, Chicago, IL 60618; (312) 478-5063
This is an outlet for Buttermaid and Butternut breads as well as Dolly Madison snack cakes and cookies. Typical discounts are 25%–60% off retail. Examples: bread 25%–50% off, buns 50% off, stuffing 50% off, snack cakes 60% off, donuts 50% off, pies 30% off. They also sell croutons, bread crumbs, Barrel O Fun chips, and Sather's candies at retail prices. Most merchandise is first quality, with some day-old, end of code, and test runs occasionally available at a greater savings. See also Buttermaid bread above.

SUN.	MON.	TUE.	WED.	THU.	FRI.	SAT.
10-3	9-7	9-7	9-7	9-7	9-7	9-6

SAVINGS: up to 60% off
BRAND NAMES: Dolly Madison, Butternut, Buttermaid
PARKING: lot
PAYMENT: cash only

Dolly Madison Cakes Outlet, 40 E. Garfield Boulevard, Chicago, IL 60615; (312) 536-7700
See listing above.

SUN.	MON.	TUE.	WED.	THU.	FRI.	SAT.
9-5	7:30-8	7:30-8	7:30-8	7:30-8	7:30-8	8-6

SAVINGS: up to 50% off
BRAND NAMES: Dolly Madison, Butternut
PARKING: lot
PAYMENT: cash, food stamps

Dolly Madison Cakes Outlet, 1857 W. 35th Street, Chicago, IL 60609; (312) 927-6014
See listing above.

SUN.	MON.	TUE.	WED.	THU.	FRI.	SAT.
closed	9–6	9–6	9–6	9–6	9–6	9–5

SAVINGS: up to 50% off
BRAND NAMES: Dolly Madison, Butternut, Buttermaid
SALE DAYS: Wednesday, Saturday, two-for-one
SPECIAL DISCOUNTS: senior citizens, 10% off
PARKING: street
PAYMENT: cash, food stamps

Dressel's Budget Bakery, 5859 W. Irving Park Road, Chicago, IL 60634; (312) 685-4124
This is the outlet for Dressel's bakeries. A large assortment of frozen bakery and other foods is available at savings from 15%–60% off retail price. Dressel's cakes are discounted 25%–60%, pies 15%, Tango tamales and chili 15%, Maurice Lenell cookies 25%, Butternut bread 10%–30%. They also carry frozen entrées, chicken kiev, and pizza. Most merchandise is first quality and overruns, and all seconds, irregulars, etc., are clearly marked. They have other outlets in Chicago, Oak Lawn, and Willowbrook, Illinois.

SUN.	MON.	TUE.	WED.	THU.	FRI.	SAT.
9:30–3	9:30–6	9:30–6	9:30–6	9:30–6	9:30–6	9–5:30

SAVINGS: 15%–60% off
BRAND NAMES: Dressel's, Butternut, Maurice Lenell, Tango
SPECIAL DISCOUNTS: church groups, extra 10% off
PARKING: lot
PAYMENT: cash, checks (amount of purchase only, with proper I.D., no out-of-state checks)

Dressel's Budget Bakery, 6630 S. Ashland Avenue, Chicago, IL 60629; (312) 434-5300
See listing above.

SUN.	MON.	TUE.	WED.	THU.	FRI.	SAT.
closed	9–5:30	9–5:30	9–5:30	9–5:30	9–5:30	9–5

SAVINGS: 50%–60% off
BRAND NAMES: Dressel's, Butternut, Maurice Lenell, Tango
PARKING: street, meters
PAYMENT: cash only

Eli's Factory Outlet, 6510 W. Dakin, Chicago, IL 60634; (312) 736-3481
This is the factory outlet for Eli's Cheesecake and Muffins. At this writing, seconds were $4.50 for 6" cheesecakes, $8.00 for plain 9", and $8.50 for fancy 9" cheesecakes. Muffins were 75¢. They have another outlet, called Eli's Cheesecake and Muffin Store in Vernon Hills, Illinois, where the prices are similar on seconds and still about 20%–30% off retail price on first quality items.

SUN.	MON.	TUE.	WED.	THU.	FRI.	SAT.
closed	9–4	9–4	9–4	9–4	9–4	9–1

SAVINGS: 35%–60% off
BRAND NAMES: Eli's
SPECIAL SALES: vary, monthly
SPECIAL DISCOUNTS: senior citizens, $1.00 off total purchase on Monday
PARKING: street
PAYMENT: cash only

Flavor Kist—Schulze & Burch Biscuit Company, 1133 W. 35th Street, Chicago, IL 60609; (312) 927-6622

This is the factory outlet for Flavor Kist cookies. Savings average 40%–80% off retail price.

SUN.	MON.	TUE.	WED.	THU.	FRI.	SAT.
closed	8–7:30	8–7:30	8–7:30	8–7:30	8–7:30	8–4

SAVINGS: 40%–80% off   *All First Quality*
PARKING: street, meters
PAYMENT: cash, food stamps

Holsum Bread Outlet, 3230 N. Milwaukee Avenue, Chicago, IL 60618; (312) 725-3399
This is the factory outlet for Holsum bread. Savings range from 35% off retail price for first quality merchandise to 75% for day-old bread. They have other stores in Glen Ellyn, Niles, and Oak Lawn, Illinois.

SUN.	MON.	TUE.	WED.	THU.	FRI.	SAT.
closed	9–8:30	9–8:30	9–8:30	9–8:30	9–8:30	9–6

SAVINGS: up to 50% off
BRAND NAMES: Holsum, Pate, Yo Ho, Blue Bird
PARKING: lot
PAYMENT: cash only

Hostess Cakes Outlet, 5702 W. 55th Street, Chicago, IL 60638; (312) 585-7474
This is the outlet for Hostess snack cakes as well as Wonder bread. Savings begin at 20% off retail price and rise to 40% on seconds and day-old merchandise. They have another store in Schiller Park, Illinois. (See also Wonder bread outlets.)

SUN.	MON.	TUE.	WED.	THU.	FRI.	SAT.
closed	9–5	9–5	9–5	9–5	9–5	9–5

SAVINGS: 25%–40% off
BRAND NAMES: Hostess, Wonder
SALE DAYS: Wednesday, Saturday
PARKING: lot
PAYMENT: cash, checks (amount of purchase only, with proper I.D.)

Kitchens of Sara Lee Thrift Store, 7654 W. Touhy Avenue, Chicago, IL 60648; (312) 763-4785
This is an outlet for Sara Lee baked goods. Savings begin at 15% off retail price, and can rise to 50%. Look for the tags, which show special buys. Seconds usually indicate incorrect packaging. Ask on which day the items that you particularly like will be on sale; the clerk usually knows. They also have outlets in Deerfield and Downers Grove, Illinois; Whiting, Indiana; and Madison, Wisconsin.

SUN.	MON.	TUE.	WED.	THU.	FRI.	SAT.
closed	9–6	9–6	9–6	9–6	9–7	9–5

SAVINGS: up to 50% off
BRAND NAMES: Sara Lee
SPECIAL DISCOUNTS: senior citizens, 10% off Wednesday
PARKING: lot
PAYMENT: cash, checks (amount of purchase only, with proper I.D.)

Wonder Bread Thrift Store, 1301 W. Diversey Parkway, Chicago, IL 60614; (312) 281-6700
This is the factory outlet for Wonder bread and Hostess snack cakes. Savings average 20%–50% off retail price on first quality and day-old merchandise. They have other outlets in River Grove and Schiller Park, Illinois. See also Hostess outlets.

SUN.	MON.	TUE.	WED.	THU.	FRI.	SAT.
closed	9–6	9–6	9–6	9–6	9–6	9–5

SAVINGS: 20%–50% off
BRAND NAMES: Wonder, Hostess
SALE DAYS: Wednesday, Saturday
PARKING: lot
PAYMENT: cash, checks (amount of purchase only, with proper I.D.), food stamps

ADDISON, IL

Dolly Madison Cakes Outlet, 515 S. Addison Road, Addison, IL 60101; (312) 832-7230

See listings under both Dolly Madison and Butternut bread in Chicago, Illinois.

SUN.	MON.	TUE.	WED.	THU.	FRI.	SAT.
closed	9–6	9–6	9–6	9–6	9–6	9–6

SAVINGS: up to 50% off
SPECIAL DISCOUNTS: senior citizens, 10% off
PARKING: lot
PAYMENT: cash, checks (amount of purchase only, with proper I.D., no out-of-state checks)

ARLINGTON HEIGHTS, IL

Butternut Bread Thrift Store, 1025 E. Algonquin Road, Arlington Heights, IL 60004; (312) 593-9737

See listing in Chicago, Illinois.

SUN.	MON.	TUE.	WED.	THU.	FRI.	SAT.
10–3	9–7	9–7	9–7	9–7	9–7	9–5

SAVINGS: 10%–75% off
BRAND NAMES: Butternut, Vitners, Sathers
SALE DAYS: Tuesday, Friday
SPECIAL DISCOUNTS: senior citizens, 10% off
PARKING: lot
PAYMENT: cash, checks (with proper I.D.), MasterCard

BERWYN, IL

Heinemann's Bakeries Surplus Store, 7059 W. Cermak Avenue, Berwyn, IL 60402; (312) 749-8499

This outlet sells Heinemann's breads, rolls, cakes, and cookies at savings up to 60% off. Most merchandise is end of code. They also have stores in Franklin Park and Oak Lawn, Illinois.

SUN.	MON.	TUE.	WED.	THU.	FRI.	SAT.
11–3	9–6	9–6	9–6	9–6	9–6	9–5

SAVINGS: 10%–60% off
BRAND NAMES: Heinemann's
SALE DAYS: senior citizens, free loaf of bread with a $3 purchase on Monday and Tuesday
PARKING: lot
PAYMENT: cash only

BLUE ISLAND, IL

Party Cookies, 13153 S. Francisco Street, Blue Island, IL 60406; (312) 371-9200

This is an outlet for Party Cookies. They also sell whole-grain crackers, birthday cakes, and petit fours. Savings average 10%–30% off retail price. They sell mostly surplus, overruns, and broken pieces.

SUN.	MON.	TUE.	WED.	THU.	FRI.	SAT.
closed	8:30–5	8:30–5	8:30–5	8:30–5	8:30–5	closed

SAVINGS: 10%–30% off
BRAND NAMES: Party Cookies
ANNUAL SALES: holiday
SPECIAL DISCOUNTS: senior citizens, 10% off
PARKING: lot
PAYMENT: cash only

CALUMET CITY, IL

Butternut Bread Thrift Store, 1525 Sibley Boulevard, Calumet City, IL 60409; (312) 862-1711
See listing in Chicago, Illinois.

SUN.	MON.	TUE.	WED.	THU.	FRI.	SAT.
closed	9-7	9-7	9-7	9-7	9-7	9-6

SAVINGS: 10%–75% off
BRAND NAMES: Butternut, Dolly Madison, Vitners
SALE DAYS: Tuesday and Friday, two-for-one on selected items
SPECIAL DISCOUNTS: senior citizens, 50% off
PARKING: lot
PAYMENT: cash, food stamps

DEERFIELD, IL

Kitchens of Sara Lee Thrift Store, 500 Waukegan Road, Deerfield, IL 60015; (312) 945-2525
See listing in Chicago, Illinois.

SUN.	MON.	TUE.	WED.	THU.	FRI.	SAT.
closed	9-6	9-6	9-6	9-6	9-6	9-5

SAVINGS: 15%–40% off
BRAND NAMES: Sara Lee
SALE DAYS: weekly
SPECIAL DISCOUNTS: senior citizens, 10% off Wednesday
PARKING: lot
PAYMENT: cash, checks (amount of purchase only, with proper I.D., no out-of-state checks)

DOWNERS GROVE, IL

Kitchens of Sara Lee Thrift Store, 2223 W. Ogden Avenue, Downers Grove, IL 60515; (312) 852-5977
See listing in Chicago, Illinois.

SUN.	MON.	TUE.	WED.	THU.	FRI.	SAT.
closed	9-6	9-6	9-6	9-6	9-6	9-5

SAVINGS: 15%–40% off
BRAND NAMES: Sara Lee
SPECIAL DISCOUNTS: senior citizens, 10% off Wednesday
PARKING: lot
PAYMENT: cash, checks (amount of purchase only, with proper I.D., no out-of-state checks)

Pepperidge Farm Outlet, 744 Ogden Avenue, Downers Grove, IL 60515; (312) 964-6380
This is the outlet for Pepperidge Farm breads and rolls. They also sell some dessert items and croutons at savings of 25% off retail price on first quality and 50% on day-old and overstocked items. They also sell Luycks vinegar, mustards, and Campbell soups. They have other stores in Flossmoor, Geneva, Highland Park, Niles, Oak Lawn, and Schaumburg, Illinois; and in Milwaukee, Wisconsin.

SUN.	MON.	TUE.	WED.	THU.	FRI.	SAT.
10-3	9-6	9-6	9-6	9-8	9-6	9-5

SAVINGS: 20%–50% off
BRAND NAMES: Pepperidge Farm, Campbell
SPECIAL DISCOUNTS: senior citizens, 10% off Monday, Wednesday
PARKING: lot
PAYMENT: cash, checks (amount of purchase only, with proper I.D.)

ELGIN, IL

Butternut Bread Thrift Store, 812 E. Chicago Avenue, Elgin, IL 60120; (312) 888-9255
See listing in Chicago, Illinois.

SUN.	MON.	TUE.	WED.	THU.	FRI.	SAT.
9-2	9-7	9-7	9-7	9-7	9-7	9-5

SAVINGS: 10%–75% off
BRAND NAMES: Butternut, Dolly Madison, Vitners
SALE DAYS: Tuesday, 10% off; Friday, two-for-one bread table
SPECIAL DISCOUNTS: senior citizens, 10% off
PARKING: lot
PAYMENT: cash, checks, food stamps

FLOSSMOOR, IL

Pepperidge Farm Outlet, 3315 Vollmer Road, Flossmoor, IL 60422; (312) 798-2223
See listing in Downers Grove, Illinois.

SUN.	MON.	TUE.	WED.	THU.	FRI.	SAT.
11-5	9-6	9-6	9-6	9-6	9-6	9-5

SAVINGS: 20%–50% off
BRAND NAMES: Pepperidge Farm, Campbell
SPECIAL DISCOUNTS: senior citizens, 10% off Monday, Wednesday
PARKING: lot
PAYMENT: cash, checks (amount of purchase only, with proper I.D., no out-of-state checks)

FRANKLIN PARK, IL

Heinemann's Bakeries Surplus Store, 10219 Grand Avenue, Franklin Park, IL 60131; (312) 451-0230
See listing in Berwyn, Illinois.

SUN.	MON.	TUE.	WED.	THU.	FRI.	SAT.
10-4	9-7	9-7	9-7	9-7	9-7	9-6

SAVINGS: 10%–60% off
BRAND NAMES: Heinemann's
SPECIAL DISCOUNTS: senior citizens get a free loaf of bread with a $3 purchase Monday, Tuesday
PARKING: lot
PAYMENT: cash only

GENEVA, IL

Pepperidge Farm Outlet, 625 W. State Street, Geneva, IL 60134; (312) 232-4447
See listing in Downers Grove, Illinois.

SUN.	MON.	TUE.	WED.	THU.	FRI.	SAT.
11-5	9-6	9-6	9-6	9-6	9-6	9-5

SAVINGS: 20%–50% off
BRAND NAMES: Pepperidge Farm, Campbell

SPECIAL DISCOUNTS: senior citizens, 10% off Monday, Wednesday
PARKING: lot
PAYMENT: cash, checks (amount of purchase only, with proper I.D., no out-of-state checks)

GLEN ELLYN, IL

Holsum Bread Outlet, 727 Roosevelt Road, Glen Ellyn, IL 60137; (312) 261-2424
See listing in Chicago, Illinois.

SUN.	MON.	TUE.	WED.	THU.	FRI.	SAT.
10-6	9-8:30	9-8:30	9-8:30	9-8:30	9-8:30	9-6

SAVINGS: 30%-65% off
BRAND NAMES: Holsum
PARKING: lot
PAYMENT: cash only

HIGHLAND PARK, IL

Pepperidge Farm Outlet, 1290 Deerfield Road, Highland Park, IL 60035; (312) 831-3040
See listing in Downers Grove, Illinois.

SUN.	MON.	TUE.	WED.	THU.	FRI.	SAT.
11-5	9-6	9-6	9-6	9-6	9-6	9-5

SAVINGS: 20%-50% off
BRAND NAMES: Pepperidge Farm, Campbell
SPECIAL DISCOUNTS: senior citizens, 10% off Monday, Wednesday
PARKING: lot
PAYMENT: cash, checks (amount of purchase only, with proper I.D.)

HILLSIDE, IL

Buttermaid Bakeries Thrift Store, 4751 Butterfield Road, Hillside, IL 61257; (312) 547-9167
See listing in Chicago, Illinois.

SUN.	MON.	TUE.	WED.	THU.	FRI.	SAT.
10-2	9-6	9-6	9-6	9-6	9-6	9-5

SAVINGS: 30%-50% off
BRAND NAMES: Buttermaid, Dolly Madison, Beatrice
SALE DAYS: Wednesday, two-for-one on bread only
SPECIAL DISCOUNTS: senior citizens, 10% off
PARKING: lot
PAYMENT: cash, checks (amount of purchase only, with proper I.D.), food stamps

JOLIET, IL

Butternut Bread Thrift Store, 2239 W. Jefferson Street, Joliet, IL 60434; (815) 744-6872
See listing in Chicago, Illinois.

SUN.	MON.	TUE.	WED.	THU.	FRI.	SAT.
10-2	9-7	9-7	9-8	9-8	9-8	9-6

SAVINGS: 10%-75% off
BRAND NAMES: Butternut, Dolly Madison, Vitners
SALE DAYS: Tuesday, 10% off total purchase
SPECIAL DISCOUNTS: senior citizens, 10% off
PARKING: lot
PAYMENT: cash only

Dolly Madison Cakes Outlet, 1524 Nicholson Street, Joliet, IL 60434; (815) 726-5626
See listings under both Dolly Madison and Butternut Bread in Chicago, Illinois.

SUN.	MON.	TUE.	WED.	THU.	FRI.	SAT.
10–2	9–6	9–6	9–6	9–6	9–6	9–5

SAVINGS: 10%–50% off
BRAND NAMES: Dolly Madison, Butternut, Vitners, Mothers, Millstone
SPECIAL SALES: vary
SPECIAL DISCOUNTS: senior citizens, 10% off
PARKING: lot
PAYMENT: cash, checks

KANKAKEE, IL

Buttermaid Bakeries Thrift Store, 1271 S. Washington Avenue, Kankakee, IL 60901;
(815) 939-9393
See listing in Chicago, Illinois.

SUN.	MON.	TUE.	WED.	THU.	FRI.	SAT.
closed	9–6	9–6	9–6	9–6	9–6	9–6

SAVINGS: 30%–50% off
BRAND NAMES: Buttermaid, Dolly Madison
SALE DAYS: Wednesday, 10% off
SPECIAL DISCOUNTS: senior citizens, 10% off
PARKING: lot
PAYMENT: cash, checks (amount of purchase only, with proper I.D.)

LA GRANGE PARK, IL

Brownberry Ovens Thrift Store, 1103 E. 31st Street, La Grange Park, IL 60525;
(312) 482-8384
This is one of many outlets for Brownberry Ovens bakery products. They also sell
Health Valley cereals, crackers, and snacks, Maurice Lenell cookies, El Molino salad
dressing, and Nature's Choice granola bars and fruit bars. Savings are greatest on
Brownberry products, and approach 50% off retail price on seconds, surplus, overruns,
and day-old merchandise. They have other stores in Oak Lawn, and Prospect Heights,
Illinois; Indianapolis, Indiana; and Brookfield, Madison, and Oconomowoc, Wisconsin.

SUN.	MON.	TUE.	WED.	THU.	FRI.	SAT.
closed	9–5:30	9–5:30	9–5:30	9–5:30	9–5:30	9–5:30

SAVINGS: 10%–50% off
BRAND NAMES: Brownberry, Health Valley, El Molino, Maurice Lenell, Penn Dutch,
Honey Acres
SALE DAYS: Tuesday
SPECIAL DISCOUNTS: senior citizens, 10% off Brownberry products only
PARKING: lot
PAYMENT: cash, checks (amount of purchase only, with proper I.D.)

LANSING, IL

Butternut Bread Thrift Store, 17801 Torrence Avenue, Lansing, IL 60438; (312)
895-1480
See listing in Chicago, Illinois.

SUN.	MON.	TUE.	WED.	THU.	FRI.	SAT.
closed	9–7	9–7	9–7	9–7	9–7	9–6

SAVINGS: 10%–75% off
BRAND NAMES: Butternut, Dolly Madison
SALE DAYS: Wednesday, 10% off
SPECIAL DISCOUNTS: senior citizens, 10% off
PARKING: lot
PAYMENT: cash, checks (amount of purchase only, with proper I.D.)

Entenmann's Thrift Bakery, 6849 N. Lincoln Avenue, Lincolnwood, IL 60646; (312) 674-7151

This is an outlet for Entenmann's baked goods. They have an interesting pricing system. "Red line" items are 25% off retail price, all "black line" items are 40% off, and all "green line" items are 50% off. On Wednesday, however, all "black line" items are 50% off, which in general means savings are greatest on seconds, irregulars, and day-old items. They have other stores in Morton Grove, Northlake, Oak Lawn, and Schaumburg, Illinois.

SUN.	MON.	TUE.	WED.	THU.	FRI.	SAT.
9-2	9-7	9-7	9-7	9-7	9-7	9-6

SAVINGS: 25%–50% off
BRAND NAMES: Entenmann's
SALE DAYS: Wednesday
PARKING: lot
PAYMENT: cash, checks (amount of purchase only, with proper I.D.)

Butternut Bread Thrift Store, 925 E. St. Charles Road, Lombard, IL 60148; (312) 620-9693

See listing in Chicago, Illinois.

SUN.	MON.	TUE.	WED.	THU.	FRI.	SAT.
10-3	9-8	9-8	9-8	9-8	9-8	9-5

SAVINGS: 10%–75% off
BRAND NAMES: Dolly Madison, Butternut, Vitners
SALE DAYS: Wednesday, 10% off
SPECIAL DISCOUNTS: senior citizens, 10% off
PARKING: lot
PAYMENT: cash, checks

Butternut Bread Thrift Store, 2920 W. 159th Street, Markham, IL 60426; (312) 333-9819

See listing in Chicago, Illinois.

SUN.	MON.	TUE.	WED.	THU.	FRI.	SAT.
closed	9-6	9-6	9-6	9-6	9-6	9-5

SAVINGS: 10%–75% off
BRAND NAMES: Butternut, Dolly Madison, Vitners
SALE DAYS: Wednesday, 10% off selected items
SPECIAL DISCOUNTS: senior citizens, 10% off
PARKING: lot
PAYMENT: cash, food stamps

Entenmann's Thrift Bakery, 6947 W. Dempster Street, Morton Grove, IL 60053; (312) 967-9420

See listing in Lincolnwood, Illinois.

SUN.	MON.	TUE.	WED.	THU.	FRI.	SAT.
9-2	9-7	9-7	9-7	9-7	9-7	9-6

SAVINGS: 10%–50% off
BRAND NAMES: Entenmann's
SALE DAYS: Wednesday
PARKING: lot
PAYMENT: cash, checks (amount of purchase only, with proper I.D.)

Buttermaid Bakeries Thrift Store, 437 N. Lake Street, Mundelein, IL 60060; (312) 949-9690
See listing in Chicago, Illinois.

SUN.	MON.	TUE.	WED.	THU.	FRI.	SAT.
10–2	9–7	9–7	9–7	9–7	9–7	9–5

SAVINGS: up to 50% off
BRAND NAMES: Buttermaid, Butternut, Vitners, Milbrook, Dolly Madison
SALE DAYS: Tuesday, 10% off; Friday, two-for-one on overstocks
SPECIAL DISCOUNTS: senior citizens, 10% off
PARKING: lot
PAYMENT: cash, checks (amount of purchase only, with proper I.D.)

Butternut Bread Thrift Store, 1111 E. Ogden Avenue, Naperville, IL 60540; (312) 355-6768
See listing in Chicago, Illinois.

SUN.	MON.	TUE.	WED.	THU.	FRI.	SAT.
10–3	9–8	9–8	9–8	9–8	9–8	9–6

SAVINGS: 10%–75% off
BRAND NAMES: Butternut, Dolly Madison, Vitners
SALE DAYS: Wednesday, 10% off
SPECIAL DISCOUNTS: senior citizens, 10%
PARKING: lot
PAYMENT: cash, checks (amount of purchase only, with proper I.D.)

Holsum Bread Outlet, 9207 N. Milwaukee Avenue, Niles, IL 60648; (312) 965-8080
See listing in Chicago, Illinois.

SUN.	MON.	TUE.	WED.	THU.	FRI.	SAT.
10–6	9–9	closed	closed	closed	9–9	9–6

SAVINGS: 30%–50% off
BRAND NAMES: Holsum
PARKING: lot
PAYMENT: cash only

Pepperidge Farm Outlet, 312 Lawrencewood Shopping Center, Waukegan Road and Oakton Street, Niles, IL 60648; (312) 965-5333
See listing in Downers Grove, Illinois.

SUN.	MON.	TUE.	WED.	THU.	FRI.	SAT.
11–4	9:30–6	9:30–6	9:30–6	9:30–6	9:30–6	9–5

SAVINGS: up to 50% off
BRAND NAMES: Pepperidge Farm, Campbell, Luycks
SPECIAL DISCOUNTS: senior citizens, 10% off Monday, Wednesday
PARKING: lot
PAYMENT: cash, checks (amount of purchase only, with proper I.D., no out-of-state checks), Mastercard, VISA

Salerno/Megowen Biscuit Company Thrift Store, 7777 N. Caldwell Avenue, Niles, IL 60648; (312) 967-4132
This factory outlet sells Salerno cookies and crackers. They also sell Mama's and Burry-Lu cookies. Prices average 20% off retail and go higher on irregulars and broken pieces. Be sure to try the free samples on the counter.

SUN.	MON.	TUE.	WED.	THU.	FRI.	SAT.
closed	9–5:30	9–5:30	9–5:30	9–5:30	9–5:30	9–3

SAVINGS: 20% off
BRAND NAMES: Salerno, Mama's, Burry-Lu
PARKING: lot
PAYMENT: cash only

NORRIDGE, IL

La Française Croissant, 7220 W. Agatite Avenue, Norridge, IL 60656; (312) 453-7400
A small counter in the front of the factory sells La Française croissants at savings of 30%–50% off retail price. They occasionally have day-old croissants. All products are "all butter."

SUN.	MON.	TUE.	WED.	THU.	FRI.	SAT.
closed	8–7	8–7	8–7	8–7	8–7	9–5

SAVINGS: 20%–50% off
BRAND NAMES: La Française
PARKING: lot
PAYMENT: cash, checks (with proper I.D.)

NORTHLAKE, IL

Butternut Bread Thrift Store, 385 E. North Avenue, Northlake, IL 60164; (312) 681-9255
See listing in Chicago, Illinois.

SUN.	MON.	TUE.	WED.	THU.	FRI.	SAT.
11–3	9:30–6	9:30–6	9:30–6	9:30–6	9:30–6	9–5

SAVINGS: 10%–75% off
BRAND NAMES: Butternut, Dolly Madison
SALE DAYS: Wednesday, 10% off
SPECIAL DISCOUNTS: senior citizens, 10% off
PARKING: lot
PAYMENT: cash, checks, food stamps

Entenmann's Thrift Bakery, 300 W. North Avenue, Northlake, IL 60164; (312) 562-6311
See listing in Lincolnwood, Illinois.

SUN.	MON.	TUE.	WED.	THU.	FRI.	SAT.
9–2	9–7	9–7	9–7	9–7	9–7	9–6

SAVINGS: 25%–50% off
BRAND NAMES: Entenmann's
SALE DAYS: Wednesday
PARKING: lot
PAYMENT: cash, checks (amount of purchase only, with proper I.D.)

OAK LAWN, IL

Brownberry Ovens Thrift Store, 4038 W. 111th Street, Oak Lawn, IL 60453; (312) 499-2128
See listing in La Grange Park, Illinois.

SUN.	MON.	TUE.	WED.	THU.	FRI.	SAT.
closed	9–6	9–6	9–6	9–6	9–6	9–5

SAVINGS: 10%–50% off
BRAND NAMES: Brownberry, Maurice Lenell, Health Valley
SALE DAYS: Tuesday, 10% off Brownberry products only

SPECIAL DISCOUNTS: senior citizens, 10% off
PARKING: lot
PAYMENT: cash, checks (amount of purchase only, with proper I.D.)

Dressel's Budget Bakery, 9024 S. Cicero Avenue, Oak Lawn, IL 60453; (312) 857-9006
See listing in Chicago, Illinois.

SUN.	MON.	TUE.	WED.	THU.	FRI.	SAT.
9:30-3	9:30-6	9:30-6	9:30-6	9:30-6	9:30-6	9:30-5

SAVINGS: 50%-60% off
BRAND NAMES: Dressel's, Butternut, Maurice Lenell, Tango
SPECIAL SALES: every two or three weeks
SPECIAL DISCOUNTS: senior citizens, Wednesday
PARKING: lot
PAYMENT: cash, checks (amount of purchase only, with proper I.D., maximum $300)

Entenmann's Thrift Bakery, 10800 S. Cicero Avenue, Oak Lawn, IL 60453; (312) 857-7151
See listing in Lincolnwood, Illinois.

SUN.	MON.	TUE.	WED.	THU.	FRI.	SAT.
9-2	9-7	9-7	9-7	9-7	9-7	9-6

SAVINGS: 25%-50% off
BRAND NAMES: Entenmann's
SALE DAYS: Wednesday, 50% off
PARKING: lot
PAYMENT: cash, checks (amount of purchase only, with proper I.D.)

Heinemann's Bakeries Surplus Store, 8747 S. Ridgeland Avenue, Oak Lawn, IL 60453; (312) 598-3399
See listing in Berwyn, Illinois.

SUN.	MON.	TUE.	WED.	THU.	FRI.	SAT.
9-1	9-6	9-6	9-6	9-6	9-6	9-5

SAVINGS: 10%-33% off
BRAND NAMES: Heinemann's
SPECIAL DISCOUNTS: senior citizens, one item free on Monday and Tuesday with a $3.00 purchase
PARKING: lot
PAYMENT: cash only

Holsum Bread Outlet, 5000 W. 111th Street, Oak Lawn, IL 60453; (312) 581-4232
See listing in Chicago, Illinois.

SUN.	MON.	TUE.	WED.	THU.	FRI.	SAT.
10-6	8:30-8	8:30-8	8:30-8	8:30-8	8:30-8	8:30-5

SAVINGS: 35%-65% off
BRAND NAMES: Holsum
PARKING: lot
PAYMENT: cash only

Pepperidge Farm Outlet, 9900 Southwest Highway, Oak Lawn, IL 60453; (312) 424-5655
See listing in Downers Grove, Illinois.

SUN.	MON.	TUE.	WED.	THU.	FRI.	SAT.
11-5	9-6	9-6	9-6	9-6	9-6	9-5

SAVINGS: 20%-50% off
BRAND NAMES: Pepperidge Farm, Campbell

SPECIAL DISCOUNTS: senior citizens, 10% off Monday, Wednesday
PARKING: lot
PAYMENT: cash, checks (amount of purchase only, with proper I.D., no out-of-state checks)

PROSPECT HEIGHTS, IL

Brownberry Ovens Thrift Store, 2 E. Camp McDonald Road, Prospect Heights, IL 60070; (312) 392-8874
See listing in La Grange Park, Illinois.

SUN.	MON.	TUE.	WED.	THU.	FRI.	SAT.
closed	9-6	9-6	9-5	9-6	9-6	9-5

SAVINGS: 10%–50% off
BRAND NAMES: Brownberry, Maurice Lenell, Health Valley
SALE DAYS: Tuesday, 10% off Brownberry products only
SPECIAL DISCOUNTS: senior citizens, 10% off
PARKING: lot
PAYMENT: cash, checks (amount of purchase only, with proper I.D.)

RIVER GROVE, IL

Wonder Bread—Hostess Cake Thrift Store, 2150 West Street, River Grove, IL 60171; (312) 625-7666
See listing in Chicago, Illinois.

SUN.	MON.	TUE.	WED.	THU.	FRI.	SAT.
closed	9-5	9-5	9-5	9-5	9-5	9-5

SAVINGS: 35%–50% off
BRAND NAMES: Wonder, Hostess
SALE DAYS: Wednesday, Saturday
PARKING: lot
PAYMENT: cash, checks (amount of purchase only, with proper I.D.)

ROCKFORD, IL

Butternut Bread Thrift Store, 2744 S. 11th Street, Rockford, IL 61109; (815) 397-9898
See listing in Chicago, Illinois.

SUN.	MON.	TUE.	WED.	THU.	FRI.	SAT.
closed	9-6	9-6	9-6	9-6	9-6	9-5

SAVINGS: 10%–75% off
BRAND NAMES: Butternut, Dolly Madison
SALE DAYS: Tuesday, Friday, two-for-one
SPECIAL DISCOUNTS: senior citizens, 10% off
PARKING: lot
PAYMENT: cash, checks (amount of purchase only, with proper I.D., no out-of-state checks), food stamps

SCHAUMBURG, IL

Butternut Bread Thrift Store, 1624 Wise Road, Schaumburg, IL 60193; (312) 894-9606
See listing in Chicago, Illinois.

SUN.	MON.	TUE.	WED.	THU.	FRI.	SAT.
10-4	9-7	9-8	9-7	9-7	9-7	9-6

SAVINGS: 10%–75% off
BRAND NAMES: Butternut, Roman Meal, Sun-Maid, Vitners
SALE DAYS: Tuesday, 10% off; Friday, two-for-one (selected items)

SPECIAL DISCOUNTS: senior citizens and tax-free, non-profit organizations, 10% off
PARKING: lot
PAYMENT: cash, checks (amount of purchase only, with proper I.D.), food stamps

Entenmann's Thrift Bakery, 275 W. Golf Road, Schaumburg, IL 60195; (312) 884-9049
    See listing in Lincolnwood, Illinois.

SUN.	MON.	TUE.	WED.	THU.	FRI.	SAT.
9-2	9-7	9-7	9-7	9-7	9-7	9-6

SAVINGS: 25%–50% off
BRAND NAMES: Entenmann's
SALE DAYS: Wednesday
PARKING: lot
PAYMENT: cash, checks (amount of purchase only, with proper I.D.)

Pepperidge Farm Outlet, 1033 E. Golf Road, Schaumburg, IL 60172; (312) 882-0242
    See listing in Downers Grove, Illinois.

SUN.	MON.	TUE.	WED.	THU.	FRI.	SAT.
11-4	9-6	9-6	9-6	9-6	9-6	9-5

SAVINGS: 20%–50% off
BRAND NAMES: Pepperidge Farm, Luycks
SPECIAL DISCOUNTS: senior citizens, 10% off Monday, Wednesday
PARKING: lot
PAYMENT: cash, checks (amount of purchase only, with proper I.D., no out-of-state checks)

SCHILLER PARK, IL

Hostess Cakes Outlet, 9555 Soreng Avenue, Schiller Park, IL 60176; (312) 678-0491
    See Hostess and/or Wonder bread outlets in Chicago, Illinois.

SUN.	MON.	TUE.	WED.	THU.	FRI.	SAT.
closed	9-5	9-5	9-5	9-5	9-5	9-5

SAVINGS: about 25% off
BRAND NAMES: Hostess, Wonder
SALE DAYS: Wednesday, Saturday
PARKING: lot
PAYMENT: cash, checks (amount of purchase only, with proper I.D., no out-of-state checks), MasterCard, VISA

Wonder Bread Thrift Store, 9555 Soreng Street, Schiller Park, IL 60176; (312) 678-0491
    See listing in Chicago, Illinois.

SUN.	MON.	TUE.	WED.	THU.	FRI.	SAT.
closed	9-5	9-5	9-5	9-5	9-5	9-5

SAVINGS: 35%–50% off
BRAND NAMES: Wonder, Hostess
SALE DAYS: Wednesday, Saturday
PARKING: lot
PAYMENT: cash, checks (amount of purchase only, with proper I.D.)

TINLEY PARK, IL

Buttermaid Bakeries Thrift Store, 7547 159th Street, Tinley Park, IL 60477; (312) 532-9646
    See listing in Chicago, Illinois.

SUN.	MON.	TUE.	WED.	THU.	FRI.	SAT.
9-5	9-9	9-9	9-9	9-9	9-9	9-6

SAVINGS: 30%–50% off
BRAND NAMES: Buttermaid, Butternut, Dolly Madison
SALE DAYS: Wednesday, 10% off
SPECIAL DISCOUNTS: senior citizens, 10% off
PARKING: lot
PAYMENT: cash, checks (with proper I.D.)

VERNON HILLS, IL

Eli's Cheesecake and Muffin Store, 908 Hawthorne Center (Routes 22 and 60) (2nd
Floor, Food Court) Vernon Hills, IL 60061; (312) 362-2328
See listing under Eli's Factory Outlet in Chicago, Illinois.

SUN.	MON.	TUE.	WED.	THU.	FRI.	SAT.
10:30–5	9:30–9	9:30–9	9:30–9	9:30–9	9:30–9	9–5:30

SAVINGS: 20%–65% off
BRAND NAMES: Eli's
SPECIAL SALES: vary
PARKING: lot
PAYMENT: cash, checks (amount of purchase only, with proper I.D.), American
Express

WAUKEGAN, IL

Butternut Bread Thrift Store, 2909 Grand Avenue, Waukegan, IL 60085; (312)
336-9876
See listing in Chicago, Illinois.

SUN.	MON.	TUE.	WED.	THU.	FRI.	SAT.
10–3	9–8	9–8	9–8	9–8	9–8	9–5

SAVINGS: 10%–75% off
BRAND NAMES: Butternut, Dolly Madison, Vitners
SALE DAYS: Tuesday, 10% off
SPECIAL DISCOUNTS: senior citizens, 10% off
PARKING: lot
PAYMENT: cash, checks

WILLOWBROOK, IL

Dressel's Budget Bakery, 6940 S. Kingery Road, Willowbrook, IL 60514; (312)
654-4226
See listing in Chicago, Illinois.

SUN.	MON.	TUE.	WED.	THU.	FRI.	SAT.
9:30–3	9:30–6	9:30–6	9:30–6	9:30–6	9:30–6	9–5:30

SAVINGS: 50%–60% off
BRAND NAMES: Dressel's, Butternut, Maurice Lenell, Tango
SALE DAYS: vary
SPECIAL DISCOUNTS: senior citizens, 10% off Wednesday
PARKING: lot
PAYMENT: cash only

WOODSTOCK, IL

Butternut Bread Thrift Store, 1321 S. Route 47, Woodstock, IL 60098; (815)
338-9892
See listing in Chicago, Illinois.

SUN.	MON.	TUE.	WED.	THU.	FRI.	SAT.
10–4	9–8	9–8	9–8	9–8	9–8	9–5

SAVINGS: 20%–50% off
BRAND NAMES: Butternut, Dolly Madison, Vitners

SALE DAYS: Tuesday, Friday, two-for-one on selected items.
SPECIAL DISCOUNTS: senior citizens, 10% off
PARKING: lot
PAYMENT: cash, checks only

ZION, IL

Zion Industries, 27th Street and Ebenezer Avenue, Zion, IL 60099; (312) 872-4581
This factory outlet sells cookies. Savings begin at 10% off retail price on first quality, and go to 40% on seconds.

SUN.	MON.	TUE.	WED.	THU.	FRI.	SAT.
closed	8:45–4	8:45–4	8:45–4	8:45–4	8:45–4	closed

SAVINGS: 10%–40% off
PARKING: lot
PAYMENT: cash, checks (amount of purchase only)

INDIANA

COLUMBUS, IN

Sap's Bakeries, 2741 N. Central Avenue, Columbus, IN 47201; (812) 372-4443
This is the outlet for Sap's donuts. They also sell Butternut bread and Dolly Madison snack cakes. Savings are greatest on day-old items.

SUN.	MON.	TUE.	WED.	THU.	FRI.	SAT.
6:30–9	6–9	6–9	6–9	6–9	6–9	6–9

SAVINGS: 10% off
BRAND NAMES: Sap's, Dolly Madison, Butternut
PARKING: lot
PAYMENT: cash, checks (amount of purchase only, with proper I.D.)

EVANSVILLE, IN

Evansville Colonial Baking Company, 1507 N. Green River Road, Evansville, IN 47715; (812) 479-6934
This factory outlet sells Colonial bread. They also sell chips, dips, crackers, snack cakes, and cookies. Savings average about 50% off retail price.

SUN.	MON.	TUE.	WED.	THU.	FRI.	SAT.
closed	8:30–6	8:30–6	8:30–6	8:30–6	8:30–9	8:30–5

SAVINGS: about 50% off   *Mailing List*
BRAND NAMES: Colonial
SALE DAYS: Tuesday, Saturday
PARKING: lot
PAYMENT: cash, checks

Lewis Bakeries, 500 N. Fulton Street, Evansville, IN 47710; (812) 425-4642
This is an outlet for Country Hearth bread. They also sell Roman Meal bread, rolls, cookies, snack cakes, and chips. Savings start at 20% off retail prices on day-old items.

SUN.	MON.	TUE.	WED.	THU.	FRI.	SAT.
closed	9–5	9–5	9–5	9–5	9–5	9–4

SAVINGS: average 20% off
BRAND NAMES: Country Hearth, Roman Meal, Chesty, Kelly
SALE DAYS: Tuesday
SPECIAL DISCOUNTS: senior citizens, free loaf of bread Thursday
PARKING: lot
PAYMENT: cash, food stamps

Archway Cookie Outlet, 3930 Ferguson Road, Fort Wayne, IN 46899; (219) 747-6136
This is the factory outlet for Archway cookies. They sell first quality cookies for
$1.29/lb. and savings are even greater on seconds, broken pieces, and end of code
merchandise.

SUN.	MON.	TUE.	WED.	THU.	FRI.	SAT.
closed	8-4:30	8-4:30	8-4:30	8-4:30	8-4:30	closed

SAVINGS: 20%–50% off
BRAND NAMES: Archway
PARKING: lot
PAYMENT: cash only

Butternut Bread Thrift Store, 3814 Grant Avenue, Gary, IN 46401; (219) 884-2562
See listing in Chicago, Illinois.

SUN.	MON.	TUE.	WED.	THU.	FRI.	SAT.
closed	9-7	9-7	9-7	9-7	9-7	9-6

SAVINGS: up to 40% off
BRAND NAMES: Butternut, Dolly Madison
SALE DAYS: Wednesday, 10% off
PARKING: lot
PAYMENT: cash, food stamps

Buttermaid Bakeries Thrift Store, 8020 Kennedy Avenue, Highland, IN 46322; (219)
972-0180
See listing in Chicago, Illinois.

SUN.	MON.	TUE.	WED.	THU.	FRI.	SAT.
closed	9-6	9-6	9-6	9-6	9-6	9-5

SAVINGS: at least 25% off
BRAND NAMES: Butternut, Buttermaid, Dolly Madison, Vitners
SALE DAYS: Wednesday, 10% off
SPECIAL DISCOUNTS: senior citizens, 10% off
PARKING: lot
PAYMENT: cash, food stamps

Brownberry Ovens Thrift Store, Nora Plaza Shopping Center, 1300 E. 86th Street,
Indianapolis, IN 46268; (317) 844-8701
See listing in La Grange Park, Illinois.

SUN.	MON.	TUE.	WED.	THU.	FRI.	SAT.
closed	10-6	10-6	10-6	10-6	10-6	10-6

SAVINGS: 10%–50% off
BRAND NAMES: Brownberry
SALE DAYS: vary
PARKING: lot
PAYMENT: cash, checks (amount of purchase only, with proper I.D.)

Roselyn Bakery Surplus Store, 2901 N. Keystone Avenue, Indianapolis, IN 46202;
(317) 925-3605
This outlet sells Roselyn coffee cakes, pastries, pies, cakes, and donuts. Savings
average 50% off retail price on seconds, imperfect, and day-old merchandise.

SUN.	MON.	TUE.	WED.	THU.	FRI.	SAT.
8-6	7-7	7-7	7-7	7-7	7-7	7-7

SAVINGS: 50% off
BRAND NAMES: Roselyn
PARKING: lot
PAYMENT: cash, checks (amount of purchase only, with proper I.D., no out-of-state checks)

Roselyn Bakery Surplus Store, 3702 E. 10th Street, Indianapolis, IN 46206; (317) 635-7778
See listing above.

SUN.	MON.	TUE.	WED.	THU.	FRI.	SAT.
8-6	7-7	7-7	7-7	7-7	7-7	7-7

SAVINGS: 50% off
BRAND NAMES: Roselyn
PARKING: lot
PAYMENT: cash, checks (amount of purchase only, with proper I.D., no out-of-state checks)

MICHIGAN CITY, IN

Parco Foods, 502 U.S. 20 West, Michigan City, IN 46360; (219) 879-4431
See listing under Party Cookies in Blue Island, Illinois.

SUN.	MON.	TUE.	WED.	THU.	FRI.	SAT.
closed	8-4:30	8-4:30	8-4:30	8-4:30	8-4:30	closed

SAVINGS: 10%-30% off
BRAND NAMES: Party Cookies
ANNUAL SALES: Valentine's Day, Easter, 4th of July, Labor Day, Christmas
SPECIAL DISCOUNTS: senior citizens, 10% off
PARKING: lot
PAYMENT: cash only

WHITING, IN

Kitchens of Sara Lee Thrift Store, 1749 Indianapolis Avenue, Whiting, IN 46394; (219) 659-5108
See listing in Chicago, Illinois.

SUN.	MON.	TUE.	WED.	THU.	FRI.	SAT.
closed	9-5:30	9-5:30	9-5:30	9-5:30	9-5:30	9-5

SAVINGS: up to 50% off
BRAND NAMES: Sara Lee
SALE DAYS: Friday
SPECIAL DISCOUNTS: senior citizens, 10% off Wednesday
PARKING: lot
PAYMENT: cash, checks (amount of purchase only, with proper I.D.), food stamps

WISCONSIN
APPLETON, WI

Rich's Bake Shop, 3300 W. College Avenue, Appleton, WI 54914; (414) 739-7063
This factory outlet sells Dick Brothers and Gardner's breads, buns, and rolls. They also sell Little Debbie snack cakes and cookies. Savings begin at 50% off retail price on first quality merchandise, and can go as high as 80% on seconds, day-old, surplus, and overrun merchandise.

SUN.	MON.	TUE.	WED.	THU.	FRI.	SAT.
closed	9-5	9-5	9-5	9-5	9-5	8-4

SAVINGS: 15%-80% off
BRAND NAMES: Dick Brothers, Little Debbie, Gardner
SPECIAL SALES: weekly

PARKING: lot
PAYMENT: cash, checks (amount of purchase only, with proper I.D., no out-of-state checks)

Jaeger Baking Company Thrift Store, 557 Broad Street, Beloit, WI 53511; (608) 362-1010
   This factory outlet sells Jaeger bread and sweet rolls. They also sell New Process cookies. Savings average 50% off retail price on day-old and broken pieces. They also have stores in Green Bay, Watertown, and Wausau, Wisconsin.

SUN.	MON.	TUE.	WED.	THU.	FRI.	SAT.
10-4	9-6	9-6	9-6	9-6	9-6	9-6

SAVINGS: 25%–50% off
BRAND NAMES: Jaeger, New Process
SALE DAYS: Tuesday, Friday
PARKING: lot
PAYMENT: cash, food stamps

Brownberry Ovens Thrift Store, 17365 W. Blue Mound Road, Brookfield, WI 53005; (414) 784-0778
   See listing in La Grange Park, Illinois.

SUN.	MON.	TUE.	WED.	THU.	FRI.	SAT.
11-3	9-5	9-6	9-6	9-5	9-6	9-4

SAVINGS: 10%–50% off
BRAND NAMES: Brownberry, Entenmann's, Maurice Lenell
SALE DAYS: Tuesday
SPECIAL DISCOUNTS: senior citizens, 10% off
PARKING: lot
PAYMENT: cash, checks

Dick Brothers Bakery, 21 N. Macy Street, Fond du Lac, WI 54935; (414) 922-0500
   This outlet sells Dick Brothers bread, sweet rolls, and assorted snack cakes. They also sell Barrel O Fun potato chips. Savings average 30%–40% off retail prices, with the greatest savings on day-old products. They have other stores in Green Bay and Manitowoc, Wisconsin.

SUN.	MON.	TUE.	WED.	THU.	FRI.	SAT.
closed	8-5:30	8-5:30	8-5:30	8-5:30	8-5:30	8-5

SAVINGS: 30%–40% off
BRAND NAMES: Dick Brothers, Barrel O Fun
PARKING: lot
PAYMENT: cash, food stamps

Dick Brothers Bakery, 2269 Main Street, Green Bay, WI 54302; (414) 465-6993
   See listing in Fond du Lac, Wisconsin.

SUN.	MON.	TUE.	WED.	THU.	FRI.	SAT.
closed	8-6	8-6	8-6	8-6	8-6	8-4

SAVINGS: 30%–40% off
BRAND NAMES: Dick Brothers, Barrel O Fun
PARKING: street
PAYMENT: cash, checks (amount of purchase only, with proper I.D.), food stamps

Jaeger Baking Company Thrift Store, 1641 Velp Avenue, Green Bay, WI 54303; (414) 498-1919
  See listing in Beloit, Wisconsin.

SUN.	MON.	TUE.	WED.	THU.	FRI.	SAT.
10-2:30	9-5:30	9-5:30	9-5:30	9-5:30	9-5:30	9-5

SAVINGS: about 50% off
BRAND NAMES: Jaeger, New Process
SALE DAYS: Tuesday, two-for-one sale on select items
PARKING: lot
PAYMENT: cash only

JANESVILLE, WI

Gardner Thrift Shop, 1720 Old Hume Road, Janesville, WI 53545; (608) 754-5541
  This is the factory outlet for Gardner bread, buns, rolls, snack cakes, and donuts. They also sell Barrel O Fun chips. Savings begin at 30% off retail price on first quality and go higher on some day-old items. They have other stores in Stevens Point, Waukesha, and West Baraboo, Wisconsin.

SUN.	MON.	TUE.	WED.	THU.	FRI.	SAT.
closed	9-5:30	9-5:30	9-5:30	9-5:30	9-5:30	9-5:30

SAVINGS: 25% off
BRAND NAMES: Gardner
SALE DAYS: Wednesday
SPECIAL DISCOUNTS: senior citizens, 10% off
PARKING: lot
PAYMENT: cash, checks (with proper I.D., no out-of-state checks)

KENOSHA, WI

Kappus Bread, 5120 8th Avenue, Kenosha, WI 53140; (414) 658-1396
  This factory outlet sells Kappus brand bread and New Process chips and cookies. Greatest savings are on day-old merchandise.

SUN.	MON.	TUE.	WED.	THU.	FRI.	SAT.
9-5	8-8	8-8	8-8	8-8	8-8	8-6

SAVINGS: 25%-65% off
BRAND NAMES: Kappus, New Process
PARKING: lot
PAYMENT: cash only

MADISON, WI

Brownberry Ovens Thrift Store, 2733 E. Atwood Avenue, Madison, WI 53704; (608) 241-1275
  See listing in La Grange Park, Illinois.

SUN.	MON.	TUE.	WED.	THU.	FRI.	SAT.
10-3	9-5:30	9-5	9-5:30	9-5:30	9-5:30	9-5

SAVINGS: 10%-50% off
PARKING: lot
PAYMENT: cash, checks

Kitchens of Sara Lee Thrift Store, Factory Outlet Centre, 4609 Verona Road, Madison, WI 53711; (608) 274-2739
  See listing in Chicago, Illinois.

SUN.	MON.	TUE.	WED.	THU.	FRI.	SAT.
9-5	9:30-9	9:30-9	9:30-9	9:30-9	9:30-9	9:30-6

SAVINGS: up to 50% off
BRAND NAMES: Sara Lee

SPECIAL DISCOUNTS: senior citizens, 10% off Wednesday
PARKING: lot
PAYMENT: cash, checks (amount of purchase only, with proper I.D.), MasterCard, VISA

MANITOWOC, WI

Dick Brothers Bakery, 306 N. 8th Street, Manitowoc, WI 54220; (414) 683-5542
See listing in Fond du Lac, Wisconsin.

SUN.	MON.	TUE.	WED.	THU.	FRI.	SAT.
closed	8–5	8–5	8–5	8–5	8–6	8–4

SAVINGS: 30%–40% off
BRAND NAMES: Dick Brothers, Barrel O Fun
PARKING: lot
PAYMENT: cash, food stamps

MILWAUKEE, WI

Mrs. Karls Thrift Store, 1923 W. Pierce Street, Milwaukee, WI 53204; (414) 645-1811
This is the factory outlet for Mrs. Karls baked goods. Savings begin at about 10% off retail price on first quality and can go up to 50% on some day-old merchandise.

SUN.	MON.	TUE.	WED.	THU.	FRI.	SAT.
closed	8:30–6:30	8:30–6:30	8:30–6:30	8:30–6:30	8:30–6:30	8:30–5

SAVINGS: 10%–50% off
BRAND NAMES: Mrs. Karls
SPECIAL DISCOUNTS: senior citizens, 10% off
PARKING: lot
PAYMENT: cash, checks (amount of purchase only, with proper I.D., no out-of-state checks)

Pepperidge Farm Outlet, 3902 N. 76th Street, Milwaukee, WI 53216; (414) 461-0050
See listing in Downers Grove, Illinois.

SUN.	MON.	TUE.	WED.	THU.	FRI.	SAT.
11–5	9–6	9–6	9–6	9–6	9–6	9–5

SAVINGS: 20%–50% off
BRAND NAMES: Pepperidge Farm, Campbell
SPECIAL DISCOUNTS: senior citizens, 10% off Monday, Wednesday
PARKING: lot
PAYMENT: cash, checks (amount of purchase only, with proper I.D., no out-of-state checks)

OAK CREEK, WI

Melody Cookies, 310 E. Oak Street, Oak Creek, WI 53145; (414) 762-2720
This factory outlet sells Melody cookies. Savings begin at 30% off retail price on first quality, and go as high as 50% off some broken pieces.

SUN.	MON.	TUE.	WED.	THU.	FRI.	SAT.
closed	8–4	8–4	8–4	8–4	8–4	closed

SAVINGS: 30% to 50% off
ANNUAL SALES: holidays
PARKING: lot
PAYMENT: cash, checks (amount of purchase only, with proper I.D.)

OCONOMOWOC, WI

Brownberry Ovens Thrift Store, 1 Meadow Road, Oconomowoc, WI 53066; (414) 567-0667
See listing in La Grange Park, Illinois.

SUN.	MON.	TUE.	WED.	THU.	FRI.	SAT.
10-2	9-5	9-5	9-5	9-5	9-5	9-5

SAVINGS: 10%–50% off
BRAND NAMES: Brownberry, Health Valley, Maurice Lenell, Ora-Wheat
SALE DAYS: Tuesday
SPECIAL DISCOUNTS: senior citizens, 10% off
PARKING: lot
PAYMENT: cash, checks (amount of purchase only, with proper I.D.)

RIPON, WI

Ripon Foods, Highway 44 Oshkosh Street, Ripon, WI 54971; (414) 748-3151
This is the factory outlet for Rippin' Good cookies. Savings average 33% off retail price on first quality and go higher on seconds, irregulars, and some broken pieces.

SUN.	MON.	TUE.	WED.	THU.	FRI.	SAT.
closed	9-4	9-4	9-4	9-4	9-4	9-noon

SAVINGS: 33%–66% off
BRAND NAMES: Rippin' Good
PARKING: lot
PAYMENT: cash, checks (with proper I.D.)

STEVENS POINT, WI

Gardner Thrift Shop, 2214 S. Madison Street, Stevens Point, WI 54481; (715) 345-2627
See listing in Janesville, Wisconsin.

SUN.	MON.	TUE.	WED.	THU.	FRI.	SAT.
closed	9-5:30	9-5:30	9-5:30	9-5:30	9-5:30	8-4:30

SAVINGS: 30%–40% off
BRAND NAMES: Gardner, Barrel O Fun
PARKING: lot
PAYMENT: cash, food stamps

WATERTOWN, WI

Jaeger Baking Company Thrift Store, 303 E. Summit Avenue, Watertown, WI 53094; (414) 261-6717
See listing in Beloit, Wisconsin.

SUN.	MON.	TUE.	WED.	THU.	FRI.	SAT.
9-1:40	9-5:40	9-5:40	9-5:40	9-5:40	9-5:40	9-5:40

SAVINGS: about 50% off
BRAND NAMES: Jaeger
PARKING: lot
PAYMENT: cash, food stamps

WAUKESHA, WI

Gardner Thrift Shop, 1915 Delafield Road, Waukesha, WI 53188; (414) 549-0260
See listing in Janesville, Wisconsin.

SUN.	MON.	TUE.	WED.	THU.	FRI.	SAT.
closed	9-5:30	9-5:30	9-5:30	9-5:30	9-5:30	8-4

SAVINGS: 30%–40% off
BRAND NAMES: Gardner, Bingles
SPECIAL DISCOUNTS: senior citizens, 10% off
PARKING: lot
PAYMENT: cash, checks (amount of purchase only, with proper I.D., no out-of-state checks), MasterCard, VISA

Jaeger Baking Company Thrift Store, 105 Central Bridge, Wausau, WI 54401;
(715) 845-1449
See listing in Beloit, Wisconsin.

SUN.	MON.	TUE.	WED.	THU.	FRI.	SAT.
closed	8-6	8-6	8-6	8-6	8-6	8-6

SAVINGS: about 50% off
BRAND NAMES: Jaeger, New Process
SALE DAYS: Tuesday
SPECIAL DISCOUNTS: senior citizens, 10% off
PARKING: lot
PAYMENT: cash only

Gardner Thrift Shop, 401 Linn Street, West Baraboo, WI 53913; (608) 356-4743
See listing in Janesville, Wisconsin.

SUN.	MON.	TUE.	WED.	THU.	FRI.	SAT.
closed	9-5	9-5	9-5	9-5	9-5	9-4

SAVINGS: 25%-50% off
BRAND NAMES: Gardner
SALE DAYS: Wednesday, Saturday
SPECIAL DISCOUNTS: senior citizens, 10% off
PARKING: lot
PAYMENT: cash, checks (amount of purchase only)

Cookie Jar Outlet (The), West Bend Factory Outlet Mall, 180 Island Avenue, West
Bend, WI 53095; (414) 334-4674
This is another outlet for Rippin' Good cookies (see p. 000). The best buys are on
bulk cookies. They also sell packaged cookies, cookie jars, cookie cutters, and other
cookie paraphernalia.

SUN.	MON.	TUE.	WED.	THU.	FRI.	SAT.
11-5	9:30-9	9:30-9	9:30-9	9:30-9	9:30-9	9:30-6

SAVINGS: 50%-80% off
BRAND NAMES: Rippin' Good
PARKING: lot
PAYMENT: cash, checks (amount of purchase only, with proper I.D.)

FOOD—CANDY, NUTS, AND FRUIT

These outlets sell mostly candy, but a few sell other items as well.
Seconds in candy save from 25% to 60%, and usually means they look
funny but taste the same as full-price merchandise. The greatest
savings I found were on special holiday candies a week or two after the
holiday. Shop carefully. Many of these outlets sell first quality merchandise at retail price. Don't be tempted; look for the bargains.

Affy Tapple, 7110 N. Clark Street, Chicago, IL 60626; (312) 338-1100
This small plant makes Affy Tapple caramel apples and Frosty frozen bananas.
"Broken stick" Affy Tapples are 60% off retail price and frozen bananas are 70% off
retail price. Bruised or very small apples are usually available at 6 pounds for 60¢.
They also sell candy.

SUN.	MON.	TUE.	WED.	THU.	FRI.	SAT.
closed*	8-4:30	8-4:30	8-4:30	8-4:30	8-4:30	8-noon

SAVINGS: 50%-70% off
BRAND NAMES: Affy Tapple, Frosty
PARKING: lot in back, or street in front
PAYMENT: cash only

---

*They are open on Sunday from 8:00-5:00 in September and October.

Andrews Caramel Apples, 3258 W. Fullerton Avenue, Chicago, IL 60647; (312) 772-7484

This factory outlet sells caramel apples. First quality are 50% off retail price, and seconds are 60% off. Seconds on a caramel apple usually means it was dipped crooked.

SUN.	MON.	TUE.	WED.	THU.	FRI.	SAT.
closed	7-4	7-4	7-4	7-4	7-4	9-3

SAVINGS: 50%-60% off
BRAND NAMES: Andrews
PARKING: street, meters
PAYMENT: cash only

Fannie May Candies, 1813 W. Montrose Avenue, Chicago, IL 60613; (312) 243-2700

This is the factory outlet for Fannie May candy. Buy the seconds, without the fancy boxes, and sometimes slightly messy, at savings of 25% off retail price. They taste just as good as the full-priced candy at the next counter. There are other stores in Chicago, and one in Berwyn, Illinois.

SUN.	MON.	TUE.	WED.	THU.	FRI.	SAT.
closed	8:30-5	8:30-5	8:30-5	8:30-5	8:30-5	8:30-2

SAVINGS: up to 25% off
BRAND NAMES: Fannie May
ANNUAL SALES: holiday seasons
PARKING: street, under the "L" at the side
PAYMENT: cash, checks (amount of purchase only, with proper I.D.)

Fannie May Candies, 9158 S. Commercial Avenue, Chicago, IL 60617; (312) 721-3120
See listing above.

SUN.	MON.	TUE.	WED.	THU.	FRI.	SAT.
10-5	10-8	10-8	10-6	10-8	10-8	10-6

SAVINGS: 33%-50% off
BRAND NAMES: Fannie May
PARKING: street
PAYMENT: cash only

Fannie May Candies, 4197 S. Archer Avenue, Chicago, IL 60632; (312) 847-8943
See listing above.

SUN.	MON.	TUE.	WED.	THU.	FRI.	SAT.
10-5	10-8	10-8	10-8	10-8	10-8	10-7

SAVINGS: 33%-50% off
BRAND NAMES: Fannie May
PARKING: street, meters
PAYMENT: cash only

Fannie May Candies, 3142 W. 63rd Street, Chicago, IL 60629; (312) 778-9211
See listing above.

SUN.	MON.	TUE.	WED.	THU.	FRI.	SAT.
10–3	9:30–7	9:30–7	9:30–7	9:30–7	9:30–7	9:30–6

SAVINGS: 33%–50% off
BRAND NAMES: Fannie May
PARKING: street
PAYMENT: cash only

Fannie May Candies, 1101 W. Jackson Boulevard, Chicago, IL 60607; (312) 243-2700
See listing above.

SUN.	MON.	TUE.	WED.	THU.	FRI.	SAT.
closed	8:30–5	8:30–5	8:30–5	8:30–5	8:30–5	8:30–5

SAVINGS: up to 40% off
BRAND NAMES: Fannie May
ANNUAL SALES: holiday seasons
PARKING: lot
PAYMENT: cash, checks (amount of purchase only, with proper I.D.)

Georgia Nut Company, 3325 N. California Avenue, Chicago, IL 60618; (312)
539-0240
This store sells nuts, candy, and dried fruit at savings that average about 20%–40%
off retail price. They have another store in Morton Grove, Illinois.

SUN.	MON.	TUE.	WED.	THU.	FRI.	SAT.
closed	7:30–5:30	7:30–5:30	7:30–5:30	7:30–5:30	7:30–4:30	9–3

SAVINGS: 20%–40% off
SPECIAL SALES: monthly   *All First Quality*
PARKING: lot
PAYMENT: cash, checks (amount of purchase only, with proper I.D.)

L & P Wholesale Candy Company, 7047 S. State Street, Chicago, IL 60637; (312)
783-4383
This store sells hundreds of kinds of candy. They also sell cigarettes and soda pop
at discounts from 10%–30% off retail price.

SUN.	MON.	TUE.	WED.	THU.	FRI.	SAT.
8–3	7–5:45	7–5:45	7–5:45	7–5:45	7–5:45	7–5:45

SAVINGS: 10%–30% off   *Mailing List*   *All First Quality*
PARKING: street
PAYMENT: cash only

Nuts to "U", 4757 N. Lincoln Avenue, Chicago, IL 60625; (312) 275-7383
This is an outlet for Regal health foods. They sell candy, nuts, coffee, and teas at
discounts approximately 20% off retail price.

SUN.	MON.	TUE.	WED.	THU.	FRI.	SAT.
closed	9:30–7	9:30–7	9:30–7	9:30–7	9:30–7	9:30–7

SAVINGS: 20% off
SALE DAYS: vary   *All First Quality*
PARKING: lot
PAYMENT: cash only

Ricci Nuts, 162 W. Superior Street, Chicago, IL 60610; (312) 787-7660
This store sells jumbo cashews, pistachio nuts, and candy at discount prices.

SUN.	MON.	TUE.	WED.	THU.	FRI.	SAT.
closed	7–4:30	7–4:30	7–4:30	7–4:30	7–4:30	7–11:30

SAVINGS: about 10% off   *All First Quality*
PARKING: street, can be difficult
PAYMENT: cash, checks (amount of purchase only, with proper I.D.), MasterCard, VISA

Superior Nut and Candy Company Outlet, 3102 N. Central Avenue, Chicago, IL
60634; (312) 237-4340
This store sells nuts, candy, and dried fruit. Savings average 20%–50% off retail
price. They also have stores in Oaklawn and Schaumburg, Illinois.

SUN.	MON.	TUE.	WED.	THU.	FRI.	SAT.
11-5	9-8	9-6	9-8	9-8	9-6	9-6

SAVINGS: 15%–60% off   *All First Quality*
PARKING: lot
PAYMENT: cash, checks (amount of purchase only, with proper I.D.)

BARRINGTON, IL

Brans Nut Company, 411 W. Lake Street, Barrington, IL 60010; (312) 381-0800
This outlet offers roasted nuts at savings, with an average of 40% off retail. They
also sell Jelly Belly candy, yogurt, chocolate, and carob. They have other stores in
Wauconda, Illinois, and Mukwonago, Wisconsin.

SUN.	MON.	TUE.	WED.	THU.	FRI.	SAT.
closed	9-5	9-5	9-5	9-5	9-5	9-5

SAVINGS: 40% off   *All First Quality*
BRAND NAMES: Brans, Jelly Belly
SPECIAL SALES: monthly
PARKING: lot
PAYMENT: cash, checks (no out-of-state checks)

BERWYN, IL

Fannie May Candies, 6747 W. Cermak Road, Berwyn, IL 60402; (312) 484-9490
See listing in Chicago, Illinois.

SUN.	MON.	TUE.	WED.	THU.	FRI.	SAT.
11-5	9:30-8:30	9:30-8:30	9:30-8:30	9:30-8:30	9:30-8:30	9:30-7

SAVINGS: 33%–50% off
BRAND NAMES: Fannie May
PARKING: street, meters
PAYMENT: cash only

BLOOMINGTON, IL

Beich's Candy, 2501 Beich Road, Bloomington, IL 61701; (309) 829-1031
Pass up the first quality candy sold at retail price, and look for the seconds.
Chocolates that retail for $5.00/lb. sell for $3.00/lb.

SUN.	MON.	TUE.	WED.	THU.	FRI.	SAT.
closed	8-8	8-8	8-8	8-8	8-8	8-1

SAVINGS: 20%–60% off   *Mailing List*
BRAND NAMES: Beich's
PARKING: lot
PAYMENT: cash, checks (amount of purchase only, with proper I.D.), MasterCard, VISA

DES PLAINES, IL

The Thrift Store—John B. Sanfilippo and Son, 300 E. Touhy Avenue, Des Plaines,
IL 60018; (312) 298-1510
This store sells nuts, candy, and bulk coffee, tea, and spices. Most merchandise is
test runs, end of code, overruns, overstocks, and closeouts. They have another store in
Elk Grove Village, Illinois.

SUN.	MON.	TUE.	WED.	THU.	FRI.	SAT.
closed	9:30-5:30	9:30-5:30	9:30-5:30	9:30-5:30	9:30-5:30	10-4:30

SAVINGS: 40%–50% off   *Mailing List*
PARKING: street, meters
PAYMENT: cash, checks (with proper I.D.), MasterCard, VISA, American Express

ELK GROVE VILLAGE, IL

Ace Pecan Company Factory Outlet Store, 2055 Lunt Avenue, Elk Grove Village, IL 60007; (312) 364-3275

This is the outlet for County Fair. They sell nuts, dried fruits, and Goelitz jelly beans. Most merchandise is first quality, but there is a special room full of broken pieces and end of code merchandise. Ask about the weekly special savings.

SUN.	MON.	TUE.	WED.	THU.	FRI.	SAT.
closed	8–4:30	8–4:30	8–4:30	8–4:30	8–4:30	8–3:30

SAVINGS: 10%–50% off
BRAND NAMES: County Fair, Goelitz
SPECIAL SALES: daily and weekly
PARKING: lot
PAYMENT: cash, checks (amount of purchase only, with proper I.D.), MasterCard, VISA

The Thrift Store—John B. Sanfilippo and Son, 2299 Busse Road, Elk Grove Village, IL 60007; (312) 593-2300

See listing in Des Plaines, Illinois.

SUN.	MON.	TUE.	WED.	THU.	FRI.	SAT.
closed	8:30–5	8:30–5	8:30–5	8:30–5	8:30–5	9–4

SAVINGS: average 20% off
BRAND NAMES: Brach's, Zachary's
PARKING: lot
PAYMENT: cash, checks (with proper I.D.)

EVERGREEN PARK, IL

Good Treats Limited Direct Outlet, 3625 W. 95th Street (located in Hobby City), Evergreen Park, IL 60642; (312) 423-1999

This is the factory outlet for Goelitz candies. They also sell bulk coffees, teas, spices, and nuts.

SUN.	MON.	TUE.	WED.	THU.	FRI.	SAT.
closed	10:30–8	10:30–6	closed	10:30–6	10:30–8	10:30–5:30

SAVINGS: up to 50% off   *All First Quality*
BRAND NAMES: Goelitz
PARKING: lot, difficult
PAYMENT: cash, checks (amount of purchase only, with proper I.D., no out-of-state checks)

MORTON GROVE, IL

Georgia Nut Company, 6431 W. Oakton Avenue, Morton Grove, 60053; (312) 966-0400

See listing in Chicago, Illinois.

SUN.	MON.	TUE.	WED.	THU.	FRI.	SAT.
closed	8–5:30	8–5:30	8–5:30	8–5:30	8–4:30	9–3

SAVINGS: 20%–40% off   *Mailing List*   *All First Quality*
SPECIAL DISCOUNTS: senior citizens, 10% off Monday
PARKING: lot
PAYMENT: cash, checks

Superior Nut and Candy Company Outlet, 10836 S. Cicero Avenue, Oaklawn, IL
60453; (312) 424-2202
See listing in Chicago, Illinois.

SUN.	MON.	TUE.	WED.	THU.	FRI.	SAT.
10–5	9–8	9–6	9–8	9–8	9–6	9–6

SAVINGS: at least 20% off
PARKING: street
PAYMENT: cash, checks (amount of purchase only, with proper I.D., $10.00 minimum),
MasterCard, VISA

Superior Nut and Candy Company Outlet, 245 S. Roselle Road, Schaumburg, IL
60193; (312) 351-6906
See listing in Chicago, Illinois.

SUN.	MON.	TUE.	WED.	THU.	FRI.	SAT.
11–5	10–7	10–7	10–7	10–7	10–7	9–6

SAVINGS: 20%–50% off
PARKING: lot
PAYMENT: cash, checks (amount of purchase only, with proper I.D.)

Brans Nut Company, 581 Bonner Road, Wauconda, IL 60084; (312) 526-0700
See listing in Barrington, Illinois.

SUN.	MON.	TUE.	WED.	THU.	FRI.	SAT.
9–5	9–5	9–5	9–5	9–5	9–5	8–5

SAVINGS: 50%–70% off
ANNUAL SALES: most holidays
PARKING: lot
PAYMENT: cash, checks (minimum $10.00)

Ambrosia Chocolate Company, Factory Outlet Centre, 7700 120th Avenue,
Kenosha, WI 53142; (414) 857-7150
This is one of several outlets for the Ambrosia Chocolate Company. Savings on
first quality Ambrosia chocolate start at 20% off retail and can be as high as 60% on
seconds, broken pieces, surplus, overruns, and "end-of-season" (hearts in March,
Santas in January) candy. They also sell cocoa, candy-making supplies, candy molds,
hard candy, fudge, taffy, chocolate chips, and gift items. They have other stores in
Milwaukee and West Bend, Wisconsin.

SUN.	MON.	TUE.	WED.	THU.	FRI.	SAT.
11–5	9:30–9	9:30–9	9:30–9	9:30–9	9:30–9	9:30–6

SAVINGS: 10%–60% off
BRAND NAMES: Ambrosia Chocolate
SALE DAYS: Wednesday, 15% off
SPECIAL DISCOUNTS: senior citizens, 15% off
PARKING: lot
PAYMENT: cash, checks (with proper I.D.)

Ambrosia Chocolate Company, 528 W. Highland Avenue, Milwaukee, WI 53202; (414) 354-0652
See listing in Kenosha, Wisconsin.

SUN.	MON.	TUE.	WED.	THU.	FRI.	SAT.
closed	9-5	9-5	9-5	9-5	9-5	9-5

SAVINGS: 20%–40% off
BRAND NAMES: Ambrosia Chocolate
SPECIAL DISCOUNTS: senior citizens, 15% off
PARKING: lot
PAYMENT: cash, checks (with proper I.D.)

The Chocolate House Factory Retail Store, 4121 S. 35th Street, Milwaukee, WI 53221; (414) 281-7803
This factory outlet sells bulk chocolate seconds at 50% off retail price and occasional overruns of various items at 25% off retail price. They also sell first quality items at retail price.

SUN.	MON.	TUE.	WED.	THU.	FRI.	SAT.
closed	9-8	9-8	9-8	9-8	9-8	8:30-1

SAVINGS: up to 50% off
BRAND NAMES: Chocolate House
PARKING: lot
PAYMENT: cash, checks (with proper I.D., no out-of-state checks)

Brans Nut Company, Highway ES, Route 3, Mukwonago, WI 53149; (414) 363-3800
See listing in Barrington, Illinois.

SUN.	MON.	TUE.	WED.	THU.	FRI.	SAT.
9-8	9-8	9-8	9-8	9-8	9-8	9-8

SAVINGS: 30%–50% off
BRAND NAMES: Evans
ANNUAL SALES: Super Bowl, Mother's Day
PARKING: lot
PAYMENT: cash, checks (with proper I.D.)

Ambrosia Chocolate Company, West Bend Outlet Mall, 180 Island Avenue, West Bend, WI 53095; (414) 334-5262
See listing in Kenosha, Wisconsin.

SUN.	MON.	TUE.	WED.	THU.	FRI.	SAT.
noon-5	9:30-5	9:30-5	9:30-5	9:30-5	9:30-5	9:30-5

SAVINGS: 20%–40% off
BRAND NAMES: Ambrosia Chocolate
SPECIAL DISCOUNTS: senior citizens, Wednesday
PARKING: lot
PAYMENT: cash, checks (amount of purchase only, with proper I.D.)

FOOD—CANNED

These plants produce canned goods. Savings on canned fruits, vegetables, and soups start about 20% off retail price on first quality, but can go as high as 75% on dented, rusted, or unlabeled cans. If you have storage space, buying cases of unlabeled cans (write the contents on the box) can save the most money.

INDIANA
PORTLAND, IN

Naas Foods, Inc., (P.O. Box 1029), W. Seventh Street Road, Portland, IN 47371; (219) 726-8155

This factory outlet has savings from 40%–70% off retail price on boxes of 46 oz. cans of tomato juice, #303 cans of tomatoes, and #10 cans of ketchup. Most merchandise is seconds, with some dents, unwrapped, or unlabeled cans.

SUN.	MON.	TUE.	WED.	THU.	FRI.	SAT.
closed	8–4	8–4	8–4	8–4	8–4	closed

SAVINGS: 40%–70% off
PARKING: lot
PAYMENT: cash, certified or cashier's checks

SWAYZEE, IN

Swayzee Packing Company, 714 E. Lyons Street, Swayzee, IN 46986; (317) 922-7995

This factory outlet sells canned tomatoes and tomato juice at wholesale prices.

SUN.	MON.	TUE.	WED.	THU.	FRI.	SAT.
closed	8–5	8–5	8–5	8–5	8–5	closed

SAVINGS: 10%–40% off   *All First Quality*
PARKING: lot
PAYMENT: cash, checks (amount of purchase only, with proper I.D.)

WISCONSIN
GREEN BAY, WI

Larson Company Dent Department, 314 N. Broadway, Green Bay, WI 54305; (414) 435-5301

This is an employees' store at the plant. The public can go to the office, get an employee to assist, go to the basement, collect dented or unlabeled cans of vegetables, go upstairs to pay, return to the basement to get the canned goods, carry them upstairs, and drive home with savings of up to 75% off retail price.

SUN.	MON.	TUE.	WED.	THU.	FRI.	SAT.
closed	7:30–2:30	7:30–2:30	7:30–2:30	7:30–2:30	7:30–2:30	closed

SAVINGS: up to 75% off
BRAND NAMES: Fresh Like, Veg-All
PARKING: street
PAYMENT: cash only

MADISON, WI

The Cannery, 99 S. Stroughton Road, Madison, WI 54301; (414) 244-3808

This is the outlet for Stokely canned goods. They carry Stokely fruits and various labels of soups. They also sell disposable diapers and paper products. Savings start at about 20% off retail price, and go up to 60% on dented and unlabeled cans. They have other stores in Oconomowoc and Wausau, Wisconsin.

SUN.	MON.	TUE.	WED.	THU.	FRI.	SAT.
closed	9-5	9-5	9-5	9-5	9-5	9-5

SAVINGS: 20%–60% off
BRAND NAMES: Stokely
SPECIAL DISCOUNTS: 2% additional on purchases of $300–$1,000
PARKING: street
PAYMENT: cash, checks (amount of purchase only, with proper I.D.)

OCONOMOWOC, WI

The Cannery, 616 E. Wisconsin Avenue, Oconomowoc, WI 53066; (414) 567-9151
   See listing in Madison, Wisconsin.

SUN.	MON.	TUE.	WED.	THU.	FRI.	SAT.
closed	9-5	9-5	9-5	9-5	9-5	9-5

SAVINGS: 20%–60% off
BRAND NAMES: Stokely
PARKING: lot
PAYMENT: cash, checks (amount of purchase only, with proper I.D., no out-of-state
   checks)

WAUSAU, WI

The Cannery, 111 W. Bridge Street, Wausau, WI 54401; (715) 845-2529
   See listing in Madison, Wisconsin.

SUN.	MON.	TUE.	WED.	THU.	FRI.	SAT.
closed	9-5	9-5	9-5	9-5	9-5	9-5

SAVINGS: at least 20% off
BRAND NAMES: Stokely
SPECIAL DISCOUNTS: 2% additional on $300–$1,000 purchase
PARKING: street
PAYMENT: cash, checks (amount of purchase only, with proper I.D.)

FOOD—CHEESE

I was not surprised to find a large concentration of dairies in Wisconsin. Most of the stores listed here are the direct factory outlets for their dairies. Many are at the cheese plants; many have a window through which you can watch the activities of the plant; and many have free tours. I found quite a few restrictions on groups for tours, so it is advisable to call ahead, where suggested, to avoid disappointment.

Many of the cheese outlets sell complementary items; they are indicated. Many provide mail order service or will ship gifts; they are also indicated.

The addresses in rural areas frequently lack a number and/or street names. Even with the clearest directions from the dairy, I had difficulty finding some of the outlets listed below. If you are planning a trip, I suggest you call ahead; once in the town, a brief stop at the gas station, the library, the police station, or the town hall will assist in the final approach to the outlet.

Prices for dairy products in Wisconsin are considerably lower than those in the Chicago area. Most of the managers in the outlets I visited found it difficult to assist me in making a customary estimation of SAVINGS. Wisconsin retail prices average 25%–40% less than supermarket prices in the Chicagoland area; those in the factory outlets were generally 10%–25% below the Wisconsin retail prices. If you are planning a trip or a vacation in Wisconsin, check a map before you leave. Plan your shopping stops in advance. I recommend you plan your cheese stop for the last day of your vacation. The tour will be fun for the children, and the cheese will be a treat for the whole family. Bring along a cooler so your purchases will stay cold on your trip home.

ILLINOIS
ELK GROVE VILLAGE, IL

Quality Cheese, 531 Bonnie Lane, Elk Grove Village, IL 60007; (312) 228-1699
This store sells many types of cheese at savings of 10%–40% off retail price.

SUN.	MON.	TUE.	WED.	THU.	FRI.	SAT.
closed	10–4	10–4	10–4	10–4	10–4	10–2

SAVINGS: 10%–40% off   *Mailing List*   *All First Quality*
PARKING: street
PAYMENT: cash, checks (amount of purchase only, with proper I.D., no out-of-state checks)

INDIANA
ELNORA, IN

Graham Farms Cheese Corporation, Highway 57 North, Elnora, IN 47529; (812) 692-5237
This factory outlet sells Graham colby and cheddar cheese spreads. They also sell Swiss chocolate, Amish candy, and popcorn. Savings average 20%–30% off retail price.

SUN.	MON.	TUE.	WED.	THU.	FRI.	SAT.
noon–5	8–6	8–6	8–6	8–6	8–6	8–6

SAVINGS: 20%–30% off   *All First Quality*
BRAND NAMES: Graham Farms
PARKING: lot
PAYMENT: cash, checks, MasterCard, VISA

WISCONSIN
ALBANY, WI

Maple Leaf Cheese Factory, 404 S. Mill Street, Albany, WI 53502; (608) 862-3707
This outlet sells about thirty kinds of cheese, half of which are manufactured on the premises. Savings average 20%–40% off Chicago retail prices. They will also ship gift packages of cheese.

SUN.	MON.	TUE.	WED.	THU.	FRI.	SAT.
closed	9–5	9–5	9–5	9–5	9–5	9–2

SAVINGS: 20%–40% off   *Mailing List*
BRAND NAMES: Cherry Valley
ANNUAL SALES: June
PARKING: lot
PAYMENT: cash, checks (amount of purchase only, with proper I.D.)

ALGOMA, WI

Renard's Rosewood Dairy, Route 2, County Highway "S", Algoma, WI 54201; (414) 487-2825
This factory outlet sells its own brand of mild cheddar cheese for $1.75/lb.

SUN.	MON.	TUE.	WED.	THU.	FRI.	SAT.
closed	8–5	8–5	8–5	8–5	8–5	8–3

SAVINGS: 25%–50% off   *Mailing List*   *All First Quality*
PARKING: lot
PAYMENT: cash, checks

ALMA CENTER, WI

South Alma Cheese Factory, Route 1, Box 65, Alma Center, WI 54611; (715) 964-7411
    This factory sells mild and sharp cheddar cheese, mozzarella, and jack cheese at savings that average 25%–50% off retail price.

SUN.	MON.	TUE.	WED.	THU.	FRI.	SAT.
closed	8:30–4	8:30–4	8:30–4	8:30–4	8:30–4	8:30–noon

SAVINGS: 25%–50% off   *All First Quality*
PARKING: lot
PAYMENT: cash, checks (amount of purchase only, with proper I.D.)

ANTIGO, WI

Schultz Creamery, W8737 Highway 47, Antigo, WI 54409; (715) 627-4308
    This factory outlet store sells brick, monterey jack, mozzarella, colby, and cheddar cheese at prices that average $1.00/lb. off retail price. They occasionally have ends and pieces at greater discounts.

SUN.	MON.	TUE.	WED.	THU.	FRI.	SAT.
10–6	10–6	10–6	10–6	10–6	10–6	10–6

SAVINGS: 25%–40% off   *Mailing List*
SPECIAL DISCOUNTS: senior citizens (ask)
PARKING: lot
PAYMENT: cash, checks (amount of purchase only, with proper I.D.)

ARENA, WI

Farmer's Pride Cheese, Box 125, Highway 14, Arena, WI 53503; (608) 753-2501
    This factory outlet sells a dozen brands of cheese at savings that average 25%–50% off retail price. Free tours are available; call ahead for information. They also sell knicknacks in their shop.

SUN.	MON.	TUE.	WED.	THU.	FRI.	SAT.
8:30–8	8:30–8	8:30–8	8:30–8	8:30–8	8:30–8	8:30–8

SAVINGS: 25%–50% off   *Mailing List*   *All First Quality*
PARKING: lot
PAYMENT: cash, MasterCard, VISA

BANGOR, WI

Farmers Creamery Company, 1415 James Street, Bangor, WI 54614; (608) 486-2351
    This factory outlet sells over twenty-five varieties of cheese at savings that average 20%–50% off retail price.

SUN.	MON.	TUE.	WED.	THU.	FRI.	SAT.
8–5	8–5	8–5	8–5	8–5	8–5	8–5

SAVINGS: 20%–50% off   *Mailing List*   *All First Quality*
PARKING: lot
PAYMENT: cash, checks (amount of purchase only, with proper I.D.)

BEECHWOOD, WI

Beechwood Cheese Factory, Route 1, 1713 Highway "A", Beechwood, WI 53001; (414) 994-9306
    This factory store sells their own brands of colby, cheddar, monterey jack, muenster, and other cheese in 1¼-, 2½-, and 5-pound packages, all at considerable savings over supermarket prices.

SUN.	MON.	TUE.	WED.	THU.	FRI.	SAT.
closed	9–5	9–5	9–5	9–5	9–5	9–5

SAVINGS: 25%–50% off   *All First Quality*
PARKING: lot
PAYMENT: cash, checks (with proper I.D.)

BERLIN, WI

Jim's Cheese Corner, Route 1, Berlin, WI 54923; (414) 361-4360
   This factory outlet sells about forty varieties of cheese at savings up to 33% off retail price. They also sell cheese curds for $2.15/lb. Tours are available; call ahead for information.

SUN.	MON.	TUE.	WED.	THU.	FRI.	SAT.
8–8	8–8	8–8	8–8	8–8	8–8	8–8

SAVINGS: 25%–33% off   *Mailing List*
SPECIAL DISCOUNTS: will negotiate with charity groups
PARKING: lot
PAYMENT: cash, checks (amount of purchase only, with proper I.D.)

BLACK CREEK, WI

Outagamie Producers Co-operative, 307 N. Clark Street, Black Creek, WI 54106;
   (414) 984-3331
   This factory outlet sells several types of cheddar cheese at savings of 20%–50% off retail price. They also sell butter.

SUN.	MON.	TUE.	WED.	THU.	FRI.	SAT.
closed	8–5	8–5	8–5	8–5	8–5	8–noon

SAVINGS: 20%–50% off   *Mailing List*   *All First Quality*
PARKING: lot
PAYMENT: cash, checks (amount of purchase only, with proper I.D.)

Twelve Corners Cheese Factory, Route 2, Highway 47, Black Creek, WI 54106;
   (414) 731-7720
   This factory outlet sells about twenty-five varieties of cheese at savings that average 20%–40% off retail price. They also sell summer sausage.

SUN.	MON.	TUE.	WED.	THU.	FRI.	SAT.
closed	7–1	7–1	7–1	7–1	7–1	7–1

SAVINGS: 20%–40% off   *All First Quality*
PARKING: lot
PAYMENT: cash, checks (amount of purchase only, with proper I.D.)

BLAIR, WI

Associated Milk Producers, 220 Center Street, Box 6, Blair, WI 54616; (608)
   989-2538
   This factory outlet sells about twenty varieties of cheese at savings that average 30% off retail price. Free tours are available; call ahead for information.

SUN.	MON.	TUE.	WED.	THU.	FRI.	SAT.
closed	8–4	8–4	8–4	8–4	8–4	closed

SAVINGS: 30% off   *All First Quality*
ANNUAL SALES: June
PARKING: lot
PAYMENT: cash, checks (amount of purchase only, with proper I.D.)

BRANCH, WI

Branch Cheese Company, P.O. Box 78, 3826 Branch River Road, Branch, WI 54203;
   (414) 684-0121

This factory outlet sells cheese at discounts of 20%–50% off retail price.

SUN.	MON.	TUE.	WED.	THU.	FRI.	SAT.
closed	8–4:30	8–4:30	8–4:30	8–4:30	8–4:30	8–noon

SAVINGS: 20%–50% off   *All First Quality*
PARKING: lot, street
PAYMENT: cash, checks (amount of purchase only, with proper I.D., no out-of-state checks)

BRISTOL, WI

Merkt Cheese Company, Box 188, 19241 83rd Street, Bristol, WI 53104; (414) 857-2316

This factory outlet sells Merkt cheese spreads. They also sell summer sausage. Free tours are available Monday–Saturday from 8:00 to 5:00.

SUN.	MON.	TUE.	WED.	THU.	FRI.	SAT.
closed	8–5	8–5	8–5	8–5	8–5	closed

SAVINGS: 10%–33% off   *All First Quality*
BRAND NAMES: Merkt
PARKING: lot
PAYMENT: cash, checks (amount of purchase only, with proper I.D.), MasterCard, VISA

BRODHEAD, WI

Decatur Dairy, W1668 Highway F, Route 2, Box 15, Brodhead, WI 53520; (608) 897-4288

This factory outlet sells over forty varieties of cheese. Free tours are available; call ahead for information. They also sell bratwurst.

SUN.	MON.	TUE.	WED.	THU.	FRI.	SAT.
9–noon	9–5	9–5	9–5	9–5	9–5	9–5

SAVINGS: 25%–40% off   *Mailing List*   *All First Quality*
PARKING: lot
PAYMENT: cash, checks (amount of purchase only, with proper I.D.)

CHILI, WI

Chili Milk Pool Co-op, County Highway "Y", 2 miles N. of Highway 10, Chili, WI 54420; (715) 683-2401

This store sells cheese at savings from 30%–50% off retail price. Best buys are ends and pieces, although bulk packaged one-, two-, five-, and forty-pound blocks can be a good buy.

SUN.	MON.	TUE.	WED.	THU.	FRI.	SAT.
closed	8–4:30	8–4:30	8–4:30	8–4:30	8–4:30	8–4:30

SAVINGS: 30%–50% off   *Mailing List*   *All First Quality*
PARKING: lot
PAYMENT: cash, checks (amount of purchase only, with proper I.D.)

CLYDE, WI

Biglow Cheese and Butter Company, County "C" and Highway 130, Clyde, WI 53506; (608) 583-3571

This factory outlet sells a dozen varieties of cheese at savings that average 25%–50% off retail price. Free tours are available for families or youth groups only; call ahead for information.

SUN.	MON.	TUE.	WED.	THU.	FRI.	SAT.
closed	8–5	8–5	8–5	8–5	8–5	8–5

SAVINGS: 25%–50% off   *Mailing List*   *All First Quality*
PARKING: lot
PAYMENT: cash, checks (amount of purchase only, with proper I.D.)

Marshall Cheese, Route 1, Box 177, Conrath, WI 54731; (715) 452-5181
   This factory outlet sells over thirty varieties of cheese. They also sell honey, crackers, and maple syrup. Free tours are available Monday–Saturday, 10:00–2:00.

SUN.	MON.	TUE.	WED.	THU.	FRI.	SAT.
closed	8–5:30	8–5:30	8–5:30	8–5:30	8–5:30	8–5:30

SAVINGS: 15%–25% off   *All First Quality*
PARKING: lot
PAYMENT: cash, checks (amount of purchase only, with proper I.D.)

Gile Cheese, 28463 Twin Bridge Road, Cuba City, WI 53807; (608) 744-8455
   This factory outlet sells brick, colby, cheddar, and swiss cheese at prices that average 30%–50% off retail price. You can save much more on seconds and ends and pieces. They also sell crackers and nacho chips.

SUN.	MON.	TUE.	WED.	THU.	FRI.	SAT.
11–3*	9–4:30	9–4:30	9–4:30	9–4:30	9–4:30	9–4:30

SAVINGS: 30%–90% off   *Mailing List*
BRAND NAMES: Carr
PARKING: lot
PAYMENT: cash, checks (amount of purchase only, with proper I.D.)

_____
*They are closed Sunday in the winter.

Brunkow Cheese Co-op, Route 2, Darlington, WI 53530; (608) 776-3716
   Although they do not have a store as such, you can buy a dozen varieties of cheese at savings that average about 30% off retail price at the factory. Free tours are available for small groups: call ahead for information.

SUN.	MON.	TUE.	WED.	THU.	FRI.	SAT.
6:30–3:30	6:30–3:30	6:30–3:30	6:30–3:30	6:30–3:30	6:30–3:30	6:30–3:30

SAVINGS: 30% off   *All First Quality*
PARKING: lot
PAYMENT: cash, checks (amount of purchase only, with proper I.D.), no out-of-state checks)

Auricchio Cheese, Highway "NN" (north of Highway 96), Route 3, Denmark, WI 54208; (414) 863-2123
   This factory outlet sells provolone, cheddar, and swiss cheese, and cheese spreads at prices that average 20%–60% off retail price. Savings are greatest on seconds. They also sell vinegar, olive oil, and canned tomatoes. Free tours are available; call ahead for information.

SUN.	MON.	TUE.	WED.	THU.	FRI.	SAT.
closed	7:30–4	7:30–4	7:30–4	7:30–4	7:30–4	7:30–4

SAVINGS: 20%–60% off
PARKING: lot
PAYMENT: cash, checks

Potts Blue Star Cheese, Route 2, Highway 29, Denmark, WI 54208; (414) 863-2595
   This factory outlet sells over thirty varieties of cheese at savings that average 30%–50% off retail price. Free tours are available; call ahead for information.

SUN.	MON.	TUE.	WED.	THU.	FRI.	SAT.
closed	9–5	9–5	9–5	9–5	9–5	9–1

SAVINGS: 30%–50% off   *All First Quality*
PARKING: lot
PAYMENT: cash, checks (amount of purchase only, with proper I.D.)

Steve's Cheese Company, Division of Branch Cheese, Route 2, Lang's Corner
   Road, Denmark, WI 54208; (414) 863-2397
   This factory outlet sells cheddar and mozzarella cheese. Free tours are available;
call ahead for information.

SUN.	MON.	TUE.	WED.	THU.	FRI.	SAT.
closed	8–4:30	8–4:30	8–4:30	8–4:30	8–4:30	8–noon

SAVINGS: 20%–30% off   *Mailing List*   *All First Quality*
PARKING: lot
PAYMENT: cash, checks (amount of purchase only, with proper I.D.)

EAU CLAIRE, WI

Nelson Cheese Factory Outlet, 1636 Harding Avenue, Eau Claire, WI 54701; (715)
   834-2000
   See listing in Nelson, Wisconsin.

SUN.	MON.	TUE.	WED.	THU.	FRI.	SAT.
10–5	9–6	9–5	9–5	9–8	9–6	9–5

SAVINGS: 30%–50% off   *Mailing List*   *All First Quality*
PARKING: lot
PAYMENT: cash, checks (amount of purchase only, with proper I.D.)

EDGAR, WI

Cherry Grove Cheese, R 5596 Highway "H", Edgar, WI 54426; (715) 352-3081
   Although they do not have set hours when they sell cheese, you can call ahead, or
stop at the factory to buy colby, cheddar, brick, mozzarella, and aged cheddar cheese
at savings that average 30%–50% off retail price. Free tours are available; call ahead for
information and reservations.

SUN.	MON.	TUE.	WED.	THU.	FRI.	SAT.
*	*	*	*	*	*	*

SAVINGS: 30%–50% off   *All First Quality*
SPECIAL DISCOUNTS: sometimes they round off the purchase price to the lesser
   dollar amount
PARKING: lot
PAYMENT: cash, checks (amount of purchase only)

---

*They have no set hours; call ahead.

Frankfort Cheese Factory, Route 1, Box 183 Highway N, Edgar, WI 54426; (715)
   352-2744
   This factory outlet sells over forty varieties of cheese at savings that average 30%
off retail price. Free tours are available; call ahead for information.

SUN.	MON.	TUE.	WED.	THU.	FRI.	SAT.
closed	7–5	7–5	7–5	7–5	7–5	7–5

SAVINGS: 30% off   *Mailing List*   *All First Quality*
PARKING: lot
PAYMENT: cash, checks (amount of purchase only, with proper I.D.), MasterCard, VISA

Pine Valley Co-op, 3704 S. Cardinal Lane, Edgar, WI 54426; (715) 352-2031
   This factory outlet sells about forty varieties of cheese. Prices average 20% off
retail price. You can save even more on what they call "trim." Free tours are available
for groups of fifteen or less; call ahead for information.

SUN.	MON.	TUE.	WED.	THU.	FRI.	SAT.
closed	7:30–4	7:30–4	7:30–4	7:30–4	7:30–4	closed

SAVINGS: 20% off
PARKING: lot
PAYMENT: cash, checks (amount of purchase only, with proper I.D.)

ELLSWORTH, WI

Ellsworth Cooperative Creamery, 232 N. Wallace Street, Ellsworth, WI 54011; (715)
   273-4311
   This factory outlet sells cheese and butter at savings of 15%–25% off retail price.

SUN.	MON.	TUE.	WED.	THU.	FRI.	SAT.
closed	7–5:30	7–5:30	7–5:30	7–5:30	7–5:30	8–2

SAVINGS: 15%–25% off   *All First Quality*
BRAND NAMES: Ellsworth
PARKING: lot
PAYMENT: cash, checks (amount of purchase only)

FENNIMORE, WI

Fennimore Cheese, 1675 Lincoln Avenue, Fennimore, WI 53809; (608) 822-3777
   This factory sells Bahl baby swiss cheese. Savings average 30%–50% off retail
price.

SUN.	MON.	TUE.	WED.	THU.	FRI.	SAT.
10–5	8–5	8–5	8–5	8–5	8–5	8–5

SAVINGS: 30%–50% off
BRAND NAMES: Bahl
ANNUAL SALES: June
PARKING: lot
PAYMENT: cash, checks, MasterCard, VISA

Preston Cheese Company, Route 1, Highway 18, Fennimore, WI 53809; (608)
   943-6843
   This factory outlet sells brick, cheddar, colby, and monterey jack cheese at savings
that average 20%–50% off retail price. They also sell summer sausage and butter, with
even greater savings on grade "B" butter.

SUN.	MON.	TUE.	WED.	THU.	FRI.	SAT.
9–6	9–6	9–6	9–6	9–6	9–6	9–6

SAVINGS: 20%–50% off   *Mailing List*   *All First Quality*
PARKING: lot
PAYMENT: cash, checks (amount of purchase only, with proper I.D.), MasterCard, VISA

FERRYVILLE, WI

Ferryville Cheese Company, Division of Swiss Valley Farm, Box 188, Highway 35,
   Ferryville, WI 54628; (608) 734-3425
   This factory outlet sells brick, swiss, colby, and cheddar cheese at savings that
average 25% off retail price. Savings are greatest on ends and pieces. They also sell
Wisconsin souvenirs. Free tours are available; call ahead for information.

SUN.	MON.	TUE.	WED.	THU.	FRI.	SAT.
9–6	9–5:30	9–5:30	9–5:30	9–5:30	9–6	9–6

SAVINGS: 25% off
BRAND NAMES: Swiss Valley
PARKING: lot
PAYMENT: cash, checks (amount of purchase only, with proper I.D.)

Mailing List

FOND DU LAC, WI

Tolibia Cheese and Wine Villa, 465 N. Main Street, Fond du Lac, WI 54935; (414) 921-4222

This factory outlet sells their own mozzarella, provolone, and blue cheese as well as many other varieties.

SUN.	MON.	TUE.	WED.	THU.	FRI.	SAT.
noon-5	9-5	9-5	9-5	9-5	9-7	9-6

SAVINGS: 20% off
ANNUAL SALES: June
PARKING: lot
PAYMENT: cash, checks (amount of purchase only, with proper I.D.)

Mailing List   *All First Quality*

FREMONT, WI

Union Star Cheese Factory, Route 1, Fremont, WI 54940; (414) 836-2804

This factory outlet sells many varieties of cheese at savings that average 30%–50% off retail price. They also sell honey and summer sausage. Free tours are available; call ahead for information.

SUN.	MON.	TUE.	WED.	THU.	FRI.	SAT.
10:30-5	7-5	7-5	7-5	7-5	7-5	7-5

SAVINGS: 30%–50% off
PARKING: lot
PAYMENT: cash, checks (amount of purchase only, with proper I.D.)

All First Quality

Silverfield Cheese Factory, Box 197, Highway 10 and Highway 110, Fremont, WI 54940; (414) 446-3121

This factory sells many varieties of cheese at savings that average 30% off retail price. They also sell sausage and maple syrup. Tours are available; call ahead for information.

SUN.	MON.	TUE.	WED.	THU.	FRI.	SAT.
8-9	8-9	8-9	8-9	8-9	8-9	8-9

SAVINGS: 30% off
PARKING: lot
PAYMENT: cash, checks (amount of purchase only, with proper I.D.)

Mailing List   *All First Quality*

GILLMAN, WI

Drangle Foods, 300 S. Riverside Drive, P.O. Box 187, Gillman, WI 54433; (715) 447-8241

This factory outlet sells twenty-five varieties of cheese at savings 30%–50% off Wisconsin retail price.

SUN.	MON.	TUE.	WED.	THU.	FRI.	SAT.
closed	8-4	8-4	8-4	8-4	8-4	8-noon

SAVINGS: 30%–50% off
PARKING: lot
PAYMENT: cash, checks (amount of purchase only, with proper I.D.)

Mailing List   *All First Quality*

Lynn Dairy, Route 2, Granton, WI 54436*; (715) 238-7129
This factory outlet sells cheddar, colby, mozzarella, brick, and flavored cheese at savings that average 25%–40% off retail price. Savings on seconds, broken pieces, ends and pieces, and surplus cheese give an additional 10¢/lb. savings. They also sell salami. Free tours are available; call ahead for information.

SUN.	MON.	TUE.	WED.	THU.	FRI.	SAT.
8–4:30	8–4:30	8–4:30	8–4:30	8–4:30	8–4:30	8–4:30

SAVINGS: 25%–40% off
SPECIAL DISCOUNTS: farmers, 10¢/lb. off
PARKING: lot
PAYMENT: cash, checks (amount of purchase only, with proper I.D.), MasterCard, VISA

---

*This is the mailing address; the plant is on Route 1, Lynn, Wisconsin.

World's Champion Gold Brick Cheese Company, Route 1, Gratiot, WI 53541; (608) 922-6252
This factory doesn't actually have a store, but you can go into the factory 24 hours a day to buy cheese. There is a five pound minimum. Free tours are available; call ahead for information. Groups are limited to twenty or less. At this writing, brick cheese was $1.50/lb.

SUN.	MON.	TUE.	WED.	THU.	FRI.	SAT.
*	*	*	*	*	*	*

SAVINGS: 40%–60% off   *All First Quality*
PARKING: lot
PAYMENT: cash, checks (amount of purchase only, with proper I.D.)

---

*They have no set hours; call ahead.

Gerber's Cheese Shop, 135 N. Main Street, Hartford, WI 53027; (414) 673-2575
This is the factory outlet for Gerber's and Bon Bree cheese. Savings begin at about 20% off retail price. They also sell sausage, tea, syrup, and jam.

SUN.	MON.	TUE.	WED.	THU.	FRI.	SAT.
closed	8–7	8–5:30	8–5:30	8–5:30	8–8	8–5

SAVINGS: at least 20% off   *Mailing List*
BRAND NAMES: Gerber's, Bon Bree, Fillman's, Leroy Locker, Twangy's, Cecils
ANNUAL SALES: July
PARKING: street
PAYMENT: cash, checks (with proper I.D.), MasterCard, VISA

Hartford Cheese Distributors, 7273 W. Waterford Road, Hartford, WI 53027*; (414) 673-2698
Although they don't have a store, you can buy muenster, cheddar, and flavored cheese from the factory at savings that average 25%–40% off retail price. Free tours are available for small groups only; call ahead for information.

SUN.	MON.	TUE.	WED.	THU.	FRI.	SAT.
closed	4–4	4–4	4–4	4–4	4–4	8–11:30

SAVINGS: 25%–40% off   *All First Quality*
PARKING: lot
PAYMENT: cash, checks (amount of purchase only, with proper I.D.)

---

*This is the mailing address; the factory address is 6495 Arthur Road.

Schmitz Bear Valley Cheese Factory, Route 1, Box 62, Hillpoint, WI 53937; (608) 583-3147
This factory outlet sells several varieties of cheese at savings that average 25%–40% off retail price.

SUN.	MON.	TUE.	WED.	THU.	FRI.	SAT.
closed	7–5	7–5	7–5	7–5	7–5	7–3

SAVINGS: 25%–40% off   *All First Quality*
PARKING: street
PAYMENT: cash, checks (amount of purchase only)

White Clover Dairy, Route 4, County Trunk "B", Holland, WI 54130; (414) 766-5765
This factory outlet sells eight varieties of gouda and edam cheese at savings of about half of what you would pay in Chicago.

SUN.	MON.	TUE.	WED.	THU.	FRI.	SAT.
closed	7–5	7–5	7–5	7–5	7–6	7–noon

SAVINGS: 50% off   *All First Quality*
ANNUAL SALES: Easter, Christmas
PARKING: lot
PAYMENT: cash, checks (amount of purchase only, with proper I.D.)

Bieri's Cheese Mart, 3271 Highway 45, Jackson, WI 53037; (414) 677-2012
This factory outlet offers over fifty varieties of cheese at savings that average 20%–40% off retail price. They also sell summer sausage and beef sticks and package cheese for shipping.

SUN.	MON.	TUE.	WED.	THU.	FRI.	SAT.
closed	8–6	8–6	8–6	8–6	8–6	8–5

SAVINGS: 20%–40% off   *All First Quality*
PARKING: lot
PAYMENT: cash, checks (with proper I.D.)

Zim's Dairy Product, Route 1, Box 47, Juda, WI 53550; (608) 934-5271
This factory outlet sells brick, colby, and cheddar cheese at savings that average 25%–50% off retail price. They also sell cheese cutters and meat. Best savings are on ends and pieces.

SUN.	MON.	TUE.	WED.	THU.	FRI.	SAT.
closed	8–4:30	8–4:30	8–4:30	8–4:30	8–4:30	8–noon

SAVINGS: 25%–50% off   *Mailing List*
PARKING: lot
PAYMENT: cash, checks (amount of purchase only, with proper I.D.)

Hennings Cheese Factory, 20201 Ucker Point Road, Kiel, WI 53042; (414) 894-3032
This factory outlet sells thirty varieties of cheese, as well as summer sausage. They sell some ends and pieces, seconds, and what they call "trim" for $1.25/lb. Free factory tours are available Monday–Saturday; call ahead for large groups.

SUN.	MON.	TUE.	WED.	THU.	FRI.	SAT.
closed	6–2	6–2	6–2	6–2	6–2	7–noon

SAVINGS: 25%–50% off   *Mailing List*
PARKING: lot
PAYMENT: cash, checks (amount of purchase only, with proper I.D.)

KNAPP, WI

Knapp Creamery Company, 115 South Street, Box 128, Knapp, WI 54749; (715) 665-2266
   This factory outlet sells colby, jack, and cheddar cheese at savings that average 25%–40% off retail price. Ends and pieces are occasionally available at greater savings. Free tours are available; call ahead for information.

SUN.	MON.	TUE.	WED.	THU.	FRI.	SAT.
closed	8:30–5	8:30–5	8:30–5	8:30–5	8:30–5	9–4

SAVINGS: 25%–50% off
PARKING: lot
PAYMENT: cash, checks (amount of purchase only, with proper I.D.)

KRAKOW, WI

Krakow Cheese Factory, Box 112, Center Street, Krakow, WI 54137; (414) 899-3666
   This factory outlet sells their own brand of cheese for $1.65/lb. at this writing.

SUN.	MON.	TUE.	WED.	THU.	FRI.	SAT.
closed	8–3	8–3	8–3	8–3	8–3	8–3

SAVINGS: about 40% off   *All First Quality*
PARKING: lot
PAYMENT: cash, checks (amount of purchase only, with proper I.D.)

LAVALLE, WI

Carr Valley Cheese Factory, Route 1, Highway "G", LaValle, WI 53941; (608) 986-2781
   This factory outlet sells cheddar cheese at savings that average 20%–33% off retail price.

SUN.	MON.	TUE.	WED.	THU.	FRI.	SAT.
closed	8–4	8–4	8–4	8–4	8–4	8–4

SAVINGS: 20%–33% off
BRAND NAMES: Armour
PARKING: lot
PAYMENT: cash, checks (amount of purchase only, with proper I.D.)

LOGANVILLE, WI

Suemnicht Cheese Company, Route 1, Box 113, Valley View Road, Loganville, WI 53943; (608) 546-2551
   This factory outlet sells several varieties of cheese. Savings average 25% off retail price on first quality, and up to 75% off ends and pieces. They have an observation window where you can watch the cheese being made. They also sell sausage.

SUN.	MON.	TUE.	WED.	THU.	FRI.	SAT.
closed	8:30–5	8:30–5	8:30–5	8:30–5	8:30–5	8:30–5

SAVINGS: 25%–75% off   *Mailing List*
SPECIAL DISCOUNTS: charity groups, 15% off
PARKING: lot
PAYMENT: cash, checks (amount of purchase only, with proper I.D., no out-of-state checks), MasterCard, VISA

Krohn Dairy Products, Route 3, Box 189, Highway 163, Luxemburg, WI 54217; (414) 845-2901

This factory outlet sells about ten varieties of mozzarella and cheddar cheese at savings that average 25%-50% off retail price. They also sell herring, mustard, and maple syrup. Free tours are available; call ahead for information.

SUN.	MON.	TUE.	WED.	THU.	FRI.	SAT.
closed	8-5	8-5	8-5	8-5	8-5	8-4

SAVINGS: 25-50% off   *All First Quality*
PARKING: lot
PAYMENT: cash, checks (amount of purchase only, with proper I.D.)

Lynn Dairy
See listing in Granton, Wisconsin.

Associated Milk Producers, 1707 S. Park Street, Madison, WI 53713; (608) 256-0687

This factory outlet sells brick, colby, and cheddar cheese at savings that average 20%-40% off retail price. Better savings are on ends and pieces at an additional 20%-25% off. They also sell sausage. Free tours are available Monday through Friday, 9:00-3:00.

SUN.	MON.	TUE.	WED.	THU.	FRI.	SAT.
closed	8-4:30	8-4:30	8-4:30	8-4:30	8-4:30	8-noon

SAVINGS: 20%-50% off   *Mailing List*
PARKING: lot
PAYMENT: cash, checks (amount of purchase only, with proper I.D.)

Pine River Dairy, 10115 W. English Lake Road, Manitowoc, WI 54220; (414) 758-2233

This factory outlet sells Pine River cheese and Buttercup butter at savings that begin about 25% off retail price. Savings are greater on seconds, surplus, and overruns.

SUN.	MON.	TUE.	WED.	THU.	FRI.	SAT.
closed	8-4	8-4	8-4	8-4	8-4	8-noon

SAVINGS: 25%-50% off
BRAND NAMES: Buttercup, Pine River
PARKING: lot
PAYMENT: cash, checks

Dupont Cheese, Route 1, Box 77, Marion, WI 54950; (715) 754-5424

This factory outlet sells twenty varieties of cheese. Savings are only about 10¢/lb. off Wisconsin prices, but still about 20% below Chicagoland retail prices.

SUN.	MON.	TUE.	WED.	THU.	FRI.	SAT.
closed	8-3	8-3	closed	closed	8-3	8-3

SAVINGS: 20% off   *All First Quality*
PARKING: lot
PAYMENT: cash, checks (amount of purchase only, with proper I.D.)

Figi's, 2525 S. Roddis Avenue, Marshfield, WI 54449; (715) 387-1771
This factory outlet sells over twenty varieties of cheese at prices that average 30%–40% off retail price. They also have a mail order business, and sell specialty gift items, sausages, and pastries. They have a cheese club; ask about it at the store. Greatest savings are on ends and pieces, which save the buyer an additional 10%.

SUN.	MON.	TUE.	WED.	THU.	FRI.	SAT.
9–5	8–6	8–6	8–6	8–6	8–6	9–5

SAVINGS: 30%–50% off
ANNUAL SALES: Valentine's Day, Christmas
PARKING: lot
PAYMENT: cash, checks (amount of purchase only, with proper I.D.), MasterCard, VISA, American Express

Gad Cheese, Route 2, Box 140, Medford, WI 54451; (715) 748-4273
This factory outlet sells brick, American, colby, cheddar, and mozzarella cheese at savings that average 50¢/lb. off retail price. Free tours are available Monday–Saturday, 6:00–3:00.

SUN.	MON.	TUE.	WED.	THU.	FRI.	SAT.
closed	6–3	6–3	6–3	6–3	6–3	6–3

SAVINGS: about 25% off   *All First Quality*
PARKING: lot
PAYMENT: cash, checks (amount of purchase only, with proper I.D., no out-of-state checks)

Cloverleaf Cheese Factory, 2006 N. Irish Road, Menasha, WI 54956; (414) 722-9201
This factory sells fifteen varieties of cheese at savings that average 25%–50% off retail price. They also sell honey, maple syrup, and popcorn.

SUN.	MON.	TUE.	WED.	THU.	FRI.	SAT.
closed	7–3	7–3	7–3	7–5:30	7–3	7–3

SAVINGS: 25%–50% off   *Mailing List*   *All First Quality*
ANNUAL SALES: April, October
PARKING: lot
PAYMENT: cash, checks (amount of purchase only, with proper I.D.)

Pine River Farmers, Dairy Co-op, N1704 Pine Ridge Road, Merrill, WI 54452; (715) 536-7324
This factory outlet sells over fifty varieties of cheese at savings that average 25%–50% off retail price. Broken pieces are occasionally available at savings of an additional 20¢/lb. They also sell some craft items, gift boxes of cheese, and summer sausage.

SUN.	MON.	TUE.	WED.	THU.	FRI.	SAT.
9–4	7–5	7–5	7–5	7–5	7–5	7–4

SAVINGS: 25%–60% off   *Mailing List*
PARKING: lot
PAYMENT: cash, checks (amount of purchase only, with proper I.D.)

Maple Grove Cheese, 10498 N. Mayflower Road, Milladore, WI 54454; (715) 652-2214
This factory sells thirty varieties of cheese at savings that average 30%–50% off retail price. Free tours are available; call ahead for information.

SUN.	MON.	TUE.	WED.	THU.	FRI.	SAT.
closed	7-4:30	7-4:30	7-4:30	7-4:30	7-4:30	7-4:30

SAVINGS: 30%–50% off   *All First Quality*
PARKING: lot
PAYMENT: cash, checks (amount of purchase only, with proper I.D., no out-of-state checks)

MINERAL POINT, WI

Hook's Cheese Company—Buck Grove Cheese Factory, Route 2, Box 42,
Highway 39, 3 miles east of town, Mineral Point, WI 53565; (608) 987-2658
This factory outlet sells several varieties of cheese. They are proud to say that their colby won the World Championship of Cheese in 1982. Savings average 30%–50% off retail price. Free tours are available; call ahead for information.

SUN.	MON.	TUE.	WED.	THU.	FRI.	SAT.
closed	8-1	8-1	8-1	8-1	8-1	8-1

SAVINGS: 30%–50% off   *Mailing List*   *All First Quality*
PARKING: lot
PAYMENT: cash, checks (amount of purchase only, with proper I.D.)

TOWNSHIP OF MITCHELL, WI

Lensmire Cheese Factory, Route 1, Township of Mitchell, WI 53011; (414) 528-8231
This factory outlet sells a dozen varieties of cheese. Savings average about 50¢/lb. off retail price, and even more off what they call "trim." Free factory tours are available; call ahead for information.

SUN.	MON.	TUE.	WED.	THU.	FRI.	SAT.
closed	7-4	7-4	7-4	7-4	7-4	7-4

SAVINGS: 25%–40% off
PARKING: lot
PAYMENT: cash, checks (amount of purchase only, with proper I.D.)

MONROE, WI

Chalet Cheese Coop, Route 4, County "N", Monroe, WI 53566; (608) 325-4343
This factory outlet sells brick, mozzarella, swiss, and limburger cheese at savings that average 20%–40% off retail price. Free tours are available seven days a week.

SUN.	MON.	TUE.	WED.	THU.	FRI.	SAT.
6:00-3:30	6-3:30	6-3:30	6-3:30	6-3:30	6-3:30	6-3:30

SAVINGS: 20%–40% off   *All First Quality*
PARKING: lot
PAYMENT: cash, checks (amount of purchase only, with proper I.D.)

MONTICELLO, WI

Silver Lewis Cheese Co-op, Route 1, Monticello, WI 53570; (608) 938-4813
This factory outlet sells ten varieties of cheese at prices that average 20¢–40¢/lb. at this writing.

SUN.	MON.	TUE.	WED.	THU.	FRI.	SAT.
closed	6-1:30	6-1:30	closed	6-1:30	6-1:30	6-1:30

SAVINGS: 20%–40% off   *All First Quality*
PARKING: lot
PAYMENT: cash, checks (amount of purchase only, with proper I.D.)

MOSINEE, WI

Mullins Cheese, 598 Seagull Drive, Mosinee, WI 54455; (715) 693-3205
   This factory outlet sells about fifty varieties of cheese. Savings average about 40% off retail price. Free tours are available any time you arrive.

SUN.	MON.	TUE.	WED.	THU.	FRI.	SAT.
6–5:30	6–5:30	6–5:30	6–5:30	6–5:30	6–5:30	6–5:30

SAVINGS: about 40% off   *All First Quality*
PARKING: lot
PAYMENT: cash, checks

MOUNT HOREB, WI

Ryser Brothers of Wisconsin, 209 E. Main Street, Mount Horeb, WI 53572; (608) 437-3051
   This is the factory outlet for Ryser Brothers cheese. They also sell some gift items, candy, and crackers. Savings are greatest on a few ends and pieces.

SUN.	MON.	TUE.	WED.	THU.	FRI.	SAT.
9–5:30	9–5:30	9–5:30	9–5:30	9–5:30	9–5:30	9–5:30

SAVINGS: 20%–30% off   *Christmas Mailing List*
PARKING: street
PAYMENT: cash, checks (amount of purchase only, with proper I.D.), MasterCard, VISA

MOUNT STERLING, WI

Mount Sterling Cheese Factory, Highway 171, Box 103, Mount Sterling, WI 54645; (608) 734-3151
   This factory outlet sells brick and mozzarella cheese. They also sell goat cheese. Savings average 15%–40% off retail price. They also sell honey, apple butter, maple syrup, and sausages. Free tours are available; call ahead for information.

SUN.	MON.	TUE.	WED.	THU.	FRI.	SAT.
9:30–5	9:30–5	9:30–5	9:30–5	9:30–5	9:30–5	9:30–5

SAVINGS: 15%–40% off   *Mailing List*   *All First Quality*
PARKING: lot
PAYMENT: cash, checks (amount of purchase only, with proper I.D.)

MUSCODA, WI

Meister Cheese Company, Box 68 Nebraska Street, Muscoda, WI 53573; (608) 739-3134
   This factory outlet sells over twenty-five varieties of cheese at savings that average 20%–40% off retail price. Free tours are available; call ahead for information.

SUN.	MON.	TUE.	WED.	THU.	FRI.	SAT.
closed	9–5	9–5	9–5	9–5	9–5	9–5

SAVINGS: 20%–40% off   *Mailing List*   *All First Quality*
PARKING: lot
PAYMENT: cash, checks (amount of purchase only, with proper I.D.)

NELSON, WI

Nelson Cheese Factory, Great River Road (State Highway 35), Nelson, WI 54756; (715) 673-4725
   This is the factory outlet for Nelson cheese. Savings average 25%–50% off retail price on first quality muenster, colby, and monterey jack cheese. This is also the birthplace of Laura Ingalls Wilder, who wrote the *Little House* books. They have another store in Eau Claire, Wisconsin.

SUN.	MON.	TUE.	WED.	THU.	FRI.	SAT.
9–5	9–5	9–5	9–5	9–5	9–5	9–5

SAVINGS: 20%–40% off   *Mailing List*   *All First Quality*
PARKING: lot
PAYMENT: cash, checks (amount of purchase only, with proper I.D.)

NEW LONDON, WI

Borden, Inc., 405 W. Wolf River Avenue, New London, WI 54961; (414) 982-3303
    This factory outlet sells many varieties of Borden cheese at savings that average
20%–50% off retail price.

SUN.	MON.	TUE.	WED.	THU.	FRI.	SAT.
closed	9-5	9-5	9-5	9-5	9-5	closed

SAVINGS: 20%–50% off
BRAND NAMES: Borden   *All First Quality*
PARKING: lot
PAYMENT: cash, checks (no out-of-state checks)

NEWBURG CORNERS, WI

Newburg Corners Cheese Factory, Route 2, Highway 33, Newburg Corners, WI
    54614; (608) 452-3636
    This factory outlet sells brick, colby, cheddar, and mozzarella cheese at savings
that average 30% off retail price. You can save more on "trim." Free tours are available
for small groups only; call ahead for information.

SUN.	MON.	TUE.	WED.	THU.	FRI.	SAT.
closed	8-4:30	8-4:30	8-4:30	8-4:30	8-4:30	8-4:30

SAVINGS: 20%–40% off   *All First Quality*
PARKING: lot
PAYMENT: cash only

NEWTON, WI

Golden Guernsey Dairy, 11110 Highway 42, Newton, WI 53063; (414) 693-8111
    This dairy sells American, provolone, mozzarella, and string cheese at the factory.
Savings are about 10¢/lb. They have free tours; call ahead for information.

SUN.	MON.	TUE.	WED.	THU.	FRI.	SAT.
closed	9-noon	9-4	9-4	9-4	9-4	9-4

SAVINGS: about 20% off   *All First Quality*
PARKING: lot
PAYMENT: cash, checks (local checks only)

OCONOMOWOC, WI

Stallman's Mapleton Cheese Factory, 35990 Mapleton Road, Oconomowoc, WI
    53066; (414) 474-7142
    This factory outlet sells Bon Bree semisoft cheese manufactured at the plant, as
well as several other varieties. Savings average 25%–40% off retail price. They also fill
mail orders.

SUN.	MON.	TUE.	WED.	THU.	FRI.	SAT.
8-5	8-5	8-5	8-5	8-5	8-5	8-5

SAVINGS: 25%–40% off   *Mailing List*   *All First Quality*
SALE DAYS: vary
PARKING: lot
PAYMENT: cash, checks (amount of purchase only, with proper I.D.), MasterCard, VISA

OCONTO, WI

County Line Cheese Company, Route 1, Box 148, Highway 41, Oconto, WI 54153;
    (715) 582-4006

This factory outlet sells over twenty-five varieties of County Line cheese. Savings average 25%–50% off retail price. They also sell summer sausage. Although they do not have tours, there is an observation window where you can watch the cheese being made.

SUN.	MON.	TUE.	WED.	THU.	FRI.	SAT.
closed	6:30–5	6:30–5	6:30–5	6:30–5	6:30–5	6:30–5

SAVINGS: 25%–50% off   *Mailing List*   *All First Quality*
BRAND NAMES: County Line
PARKING: lot
PAYMENT: cash, checks (amount of purchase only, with proper I.D.)

OCONTO FALLS, WI

Krause Dairy Corporation, Route 2, Oconto Falls, WI 54154; (414) 846-3639
This factory outlet sells mozzarella, provolone, brick, and swiss cheese at savings that average 20%–30% off retail price. They also sell sausage. Free tours are sometimes available; call ahead for information.

SUN.	MON.	TUE.	WED.	THU.	FRI.	SAT.
closed	8–2	8–2	8–2	8–2	8–2	*

SAVINGS: 20%–30% off   *All First Quality*
PARKING: lot
PAYMENT: cash, checks (amount of purchase only, with proper I.D.)

————
*Call ahead for hours on Saturday.

Springside Cheese Corporation, Route 1, Box 108A, Oconto Falls, WI 54154; (414) 829-6395
This factory outlet sells several varieties of cheese at savings that average 15%–25% off retail price. Free tours are available; call ahead for information.

SUN.	MON.	TUE.	WED.	THU.	FRI.	SAT.
closed	7–4	7–4	7–4	7–4	7–4	7–4

SAVINGS: 15%–25% off   *All First Quality*
PARKING: lot
PAYMENT: cash, checks (amount of purchase only, with proper I.D.)

PLOVER, WI

Rybicki's Cheese Factory, Manufacturers Direct Mall, 101 Plover Road, Plover, WI 54467; (715) 341-1278
This store sells cheese, gourmet items, wine, and beer at savings of 20%–50% off retail price.

SUN.	MON.	TUE.	WED.	THU.	FRI.	SAT.
11–6	9:30–9	9:30–9	9:30–9	9:30–9	9:30–9	9:30–6

SAVINGS: 20%–50% off   *Christmas Mailing List*   *All First Quality*
SALE DAYS: weekends
PARKING: lot
PAYMENT: cash, checks (with proper I.D.)

RANDOLPH, WI

Sunny Creek Co-op, Route 2, Randolph, WI 53956; (414) 326-3386
This factory outlet sells many varieties of cheese made on the premises. Savings average 30% off retail price. Free tours are available: call ahead for information.

SUN.	MON.	TUE.	WED.	THU.	FRI.	SAT.
closed	6–6	6–6	6–6	6–6	6–6	6–6

SAVINGS: 30%–40% off   *All First Quality*

PARKING: lot
PAYMENT: cash, checks (amount of purchase only, with proper I.D.)

Central Cheese and Butter Co-op, Route 4, Box 302, Highway 48, Rice Lake, WI
54868; (715) 234-9471
This factory sells a variety of cheese at prices of $1.70–$2.90/lb. at this writing.
They also sell sausages and maple syrup. Free tours can be arranged for groups of ten
to twenty-five people; call ahead for reservations.

SUN.	MON.	TUE.	WED.	THU.	FRI.	SAT.
closed	8–5	8–5	8–noon	8–5	8–5	8–5

SAVINGS: 25%–40% off   *Mailing List*   *All First Quality*
PARKING: street
PAYMENT: cash, checks (amount of purchase only, with proper I.D.)

Stanga Cheese Corporation, Box 37, Rubicon, WI 53078; (414) 673-4480
This factory doesn't have a store, but you can buy mozzarella and provolone
cheese at savings that average 30%–40% off retail price. Free tours are available; call
ahead for information.

SUN.	MON.	TUE.	WED.	THU.	FRI.	SAT.
closed	7–2	7–2	7–2	7–2	7–2	closed

SAVINGS: 30%–40% off   *All First Quality*
PARKING: lot
PAYMENT: cash, checks (amount of purchase only, with proper I.D.)

Wisconsin Dairy State Cheese Company, Box 142, Rudolph, WI 54475; (715)
435-3144
This factory outlet sells over eighty varieties of cheese at savings that average
25%–40% off retail price. They have a free movie and lecture about the cheese they
manufacture.

SUN.	MON.	TUE.	WED.	THU.	FRI.	SAT.
9–noon	8–5:15	8–5:15	8–5:15	8–5:15	8–5:15	8–5:15

SAVINGS: 25%–40%   *All First Quality*
PARKING: lot
PAYMENT: cash, checks (amount of purchase only, with proper I.D.)

Shullsburg Creamery, 208 W. Water Street, Shullsburg, WI 53586; (608) 965-4485
This factory outlet sells over fifty varieties of cheese at savings that average 20%
off retail price. Ends and pieces are the best buys. They also sell pork sausage and
summer sausage.

SUN.	MON.	TUE.	WED.	THU.	FRI.	SAT.
noon–4:30	8:30–5:30	8:30–5:30	8:30–5:30	8:30–5:30	8:30–5:30	8:30–5:30

SAVINGS: 20%–40%   *Mailing List*
SPECIAL DISCOUNTS: senior citizens and charity groups (ask)
PARKING: lot
PAYMENT: cash, checks (amount of purchase only, with proper I.D.), MasterCard, VISA

Dutch Country Cheese, County Trunk "OK" (off I-43), Sheboygan, WI 53081; (414)
457-0635

This outlet sells cheese at savings of 20%–30% off retail price. They also sell souvenirs.

SUN.	MON.	TUE.	WED.	THU.	FRI.	SAT.
noon–4	8–8	8–8	8–8	8–8	8–8	8–8

SAVINGS: 20%–30% off   *Mailing List*   *All First Quality*
SPECIAL SALES: weekly
ANNUAL SALES: anniversary
PARKING: lot
PAYMENT: cash, checks (amount of purchase only, with proper I.D.), MasterCard, VISA

SHEBOYGAN FALLS, WI

Gibbsville Cheese Sales, County Trunk "OO" West (off state route 32), Route 3, Box 5420, Sheboygan Falls, WI 53085; (414) 564-3242
   This factory outlet sells several varieties of cheddar, colby, swiss, brick, mozzarella, provolone, and gouda cheese at savings that begin at 20% off retail price and can go up to 50% on seconds and ends and pieces.

SUN.	MON.	TUE.	WED.	THU.	FRI.	SAT.
closed	8–5	8–5	8–5	8–5	8–5	8–5

SAVINGS: 20%–50% off
PARKING: lot
PAYMENT: cash, checks (with proper I.D.)

SOLDIERS GROVE, WI

Soldiers Grove Farmers Co-op, Highway 61, Soldiers Grove, WI 54655; (608) 624-5429
   This factory outlet sells over thirty varieties of cheese at savings that average 30% off retail price. Free tours are available; call ahead for information.

SUN.	MON.	TUE.	WED.	THU.	FRI.	SAT.
closed	8–4	8–4	8–4	8–4	8–4	8–4

SAVINGS: about 30% off   *Mailing List*   *All First Quality*
PARKING: lot
PAYMENT: cash, checks

Wisconsin's Pride Cheese, Highways 61 & 171, Route 1, Soldiers Grove, WI 54655; (608) 624-5683
   This factory outlet sells over forty varieties of cheese at savings up to 50% off retail price. They also sell "trim," on which you can save more. Free tours are available; call ahead for information.

SUN.	MON.	TUE.	WED.	THU.	FRI.	SAT.
9–5	9–5	9–5	9–5	9–5	9–5	9–5

SAVINGS: 50%–75% off   *All First Quality*
PARKING: lot
PAYMENT: cash, checks (amount of purchase only, with proper I.D.), MasterCard, VISA

SOUTH WAYNE, WI

Valley View Cheese Co-op, Route 1, Highway 176 North, South Wayne, WI 53587; (608) 439-5569
   You can buy cheese at the factory; they don't have a store. First quality cheese averages 35% off retail price. Occasional ends and pieces save you even more.

SUN.	MON.	TUE.	WED.	THU.	FRI.	SAT.
6–noon	6–noon	6–noon	6–noon	6–noon	6–noon	6–noon

SAVINGS: 35%–60% off
PARKING: lot
PAYMENT: cash only

Zimmerman Cheese, N6853 Highway 78, South Wayne, WI 53587; (608) 325-6834
This factory outlet sells about twenty varieties of cheese at savings that average 25%–40% off retail price.

SUN.	MON.	TUE.	WED.	THU.	FRI.	SAT.
closed	8–4	8–4	closed	closed	8–4	8–4

SAVINGS: 25%–40% off   *All First Quality*
PARKING: lot
PAYMENT: cash, checks (amount of purchase only, with proper I.D.)

SPRING GREEN, WI

Gruber Cheese, Route 2, County Trunk "B", Spring Green, WI 53588; (608) 546-3836
This factory outlet sells brick, cheddar, mozzarella, monterey jack, farmers, and swiss cheese at savings that average 30% off retail price. They also sell jams and jellies. Free tours are available 9:00–noon, seven days a week.

SUN.	MON.	TUE.	WED.	THU.	FRI.	SAT.
8–4:30	8–4:30	8–4:30	8–4:30	8–4:30	8–4:30	8–4:30

SAVINGS: about 30% off   *All First Quality*
PARKING: lot
PAYMENT: cash, checks (amount of purchase only, with proper I.D.)

THERESA, WI

Widmer's Cheese Cellars, 214 W. Henni Street, Theresa, WI 53091; (414) 488-2503
This factory outlet sells over twenty varieties of cheese at savings that average 25%–40% off retail price. Free tours are available Monday–Saturday 9:00–11:00; call ahead for reservations.

SUN.	MON.	TUE.	WED.	THU.	FRI.	SAT.
closed	5–5	5–5	5–5	5–5	5–5	5–5

SAVINGS: 25%–40% off   *Mailing List*   *All First Quality*
PARKING: street
PAYMENT: cash, checks (amount of purchase only, with proper I.D.)

VAN DYNE, WI

Lone Elm Cheese Factory, Lone Elm Road and Oregon Street Road, Van Dyne, WI 54979; (414) 688-5576
This factory outlet sells over twenty varieties of cheese at savings that average 25%–40% off retail price. They also sell honey, jam, and syrup, and make pizza with their mozzarella cheese.

SUN.	MON.	TUE.	WED.	THU.	FRI.	SAT.
closed	9–5	9–5	9–5	9–5	9–5	9–5

SAVINGS: 25%–40% off   *All First Quality*
PARKING: lot
PAYMENT: cash, checks (amount of purchase only, with proper I.D.), MasterCard, VISA

WAUSAU, WI

Lemke Cheese Company, Box 688, Wausau, WI 54401; (715) 842-3214
Although they were very shy about telling me, they do sell cheese to the public from the plant.

SUN.	MON.	TUE.	WED.	THU.	FRI.	SAT.
*	*	*	*	*	*	*

SAVINGS: 25%–40% off
PARKING: lot
PAYMENT: cash

---

*They have no set hours; call ahead.

Cady Cheese Factory and Shop, Route 1, Box 60, Wilson, WI 54027; (715) 772-4218

This factory outlet sells over eighty varieties of cheese, about a dozen of which they manufacture. Seconds and ends and pieces are $1.00 off their usual prices. Free tours are available for small groups; call ahead for information.

SUN.	MON.	TUE.	WED.	THU.	FRI.	SAT.
9-5	9-5	9-5	9-5	9-5	9-5	9-5

SAVINGS: 20%–50% off
PARKING: lot
PAYMENT: cash, checks (amount of purchase only, with proper I.D.)

Wrightstown Milk Products, 228 Green Street, Wrightstown, WI 54180; (414) 532-4412

This factory outlet sells their own brand of romano and parmesan cheese at savings of 33%–50% off retail price.

SUN.	MON.	TUE.	WED.	THU.	FRI.	SAT.
closed	8-4:30	8-4:30	8-4:30	8-4:30	8-4:30	9-3

SAVINGS: 33%–50% off   *All First Quality*
PARKING: lot
PAYMENT: cash, checks (no out-of-state checks)

FOOD—MEAT AND SAUSAGE

This chapter includes fresh, canned, and frozen meat, sausage, and delicatessen items. Several outlets sold first quality merchandise at retail prices.

Merchandise which is not first quality has flaws in appearance or packaging, not in taste or wholesomeness. Look for seconds, irregulars, "broken casings," and ends and pieces for the greatest savings. You may be willing to pay $6.00/lb. for corned beef, but if irregular slices won't bother you, they will cost as little as 99¢/lb. Savings were also excellent in large "bulk" packages.

Armour Dial Men's Club Store, 1327 W. 31st Place, Chicago, IL 60608; (312) 247-0016

This factory outlet sells Armour canned meats, Dial soap, and Loft detergent. Savings range from small on canned meats to 60% off retail price on unwrapped soap.

SUN.	MON.	TUE.	WED.	THU.	FRI.	SAT.
closed	8-3:45	8-3:45	8-3:45	8-3:45	8-3:45	8-11:45

SAVINGS: 20%–60% off
BRAND NAMES: Armour, Loft, Dial
PARKING: street
PAYMENT: cash, checks (amount of purchase only, with proper I.D.)

Chicago Chili Company, 2488 N. Leavitt Street, Chicago, IL 60647; (312) 227-0773

This small plant store offers chili and institutional packaged steaks and roasts at savings up to 40% off retail price.

SUN.	MON.	TUE.	WED.	THU.	FRI.	SAT.
closed	closed	closed	closed	closed	closed	9–4

SAVINGS: 20%–40% off   *Mailing List*   *All First Quality*
BRAND NAMES: King Carne, Chicago Trim
SPECIAL SALES: vary
PARKING: lot
PAYMENT: cash, checks (amount of purchase only, with proper I.D.)

Crawford Sausage Company, 2310 S. Pulaski Road, Chicago, IL 60623; (312) 277-3095
    This plant store sells sausage at savings that average 30% off retail price on ends and pieces and surplus.

SUN.	MON.	TUE.	WED.	THU.	FRI.	SAT.
closed	12:30–3:30	12:30–3:30	12:30–3:30	12:30–3:30	12:30–3:30	9–noon

SAVINGS: about 30% off
PARKING: lot
PAYMENT: cash only

Danielson Food Products, 215 W. Root Street, Chicago, IL 60609; (312) 285-2111
    This outlet sells Danielson chili as well as hamburger patties, sausage, roast beef, and hot dogs. Everything is first quality, and they offer wholesale prices to their retail customers. Savings are about 25% off retail price on the Danielson products.

SUN.	MON.	TUE.	WED.	THU.	FRI.	SAT.
closed	7–3	7–3	7–3	7–3	7–3	closed

SAVINGS: 10%–25% off   *All First Quality*
BRAND NAMES: Danielson
PARKING: lot
PAYMENT: cash, checks (amount of purchase only, with proper I.D.)

Kosher Zion Meats Company, 5529 N. Kedzie Avenue, Chicago, IL 60625; (312) 463-3351
    This factory outlet sells hot dogs, corned beef, sausage, and other Kosher Zion products. Savings average 10%–40%, with greatest savings on seconds.

SUN.	MON.	TUE.	WED.	THU.	FRI.	SAT.
8–3:30	8–4:30	8–4:30	8–4:30	8–5:30	8–5:30	8–3:30

SAVINGS: 10%–40% off
BRAND NAMES: Kosher Zion
SPECIAL SALES: weekly
PARKING: lot
PAYMENT: cash, checks (amount of purchase only, with proper I.D.)

Moo and Oink, 3834 S. Halsted Street, Chicago, IL 60609; (312) 666-6465
    This unusual store is like a "meat supermarket." Savings average 20%–40% off supermarket prices on most items with greatest savings on five- and ten-pound packages. Some meat is ungraded; look at the labeling. They also sell huge, 1½- to 2-ounce shrimp for $7.99/lb. (frequently on special for $6.99/lb.) and some grocery items at a discount.

SUN.	MON.	TUE.	WED.	THU.	FRI.	SAT.
10–2	9–7	9–7	9–7	9–7	9–7	8–4

SAVINGS: 20%–50% off
PARKING: lot
PAYMENT: cash, checks (amount of purchase only, with proper I.D.), food stamps

Moo and Oink, 7158 S. Stony Island Avenue, Chicago, IL 60649; (312) 666-6465
    See listing above.

SUN.	MON.	TUE.	WED.	THU.	FRI.	SAT.
10–2	9–7	9–7	9–7	9–7	9–7	8–4

SAVINGS: 20%–50% off
PARKING: lot
PAYMENT: cash, checks (amount of purchase only, with proper I.D.), food stamps

Moo and Oink, 8201 S. Racine Avenue, Chicago, IL 60620; (312) 666-6465
   See listing above.

SUN.	MON.	TUE.	WED.	THU.	FRI.	SAT.
10–2	9–7	9–7	9–7	9–7	9–7	8–5

SAVINGS: 20%–50% off   *All First Quality*
PARKING: street
PAYMENT: cash, checks, MasterCard, VISA

Randolph Packing Company, 158 N. Sangamon Street, Chicago, IL 60607; (312) 421-3320
   This factory outlet sells its own brand of salami at savings about 10% off retail price. They also sell some meat at discount prices.

SUN.	MON.	TUE.	WED.	THU.	FRI.	SAT.
closed	6–2	6–2	6–2	6–2	6–2	6–10:30

SAVINGS: at least 10% off   *All First Quality*
PARKING: street
PAYMENT: cash only

Sinai Kosher Foods Corporation, 1000 West Pershing Road, Chicago, IL 60609; (312) 650-6330
   This is the factory outlet for Sinai Kosher meats. They sell hot dogs, salami, and corned beef at savings that start at 20% off retail price on first quality, and go to about 40% on seconds and irregular merchandise.

SUN.	MON.	TUE.	WED.	THU.	FRI.	SAT.
closed	6–4	6–4	6–4	6–4	6–3	closed

SAVINGS: 20%–40% off
PARKING: lot
PAYMENT: cash only

Slotkowski Sausage Company, 2021 W. 18th Street, Chicago, IL 60608; (312) 226-1667
   This is the factory outlet for Slotkowski Polish and Italian sausage. Savings average 20%–30% off on first quality merchandise.

SUN.	MON.	TUE.	WED.	THU.	FRI.	SAT.
closed	6–4:30	6–4:30	6–4:30	6–4:30	6–4:30	7–noon

SAVINGS: 20%–30% off   *All First Quality*
PARKING: lot
PAYMENT: cash only

Sparrer Sausage Company, 4325 W. Ogden Avenue, Chicago, IL 60623; (312) 762-3334
   You can buy pizza sausage, summer sausage, ribs, and smoky beef right at the factory at savings that average 10%–25% off retail price. You must phone in your orders the day before you plan to pick them up.

SUN.	MON.	TUE.	WED.	THU.	FRI.	SAT.
*	*	*	*	*	*	*

SAVINGS: 10%–25% off   *All First Quality*
PARKING: street
PAYMENT: cash only

---

*Call ahead for hours.

Steaks 'N' Stuff Frozen Foods, 7646 W. Touhy Avenue, Chicago, IL 60648; (312)
792-1310
    This store sells frozen gift packages of meat. Savings are greatest on some
irregulars and imperfect items. They have another store in Mount Prospect, Illinois.

SUN.	MON.	TUE.	WED.	THU.	FRI.	SAT.
closed	9–6	9–6	9–6	9–6	9–6	9–5

SAVINGS: 10%–30% off   *Mailing List*
ANNUAL SALES: all holidays
PARKING: lot
PAYMENT: cash, checks (with proper I.D.)

Vienna Beef Factory Store, 2501 N. Damen Avenue, Chicago, IL 60647; (312)
278-7800
    This is the factory outlet store for Vienna beef products. Savings on corned beef,
roast beef, pastrami, salami, knockwurst, polish sausage, and bagel dogs average
about 15% off retail price. There are two bins of seconds next to the retail counter.
Look at the signs or ask the clerk for specials.

SUN.	MON.	TUE.	WED.	THU.	FRI.	SAT.
closed	9–5	9–5	9–5	9–5	9–5	9–4

SAVINGS: 15%–40% off
BRAND NAMES: Vienna
PARKING: lot
PAYMENT: cash, MasterCard, VISA

MOUNT PROSPECT, IL

Steaks 'N' Stuff Frozen Foods, 108 W. Northwest Highway, Mount Prospect, IL
60056; (312) 398-3115
    See listing in Chicago, Illinois.

SUN.	MON.	TUE.	WED.	THU.	FRI.	SAT.
closed	9–6	9–6	9–6	9–6	9–6	9–5

SAVINGS: 10%–30% off   *Mailing List*   *All First Quality*
ANNUAL SALES: holidays, anniversary
PARKING: lot
PAYMENT: cash, checks (with proper I.D.)

WISCONSIN
FORT ATKINSON, WI

Jones Dairy Farm Retail Store, Jones Avenue, Fort Atkinson, WI 53538; (414)
563-2963
    This is the factory outlet for Jones pork products. They sell ham, bacon, sausage,
liverwurst, and Canadian bacon. Savings can run up to 60% off retail price on seconds
and ends and pieces, although there is no discount on first quality merchandise. They
also sell maple syrup and Bavarian mustard.

SUN.	MON.	TUE.	WED.	THU.	FRI.	SAT.
closed	8–5	8–5	8–5	8–5	8–5	8–5

SAVINGS: up to 60% off
BRAND NAMES: Jones

PARKING: lot
PAYMENT: cash, checks (amount of purchase only, with proper I.D.)

MILWAUKEE, WI

Usinger's, 1030 N. Third Street, Milwaukee, WI 53203; (414) 276-9100
This plant store sells more than eighty sausage items. Savings begin at 10% off retail price on first quality, and can go up to 40% off on some imperfects, test runs, ends and pieces, and surplus merchandise.

SUN.	MON.	TUE.	WED.	THU.	FRI.	SAT.
closed	8:30-5	8:30-5	8:30-5	8:30-5	8:30-5	8:30-5

SAVINGS: 10%-40% off
BRAND NAMES: Usinger's
SPECIAL DISCOUNTS: senior citizens, 10% off
PARKING: lot
PAYMENT: cash only

FOOD—MISCELLANEOUS

This chapter includes beverages, gourmet and ethnic foods, mushrooms, and frozen food. As with other food categories, seconds usually have more to do with the appearance or packaging of the item than with its wholesomeness. Several of these outlets sold first quality merchandise at savings 25%-50% off retail prices.

ILLINOIS

CHICAGO, IL

Charlotte Charles, 2501 N. Elston Avenue, Chicago, IL 60647; (312) 772-8310
The plant is open every two months. They sell a variety of seconds, irregulars, dents, bruised, and surplus gourmet food items at tremendous savings. Ask to be put on their mailing list, so you'll know when their sales occur.

SUN.	MON.	TUE.	WED.	THU.	FRI.	SAT.
closed	closed	closed	closed	closed	*	*

SAVINGS: 25%-50% off   *Mailing List*
PARKING: lot
PAYMENT: cash only

---

*The store is open on Friday and Saturday every two months.

Filbert's Old Time Root Beer, 3307 S. Archer Avenue, Chicago, IL 60608; (312) 847-1520
This factory outlet sells Filbert's root beer and Jolly Good canned soda. Savings average 20%-33% off regular retail price.

SUN.	MON.	TUE.	WED.	THU.	FRI.	SAT.
closed	9-5	9-5	9-5	9-5	9-5	9-3

SAVINGS: 20%-33% off   *All First Quality*
BRAND NAMES: Filbert, Jolly Good
PARKING: street
PAYMENT: cash, checks (amount of purchase only, with proper I.D.)

Tom Tom Tamale and Bakery Company, 4750 S. Washtenaw Avenue, Chicago, IL 60632; (312) 523-5675
This factory outlet sells tamales at half the retail price.

SUN.	MON.	TUE.	WED.	THU.	FRI.	SAT.
closed	9-4	9-4	9-4	9-4	9-4	9-2

SAVINGS: about 50% off   *All First Quality*
PARKING: street
PAYMENT: cash only

MOUNT PROSPECT, IL

Arlington Club Beverage Company, Inc., 1326 W. Central Road, Mount Prospect,
  IL 60056; (312) 253-0030
    This factory outlet sells Arlington Club soft drinks in returnable bottles. Savings
average about 35% off retail prices.

SUN.	MON.	TUE.	WED.	THU.	FRI.	SAT.
9-3	closed	9-6	9-6	9-6	9-6	9-6

SAVINGS: about 30% off   *All First Quality*
BRAND NAMES: Arlington Club
PARKING: lot
PAYMENT: cash, checks (with proper I.D., no out-of-state checks)

WEST CHICAGO, IL

Camsco Produce Company, Prince Crossing Road, Route 1 Box 176, West
  Chicago, IL 60185; (312) 231-1080
    This is the farm where they grow the mushrooms for Campbell's soup. They sell
fresh mushrooms for $1.25/lb. at this writing. They have another farm in Howe,
Indiana.

SUN.	MON.	TUE.	WED.	THU.	FRI.	SAT.
closed	closed	closed	closed	closed	8-4	8-4

SAVINGS: about 33% off
PARKING: lot
PAYMENT: cash only

INDIANA

HOWE, IN

Camsco Produce Company Mushroom Farm, R.R. 3, Highway 120, Howe, IN
  46746; (219) 367-2112
    See listing in West Chicago, Illinois.

SUN.	MON.	TUE.	WED.	THU.	FRI.	SAT.
closed	7-4	7-4	7-4	7-4	7-4	7-11

SAVINGS: about 33% off
PARKING: lot
PAYMENT: cash only

WISCONSIN

WATERTOWN, WI

Rock River Foods, 925 S. Twelfth Street, Watertown, WI 53094; (414) 261-2314
    This factory outlet sells frozen, battered or breaded onion rings, cheese sticks,
cauliflower, perch, green peppers, and zucchini. Savings average 25% off retail price
on first quality, and go to 50% or better on irregulars.

SUN.	MON.	TUE.	WED.	THU.	FRI.	SAT.
closed	9-5	9-5	9-5	9-5	9-5	9-3*

SAVINGS: 20%-50% off
SPECIAL DISCOUNTS: senior citizens, 10% off
PARKING: lot
PAYMENT: cash only

---

*Open Saturday only during special sales; call ahead.

13
FURNITURE

These outlets sell furniture. Also look in Chapter 3, *Baby Accessories*; Chapter 4, *Beds, Mattresses, and Box Springs*; Chapter 9, *Decorating*; Chapter 10, *Department Stores*; Chapter 14, *Gift Items*; and Chapter 17, *Lamps and Lighting*, for other outlets that sell furniture.

Savings were very good on seconds, irregular, damaged, floor samples, and "as is" merchandise. Look closely before you buy so you can decide if the flaw is worth the savings. Take samples of colors to be matched when you shop. Know brand names and retail prices so you will recognize a bargain when you see it.

ILLINOIS

CHICAGO, IL

American Sleep—Waveland Mattress Company
See listing under *Beds, Mattresses, and Box Springs* in Chicago, Illinois.

Butcher Block & More, 1600 S. Clinton Avenue, Chicago, IL 60616; (312) 421-1138
This outlet sells their own brand of tables, chairs, and wall units at savings that start at 10% for first quality, and go up to 40% on closeouts, discontinued, samples, last year's lines, and some "bruised" and "as is" merchandise.

SUN.	MON.	TUE.	WED.	THU.	FRI.	SAT.
closed	9–4:30	9–4:30	9–4:30	9–4:30	9–4:30	9–4:30

SAVINGS: 10%–40% off   *Mailing List*
PARKING: street
PAYMENT: cash, checks (amount of purchase only, with proper I.D.), MasterCard, VISA

Country's Harvest, 300 W. Grand Avenue, Chicago, IL 60610; (312) 321-0403
This shop sells Brass Roots brass beds at 40% off retail price. They have many handmade items: furniture, quilts, rugs, toys, baby items, pillows, kitchen items, and sculpture at discounts of 20%–30% off retail price.

SUN.	MON.	TUE.	WED.	THU.	FRI.	SAT.
noon–4	10–6	10–6	10–6	10–6	10–6	10–5

SAVINGS: 20%–40% off   *All First Quality*
BRAND NAMES: Brass Roots
PARKING: street, meters, can be difficult
PAYMENT: cash, checks (with proper I.D.), MasterCard, VISA

D & L Office Furniture Company, 30 W. Hubbard Street, Chicago, IL 60610; (312) 527-3636
This is an outlet for many office furniture companies. Savings average 30%–60%

off retail price, with greatest savings on seconds, irregulars, samples, "bruised" furniture, overruns, overstocks, discontinued, and closeouts. See listing below.

SUN.	MON.	TUE.	WED.	THU.	FRI.	SAT.
11–5	9–5	9–5	9–5	9–5	9–5	closed

SAVINGS: 30%–60% off *Mailing List*
BRAND NAMES: Thayer Cogin, Josfco, Gunlocke, Vecta, Metropolitan, George Kovacs, Harris, Glassarts
ANNUAL SALES: May–June, year-end
PARKING: lot
PAYMENT: cash, checks (amount of purchase only, with proper I.D.), MasterCard, VISA, American Express

D & L Office Furniture Company, 4336 W. Addison Street, Chicago, IL 60641; (312) 286-5025
See listing above.

SUN.	MON.	TUE.	WED.	THU.	FRI.	SAT.
closed	9–5	9–5	9–5	9–5	9–5	10–3

SAVINGS: 30%–60% off *Mailing List*
BRAND NAMES: Thayer Cogin, Vecta, Harris
ANNUAL SALES: May–June, year-end
PARKING: lot
PAYMENT: cash, checks (amount of purchase only, with proper I.D.), MasterCard, VISA

Elco Supply Company, 3014 S. Wentworth Avenue, Chicago, IL 60616; (312) 326-1934
This factory outlet sells automotive and marine upholstered furniture. Savings begin at 60% off retail price, and can go as high as 85% off retail price on seconds, surplus, overruns, overstocks, last year's lines, end-of-season, closeout, and discontinued merchandise. They also sell Naugahyde vinyl upholstery fabric, usually from $10.00–$20.00/yard, for $3.25/yard.

SUN.	MON.	TUE.	WED.	THU.	FRI.	SAT.
closed	8:30–3:30	8:30–3:30	8:30–3:30	8:30–3:30	8:30–3:30	9–noon

SAVINGS: 60%–85% off *Mailing List*
BRAND NAMES: Naugahyde
PARKING: lot
PAYMENT: cash, checks (amount of purchase only, with proper I.D.)

Freedman Seating Company Factory Outlet
See listing under *Automotive* in Chicago, Illinois.

Homer's Furniture, 3053 W. Grand Avenue, Chicago, IL 60639; (312) 638-2150
This store sells several major brands of dining room and bedroom furniture. Savings average 20%–25% off retail price on first quality merchandise, and can go as high as 50% off on some show room samples, discontinued, overrun, and test run merchandise.

SUN.	MON.	TUE.	WED.	THU.	FRI.	SAT.
noon–5	9–5	9–5	9–5	9–5	9–5	9:30–5

SAVINGS: 20%–50% off *Mailing List*
BRAND NAMES: Homer's, Thomasville, Bernhardt
ANNUAL SALES: twice a year
PARKING: lot
PAYMENT: cash, MasterCard, VISA

Hufford Furniture Company, 310 W. Washington Street, Chicago, IL 60606; (312) 236-4191

This store sells many brands of kitchen, living room, bedroom, and dining room furniture. Savings can go up to 40% off retail prices on some discontinued items.

SUN.	MON.	TUE.	WED.	THU.	FRI.	SAT.
closed	9-7	9-5	9-5	9-5	9-5	9-1

SAVINGS: up to 40% off   *Mailing List*
ANNUAL SALES: summer and winter
PARKING: lot, one block away at Franklin and Randolph streets
PAYMENT: cash, checks (amount of purchase only, with proper I.D.), MasterCard, VISA

La-Z-Boy Showcase Shoppe, 4109 N. Harlem Avenue, Chicago, IL 60634; (312) 457-0284
   This is the factory outlet for La-Z-Boy recliner chairs, couches, and sleeper sofas. Savings average 10% off retail prices on first quality merchandise. They have occasional special sales where discounts on overrun merchandise can go as high as 30% off retail price. They have other stores in Aurora, Libertyville, Morton Grove, Orland Park, Palatine, Rockford, Villa Park, and Willowbrook, Illinois; and in Hammond, Indiana.

SUN.	MON.	TUE.	WED.	THU.	FRI.	SAT.
noon-5	10-9	10-9	10-9	10-9	10-9	10-5

SAVINGS: 10%-30% off
BRAND NAMES: La-Z-Boy
PARKING: lot
PAYMENT: cash, checks (amount of purchase only, with proper I.D.), MasterCard, VISA

Marjen of Chicago Discount Furniture and Bedding, 1536 W. Devon Avenue, Chicago, IL 60626; (312) 338-6636
   This store sells Sealy and Therapeutic mattresses and box springs. They also sell several brands of furniture and upholstery. Savings average 35%-50% off retail price. They have another store in Addison, Illinois.

SUN.	MON.	TUE.	WED.	THU.	FRI.	SAT.
11-5	10:30-8	10:30-7	10:30-7	10:30-8	10:30-7	10-6

SAVINGS: 35%-50% off   *Mailing List*   *All First Quality*
BRAND NAMES: Sealy, Therapeutic, Stratford
PARKING: street, meters
PAYMENT: cash, checks (amount of purchase only, with proper I.D., Telecheck), MasterCard, VISA, American Express

Polk Brothers Outlet
   See listing under *Appliances* in Chicago, Illinois.

Sofa and Sleeper Factory, 6308 N. Broadway, Chicago, IL 60660; (312) 274-9730
   This factory outlet sells its own brand of sofas, love seats, and chairs. They also sell Harris and American lamps. Savings begin at 50% off retail price on first quality, and go as high as 80% on samples, "bruised," surplus, overruns, last year's lines, discontinued, and closeout items. They offer free delivery in a limited area and for senior citizens.

SUN.	MON.	TUE.	WED.	THU.	FRI.	SAT.
noon-4	10-7	10-7	10-7	10-9	10-7	10-5:30

SAVINGS: 50%-80% off   *Mailing List*
BRAND NAMES: Harris, American
PARKING: lot
PAYMENT: cash, checks (amount of purchase only, with proper I.D.), MasterCard, VISA, American Express, Diners Club ($75 minimum)

Swingles Furniture Rental, 145 E. Ohio Street, Chicago, IL 60611; (312) 944-6350
   This company's primary business is furniture rental. There are some savings to be

had on damaged, used, and formerly rental furniture. They also sell seconds. They have other stores in Elk Grove Village and Westmont, Illinois.

SUN.	MON.	TUE.	WED.	THU.	FRI.	SAT.
closed	9:30–5:30	9:30–5:30	9:30–5:30	9:30–5:30	9:30–5:30	10–5

SAVINGS: 20%–30% off
BRAND NAMES: Carlton, Oakley
PARKING: lot
PAYMENT: cash, checks (amount of purchase only, with proper I.D., no out-of-state checks), MasterCard, VISA

Virgilio Furniture, 7128 W. Grand Avenue, Chicago, IL 60635; (312) 622-1600
This is an outlet for Stanley furniture. Savings are greatest on discontinued merchandise.

SUN.	MON.	TUE.	WED.	THU.	FRI.	SAT.
closed	10–9	10–5	10–5	10–9	10–9	10–5

SAVINGS: at least 10% off   *Mailing List*
BRAND NAMES: Stanley
PARKING: lot
PAYMENT: cash, checks (amount of purchase only, with proper I.D., no out-of-state checks), MasterCard, VISA

Wholesale Furniture Warehouse Clearance Center—Furniture Liquidators,
5906 N. Clark Street, Chicago, IL 60660; (312) 275-0584
This store sells several major brands of bedroom and living room furniture. Savings are greatest on closeouts.

SUN.	MON.	TUE.	WED.	THU.	FRI.	SAT.
11–5	9–7	9–7	9–7	9–7	9–7	11–5

SAVINGS: up to 60% off   *Mailing List*
SPECIAL DISCOUNTS: senior citizens, 10% off
PARKING: street, meters
PAYMENT: cash, checks (amount of purchase only, with proper I.D.), MasterCard, VISA

ADDISON, IL

Marjen Discount Furniture and Bedding Warehouse, 120 E. Lake Street, Addison, IL 60101; (312) 832-9770
See listing in Chicago, Illinois.

SUN.	MON.	TUE.	WED.	THU.	FRI.	SAT.
11–5	10:30–8	10:30–8	10:30–8	10:30–8	10:30–8	10–5

SAVINGS: 35%–50% off   *Mailing List*   *All First Quality*
BRAND NAMES: Sealy, Therapeutic, Stratford
PARKING: lot
PAYMENT: cash, checks (with proper I.D., Telecheck), MasterCard, VISA, American Express

AURORA, IL

La-Z-Boy Showcase Shoppe, 1885 N. Farnsworth Road, Aurora, IL 60505; (312) 898-2525
See listing in Chicago, Illinois.

SUN.	MON.	TUE.	WED.	THU.	FRI.	SAT.
noon–5	10–9	10–9	10–9	10–9	10–9	10–5

SAVINGS: 10%–30% off
BRAND NAMES: La-Z-Boy
PARKING: lot
PAYMENT: cash, checks (amount of purchase only, with proper I.D.), MasterCard, VISA

Gaines Furniture Outlet, 7414 S. Cicero Avenue, Bedford, IL 60629; (312) 496-0355
   This outlet sells major brands of living room and bedroom furniture at savings up to 50% off retail price. Best buys are on "bruised" and discontinued merchandise.

SUN.	MON.	TUE.	WED.	THU.	FRI.	SAT.
10–6	10–6	10–6	10–6	10–6	10–6	9–6

SAVINGS: up to 50% off
PARKING: lot
PAYMENT: cash, checks (amount of purchase only, with proper I.D.), MasterCard, VISA

Direct Factory Outlet, 405 W. Washington Street, Bloomington, IL 61701; (309) 829-5451
   This shop sells furniture and bedding. Greatest values are on overruns, overstocks, and closeouts, where savings can run as high as 70% off retail price on Bassett and Singer furniture, and Sealy mattresses and box springs.

SUN.	MON.	TUE.	WED.	THU.	FRI.	SAT.
closed	10–8	10–8	10–8	10–8	10–8	10–6

SAVINGS: up to 70% off
BRAND NAMES: Bassett, Singer, Sealy
PARKING: lot
PAYMENT: cash, checks (with proper I.D.), MasterCard, VISA

Guinta's Furniture, Guinta's Factory Outlet Mall, 1800 S. Cicero Avenue, Cicero, IL 60650; (312) 863-7720
   This store sells furniture at savings that average 30%–70% off retail price.

SUN.	MON.	TUE.	WED.	THU.	FRI.	SAT.
10–6	10–8	closed	10–8	10–8	10–8	10–6

SAVINGS: 30%–70% off   *Mailing List*   *All First Quality*
SPECIAL DISCOUNTS: senior citizens, police, firefighters, 10%–15% off (ask)
PARKING: lot
PAYMENT: cash, checks (amount of purchase only, with proper I.D.), MasterCard,
   VISA, American Express, Diners Club

Designer Leather Furniture, 6028 Brookbank Road, Downers Grove, IL 60515; (312) 968-2575
   Although they are not generally open to the public, you can call for an appointment to save 33%–66% on Leatherman's Guild leather furniture and Prestige kitchen cabinets. Everything is first quality, and they do take special orders.

SUN.	MON.	TUE.	WED.	THU.	FRI.	SAT.
*	*	*	*	*	*	*

SAVINGS: 33%–66% off   *Mailing List*   *All First Quality*
BRAND NAMES: Leatherman's Guild, Prestige
SPECIAL DISCOUNTS: quantity and cash in advance
PARKING: street
PAYMENT: cash, checks

---

*Open by appointment only.

Baker Road Manufacturing Company, 607 Church Road, Elgin, IL 60120; (312) 695-2377

This plant manufactures custom furniture. Savings average 20% off retail price for comparable goods.

SUN.	MON.	TUE.	WED.	THU.	FRI.	SAT.
closed	7–5	7–5	7–5	7–5	7–5	closed

SAVINGS: 20% off   *All First Quality*
PARKING: street
PAYMENT: cash, checks (with proper I.D.)

ELK GROVE VILLAGE, IL

Swingles Furniture Rental, 2461 E. Oakton Avenue, Elk Grove Village, IL 60007; (312) 437-5811
    See listing in Chicago, Illinois.

SUN.	MON.	TUE.	WED.	THU.	FRI.	SAT.
noon–5	10–8	10–6	10–6	10–8	10–6	10–5

SAVINGS: 40%–75% off
BRAND NAMES: Bassett, Schweiger, Singer
PARKING: lot
PAYMENT: cash, checks (amount of purchase only, with proper I.D.), MasterCard, VISA

EVANSTON, IL

Scandinavian Design Clearance Center, 2510 Green Bay Road, Evanston, IL 60201; (312) 491-1583
    This is the outlet for the Scandinavian Design furniture stores. The stock is inconsistent, they say: whatever comes in from the stores or the factory. Most items are "bruised" or slightly damaged. Savings average about 50% off retail price.

SUN.	MON.	TUE.	WED.	THU.	FRI.	SAT.
closed	10–6	10–6	10–6	10–8	10–6	10–6

SAVINGS: up to 50% off
PARKING: lot
PAYMENT: cash, checks (amount of purchase only, with proper I.D.), MasterCard, VISA

ITASCA, IL

Marshall Field's Commercial Interiors, 749 Baker Street, Itasca, IL 60143; (312) 250-2300
    This outlet sells commercial interiors and office furniture, desks, chairs, and lamps. Very few items are first quality; most merchandise is seconds, irregulars, "bruised" items, overruns, overstocks, and closeouts. They have another store in Chicago which sells noncommercial merchandise.

SUN.	MON.	TUE.	WED.	THU.	FRI.	SAT.
closed	9:15–5:15	9:15–5:15	9:15–5:15	9:15–5:15	9:15–5:15	10–2

SAVINGS: 50%–70% off
BRAND NAMES: Steel Case, Executive, Frederick Cooper, Signor
PARKING: lot
PAYMENT: cash, checks (with proper I.D.)

Scan Furniture Warehouse Outlet, 1401 W. Ardmore Street, Itasca, IL 60143; (312) 773-1550
    This outlet sells mostly Scandinavian-designed styles of furniture. Savings begin at 10% off retail price on first quality, but quickly go as high as 66% off on "bruised" merchandise, and some overstocks, discontinued, closeouts, and "as is" items.

SUN.	MON.	TUE.	WED.	THU.	FRI.	SAT.
closed	9–3	9–3	9–3	9–3	9–3	9–3

SAVINGS: 10%–66% off
BRAND NAMES: Balans, Domino, Jesper, Travertine, Rabami
ANNUAL SALES: January, March, June, September
PARKING: lot
PAYMENT: cash, checks, MasterCard, VISA

LIBERTYVILLE, IL

La-Z-Boy Showcase Shoppe, 1344 S. Milwaukee Avenue, Libertyville, IL 60048;
(312) 680-7507
See listing in Chicago, Illinois.

SUN.	MON.	TUE.	WED.	THU.	FRI.	SAT.
noon–5	10–9	10–9	10–9	10–9	10–9	10–5

SAVINGS: 10%–30% off
BRAND NAMES: La-Z-Boy
PARKING: lot
PAYMENT: cash, checks (amount of purchase only, with proper I.D.), MasterCard, VISA

MORTON GROVE, IL

La-Z-Boy Showcase Shoppe, 5925 W. Dempster Street, Morton Grove, IL 60053;
(312) 967-6913
See listing in Chicago, Illinois.

SUN.	MON.	TUE.	WED.	THU.	FRI.	SAT.
noon–5	10–9	10–9	10–9	10–9	10–9	10–5

SAVINGS: 10%–30% off
BRAND NAMES: La-Z-Boy
PARKING: lot
PAYMENT: cash, checks (amount of purchase only, with proper I.D.), MasterCard, VISA

ORLAND PARK, IL

La-Z-Boy Showcase Shoppe, 15605 S. 71st Court, Orland Park, IL 60462; (312)
532-3220
See listing in Chicago, Illinois.

SUN.	MON.	TUE.	WED.	THU.	FRI.	SAT.
noon–5	10–9	10–9	10–9	10–9	10–9	10–5

SAVINGS: 10%–30% off
BRAND NAMES: La-Z-Boy
PARKING: lot
PAYMENT: cash, checks (amount of purchase only, with proper I.D.), MasterCard, VISA

PALATINE, IL

La-Z-Boy Showcase Shoppe, 1288 E. Dundee Road, Palatine, IL 60067; (312)
991-0780
See listing in Chicago, Illinois.

SUN.	MON.	TUE.	WED.	THU.	FRI.	SAT.
noon–5	10–9	10–9	10–9	10–9	10–9	10–5

SAVINGS: 10%–30% off
BRAND NAMES: La-Z-Boy
PARKING: lot
PAYMENT: cash, checks (amount of purchase only, with proper I.D.), MasterCard, VISA

ROCKFORD, IL

La-Z-Boy Showcase Shoppe, 5643 E. State Street, Rockford, IL 61108; (815)
397-0074
See listing in Chicago, Illinois.

SUN.	MON.	TUE.	WED.	THU.	FRI.	SAT.
noon–5	10–9	10–9	10–9	10–9	10–9	10–5

SAVINGS: 10%–30% off
BRAND NAMES: La-Z-Boy
PARKING: lot
PAYMENT: cash, checks (amount of purchase only, with proper I.D.), MasterCard, VISA

THOMASBORO, IL

Sandman Couch Company, R.R.1, Box 6, Route 45, Thomasboro, IL 61878; (217) 643-7860
This small plant manufactures chairs, love seats, and three- and four-cushion sofas. They also sell upholstery fabrics. Call for information on custom-made furniture.

SUN.	MON.	TUE.	WED.	THU.	FRI.	SAT.
closed	8–4:30	8–4:30	8–4:30	8–4:30	8–4:30	8–4:30

SAVINGS: 40%–50% off comparable brand name prices   *All First Quality*
BRAND NAMES: Sandman
PARKING: lot
PAYMENT: cash, checks (amount of purchase only, with proper I.D.)

VILLA PARK, IL

La-Z-Boy Showcase Shoppe, 300 E. North Avenue, Villa Park, IL 60181; (312) 833-1780
See listing in Chicago, Illinois.

SUN.	MON.	TUE.	WED.	THU.	FRI.	SAT.
noon–5	10–9	10–9	10–9	10–9	10–9	10–5

SAVINGS: 10%–30% off
BRAND NAMES: La-Z-Boy
PARKING: lot
PAYMENT: cash, checks (amount of purchase only, with proper I.D.), MasterCard, VISA

WESTMONT, IL

Swingles Furniture Rentals, 151 W. Ogden Avenue, Westmont, IL 60559; (312) 963-9840
See listing in Chicago, Illinois.

SUN.	MON.	TUE.	WED.	THU.	FRI.	SAT.
noon–5	10–8	10–6	10–6	10–8	10–6	10–5

SAVINGS: 40% off (new), 50%–70% off (rental returns)   *Mailing List*
PARKING: lot
PAYMENT: cash, checks (with proper I.D., no out-of-state checks), MasterCard, VISA

WILLOWBROOK, IL

La-Z-Boy Showcase Shoppe, 6944 Kingery Highway Road, Willowbrook, IL 60514; (312) 325-7890
See listing in Chicago, Illinois.

SUN.	MON.	TUE.	WED.	THU.	FRI.	SAT.
noon–5	10–9	10–9	10–9	10–9	10–9	10–5

SAVINGS: 10%–30% off
BRAND NAMES: La-Z-Boy
PARKING: lot
PAYMENT: cash, checks (amount of purchase only, with proper I.D.), MasterCard, VISA

INDIANA
BOONVILLE, IN

Factory Furniture Outlet, Highway 62, Boonville, IN 47601; (812) 897-2275
This outlet sells furniture made by the Amish. Savings on first quality merchandise average about 25% off retail price.

SUN.	MON.	TUE.	WED.	THU.	FRI.	SAT.
closed	9-5	9-5	9-5	9-5	9-5	9-4

SAVINGS: about 25% off   *Mailing List*   *All First Quality*
PARKING: lot
PAYMENT: cash, checks (amount of purchase only, with proper I.D.)

COLUMBUS, IN

Cosco Store
See listing under *Baby Accessories* in Columbus, Indiana.

FORT WAYNE, IN

Value City Furniture Store, 811 Northcrest Shopping Mall, Fort Wayne, IN 46825; (219) 482-9641
This store sells major brands of furniture at prices starting at 40% off retail.

SUN.	MON.	TUE.	WED.	THU.	FRI.	SAT.
noon-6	10-9	10-9	10-9	10-9	10-9	10-6

SAVINGS: 40%-60% off
BRAND NAMES: Corvair, Pilliod, Roanoke
PARKING: lot
PAYMENT: cash, checks (amount of purchase only, with proper I.D.), MasterCard, VISA

GARY, IN

Brady's This Is It—Factory Outlet Store—Furniture, 5404 W. 25th Avenue, Gary, IN 46406; (219) 844-7005
This store sells major brands of furniture. They also sell flooring. Savings begin at 30% off retail price for first quality, but check the back room where seconds, irregulars, and imperfect merchandise can save you 50% off retail price. See other Brady's stores

SUN.	MON.	TUE.	WED.	THU.	FRI.	SAT.
closed	10-8	10-8	10-8	10-8	10-8	10-8

SAVINGS: 30%-50% off
BRAND NAMES: Schweiger, Douglas, Mannington Mills, Le High
SALE DAYS: vary
ANNUAL SALES: May, September
PARKING: lot
PAYMENT: cash, checks, MasterCard, VISA

HAMMOND, IN

La-Z-Boy Showcase Shoppe, 6752 N. Indianapolis Boulevard, Hammond, IN 46324; (219) 845-0845
See listing in Chicago, Illinois.

SUN.	MON.	TUE.	WED.	THU.	FRI.	SAT.
noon-5	10-9	10-9	10-9	10-9	10-9	10-5

SAVINGS: 10%-30% off
BRAND NAMES: La-Z-Boy
PARKING: lot
PAYMENT: cash, checks (amount of purchase only, with proper I.D.), MasterCard, VISA

Mastercraft, State Road 5 South, Shippshewana, IN 46565; (219) 768-4101
This is the factory outlet for Mastercraft. They make sofas, chairs, mattresses, box springs, waterbeds, and van and RV furniture and cushions at this location. Fabrics can be selected, and custom-made merchandise can be picked up in ten days. They also sell samples, surplus, overruns, overstocks, closeouts, and some bolt-end fabrics.

SUN.	MON.	TUE.	WED.	THU.	FRI.	SAT.
closed	8:30–5	8:30–5	8:30–5	8:30–5	8:30–5	8:30–noon

SAVINGS: 30%–40% off
BRAND NAMES: Mastercraft
PARKING: lot
PAYMENT: cash, checks (amount of purchase only, with proper I.D.)

WISCONSIN
APPLETON, WI

D'Lu Furniture, 2200 American Drive, Appleton, WI 54956; (414) 731-3358
This is the factory outlet for D'Lu Furniture. They have a good selection of living room furniture. Savings are greatest on seconds, irregulars, "bruised," overruns, overstocks, discontinued, and closeout merchandise. Furniture can also be custom-made. They have other stores in Green Bay, Oshkosh, and Plover, Wisconsin.

SUN.	MON.	TUE.	WED.	THU.	FRI.	SAT.
noon–5	10–9	10–9	10–9	10–9	10–9	10–5

SAVINGS: 10%–40% off
BRAND NAMES: D'Lu
PARKING: lot
PAYMENT: cash, checks (amount of purchase only, with proper I.D.), MasterCard, VISA

D'Lu Furniture, 730 E. Northland Avenue, Appleton, WI 54911; (414) 731-0913
See listing above.

SUN.	MON.	TUE.	WED.	THU.	FRI.	SAT.
noon–4	10–8	10–8	10–8	10–8	10–8	10–5

SAVINGS: 10%–40% off
BRAND NAMES: D'Lu
PARKING: lot
PAYMENT: cash, checks (amount of purchase only, with proper I.D.), MasterCard, VISA

GREEN BAY, WI

D'Lu Furniture, Kohl's Plaza, 1165 Lombardi Avenue, Green Bay, WI 54304; (414) 498-9707
See listing in Appleton, Wisconsin.

SUN.	MON.	TUE.	WED.	THU.	FRI.	SAT.
11–4	9–9	9–6	9–9	9–6	9–9	9–5

SAVINGS: 10%–40% off
BRAND NAMES: D'Lu
PARKING: lot
PAYMENT: cash, checks (amount of purchase only, with proper I.D.), MasterCard, VISA

OSHKOSH, WI

Buckstaff—Authentic Factory Outlet, 1302 S. Main Street, Oshkosh, WI 54901; (414) 235-5200
This factory outlet sells contract furniture, usually for restaurants, lobbies, and clubs. They also make kitchen stools and counters and family room furniture for the home. Savings begin at 25% off retail price on first quality, and can go to 60% on

occasional seconds, "bruised," discontinued, closeout, "as is," and one-of-a-kind items. You can also order custom-made furniture.

SUN.	MON.	TUE.	WED.	THU.	FRI.	SAT.
closed	9–5	9–5	9–5	9–5	9–9	9–3

SAVINGS: 25%–50% off   *Mailing List*
BRAND NAMES: Buckstaff
ANNUAL SALES: July
PARKING: lot
PAYMENT: cash, checks (amount of purchase only, with proper I.D.), MasterCard, VISA

D'Lu Furniture, 1528 S. Koeller Street, Oshkosh, WI 54903; (414) 426-5229
See listing in Appleton, Wisconsin.

SUN.	MON.	TUE.	WED.	THU.	FRI.	SAT.
10–5	10–8	10–8	10–8	10–8	10–8	10–5

SAVINGS: 10%–40% off
BRAND NAMES: D'Lu
PARKING: lot
PAYMENT: cash, checks (amount of purchase only, with proper I.D.), MasterCard, VISA

PLOVER, WI

D'Lu Furniture, Manufacturers Direct Mall, 101 Plover Road, Plover, WI 54467; (715) 341-7567
See listing under Appleton, Wisconsin.

SUN.	MON.	TUE.	WED.	THU.	FRI.	SAT.
11–6	9:30–9	9:30–9	9:30–9	9:30–9	9:30–9	9:30–6

SAVINGS: 10%–40% off
BRAND NAMES: D'Lu
PARKING: lot
PAYMENT: cash, checks (amount of purchase only, with proper I.D.), MasterCard, VISA

14
GIFT ITEMS

The outlets listed here sell crystal, glass, copper, brass, and wooden merchandise that are predominantly gift items. For other gift items, look in Chapter 1, *Appliances*; Chapter 6, *Ceramics*; Chapter 8, *Crafts*; Chapter 9, *Decorating*; Chapter 10, *Department Stores*; Chapter 15, *Housewares*; Chapter 17, *Lamps and Lighting*; and Chapter 24, *Plates, Glassware, and Tableware*.

Savings were often excellent on discontinued, last year's lines, and closeout merchandise. Look closely at seconds, irregulars, samples, and "bruised" merchandise. At savings up to 90% off retail price, the flaw may not bother you.

ILLINOIS

CHICAGO, IL

Crate and Barrel Warehouse Store, 1510 N. Wells Street, Chicago, IL 60610; (312) 787-4775
This store sells a vast collection of gourmet cookware, glassware, stemware, bedding, and other home accessories. The bargains are downstairs. Savings can go as high as 70% on seconds, irregulars, imperfects, samples, bolt-end fabrics, end-of-season, discontinued, overstocks, and closeout merchandise.

SUN.	MON.	TUE.	WED.	THU.	FRI.	SAT.
noon-5	10-6	10-6	10-6	10-6	10-6	10-6

SAVINGS: 10%-70% off
ANNUAL SALES: end of summer
PARKING: street, meters, can be difficult
PAYMENT: cash, checks (amount of purchase only, with proper I.D.), MasterCard, VISA, American Express

House-O-Lite—Lava-Simplex International
See listing under *Lamps and Lighting* in Chicago, Illinois.

Silvestri Corporation, 2720 N. Paulina Street, Chicago, IL 60614; (312) 871-5200
This factory outlet sells Silvestri Christmas lights, ornaments, and gift items. Savings average 50% off retail price on seconds, imperfects, discontinued, and closeout items.

SUN.	MON.	TUE.	WED.	THU.	FRI.	SAT.
closed	9:30-3:30	9:30-3:30	9:30-3:30	9:30-3:30	9:30-3:30	*

SAVINGS: about 50% off   *Mailing List*
BRAND NAMES: Silvestri

ANNUAL SALES: July, Christmas
PARKING: lot
PAYMENT: cash, checks (amount of purchase only, with proper I.D.)

---

*They are open Saturday from October through December (call for hours).

Studio 5000
See listing under *Picture Frames* in Chicago, Illinois.

ANTIOCH, IL

Pickard Factory Outlet
See listing under *Plates, Glassware, and Tableware* in Antioch, Illinois.

ARLINGTON HEIGHTS, IL

Gift Outlet, 342 E. Rand Road, Arlington Heights, IL 60004; (312) 640-5287
This is the outlet for Enesco imports. Savings on gift items, household
accessories, picture frames, and crystal begin at about 30% off retail price for first
quality, and can go uo to 90% off on some seconds, irregulars, samples, surplus,
overruns, overstocks, last year's lines, end-of-season, discontinued, closeouts,
"bruised," and "as is" merchandise. They have other stores in Elk Grove Village and
Skokie, Illinois.

SUN.	MON.	TUE.	WED.	THU.	FRI.	SAT.
11–5	10–9	10–9	10–9	10–9	10–9	10–5:30

SAVINGS: up to 90% off
PARKING: lot
PAYMENT: cash, checks (amount of purchase only, with proper I.D.), MasterCard, VISA

BLOOMINGDALE, IL

Factory Card Outlet, 366–310 Army Trail Road, Bloomingdale, IL 60108; (312)
980-8870
This is one of several outlets for Gallant Greeting Cards. Savings on cards are
always 50% off retail price. They also sell all types of party goods and paper products
and some gift items at savings of 20%–25%. They have other stores in Buffalo Grove,
Niles, Rolling Meadows, and Villa Park, Illinois.

SUN.	MON.	TUE.	WED.	THU.	FRI.	SAT.
11–5	10–9	10–9	10–9	10–9	10–9	10–6

SAVINGS: 20%–50% off   *Mailing List*
BRAND NAMES: Gallant Greeting Cards
SPECIAL SALES: vary
PARKING: lot
PAYMENT: cash, checks (amount of purchase only, with proper I.D.)

BUFFALO GROVE, IL

Factory Card Outlet, 1245 W. Dundee Road, Buffalo Grove, IL 60089; (312) 577-3807
See listing in Bloomingdale, Illinois.

SUN.	MON.	TUE.	WED.	THU.	FRI.	SAT.
noon–5	10–6	10–6	10–6	10–9	10–9	10–6

SAVINGS: 20%–50% off   *All First Quality*
BRAND NAMES: Gallant Greeting Cards
ANNUAL SALES: after Christmas
PARKING: lot
PAYMENT: cash, checks (amount of purchase only, with proper I.D.)

Discount Outlet, Guinta's Factory Outlet Mall, 1800 S. Cicero Avenue, Cicero, IL 60650; (312) 780-0797

This store sells gift items and general merchandise at discounts starting at about 20% off retail prices.

SUN.	MON.	TUE.	WED.	THU.	FRI.	SAT.
10-6	10-8	closed	10-8	10-8	10-8	10-6

SAVINGS: at least 20% off   *All First Quality*
PARKING: lot
PAYMENT: cash only

The Paul Revere Shoppe—Revere Copper & Brass, 424 W. Van Buren Street, junction of routes 54, 10, and 51, Clinton, IL 61727; (217) 935-3822

This is the outlet for Revere copper and brass. They have a large selection of cookware and kitchen items. They also sell Chicago Cutlery and Superior coffee and tea. Discounts begin at 50% off retail price, and can go as high as 70% on irregular, overrun, overstock, and closeout merchandise.

SUN.	MON.	TUE.	WED.	THU.	FRI.	SAT.
closed	10:30-5	10:30-5	10:30-5	10:30-5	10:30-5	10:30-5

SAVINGS: 50%-70% off   *Mailing List*
BRAND NAMES: Revere, Chicago Cutlery, Superior
ANNUAL SALES: April, November
PARKING: lot
PAYMENT: cash, checks (amount of purchase only, with proper I.D.), MasterCard, VISA

Haeger Potteries—Factory Outlet Complex
See listing under *Ceramics* in East Dundee, Illinois.

Gift Outlet, 2402 E. Oakton Street, Elk Grove Village, IL 60005; (312) 956-8030
See listing in Arlington Heights, Illinois.

SUN.	MON.	TUE.	WED.	THU.	FRI.	SAT.
noon-5	10-6	10-6	10-6	10-9	10-9	9:30-5:30

SAVINGS: up to 50% off
BRAND NAMES: Enesco
PARKING: lot
PAYMENT: cash, checks (amount of purchase only, with proper I.D.), MasterCard, VISA

Factory Card Outlet, 8221 W. Golf Road, Niles, IL 60048; (312) 965-5858
See listing in Bloomingdale, Illinois.

SUN.	MON.	TUE.	WED.	THU.	FRI.	SAT.
noon-5	10-6	10-6	10-6	10-9	10-9	10-6

SAVINGS: 20%-50% off   *All First Quality*
BRAND NAMES: Gallant Greeting Cards
PARKING: lot
PAYMENT: cash, checks (amount of purchase only, with proper I.D.)

ROLLING MEADOWS, IL

Factory Card Outlet, Algonquin Mills Mall, 1400 E. Golf Road, Rolling Meadows, IL
60008; (312) 952-8674
    See listing in Bloomingdale, Illinois.

SUN.	MON.	TUE.	WED.	THU.	FRI.	SAT.
11–5	10–9:30	10–9:30	10–9:30	10–9:30	10–9:30	10–6

SAVINGS: 20%–50% off   *All First Quality*
BRAND NAMES: Gallant Greeting Cards
ANNUAL SALES: after Christmas
PARKING: lot
PAYMENT: cash, checks (amount of purchase only, with proper I.D.)

SKOKIE, IL

Gift Outlet, 9432 N. Skokie Boulevard, Skokie, IL 60077; (312) 982-0311
    See listing in Arlington Heights, Illinois.

SUN.	MON.	TUE.	WED.	THU.	FRI.	SAT.
noon–5	10–9	10–9	10–9	10–9	10–9	10–6

SAVINGS: 50%–70% off
PARKING: lot
PAYMENT: cash, checks (amount of purchase only, with proper I.D.), MasterCard, VISA

ST. CHARLES, IL

The Craft Clocks, 1519 W. Main Street, St. Charles, IL 60174; (312) 584-6030
    This shop sells clocks, wall clocks, and grandfather clocks. Most merchandise is
first quality, with some end-of-season, discontinued, closeout, and overstock
merchandise bringing savings to 60% off retail price.

SUN.	MON.	TUE.	WED.	THU.	FRI.	SAT.
9–5	9–9	9–5	9–5	9–5	9–9	8–5

SAVINGS: 20%–60% off   *Mailing List*
BRAND NAMES: Howard Miller, Trend, Colonial, Hubbel, Seth Thomas
SPECIAL DISCOUNTS: senior citizens, 10% off two or three times a year (ask)
PARKING: lot
PAYMENT: cash, checks (amount of purchase only, with proper I.D., no out-of-state
checks), MasterCard, VISA

VILLA PARK, IL

Factory Card Outlet, 104 W. Roosevelt Road, Villa Park, IL 60181; (312) 832-0509
    See listing in Bloomingdale, Illinois.

SUN.	MON.	TUE.	WED.	THU.	FRI.	SAT.
10–5	9–6	9–6	9–6	9–9	9–9	9–6

SAVINGS: 20%–50% off   *All First Quality*
BRAND NAMES: Gallant Greeting Cards
PARKING: lot
PAYMENT: cash, checks (amount of purchase only, with proper I.D.)

INDIANA

DUNKIRK, IN

Indiana Glass—Factory Outlet
    See listing under *Plates, Glassware, and Tableware* in Dunkirk, Indiana.

MISHAWAKA, IN

Zondervan Outlet, Buyer's Marketplace, 5901 N. Grape Road, Mishawaka, IN 46545;
(219) 277-8450

This outlet sells bibles, religious books, and gift items. Savings can go as high as 85% off retail price on some imperfect, surplus, last year's lines, and discontinued items.

SUN.	MON.	TUE.	WED.	THU.	FRI.	SAT.
closed	9:30–9	9:30–9	9:30–9	9:30–9	9:30–9	9:30–9

SAVINGS: up to 85% off   *Mailing List*
PARKING: lot
PAYMENT: cash, checks (amount of purchase only, with proper I.D.), MasterCard, VISA, travelers' checks

WISCONSIN
KENOSHA, WI

Cape Craftsman, Factory Outlet Centre, 7700 120th Avenue, Kenosha, WI 53142; (414) 857-2924
This outlet carries wood and brass items, crystal figurines, candles, lamps, and other gift items at prices up to 50% off retail price on seconds, last year's lines, end-of-season, closeouts, and discontinued merchandise.

SUN.	MON.	TUE.	WED.	THU.	FRI.	SAT.
11–5	9:30–9	9:30–9	9:30–9	9:30–9	9:30–9	9:30–6

SAVINGS: 20%–50% off
BRAND NAMES: Imperial, Enesco, Cape Craft, Libby, Tuscany, Plymouth, Harlee, Russ Berrie
PARKING: lot
PAYMENT: cash, checks (amount of purchase only, with proper I.D.), MasterCard, VISA

LA CROSSE, WI

Oak and Iron Shop, La Crosse Factory Outlet Mall, 301 Sky Harbor Drive, La Crosse, WI 56401; (608) 781-7770
This is the outlet for the Occupation Rehabilitation Center. They sell various wooden gift items, wood-burning stoves, gift cards, and wrapping paper. Greatest discounts are on seconds, discontinued, overstock, and closeout merchandise.

SUN.	MON.	TUE.	WED.	THU.	FRI.	SAT.
11–5	10–9	10–9	10–9	10–9	10–9	9–6

SAVINGS: 15%–70% off
PARKING: lot
PAYMENT: cash, checks (amount of purchase only, with proper I.D.), MasterCard, VISA, American Express, Diners Club

MADISON, WI

Seventh Avenue—Swiss Colony, Factory Outlet Centre, 4609 Verona Road, Madison, WI 53704; (608) 273-3488
The outlet sells all of the gift items from the Swiss Colony catalog, but none of the food items. Savings can go as high as 70% off retail price on test-runs, overstocks, last year's lines, discontinued, and closeout merchandise. They have another outlet in Monroe, Wisconsin.

SUN.	MON.	TUE.	WED.	THU.	FRI.	SAT.
noon-5	9:30–9	9:30–9	9:30–9	9:30–9	9:30–9	9:30–6

SAVINGS: 20%–70% off   *Mailing List*
SPECIAL DISCOUNTS: senior citizens, 10% off Wednesday
PARKING: lot
PAYMENT: cash, checks (amount of purchase only, with proper I.D.), MasterCard, VISA, American Express

Zondervan Outlet, Factory Outlet Centre, 4609 Verona Road, Madison, WI 53704; (608) 274-3240
    See listing in Mishawaka, Indiana.

SUN.	MON.	TUE.	WED.	THU.	FRI.	SAT.
closed	9:30–9	9:30–9	9:30–9	9:30–9	9:30–9	9:30–6

SAVINGS: 25%–80% off
PARKING: lot
PAYMENT: cash, checks (amount of purchase only, with proper I.D.), MasterCard, VISA

MONROE, WI

Seventh Avenue—Swiss Colony, 16th Avenue, On the Square, Monroe, WI 53566; (608) 328-8836
    See listing in Madison, Wisconsin.

SUN.	MON.	TUE.	WED.	THU.	FRI.	SAT.
noon–4	10–8	10–8	10–8	10–8	10–8	10–5

SAVINGS: 20%–70% off   *Mailing List*
ANNUAL SALES: August
PARKING: lot
PAYMENT: cash, checks (amount of purchase only, with proper I.D.), MasterCard, VISA

OSHKOSH, WI

The Lenox Shop, 627 Bay Shore Drive, Oshkosh, WI 54901; (414) 231-9655
    This is the outlet for Lenox china. They also sell crystal, candles, and candleholders. Savings are greatest on seconds, irregulars, samples, test runs, last year's lines, end-of-season, discontinued, surplus, overruns, overstocks, closeouts, and some "as is" merchandise. They have hundreds of discontinued gift items and one-of-a-kind designer samples. Special closeout purchases are occasionally available at varying discounts.

SUN.	MON.	TUE.	WED.	THU.	FRI.	SAT.
10–5	closed	closed	closed	closed	10–5	10–5

SAVINGS: 25%–75% off
BRAND NAMES: Lenox, Caroline
ANNUAL SALES: July, November–December, December–January
PARKING: lot
PAYMENT: cash, checks, MasterCard, VISA

15
HOUSEWARES

The outlets listed here sell cooking and baking containers and utensils, small kitchen gadgets, plastic storage containers, etc. Also look in Chapter 1, *Appliances*; Chapter 10, *Department Stores*; and Chapter 24, *Plates, Glassware, and Tableware*.

ILLINOIS

CHICAGO, IL

American Family Scale
See listing under *Baby Accessories* in Chicago, Illinois.

Crate and Barrel Warehouse Store
See listing under *Gift Items* in Chicago, Illinois.

CLINTON, IL

The Paul Revere Shoppe—Revere Copper & Brass
See listing under *Gift Items* in Clinton, Illinois.

LIBERTYVILLE, IL

Berggren Trayner Corporation
See listing under *Plates, Glassware, and Tableware* in Libertyville, Illinois.

NORTHBROOK, IL

The Chef's Catalog, 3915 Commercial Avenue, Northbrook, IL 60062; (312) 480-9400
This shop sells a variety of gourmet cookware, pots and pans, microwave cookware, and bakeware at discounts up to 50% off retail price. Best buys are on last year's lines.

SUN.	MON.	TUE.	WED.	THU.	FRI.	SAT.
closed	10:30–4	10:30–4	10:30–4	10:30–4	10:30–4	10:30–4

SAVINGS: up to 50% off
PARKING: lot
PAYMENT: cash, checks (amount of purchase only, with proper I.D.), MasterCard, VISA, Diners Club (minimum $20.00 on credit card)

ROLLING MEADOWS, IL

Waccamaw Pottery, 1400 E. Golf Road, Rolling Meadows, IL 60008; (312) 255-2322
This store sells many major brands of glassware, cookware, ovenware, dinnerware, flatware, gifts, and pottery. Savings are greatest on seconds, irregulars, samples, test runs, imperfects, surplus, overruns, overstocks, last year's lines, end-of-season, discontinued, closeouts, and odd lots.

SUN.	MON.	TUE.	WED.	THU.	FRI.	SAT.
11–5	9:30–9	9:30–9	9:30–9	9:30–9	9:30–9	9:30–6

SAVINGS: 20%–80% off
BRAND NAMES: Corning, Anchor Hocking, Libby, Mikasa, Noritake, Chicago Cutlery, Rubbermaid, Ex-Cel, Enesco, Haeger, Club, Litton, Ray-o-Vac, Mattel, Bucilla, Bostik, Ekco, Revere Ware
ANNUAL SALES: all major holidays
PARKING: lot
PAYMENT: cash, checks (with proper I.D.), MasterCard, VISA

INDIANA
INDIANAPOLIS, IN

Dansk Factory Outlet, 8504 Castleton Corner Drive, Indianapolis, IN 46250; (317) 842-8864
  This outlet sells a wide variety of tableware, cookware, flatware, stemware, and also some vases and salad bowls. Savings begin at 30% off retail price for first quality, and jump quickly to 60% for seconds, test runs, discontinued, and some overstock items.

SUN.	MON.	TUE.	WED.	THU.	FRI.	SAT.
noon–6	10–6	10–6	10–6	10–9	10–9	closed

SAVINGS: 30%–60% off   *Mailing List*
BRAND NAMES: Dansk
SALE DAYS: vary
PARKING: lot
PAYMENT: cash, checks (amount of purchase only, with proper I.D.)

MISHAWAKA, IN

Houseware Outlet and Glass Factory Outlet Store, Buyer's Marketplace, 5901 N. Grape Road, Mishawaka, IN 46545; (219) 272-8408
  This store sells all kinds of kitchen items and housewares. They also sell glass items. Savings begin at 50% off retail price on first quality, and can go up to 75% on seconds and closeouts.

SUN.	MON.	TUE.	WED.	THU.	FRI.	SAT.
noon–5	9:30–9	9:30–9	9:30–9	9:30–9	9:30–9	9:30–9

SAVINGS: 50%–75% off
SALE DAYS: Tuesday
ANNUAL SALES: Christmas, closeout
PARKING: lot
PAYMENT: cash, checks (amount of purchase only, with proper I.D.)

WISCONSIN
BARABOO, WI

Flambeau Plastics Outlet, 611 Hitchcock Street, Baraboo, WI 53913; (608) 356-3602
  This outlet sells various plastic items, including housewares, Duncan yo-yos, and fishing tackle. Savings start at 35% off retail. All seconds are on a marked table. Savings are greatest on seconds and closeouts.

SUN.	MON.	TUE.	WED.	THU.	FRI.	SAT.
closed	closed	10–5	10–5	10–5	10–5	10–5

SAVINGS: about 35% off   *Mailing List*
BRAND NAMES: Flambeau, Duncan
ANNUAL SALES: August
PARKING: lot
PAYMENT: cash, checks (amount of purchase only, with proper I.D.)

Houseware Outlet, 2871 S. Oneida Street, Green Bay, WI 54304; (414) 497-8080
This outlet sells thousands of brand name housewares, almost any item you could possibly ever need. Savings begin about 25% off retail price, and can go as high as 70% on some seconds, irregulars, overruns, overstocks, last year's lines, discontinued, and closeout merchandise. There is an entire wall of kitchen gadgets, all at 86¢. They have other stores in Kenosha, Madison, Plover, and West Bend, Wisconsin.

SUN.	MON.	TUE.	WED.	THU.	FRI.	SAT.
noon–5	10–6	10–6	10–6	10–6	10–9	10–5

SAVINGS: 25%–70% off
BRAND NAMES: Ekco, Regal
SPECIAL DISCOUNTS: senior citizens, 10% off
PARKING: lot
PAYMENT: cash, checks (amount of purchase only, with proper I.D.)

Hartford Vacuum
See listing under *Appliances* in Hartford, Wisconsin.

Houseware Outlet, Factory Outlet Centre, 7700 120th Avenue, Kenosha, WI 53142; (414) 857-2923
See listing in Green Bay, Wisconsin.

SUN.	MON.	TUE.	WED.	THU.	FRI.	SAT.
noon–5	9:30–9	9:30–9	9:30–9	9:30–9	9:30–9	9:30–6

SAVINGS: 25%–80% off
BRAND NAMES: Anchor Hocking. Mirro, Foley, Ekco, Rubbermaid, Regal, Columbia, Colonial
ANNUAL SALES: July
PARKING: lot
PAYMENT: cash, checks (amount of purchase only, with proper I.D.)

Regal Ware Outlet Store
See listing under *Appliances* in Kewaskum, Wisconsin.

Houseware Outlet, Factory Outlet Centre, 4609 Verona Road, Madison, WI 53711; (608) 273-6055
See listing in Green Bay, Wisconsin.

SUN.	MON.	TUE.	WED.	THU.	FRI.	SAT.
noon–2:30	9:30–9	9:30–9	9:30–9	9:30–9	9:30–9	9:30–6

SAVINGS: 50% off
BRAND NAMES: Ekco, Anchor Hocking, Mirro
SALE DAYS: Tuesday
PARKING: lot
PAYMENT: cash, checks, travelers' checks

Schuette Brothers, 814 Jay Street, Manitowoc, WI 54220; (414) 684-5521
This is the factory outlet for Mirro aluminum cookware and bakeware. Savings begin at 20% off retail price, and can go even higher on some seconds, irregulars, surplus, overruns, overstocks, discontinued, and closeout merchandise.

SUN.	MON.	TUE.	WED.	THU.	FRI.	SAT.
closed*	9–9	9–5	9–5	9–5	9–9	9–5

SAVINGS: 20%–40% off
BRAND NAMES: Mirro
PARKING: lot
PAYMENT: cash, checks (amount of purchase only, with proper I.D.)

————
*They are open Sunday, noon–5:00, from Thanksgiving to Christmas.

PLOVER, WI

Houseware Outlet, Manufacturers Direct Mall, 101 Plover Road, Plover, WI 54467;
(715) 341-9044
See listing in Green Bay, Wisconsin.

SUN.	MON.	TUE.	WED.	THU.	FRI.	SAT.
11–6	9:30–9	9:30–9	9:30–9	9:30–9	9:30–9	9:30–6

SAVINGS: 25%–70% off
BRAND NAMES: Columbia, Lenox, Rubbermaid, Colonial Kitchen, Anchor Hocking,
Western Publishing
SALE DAYS: monthly specials
PARKING: lot
PAYMENT: cash, checks (amount of purchase only, with proper I.D.)

WEST BEND, WI

Cookie Jar Outlet
See listing under *Food—Bakery* in West Bend, Wisconsin.

E K Outlet
See listing under *Clothing—Accessories* in West Bend, Wisconsin.

Houseware Outlet, West Bend Outlet Mall, 180 Island Avenue, West Bend, WI 53095;
(414) 334-4243
See listing in Green Bay, Wisconsin.

SUN.	MON.	TUE.	WED.	THU.	FRI.	SAT.
11–6	9:30–9	9:30–9	9:30–9	9:30–9	9:30–9	9:30–6

SAVINGS: 25%–70% off
BRAND NAMES: Anchor Hocking, Ekco, Mirro
PARKING: lot
PAYMENT: cash, checks (amount of purchase only, with proper I.D.)

Regal Ware Outlet Store
See listing under *Appliances* in West Bend, Wisconsin.

West Bend Company—Employees Cash Sales Store
See listing under *Appliances* in West Bend, Wisconsin.

West Bend Vacuum Center
See listing under *Appliances* in West Bend, Wisconsin.

16
JEWELRY

Researching the chapter on jewelry presented special problems. "Retail" prices varied greatly. The market in gold and other precious metals fluctuates, and retail prices can change from week to week. Mark-up on jewelry is frequently 100% or more, so deciding value and savings were difficult.

I tried to eliminate "discount" jewelers, and to determine savings based on certain comparable items with more easily evaluated prices. Do comparison shopping before you buy. Look for savings starting at about 50% off retail price. Watch for differences in quality.

Also look in the clothing chapters. Many of those outlets also sell jewelry.

ILLINOIS
CHICAGO, IL

Jewelry Liquidation Center, 400 S. Jefferson Street, Chicago, IL 60607; (312) 454-0643

This is the outlet for Hallmark Jewelry Company. They sell Citizen, Seiko, Bulova, and Elgin watches at about 40% off retail price, and 14K chains and diamond jewelry at 50%–70% off retail prices. Best buys are on samples, test runs, surplus, overruns, last year's lines, discontinued, and closeout merchandise.

SUN.	MON.	TUE.	WED.	THU.	FRI.	SAT.
closed	9–4:30	9–4:30	9–4:30	9–4:30	9–4:30	10–2

SAVINGS: 25%–80% off　　　　　　　　　　　　　　　*Mailing List*
BRAND NAMES: Citizen, Seiko, Bulova, Elgin
ANNUAL SALES: spring, fall
PARKING: lot
PAYMENT: cash, checks, MasterCard, VISA, American Express

CICERO, IL

The Jewelry Exchange, Guinta's Factory Outlet Mall, 1800 S. Cicero Avenue, Cicero, IL 60650; (312) 652-0199

This shop sells jewelry at savings up to 70% off retail price.

SUN.	MON.	TUE.	WED.	THU.	FRI.	SAT.
10–6	10–8	closed	closed	closed	10–8	10–6

SAVINGS: up to 70% off　　　　　　　　　　　　　　*All First Quality*
PARKING: lot
PAYMENT: cash, checks (amount of purchase only, with proper I.D.)

Italian Gold II, 415 Harrison Street, Oak Park, IL 60304; (312) 524-1991
   This store sells all gold items: rings, bracelets, and other jewelry. Savings average 50%–65% off retail price depending on the market in gold.

SUN.	MON.	TUE.	WED.	THU.	FRI.	SAT.
11-3*	closed	10-6	10-6	10-7:30	10-7:30	10-5

SAVINGS: 50%–65% off   *All First Quality*
SPECIAL SALES: monthly
PARKING: street
PAYMENT: cash, checks (amount of purchase only, with proper I.D.), MasterCard,
   VISA, American Express, Diners Club

---

*They are closed on Sunday in July, August, and September.

Blume Jewelers (James M.), Eastgate Consumer Mall, 7150 E. Washington Street,
   Indianapolis, IN 46201; (317) 356-2548
   This store sells jewelry at discounts of 20%–40% off retail prices.

SUN.	MON.	TUE.	WED.	THU.	FRI.	SAT.
noon-5	10-9	10-9	10-9	10-9	10-9	10-9

SAVINGS: 20%–40% off   *Mailing List*   *All First Quality*
SALE DAYS: vary
PARKING: lot
PAYMENT: cash, checks (with proper I.D.), MasterCard, VISA, American Express,
   Diners Club

Hirth Jewelers, Buyer's Marketplace, 5901 N. Grape Road, Mishawaka, IN 46545;
   (219) 277-2343
   This store sells jewelry at savings that average 45% off retail price.

SUN.	MON.	TUE.	WED.	THU.	FRI.	SAT.
11-5	9:30-9	9:30-9	9:30-9	9:30-9	9:30-9	9:30-9

SAVINGS: 20%–70% off   *Mailing List*   *All First Quality*
SALE DAYS: vary
SPECIAL DISCOUNTS: senior citizens, 10% off (ask)
PARKING: lot
PAYMENT: cash, checks (amount of purchase only, with proper I.D., Telecheck),
   MasterCard, VISA, American Express

Stuart Manufacturing Company
   See listing under *Clothing—Women's* in Milwaukee, Wisconsin.

17
LAMPS AND LIGHTING

These outlets sell lamps and lighting fixtures. Also look in Chapter 6, *Ceramics*; Chapter 9, *Decorating*; Chapter 10, *Department Stores*; Chapter 13, *Furniture*; Chapter 14, *Gift Items*; and Chapter 20, *Office Equipment*, for other outlets that sell lamps.

Savings on lamps were generally excellent. Look for 25% off retail price as a starting point for first quality, and expect to save 50% and more on seconds and irregular merchandise. Irregularities were cosmetic and did not affect the performance of lamps.

ILLINOIS

CHICAGO, IL

Factory Lamp and Accessories Outlet Center, 3370 N. Central Avenue, Chicago, IL 60634; (312) 283-5054

This factory showroom is open to the public only on Saturday. Savings begin at 10% off retail price on first quality lamps and lamp shades, but can go higher on some imperfects, irregulars, overstocks, samples, last year's lines, and closeout merchandise.

SUN.	MON.	TUE.	WED.	THU.	FRI.	SAT.
closed	closed	closed	closed	closed	closed	9–1

SAVINGS: 10%–50% off
PARKING: lot
PAYMENT: cash, checks (amount of purchase only, with proper I.D.), MasterCard, VISA

House-O-Lite—Lava-Simplex International, 4041 S. Emerald Avenue, Chicago, IL 60609; (312) 376-9786

This is the outlet for Lava Lite, Gem Lite, and the Wave light. Savings 40%–60% off retail price on seconds, samples, overstocks, closeouts, and some "as is" merchandise.

SUN.	MON.	TUE.	WED.	THU.	FRI.	SAT.
closed	8–4:30	8–4:30	8–4:30	8–4:30	8–4:30	closed

SAVINGS: 40%–60% off
BRAND NAMES: Lava Lite, Wave, Gem Lite
ANNUAL SALES: Christmas specials
PARKING: street
PAYMENT: cash, checks (Illinois only)

The Lamp Factory, 11042 S. Kedzie Avenue, Chicago, IL 60655; (312) 238-9146

This factory outlet sells lamps and lamp shades. Savings begin at 50% off retail price, and can go even higher on occasional irregulars. They have other stores in Cicero and Franklin Park, Illinois.

SUN.	MON.	TUE.	WED.	THU.	FRI.	SAT.
11–4	9–9	10–5	10–5	9–9	10–5	10–5

SAVINGS: at least 50% off *All First Quality*
BRAND NAMES: Lamp Factory
PARKING: lot
PAYMENT: cash, checks (amount of purchase only, with proper I.D.), MasterCard, VISA

Sofa and Sleeper Factory
See listing under *Furniture* in Chicago, Illinois.

BARRINGTON, IL

L & W Lamps, 710 S. Northwest Highway, Barrington, IL 60010; (312) 382-3195
This factory outlet sells lamps and lamp shades. Since the lamps are assembled on the premises, they say the savings are passed on to the customer. Savings average 20%-30% off retail prices on first quality, with some last year's lines, end of season, and closeout merchandise. They have another store in Crystal Lake, Illinois.

SUN.	MON.	TUE.	WED.	THU.	FRI.	SAT.
closed	9-5	9-5	9-5	9-5	9-5	9-5

SAVINGS: 20%-30% off
BRAND NAMES: L & B, Nathan Lagin, Frederick Cooper
PARKING: lot
PAYMENT: cash, checks (amount of purchase only, with proper I.D.)

BUFFALO GROVE, IL

Litemart, 777 S. Buffalo Grove Road, Buffalo Grove, IL 60090; (312) 541-5310
This store sells major brands of lighting fixtures and track lighting at discounts from 30%-50% off retail price.

SUN.	MON.	TUE.	WED.	THU.	FRI.	SAT.
closed	10-8	10-5	10-5	10-8	10-5	10-4

SAVINGS: 30%-50% off *All First Quality*
BRAND NAMES: Lightolier, Framburg, Kenroy, Forcast, Plantation, Check O'Lite, Nulco, Sternberg
PARKING: lot
PAYMENT: cash, checks (with proper I.D.), MasterCard, VISA

CICERO, IL

The Lamp Factory, 6001 W. Cermak Road, Cicero, IL 60650; (312) 780-8787
See listing in Chicago, Illinois.

SUN.	MON.	TUE.	WED.	THU.	FRI.	SAT.
11-4	10-9	10-5	10-5	10-9	10-5	10-5

SAVINGS: 50% and up
BRAND NAMES: Lamp Factory
SALE DAYS: vary
PARKING: lot
PAYMENT: cash, checks (amount of purchase only, with proper I.D.), MasterCard, VISA

CRYSTAL LAKE, IL

L & W Lamps, 6319 Northwest Highway, Crystal Lake, IL 60014; (815) 455-4099
See listing in Barrington, Illinois.

SUN.	MON.	TUE.	WED.	THU.	FRI.	SAT.
closed	9-5	9-5	9-5	9-5	9-5	9-5

SAVINGS: 20%-30% off
BRAND NAMES: L & B, Nathan Lagin
SALE DAYS: vary
PARKING: lot
PAYMENT: cash, checks (amount of purchase only, with proper I.D.)

Direct Lamps and Shades, Finley Square Mall, 1524 E. Butterfield Road, Downers Grove, IL 60515; (312) 953-1888

This factory outlet offers savings from 15%–50% off on lamps and shades. Greatest savings are on surplus, overstocks, last year's lines, and discontinued items.

SUN.	MON.	TUE.	WED.	THU.	FRI.	SAT.
noon–5	noon–8	noon–8	noon–8	noon–8	noon–8	10–5

SAVINGS: 15%–50% off
PARKING: lot
PAYMENT: cash, checks (amount of purchase only, with proper I.D.), MasterCard, VISA

Haeger Potteries—Factory Outlet Complex

See listing under *Ceramics* in East Dundee, Illinois.

The Lamp Factory, 9216 W. Grand Avenue, Franklin Park, IL 60131; (312) 451-1192

See listing in Chicago, Illinois.

SUN.	MON.	TUE.	WED.	THU.	FRI.	SAT.
11–4	9–9	9–5	9–5	9–9	9–5	10–5

SAVINGS: at least 50% off
BRAND NAMES: Lamp Factory
SALE DAYS: vary
PARKING: lot
PAYMENT: cash, checks (amount of purchase only, with proper I.D.), MasterCard, VISA

WJT Sales, 28 W. 715 Mount Boulevard, Warrenville, IL 60555; (312) 393-1919

This store sells major brands of lighting fixtures, cabinets, locks, windows, and hinges. Savings are greatest on irregular merchandise.

SUN.	MON.	TUE.	WED.	THU.	FRI.	SAT.
closed	8–6	8–6	8–6	8–6	8–6	9–4

SAVINGS: 60%–80% off
PARKING: lot
PAYMENT: cash, checks (amount of purchase only, with proper I.D.)

The Brighter Side, Factory Outlet Centre, 7700 120th Avenue, Kenosha, WI 53142; (414) 857-7724

This is an outlet for Lamplight Farms. There is a wide selection of oil lamps and lamp oil at savings up to 30% on surplus, overruns, discontinued items, and overstocks. They have another store in West Bend, Wisconsin.

SUN.	MON.	TUE.	WED.	THU.	FRI.	SAT.
11–5	9:30–9	9:30–9	9:30–9	9:30–9	9:30–9	9:30–9

SAVINGS: 15%–30% off
BRAND NAMES: Lamplight Farms
SPECIAL DISCOUNTS: senior citizens, 10% off Wednesday
PARKING: lot
PAYMENT: cash, checks, MasterCard, VISA

Lamp Factory, Factory Outlet Centre, 7700 120th Avenue, Kenosha, WI 53142.
   (414) 857-7569
      This is the outlet for Bradley manufacturers. Savings on lamps and lamp shades begin at 35% off retail price for first quality. There is a bargain bin where savings can go as high as 60% off retail price.

SUN.	MON.	TUE.	WED.	THU.	FRI.	SAT.
11-5	9:30-9	9:30-9	9:30-9	9:30-9	9:30-9	9:30-6

SAVINGS: 35%-60% off
BRAND NAMES: Bradley
SPECIAL SALES: senior citizens, 5% off Wednesday
PARKING: lot
PAYMENT: cash, checks (with proper I.D.), MasterCard, VISA

WEST BEND, WI

The Brighter Side, West Bend Outlet Mall, 180 Island Avenue, West Bend, WI 53095;
   (414) 338-1411
      See listing in Kenosha, Wisconsin.

SUN.	MON.	TUE.	WED.	THU.	FRI.	SAT.
noon-5	9:30-5	9:30-5	9:30-5	9:30-5	9:30-8	9:30-5

SAVINGS: 15%-30% off
BRAND NAMES: Lamplight Farms
PARKING: lot
PAYMENT: cash, checks (amount of purchase only, with proper I.D., no out-of-state checks), MasterCard, VISA

18
LINENS

This chapter includes most cloth items for the bedroom, bath, kitchen, and table. Many outlets also sell bedroom and bath accessories. Look in Chapter 3, *Baby Accessories*; Chapter 4, *Beds, Mattresses, and Box Springs*; Chapter 9, *Decorating*; Chapter 10, *Department Stores*; and Chapter 24, *Plates, Glassware, and Tableware,* for other outlets that sell linens. Savings on first quality generally start at 25% off retail price; savings on seconds begin about 50% off retail price and often go much higher. Some outlets sell bundles of irregular towels by the pound at excellent prices.

ILLINOIS

CHICAGO, IL

Crawford's Linen Outlet, 2523 W. Devon Avenue, Chicago, IL 60639; (312) 338-2500
This outlet sells a vast selection of items for the bed, bath, and tabletop. Many brands are represented. Savings average 20%–50% on first quality items, but can go as high as 70% on irregulars, overruns, overstocks, last year's lines, discontinued, and closeout items. They also have a store in Niles, Illinois.

SUN.	MON.	TUE.	WED.	THU.	FRI.	SAT.
11–4	10–9	10–5:30	10–5:30	10–9	10–5:30	9:30–5:30

SAVINGS: 20%–70% off   *Mailing List*
BRAND NAMES: Springmaid, Martex, Burlington, Dundee, Junweave, Pillowtex,
  Chatham Ames, Elrene, Dan River
SALE DAYS: vary
PARKING: lot
PAYMENT: cash, checks (amount of purchase only, with proper I.D., no out-of-state
  checks), MasterCard, VISA, Crawford's charge card

Factory Linen Outlet, 4777 N. Milwaukee Avenue, Chicago, IL 60630; (312) 545-5246
This store sells several major brands of sheets, pillowcases, comforters, blankets, and towels. They also sell some bathroom accessories. Savings begin at 20% off retail price for first quality, and can go as high as 70% on last year's lines, seconds, irregulars, discontinued, and closeout merchandise.

SUN.	MON.	TUE.	WED.	THU.	FRI.	SAT.
11–4	10–8	10–8	10–8	10–8	10–8	10–5

SAVINGS: 20%–70% off
BRAND NAMES: Springmaid, Martex, Fieldcrest
ANNUAL SALES: February
SPECIAL DISCOUNTS: senior citizens, 10% off
PARKING: street, meters
PAYMENT: cash, checks (amount of purchase only, with proper I.D.), MasterCard, VISA

Factory Linen Outlet, 5923 N. Clark Street, Chicago, IL 60660; (312) 878-3388
   See listing above.

SUN.	MON.	TUE.	WED.	THU.	FRI.	SAT.
11–4	10–8	10–8	10–8	10–8	10–8	10–5

SAVINGS: 20%–70% off
BRAND NAMES: Fieldcrest, Martex, Springmaid
ANNUAL SALES: February
SPECIAL DISCOUNTS: senior citizens, 10% off
PARKING: street, meters
PAYMENT: cash, checks (amount of purchase only, with proper I.D.), MasterCard,
   VISA, American Express

Private Lives Warehouse, 2725 N. Clark Street, Chicago, IL 60614; (312) 525-6464
   This outlet sells major brands of linens and bed and bath accessories. Savings
begin at 25% off retail price for first quality, and go as high as 60% on discontinued,
overstock, and clearance items. They also have stores in Evanston and Northbrook,
Illinois.

SUN.	MON.	TUE.	WED.	THU.	FRI.	SAT.
noon–5	11–7	11–7	11–7	11–7	11–7	10–5:30

SAVINGS: 30%–60% off
BRAND NAMES: Martex, Fieldcrest, Burlington, Cannon
PARKING: street, meters, can be difficult
PAYMENT: cash, checks (amount of purchase only, with proper I.D.), MasterCard,
   VISA, American Express

Reiter's Outlet Store, 2460 W. George Street, Chicago, IL 60616; (312) 267-8849
   This store sells draperies, bedding, and pillows. Most merchandise is first quality,
but they do sell some seconds, last year's lines, discontinued, and overstock
merchandise.

SUN.	MON.	TUE.	WED.	THU.	FRI.	SAT.
10–5	9–5	9–5	9–5	9–5	9–5	9–5

SAVINGS: at least 10% off
SALE DAYS: vary
PARKING: street
PAYMENT: cash, checks (with proper I.D.), MasterCard, VISA

Textile Discount Outlet
   See listing under *Fabrics* in Chicago, Illinois.

ALGONQUIN, IL

Story Design and Manufacturing, 790 W. Chicago Street, Algonquin, IL 60102;
   (312) 658-5626
   This factory outlet sells Story bedspreads and comforters. They also sell pillows,
window treatments, fabrics, fiber-fill, place mats, pot holders, and baby quilts. Savings
begin at 25% off on first quality merchandise, and can go up to 75% off retail prices on
seconds, irregulars, bolt-ends, and overruns.

SUN.	MON.	TUE.	WED.	THU.	FRI.	SAT.
closed	9–4	9–4	9–4	9–4	9–4	9–1

SAVINGS: 25%–75% off   *Mailing List*
PARKING: lot
PAYMENT: cash, checks (amount of purchase only, with proper I.D.), MasterCard, VISA

ARLINGTON HEIGHTS, IL

5th Avenue Bed and Bath Outlet, Arlington Plaza, 210 W. Rand Road, Arlington
   Heights, IL 60004; (312) 394-8822

This is an outlet for Martex and Fieldcrest. They have an extensive assortment of towels, linens, tablecloths, and accessories for the bed and bath. They also have coordinated comforters by Ralph Lauren. Savings can go up to 50% off retail price. They have another store in Merrillville, Indiana.

SUN.	MON.	TUE.	WED.	THU.	FRI.	SAT.
noon–5	10–9	10–9	10–9	10–9	10–9	10–5:30

SAVINGS: up to 50% off   *All First Quality*
BRAND NAMES: Martex, Fieldcrest
SPECIAL SALES: vary
PARKING: lot
PAYMENT: cash, checks (amount of purchase only, with proper I.D.), MasterCard, VISA

Linens Plus, 350 E. Rand Road, Arlington Heights, IL 60004; (312) 398-4940
This is one of several stores that sell major brands of linens and bath, bedroom, and kitchen boutique items at 20%–40% off retail price. Savings go up to 60% off retail on seconds. They also sell some surplus, overstocks, and discontinued items. They have other stores in Des Plaines, Matteson, and Oakbrook Terrace, Illinois.

SUN.	MON.	TUE.	WED.	THU.	FRI.	SAT.
noon–5	10–9	10–9	10–9	10–9	10–9	10–5:30

SAVINGS: 20%–60% off
BRAND NAMES: Springmaid, Fieldcrest, Burlington
ANNUAL SALES: May, September
PARKING: lot
PAYMENT: cash, checks (with proper I.D., no out-of-state checks), MasterCard, VISA

Towel Factory Outlet Center, 2404 E. Oakton Street, Arlington Heights, IL 60007; (312) 981-1620
This outlet sells several major brands of towels, sheets, bedspreads, kitchen towels, and oven mitts. They also sell some bath rugs, shower curtains, comforters, and pillows. Savings begin at 40% off retail price on first quality, and can run as high as 70% on seconds, irregulars, imperfects, overstocks, and discontinued items. They have another store in Downers Grove, Illinois.

SUN.	MON.	TUE.	WED.	THU.	FRI.	SAT.
11–5	9:30–6	9:30–6	9:30–6	9:30–9	9:30–6	9:30–5:30

SAVINGS: 40%–70% off
SPECIAL SALES: monthly
PARKING: lot
PAYMENT: cash, MasterCard, VISA

CICERO, IL

Apparel Textile Outlet, Guinta's Factory Outlet Mall, 1800 S. Cicero Avenue, Cicero, IL 60650; (312) 780-9488
This outlet sells sheets, pillowcases, comforters, and bedspreads at savings from 10%–30% off retail prices.

SUN.	MON.	TUE.	WED.	THU.	FRI.	SAT.
10–6	10–8	closed	10–8	10–8	10–8	10–6

SAVINGS: 10%–30% off   *All First Quality*
PARKING: lot
PAYMENT: cash only

DEERFIELD, IL

Linens 'N' Things, 19 N. Waukegan Road, Deerfield, IL 60015; (312) 940-0350
This shop sells sheets, towels, comforters, pot holders, tablecloths, and hampers. There is a special aisle where all the seconds, irregulars, overrruns, overstocks, and discontinued items are discounted even further. They have other stores in Downers Grove and Schaumburg, Illinois; and Indianapolis, Indiana

SUN.	MON.	TUE.	WED.	THU.	FRI.	SAT.
11-5	10-9	10-9	10-9	10-9	10-9	10-6

SAVINGS: 10%-40% off
BRAND NAMES: Cannon, Martex
SALE DAYS: vary
PARKING: lot
PAYMENT: cash, checks (amount of purchase only, with proper I.D.), MasterCard, VISA

DES PLAINES, IL

Linens Plus, 8760 Dempster Street, Des Plaines, IL 60016; (312) 296-5330
See listing in Arlington Heights, Illinois.

SUN.	MON.	TUE.	WED.	THU.	FRI.	SAT.
noon-5	10-9	10-9	10-9	10-9	10-9	10-6

SAVINGS: 20%-70% off
BRAND NAMES: Springmaid, Fieldcrest, Burlington
ANNUAL SALES: May, August
PARKING: lot
PAYMENT: cash, checks (amount of purchase only, with proper I.D.), MasterCard, VISA

DOWNERS GROVE, IL

Linens 'N' Things, 1328 Butterfield Road, Downers Grove, IL 60515; (312) 627-0033
See listing in Deerfield, Illinois.

SUN.	MON.	TUE.	WED.	THU.	FRI.	SAT.
11-5	10-9	10-9	10-9	10-9	10-9	10-6

SAVINGS: 10%-40% off
BRAND NAMES: Cannon
PARKING: lot
PAYMENT: cash, checks, MasterCard, VISA

Towel Factory Outlet Center, 1630 Ogden Avenue, Downers Grove, IL 60515; (312) 852-3616
See listing in Arlington Heights, Illinois.

SUN.	MON.	TUE.	WED.	THU.	FRI.	SAT.
11-5	9:30-6	9:30-6	9:30-6	9:30-9	9:30-6	9:30-5:30

SAVINGS: 40%-50% off
BRAND NAMES: Cannon, Martex
SPECIAL DISCOUNTS: charity groups
PARKING: lot
PAYMENT: cash, MasterCard, VISA

EAST DUNDEE, IL

Winona Knits
See listing under *Clothing—Accessories* in East Dundee, Illinois.

EVANSTON, IL

Private Lives Warehouse, 522 W. Dempster Street, Evanston, IL 60202; (312) 866-8244
See listing in Chicago, Illinois.

SUN.	MON.	TUE.	WED.	THU.	FRI.	SAT.
closed	10-6	10-6	10-6	10-8	10-6	10-5:30

SAVINGS: 25%–60% off   *All First Quality*
BRAND NAMES: Martex, Fieldcrest, Burlington, Cannon
PARKING: street
PAYMENT: cash, checks (amount of purchase only, with proper I.D.), MasterCard,
  VISA, American Express ($5 minimum)

HEBRON, IL

Linen Outlet, 10004 Main Street, Hebron, IL 60034; (815) 648-4320
  This store sells linens at discounts over 50% off retail prices. Best buys are on
seconds, samples, surplus, overruns, overstocks, discontinued, last year's lines, and
closeouts. They sell the beds in their store next door (see p. 16).

SUN.	MON.	TUE.	WED.	THU.	FRI.	SAT.
11–4	10–3	10–3	closed	10–5	10–5	10–5

SAVINGS: 50%–70% off
BRAND NAMES: Cannon, Fieldcrest
ANNUAL SALES: May, December
PARKING: lot
PAYMENT: cash, checks, MasterCard, VISA, American Express

LAKE ZURICH, IL

R. A. Briggs and Company, 650 N. Church Street, Lake Zurich, IL 60047; (312)
  438-2345
  This store sells major mill brands of towels, pot holders, and textiles for the
bathroom and kitchen. Savings are greatest on seconds, irregulars, imperfects,
samples, surplus, overruns, overstocks, last year's lines, discontinued, and closeout
merchandise.

SUN.	MON.	TUE.	WED.	THU.	FRI.	SAT.
closed	9–4	9–4	9–4	9–4	9–4	9–4

SAVINGS: 40%–60% off   *Mailing List*
ANNUAL SALES: three (dates vary)
PARKING: lot
PAYMENT: cash only

LOVES PARK, IL

The Linen Outlet, Park Plaza Outlet Mart, 6427 N. 2nd Street, Loves Park, IL 61111;
  (815) 877-4959
  This store sells major brands of linens. They also sell wicker and other bathroom
accessories. Best buys are on seconds, overruns, overstocks, last year's lines,
discontinued, and closeout merchandise.

SUN.	MON.	TUE.	WED.	THU.	FRI.	SAT.
noon–5	9:30–9	9:30–9	9:30–9	9:30–9	9:30–9	9:30–5

SAVINGS: 20%–60% off
BRAND NAMES: Cannon, Fieldcrest, Martex
SALES DAYS: weekends, randomly
SPECIAL DISCOUNTS: senior citizens, 10% off Tuesday
PARKING: lot
PAYMENT: cash, checks (amount of purchase only, with proper I.D.), MasterCard, VISA

MATTESON, IL

Linens Plus, 4210 W. 211th Street, Matteson, IL 60443; (312) 481-2750
  See listing in Arlington Heights, Illinois.

SUN.	MON.	TUE.	WED.	THU.	FRI.	SAT.
noon–5	10–9	10–9	10–9	10–9	10–9	10–5:30

SAVINGS: 20%-60% off
BRAND NAMES: Springmaid, Fieldcrest, Burlington
ANNUAL SALES: summer
PARKING: lot
PAYMENT: cash, checks (amount of purchase only, with proper I.D.), MasterCard, VISA

MORTON GROVE, IL

Beds And Spreads
See listing under *Beds, Mattresses, and Box Springs* in Morton Grove, Illinois.

NILES, IL

Crawford's Linen Outlet, 8257 Golf Road, Niles, IL 60649; (312) 965-2270
See listing in Chicago, Illinois.

SUN.	MON.	TUE.	WED.	THU.	FRI.	SAT.
noon-5	10-8	10-8	10-8	10-8	10-8	10-5

SAVINGS: 20%-50% off   *Mailing List*
PARKING: lot
PAYMENT: cash, checks (amount of purchase only, with proper I.D.), MasterCard, VISA

Towel Factory Outlet—Revere Mills, 7313 N. Harlem Avenue, Niles, IL 60648; (312) 792-1700
See listing in Arlington Heights, Illinois.

SUN.	MON.	TUE.	WED.	THU.	FRI.	SAT.
closed	9:30-5	9:30-5	9:30-5	9:30-5	9:30-5	9:30-5

SAVINGS: 10%-50% off   *Mailing List*
BRAND NAMES: Revere, Cannon, St. Marys, Briggs, Pillowtex, Cultex
ANNUAL SALES: January
PARKING: lot
PAYMENT: cash, checks (amount of purchase only, with proper I.D.), MasterCard, VISA

NORTHBROOK, IL

Private Lives Warehouse, 1135 Church Street, Northbrook, IL 60062; (312) 480-0670
See listing in Chicago, Illinois.

SUN.	MON.	TUE.	WED.	THU.	FRI.	SAT.
closed	10-5:30	10-5	10-5:30	10-5:30	10-5:30	10-5:30

SAVINGS: 25%-30% off   *All First Quality*
BRAND NAMES: Martex, Fieldcrest, Burlington, Cannon
PARKING: lot
PAYMENT: cash, checks (amount of purchase only, with proper I.D.), MasterCard, VISA, American Express ($5 minimum)

OAKBROOK TERRACE, IL

Linens Plus, 17 W. 693 Roosevelt Road, Oakbrook Terrace, IL 60181; (312) 620-5662
See listing in Arlington Heights, Illinois.

SUN.	MON.	TUE.	WED.	THU.	FRI.	SAT.
noon-5	9:30-9	9:30-9	9:30-9	9:30-9	9:30-9	9:30-5

SAVINGS: 20%-60% off
BRAND NAMES: Springmaid, Fieldcrest, Burlington
SALE DAYS: vary
PARKING: lot
PAYMENT: cash, checks (amount of purchase only, with proper I.D., no out-of-state checks), MasterCard, VISA

SOUTH CHICAGO HEIGHTS, IL

Oops, We Goofed
See listing under *Fabrics* in South Chicago Heights, Illinois.

SCHAUMBURG, IL

Linens 'N' Things, 163 W. Golf Road, Schaumburg, IL 60195; (312) 843-1800
See listing in Deerfield, Illinois.

SUN.	MON.	TUE.	WED.	THU.	FRI.	SAT.
11-5	10-9	10-9	10-9	10-9	10-9	10-6

SAVINGS: 20%–50% off
BRAND NAMES: Cannon, Martex
SALE DAYS: vary
PARKING: lot
PAYMENT: cash, checks (amount of purchase only, with proper I.D.), MasterCard, VISA

INDIANA

CLARKSVILLE, IN

Leslie's Midwest Towel Store, 615 Eastern Boulevard, Clarksville, IN 47130; (812) 282-3112
This is an outlet for Cannon Mills. They sell Cannon towels, sheets, and bedspreads as well as several other major brands of linens. Savings start at 30% off retail price on first quality and drop quickly on seconds, samples, overruns, and closeout merchandise. The best buy is probably the "grab bag" of ten pounds of irregular towels for $27.50. They also sell "institutional" towels.

SUN.	MON.	TUE.	WED.	THU.	FRI.	SAT.
closed	10-8	10-8	10-8	10-8	10-8	10-5

SAVINGS: 30%–60% off
BRAND NAMES: Cannon Mills, J.P. Stevens, Fieldcrest, Spring Mills, Regal Textile, Dundee
PARKING: lot
PAYMENT: cash, MasterCard, VISA

EVANSVILLE, IN

Ashley's Outlet Store
See three listings under *Clothing—Family* in Evansville, Indiana.

GARY, IN

Brady's This Is It—Factory Outlet Store—Home and Auto
See listing under *Plates, Glassware, and Tableware* in Gary. Indiana.

INDIANAPOLIS, IN

The Company Store
See listing under *Clothing—Outerwear* in Indianapolis, Indiana.

Linens 'N' Things, Eastgate Consumer Mall, 7150 E. Washington Street, Indianapolis, IN 46219; (317) 353-1441
See listing in Deerfield, Illinois.

SUN.	MON.	TUE.	WED.	THU.	FRI.	SAT.
noon-5	10-9	10-9	10-9	10-9	10-9	10-9

SAVINGS: 25%–75% off
BRAND NAMES: Springs, Cannon, Andre Richard
SALE DAYS: vary
PARKING: lot
PAYMENT: cash, checks (with proper I.D.), MasterCard, VISA

Ashley's Outlet Store
   See listing under *Clothing—Family* in Jasper, Indiana.

5th Avenue Bed 'N Bath, Century Consumer Mall, 8275 Broadway. Merrillville, IN 46410; (219) 736-0749
   See listing in Arlington Heights, Illinois.

SUN.	MON.	TUE.	WED.	THU.	FRI.	SAT.
noon–5	10–9	10–9	10–9	10–9	10–9	10–9

SAVINGS: 20%–50% off
SALE DAYS: vary
PARKING: lot
PAYMENT: cash, checks (amount of purchase only, with proper I.D.), MasterCard, VISA

Ashley's Outlet Store
   See listing under *Clothing—Family* in Mount Vernon, Indiana.

Nettle Creek Industries, 40 Peacock Road, Richmond, IN 47374; (317) 962-1555
   This factory outlet sells bedspreads, fabric ends, decorator pillows, bath towels, sheet sets, bath rugs, and kitchen towels. Savings begin at 20% off retail price, and go much higher on seconds, irregulars, bolt-ends, last year's lines, discontinued, overruns, odd lots, and "as is" merchandise. All sales are final; no exchanges or refunds.

SUN.	MON.	TUE.	WED.	THU.	FRI.	SAT.
closed	8–4:30	8–4:30	8–4:30	8–4:30	8–4:30	9–3

SAVINGS: 20%–70% off
BRAND NAMES: Nettle Creek
ANNUAL SALES: June, September
PARKING: lot
PAYMENT: cash, checks, MasterCard, VISA

Ashley's Outlet Store
   See listing under *Clothing—Family* in Tell City, Indiana.

McArthur Towels, 120 Water Street, Baraboo, WI 53913; (608) 356-8922
   This is an outlet for Cannon and West Point towels. They also sell custom-made bathrobes and tank suits, institutional towels, and beach towels. Greatest savings are on irregulars, overruns, overstocked, and discontinued items. They do embroidering or monogramming at a small additional charge.

SUN.	MON.	TUE.	WED.	THU.	FRI.	SAT.
closed	8:30–4:30	8:30–4:30	8:30–4:30	8:30–4:30	8:30–4:30	closed

SAVINGS: 40%–50% off
BRAND NAMES: Cannon, West Point
PARKING: lot
PAYMENT: cash, checks (amount of purchase only, with proper I.D.)

Fieldcrest, Freeman Outlet Mall, 5 Freeman Lane, Beloit, WI 53511; (608) 365-3100
This is the mill outlet for Fieldcrest. They sell towels and linens. They also sell Pillowtex pillows and mattress pads. Some merchandise is first quality, but the real savings are on irregulars, samples, and discontinued colors. They frequently run a special on a bundle of five irregular towels for $8.99, but if irregulars are unavailable from the mill, the towels are first quality at the irregular price. They will ship your purchases U.P.S.

SUN.	MON.	TUE.	WED.	THU.	FRI.	SAT.
11–6	9–9	9–9	9–9	9–9	9–9	9–6

SAVINGS: up to 60% off   *Mailing List*
BRAND NAMES: Fieldcrest, Pillowtex
ANNUAL SALES: August
SPECIAL DISCOUNTS: senior citizens they occasionally run a special of 10% off (ask)
PARKING: lot
PAYMENT: cash, checks (with proper I.D.), MasterCard, VISA, American Express, Diners Club

EAU CLAIRE, WI

The Company Store
See listing under *Clothing—Outerwear* in Eau Claire, Wisconsin.

GREEN BAY, WI

Winona Knits
See listing under *Clothing—Accessories* in Green Bay, Wisconsin.

JEFFERSON, WI

Fur the Fun of It
See listing under *Fabrics* in Jefferson, Wisconsin.

KENOSHA, WI

The Company Store
See two listings under *Clothing—Outerwear* in Kenosha, Wisconsin.

Winona Knits
See listing under *Clothing—Accessories* in Kenosha, Wisconsin.

LA CROSSE, WI

The Company Store
See listing under *Clothing—Outerwear* in La Crosse, Wisconsin.

NEW GLARUS, WI

Swiss Miss Textile Mart
See listing under *Fabrics* in New Glarus, Wisconsin.

OSHKOSH, WI

The Company Store
See listing under *Clothing—Outerwear* in Oshkosh, Wisconsin.

PLOVER, WI

The Company Store
See listing under *Clothing—Outerwear* in Plover, Wisconsin.

Winona Glove Company
See listing under *Clothing—Accessories* in Plover, Wisconsin.

Winona Knits
See listing under *Clothing—Accessories* in Plover, Wisconsin.

REDWING, WI

The Company Store
See listing under *Clothing—Outerwear* in Redwing, Wisconsin.

SISTER BAY, WI

Winona Knits
See listing under *Clothing—Accessories* in Sister Bay, Wisconsin.

WEST BEND, WI

Westman Glass & China
See listing under *Plates, Glassware, and Tableware* in West Bend, Wisconsin.

Winona Knits
See listing under *Clothing—Accessories* in West Bend, Wisconsin.

19
LUGGAGE

The outlets sell luggage, but many also sell purses, wallets, brief-cases, etc. Look in Chapter 7, *Clothing—Accessories*, for other outlets that sell luggage.

Savings were best on seconds and irregular merchandise. Also look for single pieces left over from a set.

ILLINOIS

CHICAGO, IL

The Leather Shop, 191 W. Madison Street, Chicago, IL 60602; (312) 782-5448

The real bargains are on the second floor of the retail shop. Savings start at 25% off retail price on last year's lines, discontinued, and overstocks of luggage, tote bags, garment bags, and purses.

SUN.	MON.	TUE.	WED.	THU.	FRI.	SAT.
closed	8-6	8-6	8-6	8-6	8-6	8-3

SAVINGS: at least 25% off *Mailing List*
BRAND NAMES: Samsonite, Ventura
ANNUAL SALES: February
SPECIAL DISCOUNTS: senior citizens, 15% off (except sale items)
PARKING: street, meters
PAYMENT: cash, checks (amount of purchase only, with proper I.D., no out-of-state checks), MasterCard, VISA, American Express, Diners Club

National Handbag Outlet Store
See listing under *Clothing—Accessories* in Chicago, Illinois.

Specialty Trunk and Suitcase Company, 443 N. Clark Street, Chicago, IL 60610; (312) 642-1446

This store sells luggage, trunks, and foot lockers. They also make made-to-order fiber cases, equipment cases, and travel bags. They also sell some briefcases, wallets, and portfolios.

SUN.	MON.	TUE.	WED.	THU.	FRI.	SAT.
closed	8:30-5	8:30-5	8:30-5	8:30-5	8:30-5	8:30-2

SAVINGS: 10%-25% off *All First Quality*
BRAND NAMES: Winn, Andiamo, Smith, N.S.M.
PARKING: street, meters, can be difficult
PAYMENT: cash, checks (amount of purchase only, with proper I.D.), MasterCard, VISA

The Kaehler Outlet, Deerbrook Mall, 176 S. Waukegan Road, Deerfield, IL 60015; (312) 498-1888

This is the outlet for Kaehler luggage. Savings on luggage, business cases, handbags, wallets, travel accessories, and trunks start at 25% off retail price on first quality, and go as high as 75% on irregulars, samples, test runs, overstocks, discontinued, and closeout merchandise.

SUN.	MON.	TUE.	WED.	THU.	FRI.	SAT.
noon–5	10–9	10–9	10–9	10–9	10–9	10–5:30

SAVINGS: 25%–75% off
BRAND NAMES: Hartman, Samsonite, Lark, Boy, Billy, Skyway, Ventura, Verdi, Fulton,
  Atlas, National
ANNUAL SALES: February, July
PARKING: lot
PAYMENT: cash, checks (amount of purchase only, with proper I.D., no out-of-state
  checks), MasterCard, VISA

Luggage Limited, 1122 Lee Street, Des Plaines, IL 60016; (312) 825-8060

This is an outlet for Samsonite and Ventura luggage. They also sell briefcases at savings approximately 20% off retail prices.

SUN.	MON.	TUE.	WED.	THU.	FRI.	SAT.
closed	7:30–4	7:30–4	7:30–4	7:30–4	7:30–4	closed

SAVINGS: 20% off   *All First Quality*
BRAND NAMES: Samsonite, Ventura
SALE DAYS: vary
PARKING: lot
PAYMENT: cash, checks (amount of purchase only, with proper I.D.), MasterCard, VISA

Luggage Express, 1400 E. Golf Road, Rolling Meadows, IL 60008; (312) 228-6646

This outlet sells luggage and garment and gym bags at savings from 40%–60% off retail price on all first quality merchandise.

SUN.	MON.	TUE.	WED.	THU.	FRI.	SAT.
11–5	10–9:30	10–9:30	10–9:30	10–9:30	10–9:30	10–6

SAVINGS: 40%–60% off   *Mailing List*   *All First Quality*
PARKING: lot
PAYMENT: cash, checks (amount of purchase only, with proper I.D., no out-of-state
  checks, Telecheck), American Express

The Wallet Works
  See listing under *Clothing—Accessories* in Mishawaka, Indiana.

Mitchell Outlet
  See listing under *Clothing—Accessories* in Kenosha, Wisconsin.

The Wallet Works
  See listing under *Clothing—Accessories* in Kenosha, Wisconsin.

The Wallet Works
See listing under *Clothing—Accessories* in Madison, Wisconsin.

Mitchell Handbags
See listing under *Clothing—Accessories* in Milwaukee, Wisconsin.

The Wallet Works
See listing under *Clothing—Accessories* in Sister Bay, Wisconsin.

Amity Leather Products
See listing under *Clothing—Accessories* in West Bend, Wisconsin.

E K Outlet
See listing under *Clothing—Accessories* in West Bend, Wisconsin.

West Bend Company—Employees Cash Sales Store
See listing under *Appliances* in West Bend, Wisconsin.

20
OFFICE EQUIPMENT

The outlets listed in this chapter sell office equipment, although many also sell office supplies. See the following chapter, *Office Supplies*, for other outlets that sell office equipment. Savings were greatest on floor samples, "dents," and some closeout merchandise.

ILLINOIS

CHICAGO, IL

Office Furniture Warehouse, 640 N. LaSalle Street, Chicago, IL 60610; (312) 751-1400

This store sells major brands of office furniture. They also sell some office supplies. Savings begin at 20% off retail price on first quality, and can go as high as 60% off retail price on some irregulars, dents, overruns, overstocks, and closeout merchandise. They have another store in Chicago, and in Downers Grove, Franklin Park, Itasca, Lincolnwood, Oak Lawn, and Park City, Illinois; and Merrillville, Indiana.

SUN.	MON.	TUE.	WED.	THU.	FRI.	SAT.
closed	9–5:30	9–5:30	9–5:30	9–5:30	9–5:30	10–3

SAVINGS: 20%–60% off   *Mailing List*
PARKING: lot
PAYMENT: cash, checks (amount of purchase only, with proper I.D.), MasterCard, VISA, American Express

Office Furniture Warehouse, 570 W. Jackson Boulevard, Chicago, IL 60606; (312) 454-1166

See listing above.

SUN.	MON.	TUE.	WED.	THU.	FRI.	SAT.
closed	9–5:30	9–5:30	9–5:30	9–5:30	9–5:30	10–3

SAVINGS: 10%–40% off   *Mailing List*
PARKING: lot
PAYMENT: cash, checks (amount of purchase only, with proper I.D.), MasterCard, VISA, American Express

DOWNERS GROVE, IL

Office Furniture Warehouse, 1100 Ogden Avenue, Downers Grove, IL 60515; (312) 960-1100

See listing in Chicago, Illinois.

SUN.	MON.	TUE.	WED.	THU.	FRI.	SAT.
noon–3	9–8:30	9–5:30	9–5:30	9–5:30	9–5:30	10–3

SAVINGS: 20%–60% off   *Mailing List*
PARKING: lot

PAYMENT: cash, checks (amount of purchase only, with proper I.D., Telecheck), MasterCard, VISA

FRANKLIN PARK, IL

Office Furniture Warehouse, 9518 W. Franklin Avenue, Franklin Park, IL 60131: (312) 455-5053
   See listing in Chicago, Illinois.

SUN.	MON.	TUE.	WED.	THU.	FRI.	SAT.
closed	9–5:30	9–5:30	9–5:30	9–5:30	9–5:30	closed

SAVINGS: 10%–50% off   *Mailing List*
PARKING: lot
PAYMENT: cash, checks (amount of purchase only, with proper I.D.), MasterCard, VISA, American Express

GENEVA, IL

Office Supply Outlet, 830 E. State Street, Geneva, IL 60134; (312) 232-1773
   This store sells office furniture and office supplies. Most merchandise is first quality, but they sell a few seconds and imperfects where savings are greatest. They have another store in South Elgin, Ilinois.

SUN.	MON.	TUE.	WED.	THU.	FRI.	SAT.
closed	9–5	9–5	9–5	9–5	9–5	10–4

SAVINGS: 30%–60% off
BRAND NAMES: Hon, Mill, P.F.I.
PARKING: lot
PAYMENT: cash, checks (amount of purchase only, with proper I.D.)

ITASCA, IL

Office Furniture Warehouse, 700 N. Rohlwing Road, Itasca, IL 60143; (312) 773-1110
   See listing in Chicago, Illinois.

SUN.	MON.	TUE.	WED.	THU.	FRI.	SAT.
noon–4	9–5:30	9–5:30	9–5:30	9–5:30	9–5:30	10–4

SAVINGS: 30%–40% off
SPECIAL SALES: every six weeks   *Mailing List*
PARKING: lot
PAYMENT: cash, checks (with proper I.D.), MasterCard, VISA, American Express

LINCOLNWOOD, IL

Office Furniture Warehouse, 6700 N. Lincoln Avenue, Lincolnwood, IL 60645; (312) 677-0400
   See listing in Chicago, Illinois.

SUN.	MON.	TUE.	WED.	THU.	FRI.	SAT.
noon–3	9–5:30	9–5:30	9–5:30	9–5:30	9–5:30	10–3

SAVINGS: 20%–60% off   *Mailing List*
PARKING: lot
PAYMENT: cash, checks (Telecheck), MasterCard, VISA

OAK LAWN, IL

Office Furniture Warehouse, 8734 S. Cicero Avenue, Oak Lawn, IL 60453; (312) 423-0600
   See listing in Chicago, Illinois.

SUN.	MON.	TUE.	WED.	THU.	FRI.	SAT.
noon–3	9–5:30	9–5:30	9–5:30	9–5:30	9–5:30	10–3

SAVINGS: 20%–50% off   *Mailing List*
PARKING: lot
PAYMENT: cash, checks (amount of purchase only, with proper I.D.), MasterCard,
VISA, American Express

PARK CITY, IL

Office Furniture Warehouse, 3235 W. Belvidere Road, Park City, IL 60031; (312)
244-6600
See listing in Chicago, Illinois.

SUN.	MON.	TUE.	WED.	THU.	FRI.	SAT.
closed	9–5:30	9–5:30	9–5:30	9–5:30	9–5:30	noon–4

SAVINGS:30%–40% off   *Mailing List*   *All First Quality*
PARKING: lot
PAYMENT: cash, checks (with proper I.D.), MasterCard, VISA

SKOKIE, IL

OOP's Office Outlet—Office Outlet Products, 4028 W. Dempster Street, Skokie, IL
60076; (312) 674-3999
This store sells office supplies, stationery, office furniture, and computer supplies
at savings that average 50%–80% off retail prices. Best savings are on some surplus,
overstocks, discontinued, and closeout merchandise, or items in damaged boxes.

SUN.	MON.	TUE.	WED.	THU.	FRI.	SAT.
10–4	9–6	9–6	9–6	9–8	9–6	9–5

SAVINGS: 50%–80% off
SPECIAL DISCOUNTS: on sales over $200 (ask)
PARKING: lot
PAYMENT: cash, checks (amount of purchase only, with proper I.D.)

SOUTH ELGIN, IL

Office Supply Outlet, 9 N. Woodbury Street, South Elgin, IL 60177; (312) 741-4202
See listing in Geneva, Illinois.

SUN.	MON.	TUE.	WED.	THU.	FRI.	SAT.
closed	9–5	9–5	9–5	9–5	9–5	10–4

SAVINGS: 20%–40% off
PARKING: lot
PAYMENT: cash, checks (amount of purchase only)

INDIANA
JASPER, IN

Hoffman Office Supplies, 116 E. Seventh Street, Jasper, IN 47546; (812) 482-4224
This store sells several major brands of office furniture at discounts of about 40%
off retail price for first quality merchandise.

SUN.	MON.	TUE.	WED.	THU.	FRI.	SAT.
closed	8–5	8–5	8–5	8–5	8–5	8–noon

SAVINGS: about 40% off   *All First Quality*
PARKING: lot
PAYMENT: cash. checks (amount of purchase only, with proper I.D.)

MERRILLVILLE, IN

Office Furniture Warehouse, 6071 Broadway, Merrillville, IN 46410; (219) 980-1040
See listing in Chicago, Illinois.

SUN.	MON.	TUE.	WED.	THU.	FRI.	SAT.
noon–3	9–5:30	9–5:30	9–5:30	9–5:30	9–5:30	10–3

SAVINGS: 20%–60% off
SPECIAL SALES: monthly   *Mailing List*
PARKING: lot
PAYMENT: cash, checks (amount of purchase only, with proper I.D., Telecheck),
  MasterCard, VISA

MUNSTER, IN

Office Equipment Sales, 9456 S. Calumet Avenue, Munster, IN 46321; (219)
836-4200
    This store sells major brands of office furniture. Greatest savings are on
occasional dents, overruns, irregulars, overstocks, and closeout merchandise.

SUN.	MON.	TUE.	WED.	THU.	FRI.	SAT.
closed	9–5:30	9–5:30	9–5:30	9–5:30	9–5:30	9–noon

SAVINGS: at least 10% off
PARKING: lot   *Mailing List*
PAYMENT: cash, checks (amount of purchase only, with proper I.D.)

21
OFFICE SUPPLIES

These outlets sell office supplies, although some also sell office equipment. See the previous chapter, *Office Equipment*, and see the following chapter, *Paper Goods*, for other outlets that sell office supplies.

I found excellent savings on office supplies, compared to retail stores. Best savings were in large quantity purchases (500 or more envelopes, for instance), but even typewriter ribbons were usually half the price I'd seen in retail stores.

ILLINOIS

CHICAGO, IL

Arvey Paper and Supplies, 3555 N. Kimball Avenue, Chicago, IL 60618; (312) 463-0822

This store sells most major brands of printing supplies, paper products, office supplies, stationery, etc. Savings vary from 10%–70% off retail price. The computer paper and ribbons used while writing this book were purchased here for less than half the price I paid at other stores. They have another store in Elk Grove Village, Illinois.

SUN.	MON.	TUE.	WED.	THU.	FRI.	SAT.
closed	8–5:30	8–5:30	8–5:30	8–5:30	8–5:30	9–4:30

SAVINGS: 10%–70% off　　　　　　　*Mailing List*　　*All First Quality*
ANNUAL SALES: January, April, August, October
PARKING: lot
PAYMENT: cash, checks (amount of purchase only, with proper I.D.)

Office Furniture Warehouse

See two listings under *Office Equipment* in Chicago, Illinois.

ARLINGTON HEIGHTS, IL

Franz Stationery Company, 1601 E. Algonquin Road, Arlington Heights, IL 60005; (312) 593-0060

This store sells most major brands of office supplies and stationery products. Savings average 15%–70% off retail price, with best savings on overstocks, discontinued, and closeout merchandise.

SUN.	MON.	TUE.	WED.	THU.	FRI.	SAT.
closed	8–5:30	8–5:30	8–5:30	8–5:30	8–5:30	9–1

SAVINGS: 15%–70% off　　　　　　　　　　　*Mailing List*
ANNUAL SALES: summer
PARKING: lot
PAYMENT: cash, checks (with proper I.D.), MasterCard, VISA

Office Furniture Warehouse
See listing under *Office Equipment* in Downers Grove, Illinois.

Arvey Paper and Supplies, 1200 E. Higgins Road, Elk Grove Village, IL 60007; (312) 439-1880
See listing in Chicago, Illinois.

SUN.	MON.	TUE.	WED.	THU.	FRI.	SAT.
closed	8-5:30	8-5:30	8-5:30	8-5:30	8-5:30	9-1

SAVINGS: 10%-70% off   *Mailing List*   *All First Quality*
SPECIAL SALES: monthly
PARKING: lot
PAYMENT: cash, checks (amount of purchase only, with proper I.D.)

Office Furniture Warehouse
See listing under *Office Equipment* in Franklin Park, Illinois.

Office Supply Outlet
See listing under *Office Equipment* in Geneva, Illinois.

Office Furniture Warehouse
See listing under *Office Equipment* in Itasca, Illinois.

Office Furniture Warehouse
See listing under *Office Equipment* in Lincolnwood, Illinois.

Office Furniture Warehouse
See listing under *Office Equipment* in Oak Lawn, Illinois.

Office Furniture Warehouse
See listing under *Office Equipment* in Park City, Illinois.

OOP's Office Outlet—Office Outlet Products
See listing under *Office Equipment* in Skokie, Illinois.

Office Supply Outlet
See listing under *Office Equipment* in South Elgin, Illinois.

Doenges Surplus Office Supply, 809 E. Roosevelt Road, Wheaton, IL 60187; (312) 462-7890
This is a subsidiary of Doenges Stationery Corporation. They also sell major brands of office supplies. Greatest savings are on seconds, irregulars, "bruised" furniture, surplus, overruns, overstocks, and discontinued items, where discounts can run as high as 60% off normal retail price.

SUN.	MON.	TUE.	WED.	THU.	FRI.	SAT.
closed	9–5:30	9–5:30	9–5:30	9–5:30	9–5:30	9–5:30

SAVINGS: 20%–60% off

Mailing List

PARKING: lot

PAYMENT: cash, checks (with proper I.D.), MasterCard, VISA

INDIANA

MERRILLVILLE, IN

Office Furniture Warehouse
   See listing under *Office Equipment* in Merrillville, Indiana.

MISHAWAKA, IN

The Paper Factory
   See listing under *Paper Goods* in Mishawaka, Indiana.

WISCONSIN

KENOSHA, WI

The Paper Factory
   See listing under *Paper Goods* in Kenosha, Wisconsin.

MADISON, WI

The Paper Factory
   See listing under *Paper Goods* in Madison, Wisconsin.

PLOVER, WI

The Paper Factory
   See listing under *Paper Goods* in Plover, Wisconsin.

WEST BEND, WI

The Paper Factory
   See listing under *Paper Goods* in West Bend, Wisconsin.

22
PAPER GOODS

The outlets listed here sell paper cups, napkins, tablecloths, wrapping paper, and decorative paper goods, etc. Most also sell paper office supplies (also see Chapter 21, *Office Supplies*).

Savings were best on overstocks, closeouts, and holiday paper goods after the holiday had passed. Seconds and large quantities were also excellent buys.

Arvey Paper and Supplies
  See listing under *Office Supplies* in Chicago, Illinois.

Schweppe's Party Shop, 158 E. Lake Street, Bloomingdale, IL 60072; (312) 351-9608
  This store sells party supplies: paper cups, plates, napkins, tablecloths, place mats, plastic cups, etc.. Most merchandise is first quality, but they do sell some overruns, overstocks, discontinued, and closeout merchandise. The greatest savings are by buying in bulk. They have another store (called Schweppe & Sons) in Lombard, Illinois.

SUN.	MON.	TUE.	WED.	THU.	FRI.	SAT.
11–5	9:30–9	9:30–9	9:30–9	9:30–9	9:30–9	10–6

SAVINGS: 25%–30% off
PARKING: lot
PAYMENT: cash, checks (amount of purchase only, with proper I.D.), MasterCard, VISA

Arvey Paper and Supplies
  See listing under *Office Supplies* in Elk Grove Village, Illinois.

Schweppe & Sons, 376 W. North Avenue, Lombard, IL 60148; (312) 627-3550
  See listing under Schweppe's Party Shop in Bloomingdale, Illinois.

SUN.	MON.	TUE.	WED.	THU.	FRI.	SAT.
10–6	8–6	8–6	8–6	8–6	8–6	8–5

SAVINGS: at least 15% off
PARKING: lot
PAYMENT: cash, checks (amount of purchase only, with proper I.D.), MasterCard, VISA

INDIANA

MISHAWAKA, IN

The Paper Factory, Buyer's Marketplace, 5901 N. Grape Road, Mishawaka, IN 46545; (219) 277-2763

This outlet sells all types of paper goods, paper napkins, paper plates, cards, wrapping paper, and paper office supplies. They also sell games, puzzles, and children's books. Most merchandise is first quality, but there are a few seconds, closeouts, and overstocked items at greater savings. They also have stores in Kenosha, Madison, Plover, and West Bend, Wisconsin.

SUN.	MON.	TUE.	WED.	THU.	FRI.	SAT.
noon–5	9:30–9	9:30–9	9:30–9	9:30–9	9:30–9	9:30–9

SAVINGS: 40%–60% off
SALE DAYS: Tuesday
PARKING: lot
PAYMENT: cash, checks (with proper I.D.)

WISCONSIN

KENOSHA, WI

The Paper Factory, Factory Outlet Centre, 7700 120th Avenue, Kenosha, WI 53142; (414) 857-9238

See listing in Mishawaka, Indiana.

SUN.	MON.	TUE.	WED.	THU.	FRI.	SAT.
11–5	9:30–9	9:30–9	9:30–9	9:30–9	9:30–9	9:30–6

SAVINGS: up to 50% off
BRAND NAMES: Art Fair, Western
SALE DAYS: Tuesday
SPECIAL DISCOUNTS: senior citizens, 10% off Wednesday
PARKING: lot
PAYMENT: cash, checks (with proper I.D.)

MADISON, WI

The Paper Factory, Factory Outlet Centre, 4609 Verona Road, Madison, WI 53711; (609) 274-7668

See listing in Mishawaka, Indiana.

SUN.	MON.	TUE.	WED.	THU.	FRI.	SAT.
9–5	9:30–9	9:30–9	9:30–9	9:30–9	9:30–9	9:30–6

SAVINGS: 40%–50% off   *Mailing List*
SALE DAYS: Tuesday
SPECIAL DISCOUNTS: senior citizens, 10% off Wednesday
PARKING: lot
PAYMENT: cash, checks (amount of purchase only, with proper I.D.)

PLOVER, WI

The Paper Factory, Factory Direct Mall, 101 Plover Road, Plover, WI 54467; (715) 341-0616

See listing in Mishawaka, Indiana.

SUN.	MON.	TUE.	WED.	THU.	FRI.	SAT.
11–6	9:30–9	9:30–9	9:30–9	9:30–9	9:30–9	9:30–6

SAVINGS: 40%–50% off
PARKING: lot
PAYMENT: cash, checks (amount of purchase only, with proper I.D.), MasterCard, VISA

The Paper Factory, West Bend Outlet Mall, 180 Island Avenue, West Bend, WI 53095;
(414) 334-5266
See listing in Mishawaka, Indiana.

SUN.	MON.	TUE.	WED.	THU.	FRI.	SAT.
11–5	9:30–6	9:30–6	9:30–6	9:30–6	9:30–8	9:30–5

SAVINGS: 40%–50% off
BRAND NAMES: Art Fair, Riverside, B & G
ANNUAL SALES: August, February
PARKING: lot
PAYMENT: cash, checks (amount of purchase only, with proper I.D.)

23
PICTURE FRAMES

These outlets sell picture frames. They also do custom framing at considerable savings, compared to retail shops.

ILLINOIS

CHICAGO, IL

Artists' Frame Service, 1919 N. Clybourn Avenue, Chicago, IL 60614; (312) 248-7713
They manufacture picture frames on the premises here. They also do custom framing at average savings of 30% off retail price.

SUN.	MON.	TUE.	WED.	THU.	FRI.	SAT.
closed	9–6	9–6	9–6	9–6	9–6	10–4

SAVINGS: average 30% off *Mailing List* *All First Quality*
PARKING: lot
PAYMENT: cash, checks, MasterCard, VISA

Custom Frame and Poster Manufacturing Company, 2311 W. Howard Street, 2nd floor, Chicago, IL 60645; (312) 465-6666
This outlet sells frames and does custom framing. Savings are greatest on overstocks and surplus materials.

SUN.	MON.	TUE.	WED.	THU.	FRI.	SAT.
closed	10–9	10–6	10–6	10–9	10–6	10–6

SAVINGS: 30%–40% off *Mailing List*
PARKING: street
PAYMENT: cash, checks (amount of purchase only, with proper I.D.), MasterCard, VISA, American Express

The Frame Factory, 760 W. Waveland Avenue, Chicago, IL 60613: (312) 929-8930
This store sells many types of Mexican and Taiwanese picture frames at savings from 25%–50% off retail price. They also do custom framing at a discount. They have another store in Skokie, Illinois.

SUN.	MON.	TUE.	WED.	THU.	FRI.	SAT.
closed	9–5:30	9–5:30	9–5:30	9–5:30	9–5:30	9–5:30

SAVINGS: 25%–50% off *Mailing List* *All First Quality*
SPECIAL DISCOUNTS: charity organizations (ask)
PARKING: lot
PAYMENT: cash, checks (amount of purchase only, with proper I.D.), MasterCard, VISA

Studio 5000, 5000 N. Cumberland Avenue, Chicago, IL 60656; (312) 453-1620
This store sells oil paintings, sculptures, Chinese vases, and picture frames. All merchandise is first quality, except some frames are slightly damaged. They have a guarantee that you can return any merchandise for any reason within thirty days for a full refund.

SUN.	MON.	TUE.	WED.	THU.	FRI.	SAT.
10-5	closed	*	*	noon-6	noon-6	10-5

SAVINGS: 20%–50% off
SPECIAL DISCOUNTS: groups (ask)   *Mailing List*
PARKING: lot
PAYMENT: cash, checks, MasterCard, VISA

———
*Open by appointment only on Tuesday and Wednesday.

ARLINGTON HEIGHTS, IL

Artists' Frame Service, 4234 N. Arlington Heights Road, Arlington Heights, IL 60004;
(312) 577-6510
See listing in Chicago, Illinois.

SUN.	MON.	TUE.	WED.	THU.	FRI.	SAT.
noon-4	10-9	10-5	10-5	10-9	10-5	10-5

SAVINGS: about 30% off
ANNUAL SALES: spring   *Mailing List*
PARKING: lot
PAYMENT: cash, checks (amount of purchase only, with proper I.D., no out-of-state
checks), MasterCard, VISA, American Express

Gift Outlet
See listing under *Gift Items* in Arlington Heights, Illinois.

LOVES PARK, IL

Frame Warehouse, Park Plaza Outlet Mart, 6409 N. 2nd Street, Loves Park, IL 61111;
(815) 877-2828
This outlet sells frames, framed prints and oil paintings, decorator mirrors and
mirror tiles, and related hardware. Savings average 40%–50% off retail price on mostly
first quality merchandise, although they sell some surplus, overstocks, discontinued,
close-outs, and last year's lines. They have another store in Madison, Wisconsin.

SUN.	MON.	TUE.	WED.	THU.	FRI.	SAT.
noon-5	9:30-9	9:30-9	9:30-9	9:30-9	9:30-9	9:30-6

SAVINGS: 40%–50% off
SALE DAYS: vary
PARKING: lot
PAYMENT: cash, checks (amount of purchase only, with proper I.D.), MasterCard, VISA

SKOKIE, IL

The Frame Factory, 3735 W. Dempster Street, Skokie, IL 60076; (312) 673-8930
See listing in Chicago, Illinois.

SUN.	MON.	TUE.	WED.	THU.	FRI.	SAT.
11-4	9-8	9-5:30	9-5:30	9-8	9-5:30	9-5:30

SAVINGS: 25%–50% off
SPECIAL DISCOUNTS: charity groups (ask)   *All First Quality*
PARKING: lot
PAYMENT: cash, checks (amount of purchase only, with proper I.D.), MasterCard, VISA

Gift Outlet
See listing under *Gift Items* in Skokie, Illinois.

Frame Warehouse, Factory Outlet Centre, 4609 Verona Road, Madison, WI 53704;
(608) 274-6665
   See listing in Loves Park, Illinois.

SUN.	MON.	TUE.	WED.	THU.	FRI.	SAT.
noon–5	9:30–9	9:30–9	9:30–9	9:30–9	9:30–9	9:30–6

SAVINGS: about 40% off   *Mailing List*
ANNUAL SALES: before Christmas
PARKING: lot
PAYMENT: cash, checks (amount of purchase only, with proper I.D., no out-of-state
   checks), MasterCard, VISA

24
PLATES, GLASSWARE, AND TABLEWARE

These outlets sell most items for the table. Also look in Chapter 6, *Ceramics*; Chapter 10, *Department Stores*; Chapter 14, *Gift Items*; Chapter 15, *Housewares*; Chapter 18, *Linens*; and Chapter 22, *Paper Goods* for other, related items.

Savings of 50%–75% off retail price on seconds were frequent. There were also very good buys on overstocks, closeouts, and discontinued patterns.

ILLINOIS

CHICAGO, IL

Crate and Barrel Warehouse Store
See listing under *Gift Items* in Chicago, Illinois.

ANTIOCH, IL

Pickard Factory Outlet, 782 Corona Avenue, Antioch, IL 60002; (312) 395-3800
This is the outlet for Pickard fine china dinnerware and giftware. Most merchandise is seconds. Savings average 40%–50% off retail prices.

SUN.	MON.	TUE.	WED.	THU.	FRI.	SAT.
closed	8:30–4	8:30–4	8:30–4	8:30–4	8:30–4	closed

SAVINGS: 40%–50% off
BRAND NAMES: Pickard
PARKING: street
PAYMENT: cash, checks (amount of purchase only, with proper I.D.), MasterCard, VISA

ARLINGTON HEIGHTS, IL

Gift Outlet
See listing under *Gift Items* in Arlington Heights, Illinois.

BERWYN, IL

The Crystal Center, 6300 W. Cermak Road, Berwyn, IL 60402; (312) 749-7008
This outlet sells crystal at discounts of 40%–60% off retail price. They have other stores in Bloomingdale and Western Springs, Illinois.

SUN.	MON.	TUE.	WED.	THU.	FRI.	SAT.
closed	10–8	10–6	10–6	10–8	10–6	10–5

SAVINGS: 40%–60% off
SPECIAL SALES: vary
PARKING: lot
PAYMENT: cash, checks (amount of purchase only, with proper I.D.), MasterCard, VISA

All First Quality

The Crystal Center, 156D E. Lake Street, Bloomingdale, IL 60108; (312) 893-6161
See listing in Berwyn, Illinois.

SUN.	MON.	TUE.	WED.	THU.	FRI.	SAT.
closed	10–8	10–6	10–6	10–8	10–6	10–5

SAVINGS: 40%–60% off   *All First Quality*
PARKING: lot
PAYMENT: cash, checks (amount of purchase only, with proper I.D.), MasterCard,
VISA

The Paul Revere Shoppe—Revere Copper & Brass
See listing under *Gift Items* in Clinton, Illinois.

China Bazaar, 1024 Emerson Street, Evanston, IL 60204; (312) 328-2000
This is the outlet for Wittur & Company. They sell fine crystal stemware in seconds
for up to 75% off retail price. They also sell fine Bavarian china in discontinued
patterns. Five-piece place settings (normally $40.00) in discontinued patterns are
$15.00. They sell some seconds, discontinued, closeouts, and some "as is"
merchandise.

SUN.	MON.	TUE.	WED.	THU.	FRI.	SAT.
closed	8–5	8–5	8–5	8–5	8–5	8–noon

SAVINGS: 50%–75% off
PARKING: street
PAYMENT: cash, checks

Berggren Trayner Corporation, 624 E. Park Avenue, Libertyville, IL 60048; (312)
367-0064
This factory outlet sells china, tiles, teapots, and coffee pots. Savings average
40%–60% off retail price on some seconds, irregulars, samples, and test runs.

SUN.	MON.	TUE.	WED.	THU.	FRI.	SAT.
closed	9–4	9–4	9–4	9–4	9–4	9–4

SAVINGS: 40%–60% off
BRAND NAMES: Berggren
PARKING: lot
PAYMENT: cash, checks (amount of purchase only, with proper I.D.)

Waccamaw Pottery
See listing under *Housewares* in Rolling Meadows, Illinois.

Irish Crystal Company of Chicago, 815 E. Nerge Road, Roselle, IL 60172; (312)
351-3722
This is the factory outlet for Tyrone. They sell stemware, accessories, bowls, and
vases. Savings average 30%–40% off retail price on first quality.

SUN.	MON.	TUE.	WED.	THU.	FRI.	SAT.
closed	closed	10–5	10–5	10–5	10–5	10–5

SAVINGS: 30%–40% off   *Mailing List*   *All First Quality*
PARKING: lot
PAYMENT: cash, checks, MasterCard, VISA

Gift Outlet
 See listing under *Gift Items* in Skokie, Illinois.

The Crystal Center, 43 Garden Market, 47th & Willow Springs Road, Western
 Springs, IL 60558; (312) 246-0102
 See listing in Berwyn, Illinois.

SUN.	MON.	TUE.	WED.	THU.	FRI.	SAT.
noon–4	10–8	10–5	10–5	10–8	10–5	10–5

SAVINGS: 40%–60% off   *All First Quality*
PARKING: lot
PAYMENT: cash, checks (amount of purchase only, with proper I.D.), MasterCard, VISA

Indiana Glass—Factory Outlet, 1059 S. Main Street, Dunkirk, IN 47336; (317)
 768-6789
 This is the factory outlet for Indiana Glass tableware and gift items. They also sell
some aluminum cookware and bakeware, and Loma/Rubberqueen kitchen accessories.
Savings are greatest on seconds, irregulars, imperfects, overruns, discontinued, and
closeout merchandise.

SUN.	MON.	TUE.	WED.	THU.	FRI.	SAT.
noon–6	9:30–5:30	9:30–5:30	9:30–5:30	9:30–5:30	9:30–5:30	9:30–5:30

SAVINGS: 25%–30% off
BRAND NAMES: Indiana Glass, Candlelight, Enterprize Aluminum, Loma/Rubberqueen
SPECIAL SALES: vary
PARKING: lot
PAYMENT: cash, checks (amount of purchase only, with proper I.D.)

Brady's This Is It—Factory Outlet Store—Home and Auto, 5218 W. 25th Street,
 Gary, IN 46406; (219) 844-6831
 This store sells Anchor Hocking glassware, housewares, automobile parts and
accessories, sporting goods, towels, household cleaning supplies, and health and
beauty aids. Savings begin at 20% off retail price on first quality, and can go up to 40%
on some seconds. See other Brady's stores.

SUN.	MON.	TUE.	WED.	THU.	FRI.	SAT.
10–6	10–9	10–9	10–9	10–9	10–9	I0–9

SAVINGS: 20%–40% off
BRAND NAMES: Champion, Wilson, Cannon Mills, Procter & Gamble, Anchor Hocking
SALE DAYS: vary
ANNUAL SALES: May, September
PARKING: lot
PAYMENT: cash, checks (amount of purchase only, with proper I.D.), MasterCard, VISA

Crystal and China Outlet, Eastgate Consumer Mall, 7150 E. Washington Street,
 Indianapolis, IN 46201; (317) 356-3910
 This outlet sells Noritake and other major brands of china and crystal. Savings are
greatest on overstocks, and there are some discontinued items available.

SUN.	MON.	TUE.	WED.	THU.	FRI.	SAT.
noon–5	10–9	10–9	10–9	10–9	10–9	10–9

SAVINGS: 10%–50% off
BRAND NAMES: Noritake
PARKING: lot
PAYMENT: cash, checks (no out-of-state checks), MasterCard, VISA

MISHAWAKA, IN

Houseware Outlet and Glass Factory Outlet Store
See listing under *Housewares* in Mishawaka, Indiana.

WARSAW, IN

Dirilyte Factory Seconds Store, 939 W. Market Street, Warsaw, IN 46580; (219) 267-3803
   Although they sell first quality Dirilyte flatware and hollowware at retail prices, savings on the seconds average 50% off retail price.

SUN.	MON.	TUE.	WED.	THU.	FRI.	SAT.
closed	8–5	8–5	8–5	8–5	8–5	closed

SAVINGS: up to 50% off
BRAND NAMES: Dirilyte
PARKING: lot
PAYMENT: cash, checks, MasterCard, VISA

WISCONSIN

GREEN BAY, WI

Houseware Outlet
See listing under *Housewares* in Green Bay, Wisconsin.

KENOSHA, WI

Houseware Outlet
See listing under *Housewares* in Kenosha, Wisconsin.

MADISON, WI

Houseware Outlet
See listing under *Housewares* in Madison, Wisconsin.

OSHKOSH, WI

The Lenox Shop
See listing under *Gift Items* in Oshkosh, Wisconsin.

PLOVER, WI

Houseware Outlet
See listing under *Housewares* in Plover, Wisconsin.

WEST BEND, WI

Dinnerware, Etc., Factory Outlet, West Bend Factory Outlet Mall, 180 Island Avenue, West Bend, WI 53095; (414) 334-4525
   This is the outlet for Kenro and Melamine. They sell place settings, trays, and restaurant items at savings up to 85% off retail price, and acrylic giftware and catering supplies at discounts up to 75%. Some items are first quality, but greatest savings are on seconds, samples, test runs, surplus, overruns, overstocks, odd lots, and discontinued merchandise.

SUN.	MON.	TUE.	WED.	THU.	FRI.	SAT.
11–5	9:30–9	9:30–9	9:30–9	9:30–9	9:30–9	9:30–6

SAVINGS: up to 85% off   *Mailing List*
BRAND NAMES: Kenro, Melamine
SPECIAL SALES: end of season
ANNUAL SALES: February, April
SPECIAL DISCOUNTS: senior citizens, 10% off; quantity buyers
PARKING: lot
PAYMENT: cash, checks (amount of purchase only, with proper I.D.), MasterCard, VISA

Houseware Outlet
See listing under *Housewares* in West Bend, Wisconsin.

Westman Glass & China, 111 N. Main Street, West Bend, WI 53095; (414) 334-7712
This outlet sells major brands of glassware, china, and linens. Savings on irregular items begin at 50% off retail prices.

SUN.	MON.	TUE.	WED.	THU.	FRI.	SAT.
closed	9:30–5	9:30–5	9:30–5	9:30–5	9:30–8	9:30–5

SAVINGS: 15%–60% off   *Mailing List*
BRAND NAMES: Noritake, Dansk, Chicago Weaving, Leacock
PARKING: street
PAYMENT: cash, checks (amount of purchase only, with proper I.D.), MasterCard, VISA

25
SEWING SUPPLIES
AND EQUIPMENT

These outlets sell sewing machines and sewing supplies. Also look in Chapter 1, *Appliances*, for other outlets that sell sewing machines, and Chapter 8, *Crafts*, for other outlets that sell sewing supplies.

ILLINOIS
ARLINGTON HEIGHTS, IL

The Treadle Machine, 10398 S. Arlington Heights Road, Arlington Heights, IL 60005; (312) 364-6262

This store sells sewing machines, and some vacuum cleaners and fans. Discounts are highest on test runs, dents, discontinued, and "as is" merchandise.

SUN.	MON.	TUE.	WED.	THU.	FRI.	SAT.
closed	9–7	9–7	9–5:30	9–5:30	9–7	9–5:30

SAVINGS: 30%–50% off　　　　　　　　　　　　　　　　*Mailing List*
BRAND NAMES: Panasonic, White, Elna, Singer, New Home
SALE DAYS: vary
PARKING: lot
PAYMENT: cash, checks, MasterCard, VISA

EVANSTON, IL

Kitworks, 1020 Davis Street, Evanston, IL 60201; (312) 864-8616

This is the outlet for Altra sewing kits. Savings begin at 10% off retail price on first quality, but rise quickly to 50% on samples and discontinued items. They also have some sample garments that were made from the kits on sale.

SUN.	MON.	TUE.	WED.	THU.	FRI.	SAT.
closed	closed	10–5:30	10–5:30	10–5:30	10–5:30	10–5:30

SAVINGS: 10%–50% off　　　　　　　　　　　　　　　　*Mailing List*
ANNUAL SALES: winter, summer
PARKING: street
PAYMENT: cash, checks (with proper I.D.), MasterCard, VISA

INDIANA
MIDDLEBURY, IN

Gohn Brothers Manufacturing Company
See listing under *Fabrics* in Middlebury, Indiana.

26
SPORTING GOODS

These outlets sell sporting goods, exercise equipment, and related items. You may want to look in Chapter 7, *Clothing—Activewear*, for sports-related clothing.

Savings were greatest on seconds and seasonal items at the end of the season. Also look for excellent buys on overruns, overstocks, and closeout merchandise.

ILLINOIS

CHICAGO, IL

B & W Golf Ball Company, 6244 W. Belmont Avenue, Chicago, IL 60634; (312) 283-7111

This shop has a large assortment of major brands of golf clubs, carts, bags, and balls. They also sell Dexter golf shoes and Munsingwear golf shirts. Savings are greatest on seconds, discontinued, and closeout merchandise.

SUN.	MON.	TUE.	WED.	THU.	FRI.	SAT.
closed	9-6	9-6	9-6	9-6	9-6	9-6

SAVINGS: 30%–40% off
BRAND NAMES: Ram, Link's, Northwestern, Dunlop, McGreggor
SPECIAL DISCOUNTS: high schools, 10% off
PARKING: street
PAYMENT: cash, checks (amount of purchase only, with proper I.D.), MasterCard, VISA

Frank O'Conner Pro Golf, 7452 W. Belmont Avenue, Chicago, IL 60634; (312) 237-1525

This store sells Ram golf clubs, golf bags, and golf supplies. Savings average 30%–40% off retail price with better savings on irregulars, overruns, overstocks, discontinued, and closeout merchandise.

SUN.	MON.	TUE.	WED.	THU.	FRI.	SAT.
closed	9-5	9-5	9-5	9-8	9-5	9-5*

SAVINGS: 35%–40% off   *Mailing List*
PARKING: lot
PAYMENT: cash, checks (with proper I.D.), MasterCard, VISA

---

*From October through March, Saturday hours are 9:00–3:00.

Stark's Bargain Warehouse, 1601 S. Canal, Chicago, IL 60631; (312) 586-5900

This store sells fishing and camping gear at savings starting at 10% off retail on first quality. Better savings are on seconds, irregulars, last year's lines, end of season, discontinued, and closeout merchandise.

SUN.	MON.	TUE.	WED.	THU.	FRI.	SAT.
9–5:30	9–5:30	9–5:30	9–5:30	9–5:30	9–5:30	9–5:30

SAVINGS: at least 10% off
SALE DAYS: Wednesday, Thursday
PARKING: street
PAYMENT: cash, checks (amount of purchase only, with proper I.D., no out-of-state
  checks, $5.00 minimum), MasterCard, VISA ($10.00 minimum)

ELMWOOD PARK, IL

Golfer's Outlet, 7216 W. Grand Avenue, Elmwood Park, IL 60635; (312) 456-2255
   This outlet sells major brands of golf clubs, balls, bags, clothing, shoes, and
accessories. All merchandise is first quality, but many items are surplus, overstocks,
last year's lines, end-of-season, discount, and close-outs. Savings start at 50% off retail
price and can go as high as 70% off. You can also special order merchandise not in
stock at 10% over cost.

SUN.	MON.	TUE.	WED.	THU.	FRI.	SAT.
10–5	10–9	10–9	10–9	10–9	10–9	10–5

SAVINGS: 50%–70% off   *Mailing List*   *All First Quality*
PARKING: lot
PAYMENT: cash, checks (amount of purchase only, with proper I.D.), MasterCard,
  VISA, American Express, Discover

HIGHWOOD, IL

Forsize Weightlifting Equipment Supply, 400 Sheridan Road, Highwood, IL 60040;
  (312) 433-4222
   This is the outlet for Vector Manufacturing Company. They sell several brands of
exercise machines, rowing machines, weight lifting and muscle-building supplies.
Savings begin at 10% off retail price for first quality, and can go as high as 50% on
some overstocks and closeouts.

SUN.	MON.	TUE.	WED.	THU.	FRI.	SAT.
closed	closed	9–6	9–6	9–6	9–6	9–5

SAVINGS: 10%–50% off   *Mailing List*
BRAND NAMES: Vector, Sonata, Precor, Nussbaum, Gym Jazz
ANNUAL SALES: May
PARKING: lot
PAYMENT: cash, checks, MasterCard, VISA ($20.00 minimum)

NAPERVILLE, IL

Strictly Golf of Naperville, 29 W 221 N. Aurora Road, Naperville, IL 60540; (312)
  355-5353
   This shop sells several major brands of golf clubs, men's and women's golf
apparel, golf balls, and golf equipment. Savings are greatest on discontinued, closeout,
and some irregular merchandise.

SUN.	MON.	TUE.	WED.	THU.	FRI.	SAT.
9–4	9–9	9–9	9–9	9–9	9–9	9–5

SAVINGS: 20%–70% off   *Mailing List*
ANNUAL SALES: July
PARKING: lot
PAYMENT: cash, checks (with proper I.D.), MasterCard, VISA

OAK FOREST, IL

Fitness Warehouse, 5542 W. 159th Street, Oak Forest, IL 60452; (312) 535-2006
   This store sells major brands of exercise machines, treadmills, and weight training

equipment. Savings average 5%–25% off retail prices. They have another store in Skokie, Illinois.

SUN.	MON.	TUE.	WED.	THU.	FRI.	SAT.
closed	10–8:30	10–6:30	10–6:30	10–8:30	10–6:30	10–5

SAVINGS: 5%–25% off   *Mailing List*   *All First Quality*
BRAND NAMES: Paramount, Precor, Tunturi
SPECIAL DISCOUNTS: charity groups (ask)
PARKING: lot
PAYMENT: cash, checks (amount of purchase only, with proper I.D.), MasterCard, VISA

SKOKIE, IL

Fitness Warehouse, 3936 W. Dempster Street, Skokie, IL 60076; (312) 677-0101
See listing in Oak Forest, Illinois.

SUN.	MON.	TUE.	WED.	THU.	FRI.	SAT.
closed	10–8:30	10–6:30	10–6:30	10–6:30	10–6:30	10–5

SAVINGS: 5%–25%   *Mailing List*   *All First Quality*
BRAND NAMES: Paramount, Precor, Tunturi
SPECIAL DISCOUNTS: charity groups (ask)
PARKING: lot
PAYMENT: cash, checks (amount of purchase only, with proper I.D.), MasterCard, VISA

Pro Shop World of Golf, 8130 N. Lincoln Avenue, Skokie, IL 60077; (312) 675-5286
This store sells many major brands of golf clubs, golf shoes, and golf bags. They also make custom-made golf clubs and sell some customer trade-ins. Savings are greatest on last year's lines, discontinued, and closeout items. They have another store, called Pro Shop West, in Villa Park, Illinois.

SUN.	MON.	TUE.	WED.	THU.	FRI.	SAT.
11–5	10–9	10–9	10–9	10–9	10–9	l0–6

SAVINGS: 20%–40% off   *Mailing List*
BRAND NAMES: Wilson, Hogan, PGA, Ram, Spaulding
SPECIAL SALES: weekly
ANNUAL SALES: August
PARKING: street, meters
PAYMENT: cash, checks (amount of purchase only, with proper I.D.), MasterCard, VISA, American Express ($100 minimum)

VILLA PARK, IL

Pro Shop West, 900 S. Rt. 83, Villa Park, IL 60181; (312) 833-0505
See listing under Pro Shop World of Golf in Skokie, Illinois.

SUN.	MON.	TUE.	WED.	THU.	FRI.	SAT.
11–5	10–9	10–6	10–6	10–6	10–9	10–6

SAVINGS: 20%–50% off   *Mailing List*
BRAND NAMES: Wilson, Hogan, Ram, Spaulding, PGA
ANNUAL SALES: August
PARKING: lot
PAYMENT: cash, checks (amount of purchase only, with proper I.D.), MasterCard, VISA, American Express ($100 minimum)

INDIANA
GARY, IN

Brady's This Is It—Factory Outlet Store—Home and Auto
See listing under *Plates, Glassware, and Tableware* in Gary, Indiana.

Flambeau Plastics Outlet
See listing under *Housewares* in Baraboo, Wisconsin.

AAA Sports, 3138 Center Avenue, Janesville, WI 53545; (608) 755-0320
This store sells major brands of sports equipment and sports-related clothes. Greatest savings are on some irregular and closeout merchandise. They have other stores in La Crosse and Madison, Wisconsin.

SUN.	MON.	TUE.	WED.	THU.	FRI.	SAT.
11-5	10-9	10-9	10-9	10-9	10-9	10-5

SAVINGS: 30%–40% off   *Mailing List*
BRAND NAMES: Spaulding, Wilson, McGreggor
PARKING: lot
PAYMENT: cash, checks (amount of purchase only, with proper I.D.), MasterCard, VISA

Mitchell Outlet
See listing under *Clothing—Accessories* in Kenosha, Wisconsin.

AAA Sports, 319 Lang Drive, LaCrosse, WI 54601; (608) 782-4575
See listing in Janesville, Wisconsin.

SUN.	MON.	TUE.	WED.	THU.	FRI.	SAT.
11-5	10-9	10-9	10-9	10-9	10-9	9-5

SAVINGS: 30%–40% off   *Mailing List*
BRAND NAMES: Wilson, Spaulding, McGreggor
PARKING: lot
PAYMENT: cash, checks (amount of purchase only, with proper I.D.), MasterCard, VISA

AAA Sports, Factory Outlet Centre, 4609 Verona Road, Madison, WI 53711; (608) 273-9225
See listing in Janesville, Wisconsin.

SUN.	MON.	TUE.	WED.	THU.	FRI.	SAT.
9-5	9:30-9	9:30-9	9:30-9	9:30-9	9:30-9	9:30-6

SAVINGS: 30%–40% off   *Mailing List*
BRAND NAMES: Spaulding, Wilson, McGreggor
SPECIAL SALES: weekends
SPECIAL DISCOUNTS: senior citizens, 10% off Wednesday
PARKING: lot
PAYMENT: cash, checks (with proper I.D.), MasterCard, VISA

Mitchell Handbags
See listing under *Clothing—Accessories* in Milwaukee, Wisconsin.

St. Croix Corporation, North Highway 13, P.O. Box 279, Park Falls, WI 54552; (715) 762-3226
This is the factory outlet for St. Croix fishing rods. Savings are greatest on seconds and some closeouts.

SUN.	MON.	TUE.	WED.	THU.	FRI.	SAT.
closed	8:30–4:30	8:30–4:30	8:30–4:30	8:30–4:30	8:30–4:30	8:30–noon

SAVINGS: about 20% off   *Mailing List*
BRAND NAMES: St. Croix
PARKING: lot
PAYMENT: cash, checks (amount of purchase only, with proper I.D.), MasterCard,
   VISA, American Express

27
TOYS

These outlets sell toys and games. Also look in Chapter 7, *Clothing—Babies'*, and *Children's*; and Chapter 22, *Paper Goods*, for other outlets that sell toys.

Cut-Rate Toys, 2424 W. Devon Avenue, Chicago, IL 60659; (312) 743-3822
This store sells toys and games. Savings start at 20% off retail price for first quality, and can go to 80% off surplus and discontinued items. They also sell Dr. Denton and Happy Days children's pajamas and underwear.

SUN.	MON.	TUE.	WED.	THU.	FRI.	SAT.
11–4	9:30–9	9:30–9	9:30–7	9:30–9	9:30–7	9:30–7

SAVINGS: 20%–80% off
BRAND NAMES: Mattel, Ideal, Dr. Denton, Happy Days, Hasbro
SPECIAL SALES: monthly, dates vary
ANNUAL SALES: Christmas season
PARKING: street, meters, can be difficult
PAYMENT: cash, checks (amount of purchase only, with proper I.D.)

Toys and Gifts Outlet, 1400 E. Golf Road, Rolling Meadows, IL 60008; (312) 437-0775
This outlet sells major brands of toys. Savings begin about 10% off retail price, but can go up to 75% on some overruns, overstocks, and closeout merchandise. They have other outlets in Merrillville, Indiana, and Kenosha, Wisconsin.

SUN.	MON.	TUE.	WED.	THU.	FRI.	SAT.
10–5	10–9:30	10–9:30	10–9:30	10–9:30	10–9:30	10–6

SAVINGS: 20%–50% off   *All First Quality*
ANNUAL SALES: October, Christmas
PARKING: lot
PAYMENT: cash, checks (amount of purchase only, with proper I.D., no out-of-state checks), MasterCard, VISA, American Express

Toys and Gifts Outlet, Century Consumer Mall, 8275 Broadway, Merrillville, IN 46410; (219) 269-2459
See listing in Rolling Meadows, Illinois.

SUN.	MON.	TUE.	WED.	THU.	FRI.	SAT.
11-5	10-9	10-9	10-9	10-9	10-9	10-9

SAVINGS: 20%-40% off   *All First Quality*
PARKING: lot
PAYMENT: cash, checks (amount of purchase only, with proper I.D., no out-of-state
checks), MasterCard, VISA

MISHAWAKA, IN

Four Seasons, Buyer's Marketplace, 5901 N. Grape Road, Mishawaka, IN 46545; (219)
272-6341
This outlet sells Fine Line toys at discounts of 20% off retail price.

SUN.	MON.	TUE.	WED.	THU.	FRI.	SAT.
noon-5	9:30-9	9:30-9	9:30-9	9:30-9	9:30-9	9:30-9

SAVINGS: about 20% off   *All First Quality*
PARKING: lot
PAYMENT: cash, checks (amount of purchase only, with proper I.D.), MasterCard, VISA

The Paper Factory
See listing under *Paper Goods* in Mishawaka. Indiana.

WISCONSIN
BARABOO, WI

Flambeau Plastics Outlet
See listing under *Housewares* in Baraboo, Wisconsin.

JANESVILLE, WI

Norwood Mills Outlet Store
See listing under *Fabrics* in Janesville, Wisconsin.

JEFFERSON, WI

Fur the Fun of It
See listing under *Fabrics* in Jefferson, Wisconsin.

KENOSHA, WI

The Paper Factory
See listing under *Paper Goods* in Kenosha, Wisconsin.

Toys and Gifts Outlet, Factory Outlet Centre, 7700 120th Avenue, Kenosha, WI
53142; (414) 857-2730
This store sells major brands of toys. Savings begin about 10% off retail price, but
can go up to 75% on some overruns, overstocks, and closeout merchandise.

SUN.	MON.	TUE.	WED.	THU.	FRI.	SAT.
11-5	9:30-9	9:30-9	9:30-9	9:30-9	9:30-9	9:30-6

SAVINGS: 10%-75% off
BRAND NAMES: Fisher-Price, Milton Bradley, Hasbro
SPECIAL SALES: holidays
PARKING: lot
PAYMENT: cash, checks (amount of purchase only, with proper I.D.), MasterCard, VISA

MADISON, WI

The Paper Factory
See listing under *Paper Goods* in Madison, Wisconsin.

PLOVER, WI

The Paper Factory
See listing under *Paper Goods* in Plover, Wisconsin.

WEST BEND, WI

The Paper Factory
See listing under *Paper Goods* in West Bend, Wisconsin.

28
MISCELLANEOUS MERCHANDISE

This chapter contains all merchandise which did not fall into the other categories. You may find several of the items in Chapter 10, *Department Stores*, as well.

The outlets are still listed Chicago first, then towns in Illinois, Indiana, and Wisconsin; within each town the listings are alphabetical by the outlet's name. Here is a list of the merchandise in this chapter:

air conditioners (central)
awnings
bathtub surrounds
bird feeders
bird houses
books
boxes (shoe shine)
cedar boxes
cleaning supplies
cologne
cosmetics
detergent
floor cleaning supplies
floral arrangements (artificial)
furnaces
gardening supplies
grooming supplies (horses)
health foods
horse accessories
house plants
humidifiers (central)
instruments (medical)
instruments (musical)
laboratory equipment
lawn ornaments
magazines
mailboxes
medical supplies
musical instruments
perfume
pet foods
pet supplies
power tools
shoe shine boxes
shoe shine kits
shower surrounds
shutters
soap
stable supplies
storm windows
tack (horses')
thermostats
tools
trees (artificial)
trees and shrubs
vanities (bathroom)
vitamins
windows

Affordable Awning Factory, 3817 N. Cicero Avenue, Chicago, IL 60641; (312) 777-3135
This outlet sells its own brand of aluminum awnings, shutters, and mini blinds. Savings begin about 25% off retail price on first quality, and can go as high as 60% on seconds, irregulars, "bruised," and mismeasured custom-made merchandise.

SUN.	MON.	TUE.	WED.	THU.	FRI.	SAT.
9–5	9–5	9–5	9–5	9–5	9–4	closed

SAVINGS: 35%–50% off
ANNUAL SALES: spring, summer, fall, winter
SPECIAL DISCOUNTS: senior citizens, 10% off
PARKING: street
PAYMENT: cash, checks, MasterCard, VISA, lay-away, financing

American Science Center, 5696 N. Northwest Highway, Chicago, IL 60646; (312) 763-0313
    This outlet sells all types of medical, scientific, and laboratory equipment. Although first quality merchandise is at retail prices, savings on seconds, surplus, overruns, and discontinued merchandise can go as high as 75% off retail price. They also sell used telescopes and microscopes at tremendous savings. They have another store in Milwaukee, Wisconsin.

SUN.	MON.	TUE.	WED.	THU.	FRI.	SAT.
closed	closed	10–6	10–6	10–9	10–6	10–6

SAVINGS: up to 75% off   ***Mailing List***
BRAND NAMES: Meade, Swift
PARKING: street, can be difficult
PAYMENT: cash, checks (amount of purchase only, with proper I.D.), MasterCard, VISA

Deesigned Trees, 3100 W. Grand Avenue, Chicago, IL 60622; (312) 722-7300
    This outlet sells artificial trees and floral arrangements. Savings begin at about 30% off retail price on all discontinued merchandise.

SUN.	MON.	TUE.	WED.	THU.	FRI.	SAT.
closed	8–4:30	8–4:30	8–4:30	8–4:30	8–4:30	closed

SAVINGS: at least 30% off
SPECIAL DISCOUNTS: charity groups
PARKING: lot
PAYMENT: cash, checks (amount of purchase only, with proper I.D.)

Drums Limited—Frank's Drum Shop, 218 S. Wabash Avenue, Chicago, IL 60604; (312) 427-8480
    Although they sell first quality musical instruments at retail price, they do have a few seconds and overstocks, where savings can go up to 50% off retail price.

SUN.	MON.	TUE.	WED.	THU.	FRI.	SAT.
closed	9–5:30	9–5:30	9–5:30	9–5:30	9–5:30	9–5:30

SAVINGS: up to 50% off
BRAND NAMES: Ludwig, Yamaha, Zildjian
SPECIAL SALES: monthly
PARKING: street
PAYMENT: cash, checks (with proper I.D.), MasterCard, VISA, American Express

Kroch's and Brentano's Bargain Book Center, 29 S. Wabash Avenue, Chicago, IL 60603; (312) 332-7500
    This is the outlet for the Kroch's and Brentano's retail stores. Savings on surplus and overstocked merchandise can run as high as 90% off retail price.

SUN.	MON.	TUE.	WED.	THU.	FRI.	SAT.
closed	9–7	9–7	9–6	9–7	9–7	9–6

SAVINGS: 10%–90% off
PARKING: lot (ask first)
PAYMENT: cash, checks, MasterCard, VISA, American Express

Hahn Industries, 300 S. Walnut Street, Cullom, IL 60929; (815) 689-2133
This outlet sells ornamental concrete lawn ornaments. Savings average about 20% off retail price on all first quality merchandise.

SUN.	MON.	TUE.	WED.	THU.	FRI.	SAT.
9–4*	9–4*	9–4*	9–4*	9–4*	9–4*	9–4*

SAVINGS: about 25% off　　　　　　　　　　　　　　　*All First Quality*
ANNUAL SALES: September
PARKING: lot
PAYMENT: cash, checks

---

*They are closed in January and February.

Black & Decker, Inc., 1277 S. Elmhurst Road, Des Plaines, IL 60018; (312) 364-5220
This is the factory outlet for Black & Decker tools. Savings begin about 10% off retail price, and can go much higher on irregular, bruised, and discontinued merchandise. Sometimes the company doesn't even put a suggested price on an item.

SUN.	MON.	TUE.	WED.	THU.	FRI.	SAT.
closed	8–5	8–5	8–5	8–5	8–5	closed

SAVINGS: 10%–65% off
BRAND NAMES: Black & Decker
ANNUAL SALES: Father's Day
PARKING: lot
PAYMENT: cash, checks (with proper I.D.), MasterCard, VISA

Airwize Heating and Air Conditioning, 750 Lee Street, Elk Grove Village, IL 60007; (312) 640-6300
This store sells several major brands of furnaces, central air conditioning units, thermostats, air cleaners, and humidifiers. Best savings are on seconds, samples, dents, "bruised," last year's lines, end-of-season, discontinued, closeouts, customer returns, freight damaged, repossessed, and "as is" merchandise. They say they cater to the do-it-yourselfer.

SUN.	MON.	TUE.	WED.	THU.	FRI.	SAT.
closed	8–5	8–5	8–5	8–5	8–5	8–1

SAVINGS: up to 75% off
BRAND NAMES: Trane, Carrier, Lennox, GE, Arco Air, Westinghouse, Fedders
SPECIAL SALES: end-of-seasons
SPECIAL DISCOUNTS: charitable organizations, 15% off
PARKING: lot
PAYMENT: cash, checks (amount of purchase only, with proper I.D.), MasterCard, VISA

Sensera Medco, 910 Sherwood Drive, Unit #16, Lake Bluff, IL 60044; (312) 295-6888, or 1 (800) 323-9790
This store sells various types of medical equipment and accessories. Savings begin at about 20% off retail price on first quality merchandise, and can go as high as 66% on some irregulars and test runs.

SUN.	MON.	TUE.	WED.	THU.	FRI.	SAT.
*	9–4:30	9–4:30	9–4:30	9–4:30	9–4:30	*

SAVINGS: 20%–66% off   *Mailing List*
BRAND NAMES: Design Med, Timex, Healthcheck, Toshiba, Leading Edge, Whal
SPECIAL SALES: students and medical profession (ask)
SPECIAL DISCOUNTS: ask
PARKING: lot
PAYMENT: cash, checks (amount of purchase only), MasterCard, VISA

---

*Saturday and Sunday hours are by appointment only.

NILES, IL

Cosmetique, 6045 W. Howard Street, Niles, IL 60648; (312) 647-7575
   This store sells major brands of women's makeup and cosmetics and men's
aftershave and cologne. They sell only first quality merchandise at a discount.

SUN.	MON.	TUE.	WED.	THU.	FRI.	SAT.
closed	10–3	10–3	10–3	10–3	closed	closed

SAVINGS: up to 50% off   *All First Quality*
BRAND NAMES: Von Furstenberg, Orlaine, Paco Rabanne, Quorum;
PARKING: lot
PAYMENT: cash, checks (amount of purchase only, with proper I.D.)

WEST CHICAGO, IL

Delite Marble Company, 31 W 021 Conte Parkway, West Chicago, IL 60185; (312)
   231-7440
   This outlet sells Delite cultured marble vanity tops, cultured onyx vanity tops, and
shower tub surrounds in marble. Savings begin at about 20% off retail price on first
quality merchandise, and can go to 50% on seconds and discontinued items.

SUN.	MON.	TUE.	WED.	THU.	FRI.	SAT.
closed	9–6	9–6	9–6	9–6	9–6	10–2

SAVINGS: 20%–50% off
BRAND NAMES: Delite
PARKING: lot
PAYMENT: cash, checks (amount of purchase only, with proper I.D.)

WHEELING, IL

Evanger's Pet Products, 221 S. Wheeling Road, Wheeling, IL 60090; (312) 541-PETS
   This is the factory outlet for Evanger's pet foods. They also sell other brands of
pet diets, pet accessories, and leashes, and show leads. Savings start at 20% off retail
price on pet foods, and can go as high as 70% on leashes and rawhide seconds.

SUN.	MON.	TUE.	WED.	THU.	FRI.	SAT.
closed	9–5:30	9–5:30	9–9	9–5:30	9–5:30	9–4

SAVINGS: 20%–70% off   *Mailing List*
BRAND NAMES: Evanger's
SPECIAL DISCOUNTS: quantity discounts
PARKING: lot
PAYMENT: cash, checks (amount of purchase only, with proper I.D.)

INDIANA
BERNE, IN

Golden Rule Book Store, 366 Lehman Street, Berne, IN 46711; (219) 589-3795
   This is the factory outlet for Nussbaum wooden shoe shine boxes, cedar novelty
boxes, and miscellaneous wooden boxes. Savings on first quality merchandise are 25%
off retail price; savings on seconds are 50% off retail price. Occasionally they sell some
obsolete goods.

SUN.	MON.	TUE.	WED.	THU.	FRI.	SAT.
closed	9–5:30	9–5:30	9–5:30	9–5:30	9–5:30	9–noon

SAVINGS: 25%–50% off
BRAND NAMES: Nussbaum
ANNUAL SALES: July
PARKING: street
PAYMENT: cash, checks (amount of purchase only, with proper I.D.)

INDIANAPOLIS, IN

Farm and Home Saddlery, 6449 S. Harding Street, Indianapolis, IN 46217; (317) 784-4424
This factory outlet sells bridles, saddles, halters, and other horse equipment. Savings on first quality merchandise average 20%–25% off retail price.

SUN.	MON.	TUE.	WED.	THU.	FRI.	SAT.
closed	8:30–5	8:30–5	8:30–5	8:30–5	8:30–5	closed

SAVINGS: 20%–25% off   *Mailing List*   *All First Quality*
PARKING: lot
PAYMENT: cash, checks (amount of purchase only, with proper I.D.)

Publisher's Book Outlet, Eastgate Consumer Mall, 7150 E. Washington Street, Indianapolis, IN 46410; (317) 356-3921
This store sells magazines, books, games, and puzzles. Savings begin about 10% off retail price on first quality and can go as high as 80% on some seconds, discontinued, and closeout merchandise. They have another store in Merrillville, Indiana.

SUN.	MON.	TUE.	WED.	THU.	FRI.	SAT.
noon–5	10–9	10–9	10–9	10–9	10–9	10–9

SAVINGS: 10%–80% off
ANNUAL SALES: January
PARKING: lot
PAYMENT: cash, checks (amount of purchase only, with proper I.D.), MasterCard, VISA, American Express

MERRILLVILLE, IN

Publisher's Book Outlet, Century Consumer Mall, 8275 Broadway, Merrillville, IN 46410; (219) 769-2982
See listing in Indianapolis, Indiana.

SUN.	MON.	TUE.	WED.	THU.	FRI.	SAT.
11–5	10–9	10–9	10–9	10–9	10–9	10–9

SAVINGS: 10%–80% off
PARKING: lot
PAYMENT: cash, checks (amount of purchase only, with proper I.D.), MasterCard, VISA

MISHAWAKA, IN

Nutrition Outlet, Buyer's Marketplace, 5901 Grape Road, Mishawaka, IN 46545; (219) 272-5568
This outlet sells vitamins and health foods at savings up to 50% off retail price.

SUN.	MON.	TUE.	WED.	THU.	FRI.	SAT.
noon–5	9:30–9	9:30–9	9:30–9	9:30–9	9:30–9	9:30–9

SAVINGS: 20%–50% off   *All First Quality*
SALE DAYS: Tuesday
SPECIAL DAYS: vary
PARKING: lot
PAYMENT: cash, checks (amount of purchase only, with proper I.D., within 50-mile
  radius), MasterCard, VISA

WISCONSIN

MILWAUKEE, WI

American Science Center, 5430 W. Layton, Milwaukee, WI 53220; (414) 281-2322
    See listing in Chicago, Illinois.

SUN.	MON.	TUE.	WED.	THU.	FRI.	SAT.
closed	closed	10–6	10–6	10–9	10–6	10–6

SAVINGS: 30%–50% off   *Mailing List*
BRAND NAMES: Barter-Coleman, Texas Instruments
SALE DAYS: Saturday
PARKING: lot
PAYMENT: cash, checks (with proper I.D.), MasterCard, VISA

Milwaukee Soap Company, 1526 N. 31st St., Milwaukee, WI 53208; (414) 342-5733
    This factory outlet sells soap and cleaning supplies. They also sell other
manufacturers' paper products by the case or half case. Their merchandise is mostly
institutional dishwashing/laundry soap, cleaning supplies, floor care products, etc.
Best savings are on some seconds, overstocks, unwrapped, and unlabeled items. See
their other store, below.

SUN.	MON.	TUE.	WED.	THU.	FRI.	SAT.
closed	8–4:30	8–4:30	8–4:30	8–4:30	8–4:30	closed

SAVINGS: 10%–50% off
SPECIAL SALES: vary
PARKING: lot
PAYMENT: cash, checks (amount of purchase only, with proper I.D.), MasterCard, VISA

Milwaukee Soap Company, 5661 S. 27th St., Milwaukee, WI 53221; (414) 282-7880
    See listing above.

SUN.	MON.	TUE.	WED.	THU.	FRI.	SAT.
closed	10–6	10–6	10–6	10–6	10–6	9–5

SAVINGS: 10%–50% off
SPECIAL SALES: vary
PARKING: lot
PAYMENT: cash, checks (amount of purchase only, with proper I.D.), MasterCard, VISA

VirJeane Perfumes, 1030 S. Mitchell Street, Milwaukee, WI 53204; (414) 383-7060
    This outlet sells Halston and Giorgio men's cologne in unmarked boxes. They also
sell reproductions.

SUN.	MON.	TUE.	WED.	THU.	FRI.	SAT.
noon–5	9:30–8	9:30–5:30	9:30–8	9:30–8	9:30–8	9:30–5:30

SAVINGS: 50%–80% off   *All First Quality*
BRAND NAMES: Halston, Giorgio
PARKING: lot
PAYMENT: cash, checks (with proper I.D.), MasterCard, VISA

MISHICOT, WI

Andercraft Woods, Box 91, Route 1, Mishicot, WI 54228; (414) 755-4014
    This factory outlet sells Andercraft bird feeders, birdhouses, nativity stables,

planter boxes, and mailboxes. All merchandise is first quality. Savings are about 20% off retail price.

SUN.	MON.	TUE.	WED.	THU.	FRI.	SAT.
1–4	8–4:30	8–4:30	8–4:30	8–4:30	8–4:30	9–4

SAVINGS: at least 20% off
BRAND NAMES: Andercraft   *Mailing List*   *All First Quality*
PARKING: lot
PAYMENT: cash, checks (with proper I.D.)

PLOVER, WI

Tree Acres Nursery, Manufacturers Direct Mall, 101 Plover Road, Plover, WI 54467; (715) 341-7972
   This outlet sells house plants and some garden annuals at savings 10%–20% off retail price. Look for end-of-season items for best savings.

SUN.	MON.	TUE.	WED.	THU.	FRI.	SAT.
11–6	9:30–9	9:30–9	9:30–9	9:30–9	9:30–9	9:30–6

SAVINGS: 10%–20% off
PARKING: lot
PAYMENT: cash, checks (amount of purchase only, with proper I.D.)

PLYMOUTH, WI

H & J Outfitters, 127 E. Mill Street, Plymouth, WI 53073; (414) 893-8360
   This outlet sells western and English horseback riding equipment and accessories. They also sell men's and women's horseback riding clothing and boots, and grooming and health care products for the horse. Savings on first quality merchandise are small, but savings on end-of-season and odd lot merchandise can go to 30% off retail price.

SUN.	MON.	TUE.	WED.	THU.	FRI.	SAT.
closed	10–5	10–5	10–5	10–5	10–8	10–4

SAVINGS: 5%–30% off   *Mailing List*
BRAND NAMES: Tony Lama, Circle Y
ANNUAL SALES: November
PARKING: lot
PAYMENT: cash, checks (amount of purchase only, with proper I.D.), MasterCard, VISA

WEST BEND, WI

VirJeane Perfumes, West Bend Outlet Mall, 180 Island Avenue, West Bend, WI 53095; (414) 338-3816
   See listing in Milwaukee, Wisconsin.

SUN.	MON.	TUE.	WED.	THU.	FRI.	SAT.
11–5	9:30–6	9:30–6	9:30–6	9:30–6	9:30–8	9:30–5

SAVINGS: 50%–80% off   *All First Quality*
BRAND NAMES: Halston, Giorgio
PARKING: lot
PAYMENT: cash, checks (with proper I.D.), MasterCard, VISA

29
MALLS

There are eleven "outlet malls" within driving distance of Chicago. They vary from very small to very large, from very clean to rather dirty, from well-stocked to disappointing, from well-organized to chaotic, from fantastic bargains to negligible savings, from fun shopping places to stores that may have some bargains. The malls are in Cicero, Illinois; Loves Park, Illinois; Indianapolis, Indiana; Merrillville, Indiana; Mishawaka, Indiana; Beloit, Wisconsin; Kenosha, Wisconsin; La Crosse, Wisconsin; Madison, Wisconsin; Plover, Wisconsin; and West Bend, Wisconsin.

There is also an "off price" mall, Algonquin Mills Mall, in Rolling Meadows, Illinois. It has seven outlets among scores of "off price" stores: Classic Lady (see listing in *Clothing—Large Sizes*), Factory Card Outlet (see listing in *Gift Items*), Loomcraft (see listing in *Decorating*), Luggage Express (see listing in *Luggage*), Sneakee Feet (see listing in *Clothing—Footwear*), Toys and Gifts Outlet (see listing in *Toys*), and Waccamaw Pottery (see listing in *Housewares*).

Mall hours may vary during the winter. Indiana is in the eastern time zone. During the summer, however, remember that Indiana does not observe daylight savings time. If you plan to shop very early or very late, a call ahead to one of the stores will avoid disappointment.

GUINTA'S FACTORY OUTLET MALL, 1800 S. Cicero Avenue, Cicero, IL 60650

SUN.	MON.	TUE.	WED.	THU.	FRI.	SAT.
10-6	10-8	closed	10-8	10-8	10-8	10-6

This small mall is the closest to the city. It was a disappointment in several ways. I saw very few major brands in any of the stores. On the whole, merchandise was of poorer quality than at any of the other malls. The ambience and cleanliness left much to be desired.

OUTLETS

Apparel Textile Outlet; (312) 780-9488. (See listing in *Linens*.) They sell draperies, towels, and sheets. SAVINGS: 10%–30% off

Discount Outlet; (312) 780-0797. (See listing in *Gift Items*.) They sell wall hangings, toys, and cassette players. SAVINGS: at least 20% off

Guinta's Furniture; (312) 863-7720. They sell furniture. SAVINGS: 30%–70% off

L & S Furniture; (312) 653-5003. (See listing in *Furniture*.) They sell furniture. SAVINGS: 20%–45% off

Plus Size Fashion Outlet; (312) 652-9898. (See listing in *Clothing—Large Sizes*.) They sell large sizes of women's clothing. SAVINGS: up to 75% off

Under Things Unlimited; (312) 652-6962. (See listing in *Clothing—Lingerie*.) They sell men's, women's, and children's underwear. SAVINGS: at least 30% off

Waveland International Imports; (312) 656-3375. (See listing in *Clothing—Men's*.) They sell men's and women's clothing. SAVINGS: 30%–70% off

DISCOUNT STORES

Bargains Plus; (312) 780-0068. They sell sundries. SAVINGS: 10%–40% off

Golden Fashion; (312) no phone. They sell women's clothing. SAVINGS: about 25% off

The Jogging Shoe Company; (312) 780-6939. They sell men's and women's shoes. SAVINGS: average 20% off

Mr. Gold Jewelry Mart; (312) 780-7766. They sell jewelry. SAVINGS: about 30% off

PARK PLAZA OUTLET MART, 6400 block of N. 2nd Street, Loves Park, IL 61111

SUN.	MON.	TUE.	WED.	THU.	FRI.	SAT.
12-5	9:30-9	9:30-9	9:30-9	9:30-9	9:30-9	9:30-6

This small mall has major manufacturer's factory outlets. Most merchandise was name brand. All stores were clean and well-stocked, and merchandise was nicely displayed.

OUTLETS

Bass Shoe Factory Outlet; (815) 654-3130. (See listing in *Clothing—Footwear*.) They sell men's and women's shoes. SAVINGS: 20%–70% off

Frame Warehouse; (815) 877-2828. (See listing in *Picture Frames*.) They sell frames, prints, and mirrors. SAVINGS: 40%–50% off

The Linen Outlet; (815) 877-4959. (See listing in *Linens*.) They sell linens. SAVINGS: 20%–60% off

VIP Yarn and Craft Center—Knit Pikker—Gloray Knitting Mills; (815) 633-2966. (See listing in *Crafts*.) They sell yarn and craft kits and items, knit accessories, and sweaters. SAVINGS: 50%–70% off

DISCOUNT STORES

New York Sweater Company; (815) 654-3131. They sell sweaters. SAVINGS: 50%–67% off

Union Hall; (815) 654-9000. They sell general merchandise. SAVINGS: 10%–30% off

EASTGATE CONSUMER MALL, 7150 E. Washington Street, Indianapolis, IN 46201

SUN.	MON.	TUE.	WED.	THU.	FRI.	SAT.
12-5	10-9	10-9	10-9	10-9	10-9	10-9

This large mall has many major maufacturers' factory outlets. There were also many discount stores. Most merchandise was brand name. All stores were clean and well-stocked, and merchandise was nicely displayed.

OUTLETS

Big and Small Lots; (317) 356-9611. (See listing in *Department Stores*.) They sell general merchandise. SAVINGS: 50%–80% off

James M. Blume Jewelers; (317) 356-2548. (See listing in *Jewelry*.) They sell jewelry. SAVINGS: 20%–40% off

Burlington Coat Factory; (317) 352-9166. (See listing in *Clothing—Outerwear*.) They sell coats and clothing for every member of the family. SAVINGS: 25%–60% off

C J's Company Store; (317) 359-9720. (See listing in *Clothing—Family*.) They sell clothing for every member of the family. SAVINGS: 30%–50% off

The Children's Outlet; (317) 359-2021. (See listing in *Clothing—Babies'*.) They sell clothing for babies and children. SAVINGS: 10%–50% off

Crystal and China Outlet; (317) 356-3910. (See listing in *Gift Items*.) They sell china and crystal decorative gift items and table settings. SAVINGS: 10%–50% off

El-Bee Shoes; (317) 353-2911. (See listing in *Clothing—Footwear*.) They sell shoes for every member of the family. SAVINGS: 50%–70% off

Famous Footwear; (317) 356-5513. (See listing in *Clothing—Footwear*.) They sell shoes for every member of the family. SAVINGS: 25%–50% off

The Front Row; (317) 353-1114. (See listing in *Clothing—Accessories*.) They sell men's and women's accessories and clothing. SAVINGS: 10%–50% off

Linens 'N' Things; (317) 353-1441. (See listing in *Linens*.) They sell linens. SAVINGS: 25%–75% off

Old Mill Ladies Sportswear Factory Outlet; (317) 352-9170. (See listing in *Clothing—Sportswear*.) They sell women's sportswear. SAVINGS: about 20% off

DISCOUNT STORES

F & M Distributers; (317) 353-1003. They sell sundries. SAVINGS: up to 40% off

The Finish Line; (317) 353-6310. They sell athletic shoes for every member of the family. SAVINGS: 20%–30% off

Hit or Miss; (317) 357-0728. They sell women's clothing. SAVINGS: average 20% off

Peck's Menswear Center; (317) 359-0602. They sell men's clothing. SAVINGS: 25%–40% off

Publishers Book Outlet; (317) 356-3921. They sell books and magazines. SAVINGS: 10%–80% off

Smith Diamond Brokers; (317) 357-0209. They sell diamonds and other jewelry. SAVINGS: 20%–40% off

CENTURY CONSUMER MALL, 8275 Broadway, Merrillville, IN 46410

SUN.	MON.	TUE.	WED.	THU.	FRI.	SAT.
11–5	10–9	10–9	10–9	10–9	10–9	10–9

This is one of the largest malls. There are many major manufacturers' factory outlets. More than half of the shops were not outlets but discount stores. Most merchandise was brand name. The mall is spacious and well cared for. All stores were clean and well-stocked, and merchandise was nicely displayed. People in the mall were very friendly and helpful.

OUTLETS

Burlington Coat Factory; (219) 736-0636. (See listing in *Clothing—Outerwear.*) They sell coats and clothing for every member of the family. SAVINGS: 25%–60% off

Famous Footwear; (219) 736-1181. (See listing in *Clothing—Footwear.*) They sell shoes for every member of the family. SAVINGS: 25%–50% off

5th Avenue Bed 'N Bath; (219) 736-0749. (See listing in *Linens.*) They sell linens, decorating accessories, and gift items. SAVINGS: 20%–50% off

Frugal Frank's; (219) 736-6806. (See listing in *Clothing—Footwear.*) They sell shoes for every member of the family. SAVINGS: 10%–30% off

Kid's Ca'pers; (219) 769-2459. (See listing in *Clothing—Babies'.*) They sell infants' and children's clothing and accessories. SAVINGS: 20%–70% off

Publisher's Book Outlet; (219) 769-2982. (See listing in *Miscellaneous.*) They sell books and magazines. SAVINGS: 10%–80% off

Royal Belgium Rug Outlet; (219) 736-9092. (See listing in *Carpeting, Rugs, and Floor Coverings.*) They sell rugs. SAVINGS: 30%–70% off

Sizes Unlimited; (219) 769-7154. (See listing in *Clothing—Large Sizes.*) They sell clothing for the large woman. SAVINGS: 20%–70% off

Sole Hole Shoes; (219) 738-1790. (See listing in *Clothing—Footwear.*) They sell women's shoes. SAVINGS: up to 20% off

Tony Lama Boots; (219) 238-3263. (See listing in *Clothing—Footwear.*) They sell men's and women's boots and shoes. SAVINGS: 25%–40% off

Toys and Gifts Outlet; (219) 769-3259. (See listing in *Toys.*) They sell toys. SAVINGS: 20%–40% off

Van Heusen Factory Store; (219) 738-1959. (See listing in *Clothing—Men's.*) They sell men's and women's shirts, clothing, and accessories. SAVINGS: 30%–50% off

DISCOUNT STORES

Busch Jewelry Company; (219) 736-5222. They sell jewelry. SAVINGS: 25%–50% off

Casual Male; (219) 769-9614. They sell men's clothing. SAVINGS: 20%–50% off

Country Crafts; (219) 738-2782. They sell gift items. SAVINGS: 10%–20% off

Finish Line; (219) 738-2961. (See listing in *Clothing—Footwear.*) They sell athletic footwear. SAVINGS: 10%–50% off

Glitter 'N Gold; (219) 769-1179. They sell jewelry. SAVINGS: up to 30% off

Globe Music; (219) 769-0124. They sell musical equipment. SAVINGS: 20%–70% off

Hit or Miss; (219) 769-9514. They sell women's clothing. SAVINGS: about 20% off

Just Accessories; (219) 769-5313. They sell accessories. SAVINGS: 20%–30% off

Kaplan's Shoes; (219) 769-6493. They sell shoes for every member of the family. SAVINGS: 10%–40% off

Manufacturer's Record and Tape Outlet; (219) 736-8340. They sell records and tapes. SAVINGS: 10%–25% off

Marianne; (219) 769-6459. They sell women's clothing. SAVINGS: 20%–70% off

Peck's Menswear Center; (219) 769-9288. They sell men's clothing. SAVINGS: 20%–40% off

Rapps Round Up; (219) 769-0425. They sell men's clothing. SAVINGS: 15%–20% off

R-Way Walgreens; (219) 736-0521. It's a discount drug store. SAVINGS: 15%–50% off

Service Optical; (219) 769-0677. They sell eyewear. SAVINGS: up to 40% off

Worth's; (219) 769-5954. They sell women's clothing. SAVINGS: 20%–50% off

BUYER'S MARKETPLACE, 5901 N. Grape Road, Mishawaka, IN 46545

SUN.	MON.	TUE.	WED.	THU.	FRI.	SAT.
11-5	9:30-9	9:30-9	9:30-9	9:30-9	9:30-9	9:30-9

This large mall has many major manufacturers' factory outlets. Less than one third of the shops were discount stores. Most merchandise was brand name. All stores were clean and well-stocked, and merchandise was nicely displayed. The mall was well-kept and a pleasant place to shop.

OUTLETS

Bags Plus; (219) 277-0474. (See listing in *Clothing—Accessories.*) They sell handbags, wallets, and other accessories. SAVINGS: 30%–50% off

Big Lots; (219) 277-2664. (See listing in *Department Stores.*) They sell general merchandise. SAVINGS: 25%–70% off

Can'da Fashions; (219) 277-2875. (See listing in *Clothing—Women's.*) They sell women's clothing. SAVINGS: 30%–70% off

Candlelight Fashions; (219) 277-0930. (See listing in *Clothing—Lingerie.*) They sell intimate apparel. SAVINGS: 40%–60% off

Cornerstone; (219) 277-6957. (See listing in *Clothing—Sportswear.*) They sell clothing for men, women, and children. SAVINGS: 20%–50% off

El-Bee Shoes; (219) 277-6793. (See listing in *Clothing—Footwear.*) They sell men's and women's shoes. SAVINGS: 20%–60% off

Famous Footwear; (219) 277-0801. (See listing in *Clothing—Footwear.*) They sell men's, women's, and children's shoes. SAVINGS: 10%–40% off

Four Seasons; (219) 272-6341. (See listing in *Clothing—Women's.*) They sell women's clothing. SAVINGS: about 20% off

Hirth Wholesale Jewelers; (219) 277-2343. (See listing in *Jewelry*.) They sell jewelry. SAVINGS: 20%–70% off

Houseware Outlet and Glass Factory Outlet Store; (219) 272-8408. (See listing in *Housewares*.) They sell all kinds of housewares, cookware, gadgets, and serving pieces. SAVINGS: 50%–75% off

Julie's Jewelry; (219) 272-6341. (See listing in *Jewelry*.) They sell jewelry. SAVINGS: about 40% off

Kid's Ca'pers; (219) 277-2940. (See listing in *Clothing—Babies'*.) They sell babies' and children's clothing. SAVINGS: about 50% off

Little Red Shoe House; (219) 277-0432. (See listing in *Clothing—Footwear*.) They sell men's, women's, and children's shoes. SAVINGS: 20%–75% off

Newport Sportswear; (219) 277-7615. (See listing in *Clothing—Sportswear*.) They sell men's and women's clothing. SAVINGS: about 25% off

Nutrition Outlet; (219) 272-5568. (See listing in *Miscellaneous*.) They sell health foods, vitamins, and cosmetics. SAVINGS: 20%–50% off

The Paper Factory; (219) 277-2763. (See listing in *Paper Goods*.) They sell paper, office supplies, wrapping paper, and party goods. SAVINGS: 40%–60% off

Socks Galore and More; (219) 277-8692. (See listing in *Clothing—Accessories*.) They sell socks and hosiery for men, women, and children. SAVINGS: 20%–80% off

VIP Yarn and Craft Center; (219) 277-0491. (See listing in *Crafts*.) They sell yarn and crafts supplies. SAVINGS: 40%–70% off

The Wallet Works; (219) 277-0487. (See listing in *Clothing—Accessories*.) They sell wallets, briefcases, luggage, and other accessories. SAVINGS: 30%–40% off

Zondervan Outlet; (219) 277-8450. (See listing in *Gift Items*.) They sell religious items. SAVINGS: 25%–80% off

DISCOUNT STORES

Books Plus; (219) 272-3100. They sell books, magazines, wrapping paper, and greeting cards. SAVINGS: 10%–30% off

Budget Bridals; (219) 272-8972. They sell wedding dresses and rent tuxedos. SAVINGS: 30%–50% off

CSO; (219) 272-4063. They sell women's clothing. SAVINGS: about 20% off

County Market; (219) 277-8694. They sell food. SAVINGS: 25%–75% off

The Elegant Peddler; (219) 272-8833. They sell gift items, household accessories, and furnishings. SAVINGS: 20%–60% off

Frames Unlimited; (219) 277-6617. They sell picture frames. SAVINGS: 20% off

Hit or Miss; (219) 272-4071. They sell women's clothing. SAVINGS: 20%–50% off

Just Ears; (219) no phone. They sell earrings. SAVINGS: 20%–80% off

Kaplan's Shoes; (219) 277-0439. They sell men's and women's shoes. SAVINGS: 10%–40% off

Linen Center; (219) 277-0720. They sell linens and bed and bath accessories. SAVINGS: 20%–60% off

Northwest Fabrics; (219) no phone. They sell fabrics. SAVINGS: 30%–50% off

Peck's Menswear Center; (219) 272-1611. They sell men's clothing. SAVINGS: 10%–40% off

Pet Specialists; (219) 277-6224. They sell pets and pet supplies. SAVINGS: 20%–40% off

FREEMAN OUTLET MALL, 5 Freeman Lane, Beloit, WI 53511

SUN.	MON.	TUE.	WED.	THU.	FRI.	SAT.
11–6	9–9	9–9	9–9	9–9	9–9	9–6

This small mall is a collection of major manufacturers' factory outlets. There are no discount stores. Most merchandise was brand name. All stores were clean and well-stocked, and merchandise was nicely displayed.

OUTLETS

Clothesworks; (608) 365-9992. (See listing in *Clothing—Women's*.) They sell women's clothing. SAVINGS: 20%–60% off

Fieldcrest; (608) 365-3100. (See listing in *Linens*.) They sell linens. SAVINGS: up to 60% off

Freeman Outlet Store; (608) 364-1334. (See listing in *Clothing—Footwear*.) They sell men's and women's shoes. SAVINGS: 25%–50% off

Manhattan Factory Outlet; (608) 365-5584. (See listing in *Clothing—Men's*.) They sell men's and women's shirts and other clothing. SAVINGS: 25%–60% off

Van Heusen Factory Outlet Store; (608) 362-1700. (See listing in *Clothing—Men's*.) They sell men's and women's shirts and other clothing. SAVINGS: 30%–60% off

FACTORY OUTLET CENTRE, 7700 120th Avenue, Kenosha, WI 53142

SUN.	MON.	TUE.	WED.	THU.	FRI.	SAT.
11–5	9:30–9	9:30–9	9:30–9	9:30–9	9:30–9	9:30–6

This is the largest of the malls in the area. Almost all of the shops are major manufacturers' factory outlets. There were only a few discount stores. Most merchandise was brand name. All stores were clean and well-stocked, and merchandise was nicely displayed. The mall is well-kept, with helpful people making it a very pleasant place to shop.

OUTLETS

Ambrosia Chocolate Company; (414) 857-7150. (See listing in *Food—Candy, Nuts, and Dried Fruit*.) They sell chocolate, candy, and candy-making supplies. SAVINGS: 10%–50% off

The Athletic Shoe Outlet; (414) 857-2709. (See listing in *Clothing—Footwear*.) They sell athletic footwear and shoes for every member of the family. SAVINGS: 15%–30% off

B.G. Chicago; (414) 857-2858. (See listing in *Clothing—Women's*.) They sell women's clothing. SAVINGS: 30%–70% off

Bare Essentials; (414) 857-7565. (See listing in *Clothing—Lingerie*.) They sell lingerie and swimwear. SAVINGS: at least 50% off

The Brandwagon; (414) 857-7977. (See listing in *Clothing—Accessories*.) They sell men's accessories and clothing. SAVINGS: 35%–50% off

The Brighter Side; (414) 857-7724. (See listing in *Lamps and Lighting*.) They sell oil lamps and lamp oil. SAVINGS: 15%–30% off

C.J. Chips; (414) 857-7973. (See listing in *Clothing—Family*.) They sell men's and women's sportswear and business clothing. SAVINGS: 20%–45% off

Can'da Fashions; (414) 857-7553. (See listing in *Clothing—Women's*.) They sell women's clothing. SAVINGS: 30%–70% off

Cape Craftsman; (414) 857-2924. (See listing in *Gift Items*.) They sell gift items. SAVINGS: 20%–50% off

Carter's Factory Outlet; (414) 857-2049. (See listing in *Clothing—Babies'*.) They sell babies' and children's clothing. SAVINGS: 20%–50% off

Clothesworks; (414) 857-2326. (See listing in *Clothing—Women's*.) They sell women's clothing. SAVINGS: 30%–70% off

The Company Store; (414) 857-7027. (See listing in *Clothing—Outerwear*.) They sell down outerwear, pillows, comforters, and other products. SAVINGS: about 50% off

Draperies, Etc.; (414) 857-2006. (See listing in *Decorating*.) They sell curtains and linens. SAVINGS: average 35% off

Fashion Rack; (414) 857-7935. (See listing in *Clothing—Sportswear*.) They sell women's clothing. SAVINGS: 35%–80% off

Fashions For Less; (414) 857-2037. (See listing in *Clothing—Women's*.) They sell women's and men's clothing. SAVINGS: 35%–50% off

Frugal Frank's; (414) 857-7170. (See listing in *Clothing—Footwear*.) They sell shoes and some clothes for every member of the family. SAVINGS: 10%–30% off

Gentlemen's Wear House; (414) 857-2250. (See listing in *Clothing—Men's*.) They sell men's clothing. SAVINGS: 40%–60% off

The Genuine Article; (414) 857-9224. (See listing in *Clothing—Family*.) They sell overalls and casual clothing for men, women, and children, and maternity clothes. SAVINGS: 20%–50% off

Houseware Outlet; (414) 857-2923. (See listing in *Housewares*.) They sell housewares, kitchen gadgets, and cookware. SAVINGS: 25%–80% off

Kid's Ca'pers; (414) 857-2287. (See listing in *Clothing—Children's*.) They sell children's clothing. SAVINGS: 25%–75% off

Knit Pikker; (414) 857-2213. (See listing in *Clothing—Accessories*.) They sell knit accessories for every member of the family. SAVINGS: 15%–50% off

Lamp Factory; (414) 857-7569. (See listing in *Lamps and Lighting*.) They sell lamps. SAVINGS: 35%–60% off

Leading Labels; (414) 857-7454. (See listing in *Clothing—Accessories*.) They sell hosiery. SAVINGS: 35%–75% off

Little Red Shoe House; (414) 857-7344. (See listing in *Clothing—Footwear*.) They sell men's, women's, and children's shoes. SAVINGS: 25%–70% off

Loomcraft Textiles; (414) 857-2100. (See listing in *Fabrics*.) They sell fabrics. SAVINGS: 50%–75% off

Manhattan Factory Outlet; (414) 857-7993. (See listing in *Clothing—Men's*.) They sell men's and women's shirts and clothing. SAVINGS: 50%–70% off

Mid-America Shoe Factory Outlet; (414) 857-2920. (See listing in *Clothing—Footwear*.) They sell men's, women's and children's shoes. SAVINGS: 25%–75% off

Mill City Outlet; (414) 857-2055. (See listing in *Clothing—Women's*.) They sell women's clothing. SAVINGS: 20%–50% off

Mitchell Handbags Outlet; (414) 857-7675. (See listing in *Clothing—Accessories*.) They sell handbags, luggage, and other accessories. SAVINGS: 50% off

Munsingwear Factory Outlet; (414) 857-7991. (See listing in *Clothing—Sportswear*.) They sell sportswear and underwear for men and women. SAVINGS: 50% off

Newport Sportswear; (414) 857-9217. (See listing in *Clothing—Sportswear*.) They sell women's clothing. SAVINGS: 25% off

The Paper Factory; (414) 857-9238. (See listing in *Paper Goods*.) They sell paper, office supplies, wrapping paper, and party goods. SAVINGS: up to 50% off

Socks Galore and More; (414) 857-7600. (See listing in *Clothing—Accessories*.) They sell socks for men, women, and children. SAVINGS: 20%–80% off

Toys and Gifts Outlet; (414) 857-2730. (See listing in *Toys*.) They sell toys, puzzles, and gifts. SAVINGS: 10%–75% off

VIP Yarn and Craft Center; (414) 857-7393. (See listing in *Crafts*.) They sell yarn and craft kits. SAVINGS: 40%–80% off

The Wallet Works; (414) 857-9028. (See listing in *Clothing—Accessories*.) They sell wallets, handbags, and accessories. SAVINGS: 20%–40% off

Whitewater Glove Company; (414) 857-7003. (See listing in *Clothing—Accessories*.) They sell all types of gloves and mittens. SAVINGS: 40%–50% off

Winona Knits; (414) 857-2921. (See listing in *Clothing—Accessories*.) They sell knit outerwear, sweaters, and accessories for men, women, and children. SAVINGS: 25%–60% off

DISCOUNT STORES

Dickens Discount Book; (414) 857-2337. They sell books and magazines. SAVINGS: 10%–15% off

Enchanted Gold Jewelry; (414) 857-9002. They sell jewelry. SAVINGS: 10% off

Hit or Miss; (414) 857-9914. They sell women's clothing. SAVINGS: 25%–50% off

Laser Expressions; (414) 857-2744. They sell laser art and photographs. SAVINGS: 40%–70% off

Perfume Boutique; (414) 857-9252. They sell perfume and cologne for women and men. SAVINGS: 50%–85% off

Total Furniture Gift Outlet; (414) 857-7171. They sell furniture and gift items. SAVINGS: 20%–40% off

World Bazaar; (414) 857-7739. They sell wicker and glass decorating accessories. SAVINGS: about 25% off

LA CROSSE FACTORY OUTLET MALL, 301 Sky Harbor Drive, La Crosse, WI 54601

SUN.	MON.	TUE.	WED.	THU.	FRI.	SAT.
11-5	10-9	10-9	10-9	10-9	10-9	9-6

This small mall has major manufacturers' factory outlets and a few discount stores. Most merchandise was brand name. All stores were clean and merchandise was nicely displayed. People were friendly and helpful.

OUTLETS

C.O.M.B.; (608) 783-6464. (See listing in *Department Stores*.) They sell general merchandise. SAVINGS: 50%–75% off

The Children's Outlet; (608) 783-7440. (See listing in *Clothing—Babies'*.) They sell babies' and children's clothing. SAVINGS: 10%–50% off

Clothesworks; (608) 783-7077. (See listings in *Clothing—Women's*.) They sell women's sportswear. SAVINGS: 20%–60% off

The Company Store; (608) 783-4171. (See listing in *Clothing—Outerwear*.) They sell down outerwear, pillows, quilts, and other products. SAVINGS: at least 50% off

Little Red Shoe House; (608) 783-3388. (See listing in *Clothing—Footwear*.) They sell men's, women's, and children's shoes. SAVINGS: up to 60% off

Oak and Iron Shoppe; (608) 781-7770. (See listing in *Gift Items*.) They sell wooden and iron gift items. SAVINGS: 15%–70% off

Wag's Family Outlet; (608) 783-7633. (See listing in *Clothing—Family*. They sell men's, women's, and children's clothing. SAVINGS: 20%–50% off

DISCOUNT STORES

Hurrah!; (608) 783-4333. They sell women's clothing. SAVINGS: 20%–40% off

FACTORY OUTLET CENTRE, 4609 Verona Road, Madison, WI 53704

SUN.	MON.	TUE.	WED.	THU.	FRI.	SAT.
12-5	9:30-9	9:30-9	9:30-9	9:30-9	9:30-9	9:30-6

This large mall has many major manufacturers' factory outlets. Most merchandise was brand name. All stores were clean and well-stocked, and merchandise was nicely displayed.

OUTLETS

AAA Sports; (608) 273-9225. (See listing in *Sporting Goods*.) They sell sporting goods. SAVINGS: 30%–40% off

Formfit; (608) 273-1866. (See listing in *Clothing—Lingerie*.) They sell women's lingerie and exercise clothing. SAVINGS: 30%–70% off

Frugal Frank's; (608) 273-4071. (See listing in *Clothing—Footwear*.) They sell shoes and clothing for the entire family. SAVINGS: 10%–30% off

Houseware Outlet; (608) 273-6055. (See listing in *Housewares*.) They sell housewares, gadgets, and cookware. SAVINGS: 50% off

Kid's Ca'pers; (608) 273-8877. (See listing in *Clothing—Children's*.) They sell children's and infants' clothing. SAVINGS: 20%–70% off

Kitchens of Sara Lee Thrift Store; (608) 274-2739. (See listing in *Food—Bakery*.) They sell frozen baked goods. SAVINGS: up to 50% off

Little Red Shoe House; (608) 274-8747. (See listing in *Clothing—Footwear*.) They sell men's, women's, and children's shoes. SAVINGS: 10%–50% off

Manhattan Factory Outlet; (608) 273-4004. (See listing in *Clothing—Men's*.) They sell men's and women's shirts and clothing. SAVINGS: 25%–60% off

Mid-America Shoe Factory Outlet; (414) 273-4840. (See listing in *Clothing—Footwear*.) They sell shoes for every member of the family. SAVINGS: 25%–75% off

The Paper Factory; (608) 274-7668. (See listing in *Paper Goods*.) They sell paper, stationery, office supplies, and party goods. SAVINGS: 40%–50% off

Seventh Avenue—Swiss Colony; (608) 273-3488. (See listing in *Gift Items*.) They sell gift items. SAVINGS: 20%–70% off

VIP Mill Store—Knit Pikker; (608) 271-6357. (See listing in *Crafts* and *Clothing—Accessories*.) They sell yarn, crafts kits, and knit outerwear and accessories. SAVINGS: 15%–50% off

The Wallet Works; (608) 273-3713. (See listing in *Clothing—Accessories*.) They sell wallets, key rings, and accessories. SAVINGS: 40%–60% off

Zondervan Outlet; (608) 274-3240. (See listing in *Gift Items*.) They sell religious items. SAVINGS: 25%–80% off

DISCOUNT STORES

Enchanted Gold Jewelry; (608) 271-8816. They sell jewelry. SAVINGS: 25%–75% off

Houseworld; (608) 273-6580. They sell window treatments, gift items, and housewares. SAVINGS: 20%–50% off

MANUFACTURERS DIRECT MALL, 101 Plover Road, Plover, WI 54467

SUN.	MON.	TUE.	WED.	THU.	FRI.	SAT.
11-6	9:30-9	9:30-9	9:30-9	9:30-9	9:30-9	9:30-6

This large mall has many major manufacturers' factory outlets. Less than one third of the shops are discount stores. Most merchandise was brand name. All stores were clean and well-stocked, and merchandise was nicely displayed. The mall is well-kept, and nice people make it a pleasant place to shop.

OUTLETS

B. G. Chicago; (715) 341-8850. (See listing in *Clothing—Women's*.) They sell women's clothing. SAVINGS: 25%–75% off

Can'da Fashions; (715) 344-4423. (See listing in *Clothing—Women's*.) They sell women's clothing. SAVINGS: 30%–70% off

Carter's Factory Outlet; (715) 344-2193. (See listing in *Clothing—Babies'*.) They sell babies' and children's clothing. SAVINGS: 20%–50% off

C. J. T-Shirts; (715) 341-9292. (See listings in *Clothing—Family*.) They sell gift items and custom-made T-shirts. SAVINGS: 20% off

Clothesworks; (715) 341-8331. (See listing in *Clothing—Women's*.) They sell women's clothing. SAVINGS: 20%–60% off

The Company Store; (715) 344-5656. (See listing in *Clothing—Outerwear*.) They sell down outerwear, pillows, and comforters. SAVINGS: at least 50% off

D'Lu Furniture; (715) 341-7567. (See listing in *Furniture*.) They sell furniture. SAVINGS: 10%–40% off

The Discounter; (715) 344-4771. (See listing in *Department Stores*.) They sell general merchandise. SAVINGS: 50%–90% off.

The Genuine Article; (715) 344-0175. (See listing in *Clothing—Family*.) They sell overalls for men, women, and children, and maternity clothes. SAVINGS: 20%–50% off

House of Large Sizes; (715) 345-0717. (See listing in *Clothing—Large Sizes*.) They sell large size women's clothing. SAVINGS: 25%–75% off

Houseware Outlet; (715) 341-9044. (See listing in *Housewares*.) They sell housewares, kitchen gadgets, and cookware. SAVINGS: 25%–70% off

Little Red Shoe House; (715) 344-5366. (See listing in *Clothing—Footwear*.) They sell men's, women's, and children's shoes. SAVINGS: 25%–70% off

Manhattan Factory Outlet; (715) 344-2241. (See listing in *Clothing—Men's*.) They sell shirts and clothing for men and women. SAVINGS: 25%–60% off

Newport Sportswear; (715) 341-3455. (See listing in *Clothing—Sportswear*.) They sell women's sportswear. SAVINGS: 25% off

Norman's Shoes; (715) 344-1444. (See listing in *Clothing—Footwear*.) They sell shoes for every member of the family. SAVINGS: 20%–75% off

Old Mill Ladies Sportswear Factory Outlet; (715) 345-2900. (See listing in *Clothing— Sportswear*.) They sell women's sportswear. SAVINGS: 25%–70% off

The Paper Factory; (715) 341-0616. (See listing in *Paper Goods*.) They sell paper, office supplies, wrapping paper, and party goods. SAVINGS: 40%–50% off

Rybicki's Cheese Factory; (715) 341-1278. (See listing in *Food—Cheese*.) They sell cheese and gourmet foods. SAVINGS: 20%–50% off

Tree Acres Nursery; (715) 341-7972. (See listing in *Miscellaneous*.) They sell plants and gardening supplies. SAVINGS: 20%–50% off

VIP Yarn and Craft Center; (715) 344-6062. (See listing in *Crafts*.) They sell yarn and crafts kits. SAVINGS: 40%–80% off

Winona Glove Company; (715) 341-8833. (See listing in *Clothing—Accessories*.) They sell gloves and mittens. SAVINGS: 10%–50% off

Winona Knits; (715) 344-6299. (See listing in *Clothing—Accessories*.) They sell knit accessories and outerwear for every member of the family. SAVINGS: 25%–60% off

DISCOUNT STORES

Accessories Plus; (715) 344-2499. They sell costume jewelry. SAVINGS: 10% off

Fashion Encounter Boutique; (715) 344-6630. They sell accessories. SAVINGS: 25%–40% off

Hidden Treasures; (715) 344-7715. They sell gift items. SAVINGS: 20% off

Idea Shop; (715) 344-2499. They sell novelties and gift items. SAVINGS: 10% off

Lingerie Plus; (715) 341-5307. They sell lingerie. SAVINGS: 20%–35% off

Title Wave; (715) 344-3311. They sell new and used books. SAVINGS: 50%–75% off

Toy-Rific; (715) 345-2601. They sell toys and games. SAVINGS: 20%–40% off

WEST BEND FACTORY OUTLET MALL, 180 Island Avenue, West Bend, WI 53095

SUN.	MON.	TUE.	WED.	THU.	FRI.	SAT.
11–6	9:30–9	9:30–9	9:30–9	9:30–9	9:30–9	9:30–6

This mall has many major manufacturers' factory outlets. Most merchandise was brand name. All stores were clean and well-stocked, and merchandise was nicely displayed.

OUTLETS

Ambrosia Chocolate Company; (414) 334-5262. (See listing in *Food—Candy, Nuts, and Dried Fruit*.) They sell chocolate, candy, and candy-making supplies. SAVINGS: 20%–40% off

The Brighter Side; (414) 338-1411. (See listing in *Lamps and Lighting*.) They sell oil lamps and lamp oil. SAVINGS: 15%–30% off

Can'da Fashions; (414) 338-1998. (See listing in *Clothing—Women's*.) They sell women's clothing. SAVINGS: 30%–70% off

The Cookie Jar Outlet; (414) 334-4674. (See listing in *Food—Bakery*.) They sell cookies and cookie paraphernalia. SAVINGS: up to 65% off

Dinnerware, Etc.; (414) 334-4525. (See listing in *Plates, Glassware, and Tableware*.) They sell plastic tableware and kitchen storage containers. SAVINGS: 20%–50% off

General Shoe (Factory To You); (414) 338-2558. (See listing in *Clothing—Footwear*.) They sell shoes for every member of the family. SAVINGS: 40%–70% off

The Genuine Article; (414) 334-1121. (See listing in *Clothing—Family*.) They sell overalls and casual clothing for men, women, and children, and maternity clothing. SAVINGS: 20%–50% off

Handbag Factory Outlet; (414) 338-2929. (See listing in *Clothing—Accessories*.) They sell handbags and women's accessories. SAVINGS: 30%–70% off

Houseware Outlet; (414) 334-4243. (See listing in *Housewares*.) They sell housewares, kitchen gadgets, and cookware. SAVINGS: 25%–70% off

Knit Pikker; (414) 334-5167. (See listing in *Clothing—Accessories*.) They sell knit accessories for every member of the family. SAVINGS: 15%–50% off

Little Red Shoe House; (414) 334-3112. (See listing in *Clothing—Footwear*.) They sell men's, women's, and children's shoes. SAVINGS: 25%–70% off

Manhattan Factory Outlet; (414) 338-3636. (See listing in *Clothing—Men's*.) They sell men's and women's shirts and clothing. SAVINGS: 25%–60% off

Newport Sportswear; (414) 334-4711. (See listing in *Clothing—Sportswear*.) They sell women's sportswear. SAVINGS: 25% off

The Paper Factory; (414) 334-5266. (See listing in *Paper Goods*.) They sell paper, office supplies, wrapping paper, and party goods. SAVINGS: 40%–50% off

Regal Ware Outlet; (414) 334-9445. (See listing in *Appliances*.) They sell appliances, cookware, and microware. SAVINGS: 30%–40% off

The Sock Market; (414) 338-8869. (See listing in *Clothing—Accessories*.) They sell socks for men, women, and children. SAVINGS: 30%–70% off

VirJeane Perfumes, Ltd.; (414) 338-3816. (See listing in *Miscellaneous*.) They sell perfume and cologne. SAVINGS: 50%–80% off

Winona Knits; (414) 338-2545. (See listing in *Clothing—Accessories*.) They sell knit accessories for every member of the family. SAVINGS: 25%–40% off

APPENDIX A: OUTLETS OPEN ON SUNDAY

CHICAGO

Adams Factory Outlet
Affordable Awning Factory
Al's Men's Wear Big and
 Tall
Atlas Baking Company
B & W Golf Ball Company
Baltic Bakery
Besley's Tie Shop
Burlington Coat Factory
 Warehouse
Buttermaid Bakeries Thrift
 Store
Buy-A-Tux
Caravans Awry
Carpet Wholesalers
Chicago Shoe Outlet
Clothing Clearance Center
The Cookie Jar
Country Harvest
County Seat
Crate and Barrel
 Warehouse Store
Crawford's Linen Outlet
Cut-Rate Toys
D & L Office Furniture
 Company
Dan Howard's Maternity
 Factory Outlet
Dolly Madison Cakes Outlet
Dressel's Budget Bakery
Factory Linen Outlet
Fannie May Candies
Fishman's Fabric Outlet
General Jobbing
 Corporation Warehouse
Homer's Furniture
 Company
Karol's Men's Fashions
 Men's Clothing
 Warehouse
Keller's 2nd Place

Kosher Zion Meats
 Company
L & P Wholesale Candy
 Company
La-Z-Boy Showcase
 Shoppe
Lady Madonna Maternity
 Outlet
The Lamp Factory
Land's End Outlet
Linker's New York Textiles
Loomcraft Textiles
Marjen of Chicago Discount
 Furniture and Bedding
Mattress King
Meystel
Moo and Oink
Morris & Sons
Peppers Waterbeds
 Warehouse Clearance
 Outlet
Polk Brothers Outlet
Private Lives Warehouse
Reiter's Outlet Store
Rottapel Clothes
Sears Catalog Surplus
 Store
Sid's Discount Clothing and
 University Shop
Sizes Unlimited
Sofa and Sleeper Company
Spiegel Outlet Store
Stark's Bargain Warehouse
Studio 5000
Superior Nut and Candy
 Company Outlet
Textile Discount Outlet
Tile Outlet Company
Wallstreet
Wholesale Furniture
 Warehouse Clearance
 Center

290

ILLINOIS

A & S Factory Clothing Outlet
Apparel Textile Outlet
Arlington Club Beverage Company
Artists' Frame Service
Bass Shoe Factory Outlet
Beds and Spreads
Big "D" Closeouts
Brans Nut Company
Burlington Coat Factory Warehouse
Buttermaid Bakeries Thrift Store
Butternut Bread Thrift Store
Carpet Mill Outlet
Carpet Values of Chicago
Carpet World
The Children's Outlet
Classic Lady
Clothes-Outs
Clothing Clearance Center
The Craft Clocks
Crawford's Linen Outlet
The Crystal Center
Dan Howard's Maternity Factory Outlet
Design Interiors of Downers Grove
Direct Lamps and Shades
Discount Outlet
Dolly Madison Cakes Outlet
The Dress and Jewelry Makers
Dressel's Budget Bakery
Econo Outlet
Eli's Cheesecake and Muffin Store
Entenmann's Thrift Bakery
Factory Card Outlet
Famous Footwear
Fannie May Candies
5th Avenue Bed and Bath Outlet
The Frame Factory
Frame Warehouse
Friedman's
Front Row
Games Furniture Outlet
The Garage Sale Store
Gift Outlet
Golfer's Outlet
Guinta's Furniture
Haeger Potteries Factory Outlet Complex
Hahn Industries
Hamilton Luggage and Handbags

Heinemann's Bakeries Surplus Store
Holsum Bread Outlet
Insurance Liquidators
Italian Gold II
J. C. Penney Catalog Outlet Store
The Jewelry Exchange
Jim's Bargain Corner
JJ's Bedding & Furniture Discount
Joseph A. Bank Clothiers
Just Wallpaper
The Kaehler Outlet
Kids Things
La-Z-Boy Showcase Shoppe
The Lamp Factory
Land's End Outlet
Lebo's Factory Shoe Outlet
The Linen Outlet
Linens 'N' Things
Linens Plus
Loomcraft Luggage Express
Marjen Discount Furniture and Bedding Warehouse
Mattress Liquidations
Merchandise Clearance Center
Montgomery Ward Budget Store
Montgomery Ward Catalog Store
North Shore Bedding
Office Furniture Warehouse
OOP's Office Outlet
The Outletters
Ozite Mill Outlet Store
Pepperidge Farm Outlet
Peppers Waterbeds
Plus Size Fashion Outlet
Prevue Fashions
Pro Shop West
Pro Shop World of Golf
Schaumburg Mattress Factory
Schweppe & Sons
Schweppe's Party Shop
Sears Catalog Surplus Store
Sewing Factory Outlet Store
Sneakee Feet
Spiegel Outlet Store
Strictly Golf of Naperville
Superior Nut and Candy Company Outlet
Todd's Factory Outlet
Tony Lama Boots

Towel Factory Outlet
Center
Toys and Gifts Outlet
Under Things Unlimited
Van Heusen Factory Outlet
Store
Verlo Mattress Factory
VIP Yarn and Craft Center
Waccamaw Pottery
Waveland International
Imports
Winona Knits

INDIANA

Allee Drapes and Curtains
Ashley's Outlet Store
Bags Plus
Big and Small Lots
Big Lots
Blume Jewelers (James M.)
Brady's This Is It Factory
Outlet Store Clothing
Brady's This Is It Factory
Outlet Store Home and
Auto
Burlington Coat Factory
Can'da Fashions
Candlelight Fashions
Carter's Factory Outlet
CJ's Company Store
The Children's Outlet
Crystal and China Outlet
The Company Store
Cornerstone
Dan Howard's Maternity
Factory Outlet
Dansk Factory Outlet
Donlevy's Back Room
El-Bee Shoes
Famous Footwear
5th Avenue Bed 'N Bath
Four Seasons
Front Row
Frugal Frank's
Graham Farms Cheese
Corporation
Hirth Jewelers
Houseware Outlet and
Glass Factory Outlet
Store
Indiana Glass Factory
Outlet
Jaymar Slacks Factory
Outlet Store
Kid's Ca'pers
Kuppenheimer Men's
Clothing
La-Z-Boy Showcase
Shoppe

Linens 'N' Things
Little Red Shoe House
Londontown Factory Outlet
Store
Newport Sportswear
Nutrition Outlet
Office Furniture Warehouse
Old Mill Ladies Sportswear
Factory Outlet
The Paper Factory
Publisher's Book Outlet
Roselyn Bakery Surplus
Store
Royal Belgium Rug Outlet
Sap's Bakeries
Sears Surplus Store
Sizes Unlimited
Sole Hole Shoes
Tony Lama Boots
Value City Furniture Store
Van Heusen Factory Store
VIP Yarn and Craft Center
The Wallet Works
Winona Knits

WISCONSIN

AAA Sports
Ambrosia Chocolate
Company
Andercraft Woods
The Athletic Shoe Outlet
B.G. Chicago
Bare Essentials
The Brandwagon
Brans Nut Company
The Brighter Side
Brownberry Ovens Thrift
Store
Brunkow Cheese Co-op
Burlington Coat Factory
C. J. Chips
C. J. Sports and T-shirts
C.O.M.B.
Cady Cheese Factory and
Shop
Can'da Fashions
Cape Craftsman
Carter's Factory Outlet
Chalet Cheese Co-op
The Children's Outlet
Clothesworks
The Company Store
The Cookie Jar Outlet
D'Lu Furniture
Dan Howard's Maternity
Factory Outlet
Decatur Dairy
Dinnerware, Etc., Factory
Outlet

Dick Brothers Bakery
The Discounter
Draperies, Etc.
Dutch Country Cheese
E K Outlet
Enchanted Gold Jewelry
Farmers Creamery
  Company
Farmers Pride Cheese
Fashion Rack
Fennimore Cheese
Ferryville Cheese Company
Fieldcrest
Figi's
Formfit
Fox River Glove Factory
  Outlet Store
Frame Warehouse
Freeman Outlet Store
Frugal Frank's
General Shoe (Factory to
  You)
Gentlemen's Wear House
The Genuine Article
Gile Cheese
Gruber Cheese
Handbag Factory OUtlet
Home Textile Outlet
House of Large Sizes
Houseware Outlet
Insurance Liquidators
J. C. Penney Catalog Outlet
  Store
J. H. Collectibles Factory
  Outlet
Jack Winter Outlet
Jaeger Baking Company
  Thrift Store
Jean's Sample Shop
Jim's Cheese Corner
Just Accessories
Kappus Bread
Kid's Ca'pers
King Industries Outlet Store
Kitchens of Sara Lee Thrift
  Store
Knit Pikker
Lamp Factory
Large Size Outlet
Leading Labels
The Lenox Shop
Little Red Shoe House
Loomcraft Textiles
Lynn Dairy
Manhattan Factory Outlet
Merkt Cheese Company
Mid-American Shoe Factory
Midwest Hosiery Company
  The Sock Market
Mill City Outlet

Mitchell Outlet
Mount Sterling Cheese
  Factory
Mullins Cheese
Munsingwear Factory
  Outlet
National Fashion
  Liquidators
Nelson Cheese Factory
  Outlet
Newport Sportswear
Nike Factory Outlet
Norman's Shoes
Oak and Iron Shoppe
The Odd Lot Shoe Store
Old Mill Ladies Sportswear
  Factory Outlet
Outlets Unlimited
The Paper Factory
Pepperidge Farm Outlet
Pine River Farmers Dairy
  Co-op
Regal Ware Outlet
Rybicki's Cheese Factory.
Ryser Brothers of
  Wisconsin
Saranac Factory Store
Schultz Creamery
Sears Surplus Store
Seventh Avenue
The Shoe Bank
Shullsburg Creamery
Silverfield Cheese Factory
Socks Galore and More
Stallman's Mapleton
  Cheese Factory
Swiss Miss Textile Mart
Tolibia Cheese and Wine
  Villa
Toys and Gifts Outlet
Tree Acres Nursery
Union Star Cheese Factory
Valley View Cheese Co-op
Van Heusen Factory Outlet
  Store
VIP Mill Store Knit Pikker
VIP Yarn and Craft Center
VirJeane Perfumes
Wag's Family Outlet
The Wallet Works
Weinbrenner Factory Shoe
  Outlet
West Bend Woolen Mills
Whitewater Glove Company
Winona Glove Company
Winona Knits
Wisconsin Dairy State
  Cheese Company
Wisconsin's Pride Cheese

APPENDIX B: OUTLETS WITH SAVINGS OVER 70% OFF RETAIL PRICE

The outlets listed here had some merchandise at terrific savings. Not every item at every outlet had the same markdown, however, so look carefully and find the best buys.

Savings of 90% and more

CHICAGO

B.J. Handbag Outlet
Fishman's Fabric Outlet
General Jobbing
  Corporation Warehouse
Kroch's and Brentano's
  Bargain Book Center

INDIANA

Farmhouse Studio

WISCONSIN

The Discounter
Gile Cheese
Winona Glove Company

Savings of 80% and more

CHICAGO

B.J. Handbag Outlet
Cut-Rate Toys
Elco Supply Company
Fishman's Fabric Outlet
Flavor Kist—Schulze and
  Burch Biscuit Company
General Jobbing
  Corporation Warehouse
Jewelry Liquidation Center
Kroch's and Brentano's
  Bargain Book Center
Marshall Field Warehouse
Mary Walter
Sofa and Sleeper Company

ILLINOIS

Aparacor Outlet Store
Big "D" Closeouts
Classic Lady
The Garage Sale Outlet
  Store
JJ's Bedding & Furniture
  Discount
OOP's Office Outlet
Sears Warehouse Outlet
  Store
Stead Textile Company
  Outlet
Waccamaw Pottery
WJT Sales

INDIANA

Farmhouse Studio
Publisher's Book Outle
Socks Galore and Mor
Zondervan Outlet

WISCONSIN

The Cookie Jar Outlet
Dinnerware, Etc. Factory
  Outlet
The Discounter
Fashion Rack
Gile Cheese
Hartford Vacuum
Houseware Outlet
Just Accessories
King Industries Outlet Store
Midwest Hosiery Company,
  The Sock Market
Nike Factory Outlet
Rich's Bake Shop
Socks Galore and More
VIP Yarn and Craft Center
VirJeane Perfumes
West Bend Vacuum
Winona Glove Company
Zondervan Outlet

Savings of 70% and more

CHICAGO

Al's Men's Wear Big and
 Tall
American Science Center
American Sleep Waveland
 Mattress Company
Arvey Paper and Supplies
B. G. Chicago
Big and Small Lots
B.J.Handbag Outlet
Burlington Coat Factory
 Warehouse
Buttermaid Bakeries Thrift
 Store
Caravans Awry
Carpet Factory Outlet
Chicago Speakerworks
Crate and Barrel
 Warehouse Store
Cut-Rate Toys
Elco Supply Company
Factory Linen Outlet
Fishman's Fabric Outlet
Flavor Kist Schulze and
 Burch Biscuit Company
General Jobbing
 Corporation Warehouse
Ideal Fashions
Jewelry Liquidation Center
Kroch's and Brentano's
 Bargain Book Center
Land's End Outlet
Loomcraft Textiles
Marshall Field Warehouse
Mary Walter
Morris & Sons
National Bedding and
 Furniture Company
National Handbag Outlet
 Store
Peppers Waterbeds
 Warehouse Clearance
 Outlet
Polk Brothers Outlet
Sid's Discount Clothing and
 University Shop
Sizes Unlimited
Sofa and Sleeper Company
Spiegel Outlet Store
Textile Discount Outlet

ILLINOIS

A & S Factory Clothing
 Outlet
Aero Drapery Company,
 Division of Minnesota
 Fabrics

Airwize Heating and Air
 Conditioning
Aparacor Outlet Store
Arvey Paper and Supplies
Bass Shoe Factory Outlet
Big "D" Closeouts
Brans Nut Company
Buttermaid Bakeries Thrift
 Store
Butternut Bread Thrift
 Store
China Bazaar
Chocolate Soup
Classic Lady
Direct Factory Outlet
The Dress and Jewelry
 Makers
Econo Outlet
Evanger's Pet Products
The Factory Outlet Store
Franz Stationery Company
The Garage Sale Outlet
 Store
Gift Outlet
Golfer's Outlet
Harvey Manufacturing
 Company
The Jewelry Exchange
JJ's Bedding & Furniture
 Discount
The Kaehler Outlet
Linen Outlet
Linens Plus
Loomcraft
Marshall Field's
 Commercial Interiors
OOP's Office Outlet
Oops, We Goofed
The Paul Revere Shoppe,
 Revere Copper & Brass
Pepperidge Farm Outlet
Plus Size Fashion Outlet
Price Tag
Sears Catalog Surplus
 Store
Sears Warehouse Outlet
 Store
Sewing Factory Outlet
 Store
Speigel Outlet Store
Stead Textile Company
 Outlet
Story Design and
 Manufacturing
Strictly Golf of Naperville
Towel Factory Outlet
 Center

Van Heusen Factory Outlet
Store
Verlo Mattress Factory
Vienna Factory Store North
VIP Yarn and Craft Center
Waccamaw Pottery
Waveland International
Imports
The Wear House
WJT Sales

INDIANA

Allee Drapes and Curtains
Ashley's Outlet Store
Big and Small Lots
Big Lots
Burnham Glove Outlet
Can'da Fashions
Donlevy's Back Room
El-Bee Shoes
Farmhouse Studio
Hirth Jewelers
Houseware Outlet and
Glass Factory Outlet
Store
Jaymar Slacks Factory
Outlet Store
Kemper Factory Outlet
Kid's Ca'pers
Kid's Warehouse
Linens 'N' Things
Little Red Shoe House
Naas Foods, Inc.
Nettle Creek Industries
Publisher's Book Outlet
Royal Belgium Rug Outlet
Sizes Unlimited
Value Center
Van Heusen Factory Outlet
Store
VIP Yarn and Craft Center
Zondervan Outlet

WISCONSIN

Amity Leather Products
Factory Outlet Store
B.G. Chicago
Burlington Coat Factory
C.O.M.B.
Can'da Fashions
Clothesworks

The Cookie Jar Outlet
Dinnerware, Etc. Factory
Outlet
The Discounter
E K Outlet
Enchanted Gold Jewelry
Fashion Rack
Florence Eiseman, Inc.
Formfit
Gile Cheese
Handbag Factory Outlet
Hartford Vacuum
House of Large Sizes
Houseware Outlet
J. H. Collectibles
Just Accessories
Kid's Ca'pers
Kidstop
King Industries Outlet Store
Larson Company Dent
Department
Leading Labels
The Lenox Shop
Little Red Shoe House
Loomcraft Textiles
Manhattan Factory Outlet
Mid-American Shoe Factory
Midwest Hosiery Company,
The Sock Market
Monterey Mills Outlet Store
Nike Factory Outlet
Norman's Shoes
Oak and Iron Shoppe
Old Mill Ladies Sportswear
Factory Outlet
Rich's Bake Shop
Schweiger Fabric Outlet
Seventh Avenue
Socks Galore and More
Suemnicht Cheese
Company
Toys and Gifts Outlet
Van Heusen Factory Outlet
Store
VIP Yarn and Craft Center
VirJeane Perfumes
Weinbrenner Factory Shoe
Outlet
West Bend Vacuum
Winona Glove Company
Wisconsin's Pride Cheese
Zondervan Outlet

APPENDIX C: OUTLETS SELLING ALL FIRST QUALITY MERCHANDISE

CHICAGO

Advance Uniform Company
American Family Scale
Artists' Frame Service
Arvey Paper and Supplies
Bedding Specialists
Besley's Tie Shop
Caravans Awry
Chicago Chili Company
Chicago Knitting Mills
Clothing Clearance Center
Country's Harvest
Danielson Food Products
Designed Interiors
Factory Bedding
Factory Tire Outlet
Filbert's Old Time Root
  Beer
Flavor Kist Schulze and
  Burch Biscuit Company
The Frame Factory
Georgia Nut Company
Ideal Fashions
Joseph A. Bank Clothiers
Karol's Men's Fashions
  Men's Clothing
  Warehouse
L & P Wholesale Candy
  Company
The Lamp Factory
Linker's New York Textiles
Lisel's Sample Shop
Made-Rite Bedding
  Company Factory to You
  Sales
Marjen of Chicago Discount
  Furniture and Bedding
Moo and Oink
Morris & Sons

Nuts to "U"
Randolph Packing
  Company
Ricci Nuts
Slotkowski Sausage
  Company
Sparrer Sausage Company
Specialty Trunk and
  Suitcase Company
Superior Nut and Candy
  Company Outlet
Tom Tom Tamale and
  Bakery Company

ILLINOIS

Apparel Textile Outlet
Arlington Club Beverage
  Company
Arvey Paper and Supplies
Astro Bedding Corporation
  The Mattress Factory
Baker Road Manufacturing
  Company
Bedding Specialists
Beds and Spreads
Brans Nut Company
Burlington Coat Factory
Carpet Wholesalers
Classic Lady
Cosmetique
Creative Surfaces
The Crystal Center
Design Interiors of Downers
  Grove
Designer Leather Furniture
Famous Footwear
Factory Card Outlet
Factory Tire Outlet

5th Avenue Bed and Bath
Outlet
Fitness Warehouse
The Frame Factory
Georgia Nut Company
Golfer's Outlet
Good Children Street
Good Treats Limited Direct
Outlet
Guinta's Furniture
Hahn Industries
Hamilton Luggage and
Handbags
Irish Crystal Company of
Chicago
Italian Gold II
The Jewelry Exchange
Jim's Bargain Corner
Joseph A. Bank Clothiers
Linens 'N' Things
Litemart
Luggage Express
Luggage Limited
Marjen Discount Furniture
and Bedding Warehouse
North Shore Bedding
Private Lives Warehouse
Quality Cheese
Sandman Couch Company
Simandl Garment Company
Steaks 'N' Stuff Frozen
Foods
Toys and Gifts Outlet
Verlo Mattress Factory

INDIANA

Bags Plus
Blume Jewelers (James M.)
CJ's Company Store
Cornerstone
El-Bee Shoes
Factory Furniture Outlet
Farm and Home Saddlery
Four Seasons
Gohn Brothers
Manufacturing Company
Graham Farms Cheese
Corporation
Hoffman Office Supplies
Kuppenheimer Men's
Clothing
Little Red Shoe House
Newport Sportswear
Nutrition Outlet
Royal Belgium Rug Outlet
Swayzee Packing Company
Work Clothing Outlet Store

WISCONSIN

Andercraft Woods
Associated Milk Producers
Beechwood Cheese Factory
Bieri's Cheese Mart
Biglow Cheese and Butter
Company
Borden, Inc.
Branch Cheese Company
The Brandwagon
Branovan Outlet Store
Brunkow Cheese Co-op
Burlington Coat Factory
C. J. Chips
C. J. Sports and T-shirts
Can'da Fashions
Central Cheese and Butter
Co-op
Chalet Cheese Co-op
Cherry Grove Cheese
Chili Milk Pool Coop
Clothing Factory Outlet
Cloverleaf Cheese Factory
County Line Cheese
Company
Dan Howard's Maternity
Factory Outlet
Decatur Dairy
Drangle Foods
Dupont Cheese
Dutch Country Cheese
Ellsworth Cooperative
Creamery
Enchanted Gold Jewelry
Farmers Creamery
Company
Farmers Pride Cheese
Fashion Rack
Frankfort Cheese Factory
Freeman Outlet Store
Gad Cheese
Gentlemen's Wear House
Gruber Cheese
Hirth Jewelers
House of Large Sizes
Hook's Cheese Company
Buck Grove Cheese
Factory
Jean's Sample Shop
Junior House Company
Outlet Store
Just Accessories
Krakow Cheese Factory
Krause Dairy Corporation
Krohn Dairy Products
Large Size Outlet
Lone Elm Cheese Factory
Maple Grove Cheese

Meister Cheese Company
Merkt Cheese Company
Mount Sterling Cheese
  Factory
Mullins Cheese
Nelson Cheese Factory
  Outlet
Newburg Corners Cheese
  Factory
North Trail Sportswear
Old Mill Ladies Sportswear
  Factory Outlet
Outagamie Producers
  Co-operative
Outlets Unlimited
Potts Blue Star Cheese
Renard's Rosewood Dairy
Rybicki's Cheese Factory
Saranac Factory Store
Schmitz Bear Valley Cheese
  Factory
Silver Lewis Cheese Co-op
Silverfield Cheese Factory
Soldiers Grove Farmers
  Co-op
South Alma Cheese Factory

Springside Cheese Corporation
Stallman's Mapleton
  Cheese Factory
Stanga Cheese Corporation
Steve's Cheese Company
  Division of Branch
  Cheese
Sunny Creek Co-op
Swiss Miss Textile Mart
Tolibia Cheese and Wine
  Villa
Twelve Corners Cheese
  Factory
Union Star Cheese Factory
Verlo Mattress Factory
VirJeane Perfumes
White Clover Dairy
Widmer's Cheese Cellars
Wisconsin Dairy State
  Cheese Company
Wisconsin's Pride Cheese
World's Champion Gold
  Brick Cheese Company
Wrightstown Milk Products
Zimmerman Cheese
Zuern Building Products

APPENDIX D: ANNUAL SALES (BY MONTH & SEASON)

Annual Sales By Month

January

CHICAGO

Arvey Paper and Supplies
Burlington Coat Factory
  Warehouse
Land's End Outlet
Mary Walter
Meystel
Sid's Discount Clothing and
  University Shop

ILLINOIS

Chocolate Soup
Kid and Kaboodle
Land's End Outlet
Loomcraft
Scan Furniture Warehouse
  Outlet
Sewing Factory Outlet
  Store
Towel Factory Outlet
  Revere Mills
Van Heusen Factory Outlet
  Store

INDIANA

Allee Drapes and Curtains
Bags Plus
Front Row
Jaymar Slacks Factory
  Outlet Store
Kid's Ca'pers
Les Kids
Publisher's Book Outlet

WISCONSIN

Allen D. Everitt Knitting
  Company Outlet Store
Brans Nut Company
Burlington Coat Factory
Can'da Fashions
Fox River Glove Factory
  Outlet Store
Frugal Frank's
Jersild Store
The Lenox Shop
Odds 'N' Ends Shop

February

CHICAGO

Al's Men's Wear Big and
  Tall
Factory Linen Outlet
The Leather Shop
Linker's New York Textiles
Lorraine Lingerie
Meystel
Wallstreet

ILLINOIS

The Kaehler Outlet

INDIANA

Donlevy's Back Room
Parco Foods

WISCONSIN

Burlington Coat Factory
Dinnerware, Etc., Factory
  Outlet
Handbag Factory Outlet
Figi's
The Paper Factory
The Shoe Bank

300

March

CHICAGO

Linker's New York Textiles

ILLINOIS

Kid and Kaboodle
Scan Furniture Warehouse
Outlet

April

CHICAGO

Arvey Paper and Supplies
Smoler Brothers Fashion
Factory Outlet

ILLINOIS

The Factory Outlet Store
The Paul Revere Shoppe,
Revere Copper & Brass

INDIANA

Parco Foods

WISCONSIN

Dinnerware, Etc., Factory
Outlet
Florence Eiseman, Inc.
White Clover Dairy

May

CHICAGO

D & L Office Furniture
Company

ILLINOIS

Forsize Weightlifting
Equipment Supply
Linen Outlet
Linens Plus

INDIANA

Bags Plus
Brady's This Is It Factory
Outlet Store Funiture
Brady's This Is It Factory
Outlet Store Home and
Auto
Socks Galore and More

WISCONSIN

Brans Nut Company

June

CHICAGO

D & L Office Furniture
Company

ILLINOIS

Black & Decker, Inc.
The Factory Outlet Store
Scan Furniture Warehouse
Outlet
Van Heusen Factory Outlet
Store
Winona Knits

INDIANA

Allee Drapes and Curtains
Jaymar Slacks Factory
Outlet Store
Kid's Ca'pers
Nettle Creek Industries

WISCONSIN

Associated Milk Producers
Fennimore Cheese
Fox River Glove Factory
Outlet Store
Maple Leaf Cheese Factory
Tolibia Cheese and Wine
Villa
The Wallet Works

July

CHICAGO

Chicago Shoe Outlet
Joseph A. Bank Clothiers
Land's End Outlet
Marshall Field Warehouse
Mary Walter
Meystel
Sid's Discount Clothing and
  University Shop
Silvestri Corporation

ILLINOIS

Haeger Potteries Factory
  Outlet Complex
The Kaehler Outlet
Kid and Kaboodle
Land's End Outlet
Sewing Factory Outlet
  Store
Strictly Golf of Naperville
Van Heusen Factory Outlet
  Store

INDIANA

Donlevy's Back Room
Front Row
Golden Rule Book Store
Kid's Warehouse
Les Kids
Parco Foods

WISCONSIN

Allen D. Everitt Knitting
  Company Outlet Store
Buckstaff Authentic Factory
  Outlet
Can'da Fashions
The Company Store
Formfit
Frugal Frank's
Gerber's Cheese Shop
Hankscraft Outlet Store
Home Textile Outlet
Houseware Outlet
The Leather Shop
The Lenox Shop
Mondl Boots and Shoes
Newport Sportswear
The Shoe Bank
Swiss Miss Textile Mart

August

CHICAGO

Al's Men's Wear Big and
  Tall
Arvey Paper and Supplies
Lorraine Lingerie

ILLINOIS

Calico Corners
Chocolate Soup
Kid and Kaboodle
Linens Plus
Pro Shop West
Pro Shop World of Golf
Tony Lama Boots
Van Heusen Factory Outlet
  Store

INDIANA

Ashley's Outlet Store
CJ's Company Store
Kid's Ca'pers

WISCONSIN

Calico Corners
The Company Store
Fieldcrest
Flambeau Plastics Outlet
Fox River Glove Factory
  Outlet Store
Handbag Factory Outlet
J. H. Collectibles
Jersild Store
Mondl Boots and Shoes
National Fashion
  Liquidators
The Paper Factory
Shoe Factory Outlet
Seventh Avenue
The Sock Market

September

ILLINOIS

Hahn Industries
Linens Plus
Scan Furniture Warehouse Outlet

INDIANA

Brady's This Is It Factory
  Outlet Store Furniture
Brady's This Is It Factory
  Outlet Store Home and Auto
Nettle Creek Industries

WISCONSIN

Fox River Glove Factory
  Outlet Store
Mid-Western Sport Togs

October

CHICAGO

Arvey Paper and Supplies

ILLINOIS

Haeger Potteries Factory
  Outlet Complex
Sneakee Feet
Toys and Gifts Outlet

WISCONSIN

Florence Eiseman, Inc.
Manhattan Factory Outlet

November

CHICAGO

Factory Handbag Outlet
  Store

ILLINOIS

The Paul Revere Shoppe,
  Revere Copper & Brass

INDIANA

CJ's Company Store

WISCONSIN

H & J Outfitters
The Lenox Shop
Swiss Miss Textile Mart

December

CHICAGO

Chicago Speakerworks
Cut-Rate Toys
Factory Handbag Outlet
  Store
House-O-Lite, Lava-Simplex
  International
Joseph A. Bank Clothiers
Silvestri Corporation

ILLINOIS

Chocolate Soup
Factory Card Outlet
Linen Outlet
Mattress Liquidations
Sears Surplus Store
Toys and Gifts Outlet

INDIANA

Ashley's Outlet Store
CJ's Company Store
Houseware Outlet and
 Glass Factory Outlet
 Store
Kid's Warehouse
Parco Foods
Winona Knits

WISCONSIN

E K Outlet
Figi's
Frame Warehouse
Jockey Men's Wear Factory
 Outlet
Kidstop
King Industries Outlet Store
Lev-Co Factory Shoe Outlet
The Sock Market
Swiss Miss Textile Mart
Weinbrenner Factory Shoe
 Outlet
White Clover Dairy

Annual Sales by Season
Spring

CHICAGO

Affordable Awning Factory
Clothing Clearance Center
Glover Shade Company
Jewelry Liquidation Center

ILLINOIS

Artists' Frame Service
Clothing Clearance Center

INDIANA

Candlelight Fashions
Kuppenheimer Men's
 Clothing
Old Mill Ladies Sportswear
 Factory Outlet

WISCONSIN

Amity Leather Products
 Factory Outlet Store
Bazaar Factory Outlet Store
Fashions for Less
The Genuine Article
Grafton Yarn Company
 Outlet Store
Just Accesories
Little Red Shoe House

Summer

CHICAGO

Affordable Awning Factory
Clothing Clearance Center
Crate and Barrel
 Warehouse Store
Hufford Furniture Company

ILLINOIS

Clothing Clearance Center
Franz Stationery Company
Kitworks
Linens Plus

INDIANA

Candlelight Fashions
Old Mill Ladies Sportswear
 Factory Outlet

WISCONSIN

Fashions for Less
The Genuine Article
Jockey Men's Wear Factory
    Outlet

Just Accessories
Little Red Shoe House
The Odd Lot Shoe Store
Stuart Manufacturing
    Company

Fall

CHICAGO

Affordable Awning Factory
Clothing Clearance Center
Glover Shade Company
Jewelry Liquidation Center

ILLINOIS

Clothing Clearance Center

INDIANA

Candlelight Fashions
Old Mill Ladies Sportswear
    Factory Outlet

WISCONSIN

Amity Leather Products
    Factory Outlet Store
Bazaar Factory Outlet Store
Calico Corners
Fashions for Less
The Genuine Article
Grafton Yarn Company
    Outlet Store
Just Accessories
Little Red Shoe House

Winter

CHICAGO

Affordable Awning Factory
Clothing Clearance Center
Hufford Furniture Company

ILLINOIS

Clothing Clearance Center
Kitworks

INDIANA

Candlelight Fashions
Old Mill Ladies Sportswear
    Factory Outlet

WISCONSIN

The Children's Outlet
Fashions for Less
The Genuine Article
Grafton Yarn Company
    Outlet Store
Just Accessories
Little Red Shoe House
The Odd Lot Shoe Store
Stuart Manufacturing
    Company

APPENDIX E: OUTLETS WITH MAILING LISTS

CHICAGO

Adams Factory Outlet
Advance Uniform Company
Al's Men's Wear Big and
   Tall
American Science Center
Artists' Frame Service
Arvey Paper and Supplies
B.J.Handbag Outlet
Butcher Block & More
Charlotte Charles
Chicago Chili Company
Chicago Speakerworks
Clothing Clearance Center
Crawford's Linen Outlet
Custom Frame and Poster
   Manufacturing Company
D & L Office Furniture
   Company
Dan Howard's Maternity
   Factory Outlet
Designed Interiors
Elco Supply Company
Factory Handbag Outlet
   Store
Factory Tire Outlet
Fernchar Textiles The
   Window-Wear Warehouse
Fishman's Fabric Outlet
Frank O'Conner Pro Golf
Gingiss Formalwear
   Warehouse
Homer's Furniture
   Company
Hufford Furniture Company
Jewelry Liquidation Center
Joseph A. Bank Clothiers
Karol's Men's Fashions
   Men's Clothing
   Warehouse
Keller's 2nd Place

L & P Wholesale Candy
   Company
Lady Madonna Maternity
   Outlet
The Leather Shop
Leo's Advance Theatrical
   Company
Linker's New York Textiles
Lorraine Lingerie
Marjen of Chicago Discount
   Furniture and Bedding
Mary Walter
Meystel
Morris & Sons
National Bedding and
   Furniture Company
Office Furniture Warehouse
Outlet Store at the Apparel
   Center
Silvestri Corporation
Smoler Brothers Fashion
   Factory Outlet
Sofa and Sleeper Company
Spiegel Outlet Store
Steaks 'N' Stuff Frozen
   Foods
Studio 5000
Textile Discount Outlet
UCI Paint Factory Outlet
Virgilio Furniture
Wholesale Furniture
   Warehouse Clearance
   Center

ILLINOIS

A & S Factory Clothing
   Outlet
Aparacor Outlet Store
Artists' Frame Service
Arvey Paper and Supplies

Beich's Candy
R. A. Briggs and Company
Calico Corners
Candlelight Fashions
Chocolate Soup
Classic Lady
Clothing Clearance Center
The Craft Clocks
Crawford's Linen Outlet
Dan Howard's Maternity
  Factory Outlet
Design Interiors of Downers
  Grove
Designer Leather Furniture
Doenges Surplus Office
  Supply
Evanger's Pet Products
Factory Tire Outlet
Fitness Warehouse
Forsize Weightlifting
  Equipment Supply
Franz Stationery Company
Georgia Nut Company
Golfer's Outlet
Guinta's Furniture
Irish Crystal Company of
  Chicago
Joseph A. Bank Clothiers
Kid and Kaboodle
Kitworks
Land's End Outlet
Lebo's Factory Shoe Outlet
Loomcraft
Luggage Express
Marjen Discount Furniture
  and Bedding Warehouse
Mattress Liquidations
Office Furniture Warehouse
Oops, We Goofed
The Paul Revere Shoppe,
  Revere Copper & Brass
Prevue Fashions
Price Tag
Pro Shop West
Pro Shop World of Golf
Quality Cheese
Sensera Medco
Spiegel Outlet Store
Stead Textile Company
  Outlet
Steaks 'N' Stuff Frozen
  Foods
Story Design and
  Manufacturing
Strictly Golf of Naperville
Sunbeam Appliance Service
  Company
Swingles Furniture Rental
The Thrift Store, John B.
  Sanfilippo and Sons
Tony Lama Boots

Towel Factory Outlet,
  Revere Mills
The Treadle Machine
VIP Yarn and Craft Center
Waveland International
  Imports
The Wear House

INDIANA

Ashley's Outlet Store
Bags Plus
James M. Blume Jewelers
Can'da Fashions
CJ's Company Store
The Company Store
Dan Howard's Maternity
  Factory Outlet
Dansk Factory Outlet
Donlevy's Back Room
El-Bee Shoes
Evansville Colonial Baking
  Company
Factory Furniture Outlet
Famous Footwear
Farm and Home Saddlery
Farmhouse Studio
Gohn Brothers
  Manufacturing Company
Gossard's Factory Outlet
M. G. Grundman & Sons
Hirth Jewelers
Jaymar Slacks Factory
  Outlet Store
Kid's Ca'pers
Kid's Warehouse
Kuppenheimer Men's
  Clothing
Londontown Factory Outlet
  Store
Mandy's Sample Shop
Office Equipment Sales
Office Furniture Warehouse
Old Mill Ladies Sportswear
  Factory Outlet
Sizes Unlimited
VIP Yarn and Craft Center
The Wallet Works
Zondervan Outlet

WISCONSIN

AAA Sports
Amity Leather Products
  Factory Outlet Store
Andercraft Woods
Associated Milk Producers
B.G. Chicago
Biglow Cheese and Butter
  Company
The Brandwagon

Branovan Outlet Store
Buckstaff Authentic Factory
    Outlet
C. J. Chips
Calico Corners
Can'da Fashions
Central Cheese and Butter
    Co-op
The Children's Outlet
Chili Milk Pool Coop
(The Original) Clothes Rack
Clothesworks
Clothing Factory Outlet
Cloverleaf Cheese Factory
The Company Store
County Line Cheese
    Company
Dan Howard's Maternity
    Factory Outlet
Decatur Dairy
Dinnerware, Etc. Factory
    Outlet
Drangle Foods
Dutch Country Cheese
Enchanted Gold Jewelry
Farmers Creamery
    Company
Farmers Pride Cheese
Ferryville Cheese Company
Fieldcrest
Flambeau Plastics Outlet
Florence Eiseman, Inc.
Frame Warehouse
Frankfort Cheese Factory
Freeman Outlet Store
Fur the Fun of It
General Shoe (Factory to
    You)
Gentlemen's Wear House
The Genuine Article
Gerber's Cheese Shop
Gile Cheese
Grafton Yarn Company
    Outlet Store
H & J Outfitters
Hennings Cheese Factory
Herrschner's, Inc.
Home Textile Outlet
Hook's Cheese Company
    Buck Grove Cheese
    Factory
House of Large Sizes
Jack Winter Outlet
Jersild Store
Jim's Cheese Corner
Jockey Men's Wear Factory
    Outlet
Junior House Company
    Outlet Store
Kid's Ca'pers
Kitworks

Knit Pikker
The Leather Shop
Loomcraft Textiles
Manhattan Factory Outlet
Maple Leaf Cheese Factory
Marshall Cheese
Meister Cheese Company
Melco Clothing Company
Mitchell Handbags
Monterey Mills Outlet Store
Mount Sterling Cheese
    Factory
Musbeck Shoes
Nelson Cheese Factory
    Outlet
Nike Factory Outlet
Odds 'N' Ends Shop
Old Mill Ladies Sportswear
    Factory Outlet
Outagamie Producers
    Co-operative
Outlets Unlimited
The Paper Factory
Pine River Farmers Dairy
    Co-op
Renard's Rosewood Dairy
Rybicki's Cheese Factory
Ryser Brothers of
    Wisconsin
Saranac Factory Store
Schultz Creamery
Seventh Avenue
Shoe Factory Outlet
Shullsburg Creamery
Silverfield Cheese Factory
Socks Galore and More
Soldiers Grove Farmers
    Co-op
St. Croix Corporation
Stallman's Mapleton
    Cheese Factory
Steve's Cheese Company
    Division of Branch
    Cheese
Stuart Manufacturing
    Company
Suemnicht Cheese
    Company
Tolibia Cheese and Wine
    Villa
Van Heusen Factory Outlet
    Store
VIP Mill Store, Knit Pikker
VIP Yarn and Craft Center
The Wallet Works
Westman Glass & China
Widmer's Cheese Cellars
Wisconsin Dairy State
    Cheese Company
Zim's Dairy Products
Zwicker Knitting Mills

APPENDIX F: OUTLETS WITH SENIOR CITIZENS' DISCOUNTS

CHICAGO

Affordable Awning Factory
B.G. Chicago
Buttermaid Bakeries Thrift
  Store
Buy-A-Tux
Dolly Madison Cakes Outlet
Eli's Factory Outlet
Factory Linen Outlet
Factory Tire Outlet
Fishman's Fabric Outlet
Kitchens of Sara Lee Thrift
  Store
The Leather Shop
Mattress King
National Handbag Outlet
  Store
Wholesale Furniture
  Warehouse Clearance
  Center

ILLINOIS

Brownberry Ovens Thrift
  Store
Buttermaid Bakeries Thrift
  Store
Butternut Bread Thrift
  Store
The Craft Clocks
Dolly Madison Cakes Outlet
Dressel's Budget Bakery
Entenmann's Thrift Bakery
Factory Tire Outlet
The Garage Sale Outlet
  Store
Georgia Nut Company
Grist "Mill Ends" & Things
Guinta's Furniture
Heinemann's Bakeries
  Surplus Store

Kitchens of Sara Lee Thrift
  Store
The Linen Outlet
Merchandise Clearance
  Center
Party Cookies
Pepperidge Farm Outlet
Sears Catalog Surplus
  Store
Verlo Mattress Factory
VIP Yarn and Craft Center

INDIANA

Ashley's Outlet Store
Buttermaid Bakeries Thrift
  Store
M. G. Grundman & Sons
Hirth Jewelers
Kitchens of Sara Lee Thrift
  Store
Lewis Bakeries
Little Red Shoe House
Parco Foods
VIP Yarn and Craft Center
The Wallet Works

WISCONSIN

AAA Sports
Ambrosia Chocolate
  Company
B.G. Chicago
Bare Essentials
The Brighter Side
Brownberry Ovens Thrift
  Store
C. J. Chips
Can'da Fashions
Clothesworks
The Company Store

309

Dinnerware, Etc., Factory Outlet
Draperies, Etc.
E K Outlet
Enchanted Gold Jewelry
Fieldcrest
Formfit
Fox River Glove Factory Outlet Store
Frugal Frank's
Gardner Thrift Shoppe
General Shoe (Factory to You)
Hartford Vacuum
Herrschner's, Inc.
Houseware Outlet
Jaeger Baking Company Thrift Store
Jersild Store
King Industries Outlet Store
Kitchens of Sara Lee Thrift Store
Lamp Factory
Large Size Outlet
Lev-Co Factory Shoe Outlet
Little Red Shoe House

Loomcraft Textiles
Manhattan Factory Outlet
Midwest Hosiery Company, The Sock Market
Mill City Outlet
Mitchell Outlet
Mrs. Karl's Thrift Store
Munsingwear Factory Outlet
Newport Sportswear
Odds 'N' Ends Shop
The Paper Factory
Pepperidge Farm Outlet
Rock River Foods
Schultz Creamery
Seventh Avenue—Swiss Colony
Shullsburg Creamery
The Sock Market
VIP Mill Store, Knit Pikker
VIP Yarn and Craft Center
Wag's Family Outlet
The Wallet Works
West Bend Vacuum
Whitewater Glove Company

INDEX

Talbots